PRAISE FOR THE FIRST EDI

"A willingness to probe rather than pronounce is ~~...~~ ...~~g...~~, as is the excitement of a taking up a good fight."

—*The Women's Review of Books*

"With refreshing authority, passion, wit, clarity and outspokenness, these articles seek to encourage dialog about such complex and provocative issues as the call for regulation/censorship of pornography by MacKinnon and Dworkin, the effects of *Bowers v. Hardwick*, and the distinctions between queer theory and lesbian and gay studies. This historic compilation is an important contribution to the field of sexual politics."

—*Library Journal*

"*Sex Wars* provides a much-needed antidote to the recent tidal wave of Republicanism. This collection of a decade's worth of writing by theorists/activists Nan Hunter and Lisa Duggan offers us a sobering lesson in the recent history of sexual repression in America. But they do not leave us wringing our hands—their useful concept of sexual dissent suggests a route out of the civil rights strategies that backfire and anti-identity politics that seem dangerously close to self-annihilation."

—Cindy Patton, author of *Queer Diasporas*

"*Sex Wars* is an invaluable contribution to the current debate on feminism and sex. Its essays reveal with cogent and dismaying clarity the repressive logic that links anti-pornography feminism with religious fundamentalism and homophobic paranoia. Feminists who have been struggling to combat this all-too-prevalent logic will be grateful for this new and powerful weapon in our own 'sex war' arsenal."

—Ellen Willis, author of *No More Nice Girls: Countercultural Essays*

MORE PRAISE FOR THE TENTH-ANNIVERSARY EDITION:

"Although many anti-porn activists draw from feminist roots, *Sex Wars* proves that those good intentions were often riddled with homophobic assumptions and inadvertent limits about women's sexuality. Best of all, *Sex Wars* shows that the answer to feminism's problems and mistakes is, simply, *more feminism*."

—Jennifer Baumgardner, coauthor of *Manifesta: Young Women, Feminism, and the Future*

"*Sex Wars* is a lively, relevant and smart analysis of the many ways in which the regulation of sex continues to be central to notions of public and private freedom. *Sex Wars* remains theory written for practitioners, and makes links between sexual politics and social justice movements in enlightening ways."

—Urvashi Vaid, executive director of the Arcus Foundation and author of *Virtual Equality: The Mainstreaming of Gay and Lesbian Liberation*

SEX WARS

10TH ANNIVERSARY EDITION

SEX WARS

SEXUAL DISSENT AND POLITICAL CULTURE

LISA DUGGAN AND NAN D. HUNTER

Routledge
Taylor & Francis Group
New York   London

Routledge is an imprint of the
Taylor & Francis Group, an informa business

Routledge
Taylor & Francis Group
270 Madison Avenue
New York, NY 10016

Routledge
Taylor & Francis Group
2 Park Square
Milton Park, Abingdon
Oxon OX14 4RN

Printed in the United States of America on acid-free paper
10 9 8 7 6 5 4 3 2 1

International Standard Book Number-10: 0-415-97874-2 (Softcover) 0-415-97873-4 (Hardcover)
International Standard Book Number-13: 978-0-415-97874-3 (Softcover) 978-0-415-97873-6 (Hardcover)

Library of Congress Cataloging-in-Publication Data

Duggan, Lisa, 1954-
   Sex wars : sexual dissent and political culture / Lisa Duggan and Nan D. Hunter.--
10th anniversary ed.
     p. cm.
   Includes bibliographical references and index.
   ISBN 0-415-97873-4 (alk. paper) -- ISBN 0-415-97874-2 (pbk. : alk. paper)
    1. Sex--Political aspects--United States. 2. Sexual orientation--Political aspects--
United States. 3. Pornography--Political aspects--United States. I. Hunter, Nan D. II.
Title.

HQ23.D78 2006
306.7--dc22
                                              2005036058

Visit the Taylor & Francis Web site at
http://www.taylorandfrancis.com

and the Routledge Web site at
http://www.routledge-ny.com

Contents

Acknowledgments   vii

Introduction to the 10th Anniversary Edition of *Sex Wars*   ix
LISA DUGGAN

Introduction   1
LISA DUGGAN

Chapter 1   Contextualizing the Sexuality Debates: A Chronology
1966–2005   15
NAN D. HUNTER

Chapter 2   Censorship in the Name of Feminism   29
LISA DUGGAN

Section I
Sexual Dissent and Representation   **41**

Chapter 3   False Promises: Feminist Antipornography Legislation   43
LISA DUGGAN, NAN D. HUNTER AND CAROLE S. VANCE

Chapter 4   Feminist Historians and Antipornography Campaigns:
An Overview   65
LISA DUGGAN

Chapter 5   Sex Panics   71
LISA DUGGAN

Chapter 6   Banned in the U.S.A.: What the Hardwick Ruling Will
Mean   77
NAN D. HUNTER

Section II
Sexual Dissent and the Law   **83**

Chapter 7   Life After Hardwick   85
NAN D. HUNTER

Chapter 8   Sexual Dissent and the Family: The Sharon Kowalski
Case   99
NAN D. HUNTER

Chapter 9   Marriage, Law and Gender: A Feminist Inquiry   105
NAN D. HUNTER

Chapter 10   Identity, Speech and Equality   119
NAN D. HUNTER

Chapter 11   History's Gay Ghetto: The Contradictions of Growth in
Lesbian and Gay History   137
LISA DUGGAN

Section III
Sexual Dissent, Activism and the Academy   **147**

Chapter 12   Making It Perfectly Queer   149
LISA DUGGAN

Chapter 13   Scholars and Sense   165
LISA DUGGAN

Chapter 14   Queering the State   171
LISA DUGGAN

Chapter 15   The Discipline Problem: Queer Theory Meets Lesbian
and Gay History   185
LISA DUGGAN

Chapter 16   *Lawrence v. Texas* as Law and Culture   197
NAN D. HUNTER

Section IV
Sexual Dissent in the New Millennium   **211**

Chapter 17   Crossing the Line: The Brandon Teena Case and the
Social Psychology of Working-Class Resentment   213
LISA DUGGAN

Chapter 18   Holy Matrimony!   221
LISA DUGGAN

Chapter 19   Beyond Gay Marriage   231
             LISA DUGGAN AND RICHARD KIM

Appendix   The FACT Brief   239
             NAN D. HUNTER AND SYLVIA A. LAW

Notes   277

Index   335

Acknowledgments

The essays in this volume were written over a period of more than a decade, with more than a little help from our friends. We have thanked those we depended on for assistance at the close of each essay. We would like to thank Carole S. Vance, Gayle Rubin, and Ann Snitow for extended political collaboration and personal support; their influence pervades this entire volume. In addition, the following friends, colleagues, and fellow travelers offered us crucial insight and criticisms over the years: Dorothy Allison, Barbara Kerr, Sylvia Law, Faye Ginsburg, Bill Rubenstein, Matt Coles, John D'Emilio, Elizabeth Schneider, Jonathan Ned Katz, Jeffrey Escoffier, Cindy Patton and Henry Abelove.

We received invaluable institutional support and assistance for these essays from Brooklyn Law School, the University of Illinois Unit for Criticism and Interpretive Theory, and the Australian National University Humanities Research Centre.

Finally, without Kathleen McHugh there would be no book—but our phone bills would be a lot lower!

Introduction to the 10th Anniversary Edition of *Sex Wars*

LISA DUGGAN (2006)

In the decade since the publication of *Sex Wars*, at the turn of the twenty-first century, we have witnessed astonishing gains in the arena of sexual politics, and have absorbed sharp defeats. We have responded, wearily, as old issues appeared in new contexts, and as we encountered entirely new and unexpected situations. As the yearly listings for 1995 to 2005, added to Nan Hunter's chronology of the sexuality debates, show, conflicts over the politics of sexuality continue to occupy center stage in the United States. In addition, U.S.-based institutions and agencies have increasingly exported U.S.-style sexual politics across the globe.

Gains and losses cannot be simply tallied, however. As neoliberal policies have widened the political and economic gaps between rich and poor, empowered and marginalized, gains for the few have increasingly meant losses for the many. Though U.S. feminists and reproductive justice activists have welcomed new reproductive technologies, and so far (as of 2007) held onto the basic right to abortion won in *Roe v. Wade*, we have at the same time seen access to basic reproductive health care eroded in the United States, as the Bush administration's global "gag rule" has restricted reproductive freedom around the world. Lesbian and gay legal victories decriminalizing sodomy in the United States, and allowing same sex couples to marry in Massachusetts, have been followed by the spread of state constitutional amendments restricting access to marriage, and adding newly severe constraints on the rights of unmarried adults in all kinds of relationships. The growth of a vital grassroots global movement to stop the spread of AIDS, and to treat those afflicted, has been met with resistant governments, and stymied by U.S. support of abstinence education and drug company profits.

As social movement activists have learned over and over again during the past century, gains in legal rights do not necessarily lead to greater substantive political power and economic equality. In fact, legal gains can be completely compatible with an increasingly unequal distribution of resources of all kinds. The overall direction of neoliberal rule in the twenty-first century thus far is: unevenly growing formal legal equality and superficially inclusive "multicultural" representation within structures of sharp, deepening, structurally embedded inequalities. During the past decade, mainstream liberal feminist and gay organizations have tended to lose sight of this contradictory reality, hailing the limited gains and overlooking the massive losses of their constituencies. For instance: What kind of gain is it for queers to win the right to marry, if increasing numbers of us are immiserated by the privatization of social welfare?

As in the first edition of *Sex Wars*, we find again in 2006 that a yawning gap too often separates the thinking of activists and scholars in the field of sexual politics. Since 1995, mainstream activism has moved in an increasingly conservative direction—though progressive grassroots organizing persists, and is currently in an upswing. Along a strangely parallel track, scholarship has tended to split off as well. For instance, a narrowly based "queer theory" inhabits the more privileged academic quarters these days, addressing itself to (and universalizing from) the aesthetics and politics of mostly white gay Euro American men. But a ferociously intelligent and cross-fertilizing new transnationally feminist and globally queer thinking has also grown, at a dizzying pace in the last few years.[1]

This tenth anniversary edition of *Sex Wars* addresses these broad conditions, and charts the shifting contours of sexual politics, by adding five elements to the original collection of essays:

1. The addition of 1995 to 2005 to the years enumerated in Nan Hunter's "Contextualizing the Sexuality Debates: A Chronology." These additions track the continuing role of scandal (from the Lewinsky Affair to the charges of child abuse in the Catholic Church), the vagaries of popular culture (including television highlights such as the premiere of *Will and Grace*, and the flood of reality wedding shows), and the persistence of antiporn and antiprostitution politics (and their transportation into the global arena by "antitrafficking" activists)—among other topics.
2. The inclusion of a new chapter by Hunter, "*Lawrence v. Texas* as Law and Culture," that analyzes the changes wrought by the stunning vic-

tory in the 2003 Supreme Court decision that decriminalized sodomy in the United States. Hunter predicts that this stunning and long overdue legal gain may have some contradictory effects, opening the door to expanded state scrutiny of lesbian and gay lives even as it decriminalizes them. As Hunter argues, riffing on Foucault, "In future state regulation of sexuality, discipline will replace punishment."

3. and 4. The reprinting of two essays originally published in *The Nation*. The first authored by me, the second coauthored with Richard Kim, on the politics of marriage surrounding the 2004 election. These essays argue that the most progressive way to politicize marriage is not to argue simply for "gay rights," but rather to urge the democratization and diversification of partnership recognitions and the expansion of household security in general. Like the focus on "abortion rights" that often substitutes for a broader progressive agenda for reproductive freedom and justice, the single-minded focus on the right of same sex couples to marry has marginalized efforts to multiply forms of recognition and universalize the benefits available to us all.

5. The republication of my essay on the Brandon Teena murders from *New Labor Forum*, "Crossing the Line." This essay shifts attention away from legal reform and electoral campaigns to examine the ways that social movements limit their angles of vision, and thereby their political imagination and effectiveness. If lesbian and gay, bisexual and transgender activists have tended to erase the specific class and racial contexts of Brandon Teena's life and death, populist campaigns for economic and class justice have generally refused to consider the ways that gender and sexual conservatism have not only neglected but actively harmed dissenters abused within or isolated outside "the working family."

This tenth anniversary edition of *Sex Wars* is dedicated to ... the next ten years, and all the emerging sex radicals, social justice organizers, anticorporate globalization activists, prison abolitionists, gender dissenters, environmental justice advocates, radical democrats, and diasporic and public intellectuals who will remake our collective lives and help bring us all the promise of a politics worth living for.

Introduction

LISA DUGGAN (1995)

At the height of the "sex wars" during the mid-1980s, members of the Feminist Anti-Censorship Taskforce (FACT) used to sit around late at night, talking and planning. We came up with the idea of making an audio tape and selling it to raise funds for our efforts. It would be called "Sex Noises of Sex Radicals"; eager buyers would hear ninety minutes of the sounds of photocopying machines, staple guns and ringing phones—the sounds that filled the hours when we might otherwise have been at play.

But the "sex wars" themselves were no party and no joke. During the decade from 1980 to 1990, a series of bitter political and cultural battles over issues of sexuality convulsed the nation—battles over the regulation of pornography, the scope of legal protections for gay people, the funding of allegedly "obscene" art, the content of safe-sex education, the scope of reproductive freedom for women, the extent of sexual abuse of children in day care centers, the sexual content of public school curricula, and more. The essays collected in this volume come out of our direct engagement in these debates; they represent our analyses of the overt issues and covert meanings circulated throughout this decade of "sex panics," and our efforts to forge a politics that might effectively intervene to transform public discourses about sexuality.

Our observations and analyses, and our suggestions for shifts in political languages and strategies, grew out of collective efforts—in FACT, in legal work on behalf of the Gay Men's Health Crisis and the four artists defunded by the National Endowment for the Arts (NEA), in study groups, at conferences and elsewhere. Most of these essays had their origin in specific collective projects, and were generated as part of larger efforts to defeat or promote a piece of legislation, to influence a court or political organization, or to critique and re-form the discourses and practices of a profession. Read together, they document efforts to intervene in multiple conversations, rather than to develop a single analysis or unitary viewpoint. They address different audiences in different idioms, ranging from the legal language of court documents, to the narrative or polemics of popular journalism, to the sustained arguments and conventional prose of professional journals.

The essays also span the ten years of our partnership (we first met while working on Chapter Three, "False Promises"), and constitute a record of our personal, political and intellectual collaboration. Though only one of the essays is jointly authored, all were jointly generated. Read together, they trace the progress of a conversation about politics, sexuality and the state; individual essays echo and respond to the others included here. They thus share many common features, despite the variety of languages and venues from which they derive.

All of the essays are involved in the production of "bridge discourses,"[1] or political languages and strategies that can open dialogue across discursive gaps, generate critical challenges from one location to another, and produce negotiated interventions and actions. Specifically, they work to build connections among three arenas of political action: (1) the reform politics of liberal and progressive groups, which address social inequities through the courts and legislatures, and work to influence electoral campaigns and referenda through mainstream media; (2) the performative politics of more radical groups, aimed at reshaping the assumptions and categories of political life through cultural production and direct action, and (3) the critical politics of cultural theory and social analysis, circulated through academic writing and journalism.

In FACT, our short- and long-term goals (to defeat antipornography legislation, to expand the scope of a liberatory public discourse about sexuality) required us to work in all these arenas. We discovered that, in practical terms, transporting questions and insights from one arena to another dramatically enhanced our effectiveness. We filed court documents and addressed legislatures with arguments adapted from feminist theory. We organized a street theater action, "Sex Cops," to protest the Meese Commission on Pornography's stacked and bogus hearings, and distributed leaflets outlining our legislative arguments to public and press. We wrote op-ed pieces, feature stories in newspapers, and articles for publication in academic journals. We designed and published our own book, *Caught Looking: Feminism, Pornography and Censorship*.

During the second half of the decade, the AIDS activist group ACT UP also forged connections among these political arenas, also with dramatic effectiveness. Demonstrations and lobbying, art and publicity, cultural theory and multiple sites of activism interacted productively (although, of course, not without tensions). The essays in this book are aimed at promoting just this sort of polymorphous political engagement.

As I write in 1995, feminist and lesbian/gay politics are too often conducted without such engagements. National legislative and media campaigns (for abortion rights, or against antigay referenda) seldom interact with feminist or queer theory; performative political groups (like Queer Nation or the Lesbian Avengers) sometimes set themselves *against* "theory" and "reform," as if a truly "radical" political campaign could do without them. And, especially distressing for us, feminist and lesbian/gay politics seem to run on entirely separate tracks. As Chapter One, "Contextualizing the Sexuality Debates: A Chronology" makes clear, feminists have had little to say about the NEA fiasco, which led to the defunding of feminist artists Karen Finley and Holly Hughes; the issues were oddly understood as being about gay rights, artistic freedom or civil liberties, but not feminism.[2] And as Chapter Nine, "Marriage, Law and Gender: A Feminist Inquiry," argues, lesbian/gay campaigns for partnership recognition largely ignore the broad political implications of the gender categories that define both "marriage" and "gay" relationships.

Of course, this lack of interaction is one of the widespread complaints about the balkanized landscape of American identity politics. If feminist and lesbian/gay politics do not interact enough with each other, they interact even less with the politics of race, class and nation which must also lie at the center of any truly progressive vision. This is not merely a matter of recognizing the intersections of issues understood as separate, but of working out the complex ways that hierarchical categories have been mutually constituting. Gender categories have been racialized; nationalisms have been produced as class-based and ethnically "pure." We would not argue, however, for a unified or totalizing politics which attempts to explain everything at once, which never accords priority to one set of issues over another, or which subsumes particular struggles into a universalizing project. Attempts to invoke a mantra of "race, class, sex, colonialism" in every political setting usually degenerate into a rhetoric of self-righteousness that defeats particular, focused actions.

In avoiding the twin dangers of narrow identity-based, single-issue politics on the one hand, and universalizing utopian projects on the other, we turn in these essays to a politics sensitive to specific local and historical contexts. Rather than ask, "Is pornography good or bad for women?"

we would question whether any meaningful generalizations can be made about all "women" and pornography, and ask how and why materials defined as "pornography" are produced and used, in what settings, for what purposes. Rather than design and promote a "model" law based on our own understandings of gender and representation, we would wish to investigate the actual probable workings of any piece of legislation in actual bookstores, art museums and courtrooms.

Our commitment in these essays is to constructing forms of intervention that can be effective in particular, historical locations, that can re-form specific institutional or cultural practices. We reject any monolithic notion of "the state," so that we might understand how different public agencies operate, sometimes at cross-purposes. Lesbian/gay activists, for instance, face an array of contradictory situations, from state antisodomy laws to municipal antidiscrimination ordinances, from a hostile military hierarchy to more friendly public arts councils and state universities. Effective political action consists in appropriating, transforming and deploying the friendliest discourses, in order to counter the most hostile ones. This was the work of FACT's appropriation of "anticensorship" rhetoric, and of the specific actions recommended in essays such as Chapter Seven, "Life After Hardwick," and Chapter Fourteen, "Queering the State."

The political strategies we advocate here are sometimes called "postmodern," and opposed to the class-based universalizing projects of the "old" and "new" left, and to any separatist or nationalist politics of gender, race, ethnicity or sexuality. Critics of "postmodern" politics charge its advocates with ignoring institutions, deep structures and material life in favor of a focus on free-floating discourses and disconnected rhetorics; or a politics based on specific local interventions is said to be blind to larger structuring realities of economic and political power. But the politics we advocate here, whether labeled "postmodern" or not, is committed to a living relationship between broad political and economic critique, and the production of rhetorics and strategies that can have specific, local, institutional/discursive impact. The challenge we confront is the necessity of intervening from within the uneven developments and contradictions of a capitalist culture, grasping at every opportunity for progressive change, without generating unrealistic (and often tyrannical) fantasies of revolution, or being willing to settle for minor tinkering with the status quo. In concrete terms, this means (for instance) reclaiming and reinventing "pornography" on behalf of women and queers, not trying to abolish it (like divine-right queens of culture), or defending it "as is" as the price of "free speech."

The specific political tool that we have worked to forge throughout the essays in this volume is the concept of *sexual dissent*, a concept that invokes a unity of speech, politics and practices, and forges a connection among sexual expressions, oppositional politics, and claims to public space. Because sexual representations construct identities (they do not merely reflect preexisting ones), restriction and regulation of sexual expression is a form of political repression aimed at sexual minorities and gender nonconformists. This is abundantly clear in conservative attacks on the arts that define homoeroticism as "obscene," and in antigay campaigns that attempt to restrict the "promotion" or "advocacy" of homosexuality in safe-sex materials or in schools. What the right wing wishes to eliminate is our power to invent and represent ourselves, and to define and redefine our politics. They know our public sexual expression is political, and that is how we must defend it. Rather than invoking fixed, natural identities and asking only for privacy or an end to discrimination, we must expand our right to public *sexual dissent*. This is the path of access to public discourse and political representation.

The essays in this volume address the politics of sexual dissent in three arenas—in sexual representation, in the law, and in activism and the academy.

Porn Again?! or, We Told You So...

Ah, the porn wars. These debates among feminists, which extended from the late seventies to the mid-eighties, did indeed feel like "war." The battles were bitter, often personal and vituperative. The scars remain. Those of us on the anti-antiporn "side" were astonished to find ourselves attacked by former allies. As we naïvely set out to open up questions which we believed antiporn activists had either sidelined or closed for discussion, we expected a debate, but not an assault. Borrowing rhetorical devices from Cold War anticommunists, antiporners defined all dissent on sexual issues as "collaboration" (in this case, with "the patriarchy") and treason (against feminism, or against all women). We were ultimately shocked to find ourselves defending our activist communities—of sex workers, of butch-fem dykes, of lesbian sadomasochists—against political attacks, launched *by feminists*. We are not just talking about sharp words here. We are talking about sponsorship of state suppression of our livelihoods, our publications, our art work, our political/sexual expression.

The porn wars more or less subsided in the mid-eighties as the antiporn position lost favor among most feminists, and lost in the courts and legislatures of the United States as well. But they have had consequences which are with us still. In the United States, the rhetoric of antiporn feminism has provided a modernizing spin for continuing conservative campaigns against sexual expression. Feminists have found themselves divided, unable to weigh into public controversies over the content of safe-sex education, or over the funding of allegedly "obscene" art. In Canada, antiporn feminists helped the Supreme Court reinterpret the obscenity law, which has since been used against gay bookstores and feminist and lesbian publications.[3]

But let's go back to the beginning, which the chronology in Chapter One, "Contextualizing the Sexuality Debates," allows us to do. The first confrontations in the porn wars were between antiporn groups and Samois, a lesbian S/M group in San Francisco. These early confrontations then migrated from the West Coast throughout the U.S., from culturally marginal organizations to more mainstream ones, from feminist venues to legislatures, courtrooms and national media. The confrontations' biggest flash point came with the introduction of antipornography legislation, coauthored by Andrea Dworkin and Catharine MacKinnon in Minneapolis and Indianapolis in 1984, followed by copycat versions in Cambridge, MA, Los Angeles, CA, Madison, WI, and Suffolk County, NY.

The two chapters following the chronology and the appendix to this volume were produced in the heat of these legislative battles. "Censorship in the Name of Feminism" is reprinted from *The Village Voice*, where it appeared as one of the first feminist reports and critical analyses of events in Minneapolis and Indianapolis. "False Promises," coauthored with Carole S. Vance, first appeared in a Canadian anthology edited by Varda Burstyn, *Women Against Censorship*, where it offered a nuts and bolts examination of the U.S. antiporn ordinances designed to persuade feminists to oppose such laws. The Appendix, "Brief Amici Curiae," was submitted as a "friend of the court" brief to an appellate court. It was intended not only to persuade the court to find the Indianapolis antiporn ordinance unconstitutional, but also to serve as an organizing device among feminists. FACT circulated it, collecting a total of eighty signatories including the Women's Legal Defense Fund, Adrienne Rich, Barbara Smith, Kate Millet, Gayle Rubin, and many other feminists from academia, the arts, feminist publishing, lesbian and activist organizations and elsewhere.

These three documents speak in somewhat different languages, and served somewhat different ends at the time of their publication. (The repetition of basic information in them reflects their original independent uses; this repetition has not been edited out for this volume, in order that each article may still stand alone.) But all set out, in different ways, to counter antiporn accounts of "pornography" as a unified (patriarchal) discourse with a singular (misogynistic) impact. Against this account we argued that the sexually explicit materials called "pornography" are full of multiple, contradictory, layered and highly contextual meanings. The literary critics and artists among us pointed out these elasticities of meaning, and also argued for the ambiguity of reception. Different audiences are bound to make complicated, unpredictable use of these fantasy materials. The sex workers, publishers and artists also stressed the positive value of sexually explicit materials for women, who might appropriate even apparently misogynistic images, transforming them for their own explorations of prohibited sexual terrains. The historians pointed out the problematic nature of the rhetoric and alliances of the antiporn campaign, which seemed to echo some of the worst aspects of turn-of-the-century social purity and temperance movements. The lawyers and political activists insisted on laying out the concrete applications of the specific pieces of legislation proposed by the antiporners.

These collective efforts came together in the effort to respond to the antiporn argument that pornography's narratives construct gender as male domination/female subordination through sex, as in the repeated story "she says no but she really means yes." In addition to disputing the claim that this is the only story porn tells, or that it is predictably received by male consumers, we argued that antiporn rhetoric *also* constructs gender. Antiporn gender is a rigid binary of potentially violent, dominant men and subordinated, silenced women. This is not a reflective description, but is itself a production of gender that tells a story that mechanically reverses the porn story into "she says yes but she really means no." This move reproduces binary gender categories, and depends for its coherence on the porn narrative it attacks. At the same time, it echoes conservative, moralistic reversals of porn narratives. The alliances of antiporn feminists with moral conservatives were due not only to local opportunity, but to a convergence of binary gender categories and melodramatic narratives of female innocence and male villainy. These convergences were furthered by feminist deployment of class disgust (during a Women Against Pornography-sponsored tour through Times Square, I was invited to just *look* at these men—*yuck*) and bourgeois priggishness.[4]

In assembling our critique of antiporn politics, we appropriated the rhetoric of "anticensorship." We did this because we found much to agree with in many widely endorsed anticensorship arguments, and because "censorship" was a negative we hoped would be powerful enough to set against "pornography." In making this appropriation, though, we necessarily encountered the entire framework of civil liberties, "free speech" arguments and their embedded oppositions: consent/force, free speech/censorship, free choice/coercion. This was a problem for us, because we wanted to separate ourselves from the civil liberties framework to make a specifically feminist argument in defense of sexually explicit expression.

We wanted to attack many of the standard oppositions of civil liberties discourse. For instance, we did not argue that sex workers have "free choice" of occupations, but emphasized that, within a limited range of very constrained choices in a sexist, capitalist economy, sex work is not always the worst option. And though we recognized that "consent" is socially constructed, we nonetheless argued that it remains a centrally important concept to retain in sex law. But such dissent from deeply entrenched cultural oppositions was often lost in public debate.

In fact, the overall *strategic* nature of the arguments and language of the various articles and documents was often lost in various responses to and commentaries on them. For instance, the FACT brief (Appendix) mobilizes arguments for the purposes of *both* persuading a court *and* organizing a wide range of feminist activists in opposition to the antipornography ordinances. As an adversarial document, it mixes arguments that respond to belief structures that its authors do not necessarily share (e.g. behavioristic social science) with efforts to stretch the prevailing doctrines of law (e.g. First Amendment law), and to infuse those doctrines with more biting, progressive feminist politics. Similarly, Chapter Three, "False Promises," was written to persuade a broad range of feminist and progressive constituencies to oppose the ordinances. Had any of its authors written an analysis of the Dworkin/MacKinnon legislation *without* the goal of persuading activists and voters in specific municipal contests, that analysis would have been quite different from the one in "False Promises." Academic writers and analysts have been most likely to miss this strategic construction at the heart of these and other activist documents. We hope that the publication of our essays together in this volume will illustrate the process of such construction, while also helping to distinguish the feminist from the liberal arguments for freedom of sexual expression.

The final two contributions to the first section of this volume are "Feminist Historians and Antipornography Campaigns," a retrospective overview of the reasons behind feminist historians' opposition to antiporn legislation, originally delivered as a speech to a conference of the National Coalition Against Censorship, and "Sex Panics," a column published in *Artforum* in the wake of the controversy over National Endowment for the Arts funding for the exhibition of the work of Robert Mapplethorpe. This last essay begins to address the sequelae to the feminist porn wars—the chain of public sex panics in which feminist voices of protest against repression have been largely absent.[5]

In the past few years, as the effects of antiporn legislation in Canada and continued antiporn activities in the U.S. have accumulated clear consequences, our comrade sex radicals have chorused repeatedly *we told you so*. This is not a particularly happy vindication, for it comes as feminist and lesbian artists, sex workers, publishers and activists have had their work banned, removed, attacked and seized.

One of the biggest *we told you so* episodes occurred in Canada. After repeated defeats for their legislative ideas in the U.S., antiporn feminists succeeded in influencing the Supreme Court of Canada to shift the interpretation of the obscenity law there from a morality-based to a harm-based approach in 1992. When Kathleen Mahoney of the Women's Legal Education and Action Fund (LEAF), the successful intervener in the case called *Donald Butler vs. Her Majesty the Queen* (or the Butler decision), was asked how they succeeded, she told *Ms.* magazine,

> How did we do it? We showed them the porn—and among the seized videos were some horrifically violent and degrading gay movies. We made the point that the abused men in these films were being treated like women—and the judges got it. Otherwise, men can't put themselves in our shoes.[6]

Mahoney was completely oblivious to her use of the judges' homophobic panic, and to the probable effects of their decision on gay and lesbian communities. The decision, which defined obscenity as "images of sex with violence or sex which degrades or dehumanizes any of the participants," was hailed by Catharine MacKinnon (who helped with the LEAF legal work) as "of world historic importance."[7] She did not seem to recognize the elasticity of terms like "degrades" or "dehumanizes," nor their easy applicability by homophobes to gay sexuality.

The first prosecution under the newly interpreted law was against Glad Day Books, a gay bookstore in Toronto, for selling *Bad Attitude*, a lesbian sex magazine. Ironically, *Bad Attitude* was one of the feminist publications that the FACT brief predicted could be vulnerable to suppression had the Dworkin-MacKinnon ordinance become law in the United States (see Appendix, "Brief Amici Curiae"). There have been innumerable prosecutions and seizures of lesbian and gay materials since.[8] *We told you so.*

But then, we suspected all along that antigay assumptions were deeply embedded in feminist antiporn rhetoric. This homophobia was projected onto gay *male* sexuality, allowing "nice" lesbians to feel normalized by their distance from "disgusting" male sexuality and promiscuity. This move required that "bad" lesbian sex be attacked as male-identified—butch-fem dykes and Samois activists were cut off from the normalizing feminine, and cast into the vile male "outside" envisioned by antiporn feminism.

Antiporners construct a wacky feminist world in which heterosexual monogamous marriage (the kind that Catharine MacKinnon's reported engagement to Jeffrey Masson has prepared her to enter), is not suspect as "patriarchal," but lesbian sex is...because it's "male"!

Some feminists, antiporn and otherwise, would like to believe that the prosecutions in Canada are due to misinterpretations of the law by conservative police, prosecutors and judges. Such "misinterpretations" are, we have argued, completely predictable once antiporn language passes into law. *We told you so.* But in addition, we believe that many antiporn feminists would themselves conduct such prosecutions if they held the reins of state. At the University of Michigan in 1992, an exhibition of feminist art work on the subject of prostitution, curated by feminist artist and videographer Carol Jacobsen, included several videos critical of the notion that sex workers are only victims. Organizers of a conference at the Law School, "Prostitution: From Academia to Activism," of which the exhibition was a part, physically removed most of the videos, claiming they were "pornographic" and a "threat" to the safety of conference participants. These "pornographic" videos included Paula Allen's *Angelina Foxy* (1986), a phototext essay documenting the life of a Jersey City prostitute; Susan Aiken's and Carlos Aparicio's *The Salt Mines* (1990), a critically acclaimed documentary about homeless transvestite hustlers in New York City; Jacobsen's *Street Sex* (1989), video interviews with Detroit prostitutes recently released from jail, and Carol Leigh's *Outlaw Poverty, Not Prostitutes* (1991), a video chronicling prostitutes' international organizing. Prominent among the public supporters of the conference organizers acting to remove this "threat" was law professor Catharine MacKinnon.[9]

This is political repression masquerading as a safety patrol, and it isn't Jesse Helms holding the stop sign.

We Are All Outlaws...

The past decade has been a season of astonishing achievements and bitter defeats in the field of U.S. law as applied to lesbian, gay and bisexual citizens. The second section of this volume begins a sustained consideration of these events with Nan Hunter's reaction to the stunning setback issued by the Supreme Court in its 1986 decision, *Bowers vs. Hardwick*. Hunter urges lesbian and gay advocates to organize for political action rather than rely too heavily on litigation.

Hunter continues her consideration of this contemptuous and contemptible court decision in "Life After Hardwick" by analyzing a notable irony. Supreme Court conservatives, wedded to a legal philosophy that defers to the intentions of the "founding fathers" in interpreting the U.S. Constitution, based the decision in *Bowers vs. Hardwick* on a historical forgery—the claim that an invidious distinction between heterosexual and homosexual practices is a centuries-old "moral" tradition. In fact, the "founding fathers" recognized no such distinction; they defined "sodomy" as nonprocreative sexual practices, without regard to the gender of the participants. Hunter points out that the practices criminalized in the Georgia statute under review (including oral and anal sex) are practices which modern hetero- and homosexuals *share*. Upon this similarity, the Justices in the majority labored to establish a distinction. "The History of Sexuality According to the U.S. Supreme Court" is not a text that could pass even preliminary review.

In "Sexual Dissent and the Law" Hunter turns to another horrifying event—the legal kidnapping of Sharon Kowalski. Disabled in an accident, Kowalski was separated from her lover, Sharon Thompson, by court decisions awarding custody to her homophobic father. Though the lovers were eventually reunited, the years of Kowalski and Thompson's forced separation fueled the nightmares of lesbians and gay men without legal recognition for their partnerships.

In her article on the Kowalski case, Hunter argues that legal wrangles over the definitions of "family" and "parent" offer us possibilities for denaturalizing and thus destabilizing institutions that marginalize us, by helping us "to expose the utter contingency of sexual conventions that, in part, construct the family." Hunter extends this argument in "Marriage, Law and Gender." She asks readers to put feminist and lesbian and gay critiques of the legal institution of marriage together, and to see how its founding terms ("husband" and "wife") *produce* gender. Traditionally, gendered concepts of authority and dependency constituted the "nature" of marriage. Feminist reform has drained those two assumptions out of the formal premises of marriage law. All that remains is the rock bottom definition, the union of "husband" and "wife." The legalization of lesbian and gay marriage, Hunter argues, has the potential to undermine that gendered core. But she also insists that any truly progressive reform of marriage law must be accompanied by the expansion of alternative forms of legal partnership, and by an attack on the stigmatization of sex outside legally recognized coupledom.

Finally, in "Identity, Speech and Equality," Hunter elaborates one of the central arguments connecting the essays in this volume. She historicizes the political uses of concepts of "identity," "privacy," "speech," and "equality," and argues that a long-term shift has occurred in efforts to regulate sexuality. Rather than working to impose a deviant identity on individuals (who invoke a right to "privacy" in self-defense), proposed state regulations are now more likely to seek to control the circulation of deviant ideas in public venues. The work of self-defense has thus shifted from invoking

the right to private conduct, to defending our right to public self-defini-
tion, self-representation and political/sexual expression.

Activism and the Academy

The third and last section of this volume includes a series of essays on the
politics of the professionalization and institutionalization of lesbian and
gay studies. These essays chart the phenomenal growth in this field, from
the time Chapter Eleven, "History's Gay Ghetto," first appeared in 1986,
when most of the work in lesbian and gay studies was conducted outside
the university, to the time of the writing of Chapter Thirteen, "Scholars
and Sense," in 1992 and Chapter Fifteen, "The Discipline Problem," in
1994, when the widespread institutionalization of lesbian and gay studies
and queer theory had produced growing pains and tensions between generations of scholars with differing allegiances and expectations. The 1986
essay reflects the documentary goals of early community-based lesbian and
gay history projects, and embraces the strategy of moving an "invisible"
population into social and political visibility. The later essays shift away
from such goals and strategies, toward an emphasis on the importance of
denaturalizing categories of social identity. Nonetheless, the later essays
continue to hold the goals of earlier community organizing in productive
tension with the projects of recent academically based theories.

The essays in this section also examine the political and theoretical
significance of a shift from "lesbian and gay" to "queer" identifications,
a shift I generally advocate. But, like any other term or category, "queer"
has meanings that shift with context and usage; the usage I advocate is a
denaturalizing one. There are many contexts in which "queer" connotes
disparagement or a fixed identity, and is less useful or progressive than
other categories or terms.

Some feminist critics of "queer" theory and politics argue that this term
erases gender in the same ways that "gay" without "lesbian" has done;
they invoke a history of "queer" that aligns it with boy-contexts and boy-
meanings. But "queer" has a girl-history too. During the porn wars, many
lesbians who were alienated by lesbian-feminists' homogenizing, white,
middle-class, anti-gay-male, antisex discourses, refused the category "lesbian," and adopted "queer" as a mark of separation from such politics, a
badge of principled dissidence.[10] Such uses of "queer" constructed alliances
with gay men, and sometimes privileged them over a feminist "sisterhood."
These alliances have not been constructed on men's terms alone, however.
Many women adopt "queer" as a mark of a particular historical relation to,
not a repudiation of, feminism. Many also recognize that, though many

political situations require the specification of gender, the assumption that all do endlessly reproduces the gender binary they (I) hope to undermine.

Running throughout this volume is the conviction that the role of a dissident intellectual is not to teach "theory" to the nontheoretical classes or masses,[11] but to find ways for theories and activisms to learn from each other in the joint effort to re-form the institutions and practices that shape and constrain us all.

CHAPTER 1

Contextualizing the Sexuality Debates

A Chronology 1966–2005

NAN D. HUNTER

I will love whom I may; I will love for as long or as short a period as I can; I will change this love when the conditions indicate that it ought to be changed; and neither you nor any law you can make shall deter me.

—Victoria Woodhull, 1873

Are our girls to be as free to please themselves by indulging in the loveless gratification of every instinct ... and passion as our boys?

—Frances Willard, 1891

Arguments about the politics of sexuality began in the first wave of feminism and have not ended yet. Throughout the second wave, women have debated questions of power, passion, violence, representation, consent, agency, diversity, and autonomy associated with sex. What follows is a chronology of feminist events and milestones of the last forty years. The specific inclusions and exclusions are idiosyncratic, but the chronology seeks to provide a context and a sense of historical rhythm for the emergence of the ferocious disputes about antipornography laws that seemed to erupt out of nowhere in the early 1980s.

In the chronology, one sees the flowering of grassroots politics in the late 1960s and early 1970s, followed by the migration of debates about sexuality out of obscure movement factionalism into the mass media and the conventional political spheres of referendum campaigns and congressional debates. The core of the feminist debate about pornography occurred during a ten-year bell curve: from the founding of Women Against Violence Against Women in 1976, to the peak intensity generated by the adoption of Andrea Dworkin's and Catharine MacKinnon's censorial law in 1984, to the denouement in 1986, when the Supreme Court ruled that law unconstitutional. Beginning with the decline of that issue, in the late 1980s, three new focus points for cultural disputes about sexuality and representation emerge: the controversies over public funding for safe-sex AIDS-prevention programs, the arts funding debate, and the debate over rap music lyrics.

About these three postpornography issues, however, feminists were, for the most part, noticeably silent. Individual women became involved, many as part of lesbian and gay or African American political efforts, but the widespread articulation of a feminist position was largely absent, even when the issues involved invited one. There was virtually no feminist commentary, for example, on the characterization of AIDS as divine punishment for sex. Nor did feminists draw the obvious analogy between the early birth control movement and safe-sex campaigns. Nor was there any visible feminist defense of the claim for a public voice by women, about women's sexuality, explicit in the work of two of the defunded artists, Karen Finley and Holly Hughes. The bitterness of the internal conflict about pornography disabled most feminists from intervening forcefully in these debates, leaving a crucial perspective largely missing from the conversation. The most significant exception came in the engagement of African-American feminists in the debates over the politics of rap.

Each of these waves of controversy has constituted its own sex panic. Each, reverberating with the others, magnified the sense that the wars over sex and imagery will continue to be fought—inside and outside feminism—for many years to come.

1966: With three hundred charter members, the National Organization for Women (NOW) announces its formation. Its statement of purpose says, in part: "We will protest, and endeavor to change, the false image of women now prevalent in the main media, and in the tests, ceremonies, laws and practices of our major social institutions." Masters and Johnson publish their clinical findings in *Human Sexual Response*, documenting that women are multiorgasmic and experience both vaginal and clitoral orgasms, with great variation possible in orgasmic intensity.

1967: Women active in the New Left press their demands for equality with men in the movement, as well as a political claim that women's status is analogous to that of colonized peoples in the Third World. Their efforts at both the Students for a Democratic Society (SDS) national convention and at a National Conference for New Politics meet with hostility from leftist men. Activist women form groups in Chicago, New York, and Washington, D.C., framing their politics as "women's liberation."

1968: Radical Women in New York protest the Miss America pageant, crowning a live sheep as Miss America and setting up a "freedom trashcan" in which to burn oppressive symbols. A leaflet tells women to bring "bras, girdles, curlers, false eyelashes, wigs and representative issues of *Cosmopolitan, Ladies' Home Journal, Family Circle, etc.*" It continues: "Miss America and *Playboy's* centerfold are sisters over the skin. To win approval, we must be both sexy and wholesome, delicate but able to cope, demure yet titillatingly bitchy. Deviation of any sort brings, we are told, disaster: 'You won't get a man!'" It is a year of tremendous political upheaval. Rebellious students in Mexico are shot by police. Thousands march in France to protest education and labor policies. The Soviet Union quashes a rebellion in Prague by invasion and occupation. In the United States, Dr. Martin Luther King and Senator Robert Kennedy are assassinated.

1969: On Valentine's Day, women in New York and San Francisco demonstrate against Bridal Fair expositions. Protesters decry the size of the wedding industry, estimated at five billion dollars a year. Women's Liberation in New York leaflets the city's Marriage License Bureau, telling women the "real terms" of the contract they are entering. Marches to repeal abortion laws occur around the country. When police raid a gay bar in Greenwich Village, drag queens refuse to cooperate; the Stonewall Riot marks the beginning of the gay liberation movement. Women demonstrate against Playboy Clubs in Chicago, New York, Boston, and San Francisco. At Grinnell College in Iowa, male and female students stage a "nude-in" when a Playboy representative comes to speak on the "Playboy philosophy." They demand that he also take off his clothes; he flees.

1970: It is an extraordinary year for the publication of feminist books: *Sexual Politics*, by Kate Millet; *The Dialectic of Sex*, by Shulamith Firestone; *Notes from the Second Year*, containing Anne Koedt's "The Myth of the Vaginal Orgasm"; and *Sisterhood is Powerful*, edited by Robin Morgan, containing such feminist classics as "The Politics of Housework" by Pat Mainardi and "Psychology Constructs the Female" by Naomi Weisstein. Women sit in for eleven hours at the offices of the male editor of *Ladies' Home Journal*, winning the right to write and edit a special supplement on women's liberation that the magazine agrees to publish. The San Francisco Women's Liberation Front invades a CBS stockholders' meeting to demand changes in how the network portrays women. Women in the American Newspaper Guild hold a convention on women's rights. *off our backs* begins publication in Washington, D.C. An early issue features a spoof called "Mr. April, Playboy of the Month," and a centerfold ad for "Butterballs," a male genital deodorant. During a unionization struggle at Grove Press, women occupy the Grove offices and demand equal decision-making power, an end to publications that degrade women, and the use of profits to fund women's services, including abortion clinics and a bail fund for prostitutes. The President's Commission on Obscenity and Pornography recommends the repeal of all laws prohibiting the distribution of sexually explicit materials to consenting adults, and the implementation of a massive sex education program. Congress begins a program of federal funding for family planning services. Student protests against the war in Vietnam reach their height with a nationwide strike after violence erupts at Kent State and Jackson State colleges.

1971: At a Women's National Abortion Conference, delegates adopt demands for repeal of all abortion laws, no forced sterilizations, and no restrictions on contraceptives, but split on whether to include a demand for "freedom of sexual expression." That demand is ultimately voted down, and dozens of women walk out. Throughout the movement, the gay-straight split is at its height, as lesbians leave many existing women's groups to form their own separate organizations. A group of lesbians who leave *off our backs* begins publication of *The Furies*. Feminists organize antirape organizations in major cities, beginning with Bay Area Women Against Rape, and the Washington, D.C., rape crisis hotline. Rape crisis centers open around the country, and women use multiple strategies to discredit the myth that "no means yes." NOW announces a national campaign to change the role and images of women in the broadcasting industry. The NOW Media Task Force is formed, which begins a process of monitoring employment and programming policies at TV stations around the country. During the next five years, NOW files fifteen license renewal challenges against TV stations. The Feminist

Women's Health Center opens in Los Angeles, the first of a series of clinics founded on the principle of self-help and self-examination. The Boston Women's Health Book Collective publishes the first edition of *Our Bodies, Ourselves*, a 112-page newsprint book selling for thirty-five cents.

1972: *Ms.* magazine begins publication. Shere Hite embarks on a study of women's sexuality, sending detailed questionnaires on sexual practices and preferences to thousands of women in NOW chapters, abortion rights groups and women's centers, and asking readers of *The Village Voice, Mademoiselle, Brides, Ms.*, and *Oui* magazines to participate. The Supreme Court rules that unmarried persons have the same right as married couples to purchase contraceptives. Congress passes the Equal Rights Amendment, sending it to the states for ratification.

1973: The Supreme Court, in *Roe v. Wade*, rules that women have a constitutional right to choose abortion. The same year, in *Miller v. California*, the Court modifies the definition of obscenity to make prosecutions easier. Instead of a requirement the material be "utterly without redeeming social value," the new test requires proof only that it lack "serious" artistic or social value. Additionally, the Court rules that whether material appeals to "prurient interests" should be judged by local community standards. Chief Justice Burger's opinion ignores the recommendations of the Presidential Commission (see 1970). African American feminists in New York create the National Black Feminist Organization. Women working in prostitution announce the formation of COYOTE (Call Off Your Old Tired Ethics), an organization urging the repeal of prostitution laws. In New York, Baltimore, and Florida, three women's presses form: Daughters, Diana, and Naiad. Daughters' first book is *Rubyfruit Jungle*.

1974: The battered women's movement begins to emerge, influenced by the writings of British feminists; the first shelter for battered women opens in St. Paul. Members of the Beach Cities NOW chapter in Southern California picket the Academy Awards ceremony and demand more leading roles and more nontraditional employment opportunities for women. The first of many lawsuits against major media organizations is filed by women alleging employment discrimination. During the next five years, suits are filed against NBC, the *New York Times, Newsday*, The Associated Press, the *Washington Post, Newsweek, Reader's Digest*, Universal Studios, and many others. Betty Dodson self-publishes *Liberating Masturbation* after five thousand women respond to a notice in *Ms.* magazine offering a booklet on women and masturbation.

1975: Feminist and civil rights groups rally to the defense of Joanne Little, an African American woman from a small North Carolina town who killed a white prison guard in self-defense when he sexually assaulted her. She is tried for murder and acquitted. *Against Our Will*, Susan Brownmiller's study of rape, is published. Women in the antirape movement critique race and class bias in Brownmiller's book and, more generally, throughout the movement. *For Colored Girls Who Have Considered Suicide When the Rainbow Is Enuf*, Ntozake Shange's anthem of African American women's voices, opens on the New York stage. The war in Vietnam ends.

1976: Women Against Violence Against Women (WAVAW) begins in Los Angeles. Members deface a Rolling Stones billboard ("I'm black and blue from the Rolling Stones and I love it"), call a press conference, and Warner Brothers removes the billboard. A conference on violence against women held in San Francisco spawns Women Against Violence in Pornography and the Media (WAVPM).

1977: In another widely followed case around which feminists organize, Inez Garcia is acquitted of murder for killing the man who held her down while another man raped her. The Combahee River Collective publishes "A Black Feminist Statement," calling for analysis of "the major systems of oppression" as "interlocking." Antirape protestors in Pittsburgh organize the first "Take Back the Night" march to dramatize women's insistence on the right to enjoy public space in safety. Women in Rochester, New York stage civil disobedience at a theater showing *Snuff. Snuff* protests occur in San Diego, New York, Denver, and other cities. Phyllis Schlafly's Eagle Forum, apparently angered by the increasing availability of *Our Bodies, Ourselves* in small-town libraries, launches local campaigns to ban the book, claiming that it encourages masturbation, lesbianism, premarital sex, and abortion. In Helena, Montana, the Eagle Forum succeeds in removing the book from school libraries, in part because a local district attorney states that, although it is not legally obscene, librarians who distribute it may be prosecuted for contributing to the delinquency of a minor. The local ACLU sues in federal court to get the book reinstated.

1978: Events in California illustrate the divergent political tendencies within the movement related to sexual issues. Lesbians and gay men join forces in the "No on 6" campaign to defeat the Briggs Initiative, a right-wing ballot proposal which would have required the state to fire any employee, gay or straight, who advocated gay rights. Various elements within the coalition use different rhetorical and political strategies: gay leftists use the opportunity to defend sexual freedom, while professional campaign consultants obtain an op-ed against the proposal from Ronald Reagan, which becomes the turning point in the campaign. The same year in California, WAVPM organizes a conference on "Feminist Perspectives on Pornography" featuring workshops, speeches and a march by five thousand women demanding an end to pornography.

1979: Samois, a lesbian S/M group, holds its first public forum at the Old Wives Tales bookstore in San Francisco. Samois criticizes the equation WAVPM makes in its slide show of consensual sadomasochism with violence. Samois later publishes *What Color Is Your Handkerchief*, which some feminist bookstores refuse to carry, and for which some feminist publications refuse to accept advertising. At the first conference of the National Coalition Against Sexual Assault, a resolution that would commit member groups of the coalition to refuse funding from the Playboy Foundation is defeated; a number of women attending the conference raise six hundred dollars among themselves to repay Playboy's contribution to the conference. Whether to accept Playboy funding becomes a hot issue for many groups. After an antipornography conference and a march through Times Square modeled on WAVPM's activities in San Francisco, Women Against Pornography forms in New York and begins leading tours of 42nd Street. WAP advocates education and protest, and specifically disavows censorship. Its position statement on the First Amendment says, in part; "We have not put forth any repressive legislative proposals, and we are not carving out any new exceptions to the First Amendment." Ellen Willis' columns in *The Village Voice* criticize the WAP analysis of porn as simplistic. Andrea Dworkin's book, *Pornography: Men Possessing Women*, is published. The Screen Actors Guild releases the results of its study of TV drama, analyzing content from 1969 to 1978. The study finds that men outnumber women three to one in prime-time drama, and that "marriage, romance, and family are women's concerns in the world of television."

1980: *Take Back The Night*, an anthology of antiporn articles, many of which were originally talks at the 1978 WAVPM conference, is published. WAVPM sponsors a forum on S/M at University of California-Berkeley, which Samois pickets. In April, *Mother Jones* prints a special issue on pornography, including a critical analysis of feminist antiporn politics by Deirdre English. Another critique, Pat Califia's "Among Us, Against Us–The New Puritans," appears in *The Advocate*. Naiad Press publishes Califia's book *Sapphistry: The Book of Lesbian Sexuality*, which is greeted by a storm of protest because it contains a section on S/M. NOW passes a resolution condemning pornography and S/M as exploitation and violence. Ronald Reagan is elected president.

1981: Samois publishes *Coming to Power*, a collection of essays and erotic fiction about lesbian S/M. Again, some bookstores refuse to carry it. In New York, the Heresies literature collective publishes *Heresies 12: The Sex Issue*, a work of prose, poetry, and art on the theme of sexuality. Jerry Falwell sends out a fundraising letter asking readers to remove *Our Bodies, Ourselves* from libraries and classrooms. The letter includes two pages of "actual excerpts" from the book's sections on sexuality, fantasies, masturbation, and abortion. A collective of African American and Hispanic women forms Kitchen Table Press for the purpose of publishing the works of women of color. *This Bridge Called My Back: Writings By Radical Women of Color*, edited by Cherríe Moraga and Gloria Anzaldúa, is published. Doctors in New York and Los Angeles become aware of a strange new, fatal disease. Initially they name it GRID, gay-related immune deficiency.

1982: In April, the annual Barnard Conference is held, this year focusing on Women and Sexuality. Conference planners hope to avoid the polarization that has already occurred on the West Coast, and structure the Conference theme around "pleasure and danger." More than eight hundred women attend. WAP stages a protest wearing T-shirts that read "For Feminist Sexuality" on one side and "Against S/M" on the other. WAP also circulates leaflets criticizing selected participants by name on the basis of their alleged sexual behavior. Barnard College officials confiscate the *Diary of a Conference* produced by conference organizers. The Helena Rubinstein Foundation withdraws its funding from future conferences. The Lesbian Sex Mafia, a New York-based support group for "politically incorrect sex," holds a speak-out the day after the conference. Reporting of the conference and letters to the editor condemning or extolling it are printed for months in *off our backs*. Alice Walker publishes *The Color Purple*, depicting a southern African American woman's path from abuse to dignity and sexual self-discovery; within three years, more than three million copies are in print. The deadline for ratification of the ERA by the states expires.

1983: *Powers of Desire: The Politics of Sexuality* is published. It is the first East Coast-based book to offer a critical analysis of antiporn politics. In London, copies of Samois's *Coming to Power* are burned outside a women's bookstore. Late in the year, Andrea Dworkin and Catharine MacKinnon draft a proposed ordinance to ban pornography in Minneapolis. The Centers for Disease Control recommends avoiding sexual contact with persons "known or suspected" to have AIDS.

1984: The Minneapolis antiporn ordinance is passed by the City Council, but vetoed by Mayor Donald Fraser. A revised version is introduced in the Indianapolis City Council by Beulah Coughenour, a council member who built her political career on anti-ERA work. It is passed and signed into law in Indianapolis; a coalition of media groups led by the American Booksellers Association files suit to challenge it, and wins a court order declaring it unconstitutional. WAP endorses the ordinances. In her June, 1984 newsletter, Phyllis Schlafly also endorses the ordinances. In New York and Madison, Wisconsin, feminists form FACT (Feminist Anti-Censorship Taskforce) to oppose the ordinance on feminist grounds. The ordinance is revised and introduced by a conservative County Council member in Suffolk County, New York, where it is defeated by one vote. At the Michigan Women's Music Festival, leaflets seeking models and writers for a Chicago lesbian sex magazine lead to protests of "pimps off the land." Meanwhile, lesbian sex magazines begin publication, including *Bad Attitude* from Boston and *On Our Backs* from San Francisco. *Pleasure and Danger*, the edited proceedings of the Barnard conference, is published.

1985: FACT, together with eighty other feminists, files a friend of the court brief in the U.S. Appeals Court, which later rules that the Indianapolis ordinance is unconstitutional. The Los Angeles County Board of Supervisors considers a version of the ordinance almost identical to the original Minneapolis version. FACT-LA forms to oppose it, joined by a variety of feminists, including leaders of the Feminist Women's Health Center. It is defeated by one vote. In the fall, the ordinance appears as a referendum question on the Cambridge, Massachusetts ballot. Voters defeat it by a three-to-two margin, after opposition from FACT-Cambridge, the Greater Boston Area NOW Chapter, No Bad Women/Just Bad Laws (an organization of sex industry workers), the Boston Women's Health Book Collective (publisher of *Our Bodies, Ourselves*), the Cambridge Commission on the Status of Women, and the founders of the Boston chapter of WAVAW. Attorney General Edwin Meese appoints a commission "to address the serious national problem of pornography." The Reagan Administration proposes a budget that would cut AIDS spending by 10 percent. The number of Americans with AIDS surpasses twelve thousand; one of them is Rock Hudson.

1986: The Supreme Court affirms the Appeals Court ruling that the Indianapolis ordinance is unconstitutional. In June, the Meese Commission issues its final report, condemning "violent" pornography, a category that seems to include both rape and S/M, and splitting on whether to also condemn explicit depictions of all sex outside of marriage. The Supreme Court rules in *Bowers v. Hardwick* that the right to privacy does not extend to homosexual sex.

1987: President Reagan makes his first speech concerning AIDS, in which he calls for mandatory testing of immigrants and prisoners. There are now thirty-six thousand Americans diagnosed with AIDS. The Reagan Administration continues to oppose bills offered in Congress that would prohibit discrimination against persons with HIV disease or AIDS. Sen. Jesse Helms wins adoption of a provision barring federal funds for AIDS prevention programs that "promote" homosexuality. ACT UP forms in New York, and posters the city with the slogan "Silence=Death."

1988: The Reagan Administration adopts regulations preventing federally funded family planning clinics from counseling or referring for abortion, even upon request, a policy that becomes known as the "gag rule." The Presidential election process, beginning with the primaries and continuing through the election, dominates domestic news coverage, pushing other issues, including AIDS, out of the limelight. The media attention to AIDS never returns in the same degree.

1989: Right-wing conservatives attack the National Endowment for the Arts (NEA) for its financial support of two art museums that have exhibited controversial photographs, including homoerotic and sadomasochistic images by Robert Mapplethorpe. PepsiCo drops a planned commercial featuring Madonna to avoid association of the company with her video for "Like a Prayer," which Rev. Donald Wildmon and the American Family Association have attacked as blasphemous. Commentators declare that a "culture war" is raging.

1990: NEA Director John Frohnmayer reverses the decision of a peer review panel and blocks grants to four performance artists: Karen Finley, John Fleck, Holly Hughes, and Tim Miller. Finley's work is feminist, often condemning violence against women in blunt, confrontational style; Hughes' work draws on her lesbian identity; and

Fleck and Miller address issues of gay male experience and sexuality. The director of a Cincinnati art museum is tried and acquitted on obscenity charges for having presented an exhibition of Mapplethorpe's photographs. A federal judge rules that 2 Live Crew's "As Nasty As They Wanna Be" recording is obscene. In November, MTV refuses to air Madonna's newest video release, "Justify My Love," which depicts males and females, of various races, in eroticized relationships to her. MTV says, it is "just not for us." Congress passes legislation prohibiting discrimination against persons with disabilities, including those with AIDS.

1991: The arts funding controversy continues. Congress bans NEA funding unless the applicant is found to satisfy standards of "decency." Several Public Broadcasting System stations refuse to air *Tongues Untied*, a film essay on African American, gay, male life by Marlon Riggs. *Paris Is Burning*, a documentary about drag balls in New York (financed in part by an NEA grant), becomes the independent film hit of the year. President Bush nominates Judge Clarence Thomas to the Supreme Court, and the nation is convulsed by accusations against him of sexual harassment by Professor Anita Hill. Feminists lobby intensively against his confirmation, but his supporters counterattack with accusations against Hill and he is confirmed. Earlier in the year, during the heavily televised Gulf War, Americans see for the first time multiple images of women at war: servicewomen operate missile batteries and fly noncombat missions, the first U.S. military woman becomes a prisoner of war; and mothers whose units have been called up leave behind their children.

1992: The Supreme Court of Canada upholds that nation's obscenity law on the grounds that sexually explicit speech is comparable to "hate speech" because it degrades women. The first prosecution under the new ruling is against *Bad Attitude*, the lesbian sex magazine published by a women's collective in Boston. The U.S. Supreme Court rules that *Roe v. Wade* will not be overturned, although it weakens the standard of review applied to laws that restrict access to abortion. A federal court strikes down content restrictions that ban "offensive" AIDS educational materials. An appeals court reverses the ruling that "As Nasty As They Wanna Be" is obscene. In the November election, Democrats win their first presidential contest in sixteen years, and the number of women in the U.S. Senate triples—to six. Brandon Teena, a transgender teenager, is raped and murdered in Nebraska when a group of boys discovers that he is female.

1993: A gay rights issue enters national mass politics for the first time with an intense debate over the military's ban against gay and lesbian servicemembers that lasts for months. In July, President Clinton announces a compromise in which gay speech and conduct are still grounds for discharge; secret status is not. The President ends the "gag rule" policy of barring abortion counseling at federally funded family planning clinics. The "NEA four" win reinstatement of the grants denied them in 1990.

1994: A subcommittee in the House of Representatives holds hearings on the regulation of music lyrics, focusing on rap. Paula Jones files a lawsuit in federal court alleging that then-governor Bill Clinton sexually harassed her. Republicans win a stunning victory in the midterm elections, capturing control of both the Senate and the House of Representatives. Their "Contract with America" becomes the dominant political document of the moment. Reflecting their attempt to mute intraparty divisions over social and sexual issues, it avoids any focus on abortion, homosexuality, or pornography. Analysts debate whether Republicans can sustain a coalition built on the combination of free-market individualism and traditional moral regulation.

1995: The Hawaii Commission on Sexual Orientation and Law, appointed by the governor, recommends that same-sex couples be allowed to marry, triggering a backlash by conservatives. The National Gay and Lesbian Task Force launches its Policy Institute, the first LGBT think tank. The Beijing Conference on Women endorses women's "right to control [their] sexuality." Deaths from AIDS in the United States during any one year peak at 51,414.

1996: The Supreme Court strikes down an antigay amendment to the Colorado Constitution, sending the first signal of more openness to LGBT rights issues, and ending the right-wing strategy of trying to pass such laws across the nation. Deepa Mehta's film "Fire," about a lesbian relationship between two New Delhi women, sets off fundamentalist protests, which lead to its banning in India and Pakistan. Congress enacts, and President Clinton signs, the Defense of Marriage Act (DoMA), which establishes a one man-one woman definition for marriage in all federal laws and declares that no state shall be required to recognize a marriage between partners of the same sex from another state. Antiretroviral drugs for HIV become available, and the number of AIDS deaths in the United States and Europe plummets. On the day after Christmas, six-year-old Jon-Benet Ramsey is murdered at home in Boulder, Colorado, setting off intense speculation about the identity of the murderer(s). The media repeatedly broadcast photographs of a highly sexualized child wearing make-up and risqué outfits.

1997: The Senate Armed Services Committee holds hearings on sexual harassment in the military, spurred by charges against the Army's highest-ranking noncommissioned officer. The People's Republic of China decriminalizes sodomy. Ellen Degeneres comes out, in character, on her TV sitcom. San Francisco enacts the nation's first equal benefits ordinance, requiring all companies that do business with the city to offer benefits to domestic partners of their employees. The Audre Lorde Project, a community center for Lesbian, Gay, Bisexual, Two Spirit, and Transgender (LGBTT) people of color, opens in Brooklyn, New York.

1998: In January, the Monica Lewinsky scandal breaks, dominating the news almost daily for most of the year. In August, President Clinton admits having lied about his relationship with Lewinsky. In September, the House of Representatives passes four Articles of Impeachment based on his misrepresentations in the Paula Jones case and to the Grand Jury. The U. S. Supreme Court rules in the NEA Four case that the requirement that grantees produce only art that meets "general standards of decency" is constitutionally valid because it does not discriminate against any viewpoint. The first TV season of "Will and Grace" begins. Matthew Shepard is murdered in Wyoming.

1999: President Clinton wins acquittal in the Senate. The Vermont Supreme Court rules that the exclusion of same-sex couples from the marriage statute violates the Vermont state constitution, but asks the legislature to act to remedy the discrimination. The following year, the legislature adopts the nation's first civil union law.

2000: Hilary Swank wins the Best Actress Oscar for her portrayal of Brandon Teena in "Boys Don't Cry." The reality TV craze begins with "Who Wants to Marry a Millionaire?", in which fifty women compete to marry a wealthy real estate developer. More than twenty million people watch the wedding; the marriage is annulled shortly thereafter. When it becomes public that the man had been accused of beating a former girlfriend, Fox cancels the show. A bitterly disputed presidential election ends when the Supreme Court essentially declares George W. Bush the winner.

2001: The Netherlands becomes the first nation in the world to enact a law allowing same-sex couples to marry. Newly inaugurated President George Bush reinstates the global "gag rule" barring funding for family planning organizations that support abortion and establishes an office to promote faith-based initiatives. A controversy over anti-gay slurs in Eminem's lyrics cools after he and Elton John sing a duet at the annual Grammy awards. Minnesota becomes the first state to prohibit discrimination based on gender identity. The tragedy of September 11 shakes the world, redefining domestic and international politics.

2002: Bernard Cardinal Law, Archbishop of Boston, resigns his post in reaction to scandals revealing the failure of the Roman Catholic Church to intervene or discipline clergy after being informed that certain priests were sexually engaged with minors, in some cases children. High-ranking American Catholic clergy meet in April at the Vatican and in June in Dallas, issuing statements condemning sexual abuse. Harry Hay, founder of the Mattachine Society, dies at age 90; Sylvia Rivera, New York-based activist and drag queen, dies at age 50.

2003: In *Lawrence v. Texas*, the Supreme Court reverses *Bowers v. Hardwick* and rules that the Constitution protects the liberty rights of persons to engage in same-sex sexual activity. The highest court of Massachusetts declares that the exclusion of same-sex couples from marriage violates that state's constitution. The United States goes to war against Iraq.

2004: The exposure of one of Janet Jackson's breasts during the halftime show at the Super Bowl game leads to an FCC investigation of indecency in the media. The House of Representatives votes on a Federal Marriage Amendment, which is endorsed by President Bush, but it fails to secure the necessary two-thirds margin to advance to the Senate. When President Bush wins re-election, some argue that the gay marriage issue tipped the scales in his favor, although most polling data indicate otherwise. As sexual abuse lawsuits mount against the Roman Catholic Church, bankruptcy filings include the Archdiocese of Portland (Oregon), the Diocese of Spokane (Washington), and the Diocese of Tucson (Arizona). Half of all people living with HIV are now women.

2005: Chief Justice John Roberts is sworn in after the death of William Rehnquist. Judge Samuel Alito is nominated to replace Justice Sandra Day O'Connor after her resignation. These two changes create the first shift in the Court's membership in eleven years. The California legislature passes a bill to end the exclusion of gay couples from marriage, the first state legislature to do so, but the bill is vetoed by Governor Arnold Schwarzenegger. Andrea Dworkin dies at age 58. Twenty years after the creation of the Meese Commission, Attorney General Alberto Gonzalez creates a special Justice Department Task Force on Obscenity, to increase the number of prosecutions.

CHAPTER 2

Censorship in the Name of Feminism

LISA DUGGAN (1984)

Indianapolis is an unlikely place for an antipornography crusade. Its busy, immaculate downtown is free of porn shops; even convenience stores and newsstands carry only an occasional copy of *Playboy* or *Penthouse*. Hardcore pornography is hard to find. During a recent visit to the city, it took me three days to locate the local porn district—a pathetic collection of "adult businesses" at 38th Street and Shadeland Avenue, in a depressed commercial area of empty parking lots, boarded-up storefronts, and small shops about twenty minutes east of the city's center. Adult Toy and Gift, a heterosexual porn shop with live peep shows, sits alongside the Annex, a gay men's porn shop, and the Doll House, a go-go bar. There are other porn shops scattered in outlying areas of the city and surrounding Marion County. There are also adult movie theaters, and an occasional massage parlor. But these are few and far between. For a city of a million and a half, Indianapolis is remarkably porn-free.

Yet in the last year Indianapolis has become the site of an extraordinary antipornography effort. It is the first American city to sign into law an amendment to its civil rights ordinance defining "pornography" as a form of sex discrimination. The legislation would allow individuals to sue in civil court to ban specified sexually explicit materials and to collect damages for the harm done by the pornographers. It was written by radical feminists Catharine MacKinnon and Andrea Dworkin. The Indianapolis action was extraordinary because an ostensibly feminist initiative was supported not by local feminist groups but by neighborhood associations, conservative Republican politicians, right-wing fundamentalists, and members of the Moral Majority—a coalition unique in American politics.

The new law is not yet in effect. Less than ninety minutes after it was signed by the mayor, a collection of publishers, booksellers, broadcasters, and librarians, joined by the ACLU, challenged the measure in federal district court on Constitutional grounds, as a violation of First Amendment protection of free speech. Judge Sarah Evans Barker's decision is pending, and it is likely to have a wide impact. Scores of other U.S. cities are awaiting her decision before enacting their own versions of the law.

Regardless of the judicial outcome, the passage of this law in Indianapolis is a landmark event. It constitutes the first success of a new legislative strategy on the part of antipornography feminists. For the first time, organizations such as Women Against Pornography (WAP) are advocating state censorship of films, books, and magazines deemed degrading to women. In doing so, they've provided traditional procensorship forces with a new way to attack the First Amendment. They've also allied themselves with the most antifeminist forces in the culture, those who are opposed to ERA, abortion, gay rights, and affirmative action (the list could go on). That this has been done is appalling—that it has been done in the name of feminism is frightening.

Like that of many American cities, Indianapolis's downtown has gone through a renaissance in the last few years. Steel and glass office towers stand next to restored townhouses. Chic restaurants line up next to theaters and galleries offering sophisticated urban entertainment for the city's young professionals. But away from downtown, Indianapolis begins to feel like a Southern city—more like Louisville, say, than Chicago. Residential racial segregation is the rule; voices slow to a drawl; tract houses, bowling alleys, dreary commercial strips, and dramatically designed evangelical churches abut one another. The Bob Evans Restaurant serves grits and honey biscuits for breakfast. Political conflict takes place within an overwhelming context of Republican conservatism. The basic contrast among white politicians is the equivalent of that between George Bush and Jesse Helms—slick, sophisticated conservatives versus right-wing populists. What Democratic strength there is exists primarily among black politicians, though the city has a sprinkling of embattled white liberals as well.

Since the election of Ronald Reagan and the growth of the New Right as a force in national politics, the fundamentalist right wing in Indianapolis has been strengthened. Consequently, public morality campaigns of various sorts have appeared with a confident vigor. Two years ago, Reverend Greg

Dixon, pastor of the Indianapolis Baptist Temple and a former Moral Majority official, led the Coalition for a Clean Community on a march against immorality in the city's downtown. About two and a half thousand marchers cheered when Republican Mayor William Hudnut III declared Clean Community Day. In Indianapolis, reactionary extremists enjoy a degree of political legitimacy almost unimaginable to most Northeasterners.

The religious right in Indianapolis opposes pornography on scriptural and moral grounds as propaganda for promiscuity. But they are not the only antipornography campaigners in the city. Neighborhood groups have organized against porn for a mixed bag of reasons. Some are angry that commercial interests have the power to determine what goes into their neighborhoods. Some are motivated by fear and bigotry, and express concern that pornography promotes interracial sex and homosexuality. Some would like to close only the porn shops in their own neighborhoods; others would eliminate all sexually explicit materials from the face of the earth.

Ron Hackler of the Citizens for Decency of Marion County, for example, explains that his group was founded to oppose the little complex at 38th and Shadeland on behalf of the residents of the adjacent neighborhood. But the citizens have branched out since then. They plan to ally themselves with the national organization, Citizens For Decency Through Law, a group that advocates the elimination of porn through vigorous enforcement of obscenity laws. According to the group's brochure, pornography causes crime, venereal disease and "dangerous societal change," through its depiction of "everything from beastiality [sic], sodomy, rape, fornication, masturbation, piquerism, orgies, homosexuality and sadomasochism." It's quite a leap from a desire by residents to gain some control over their neighborhoods to a vision of sex leading to Armaggedon.

Pressure this past year from the motley collection of antiporn groups in Indianapolis led Mayor Hudnut, a Presbyterian minister, to look for new ways to battle pornography. Obscenity laws had not proved effective. Although the city's zealous antivice prosecutor and police department had been willing to make the arrests, their cases repeatedly failed to persuade juries, or were thrown out on technicalities. The zoning law used to restrict "adult businesses" had been tied up in court challenges as well (there is now a new zoning law, however). Mayor Hudnut finally received inspiration from an unlikely source—the progressive city of Minneapolis, and radical feminists Dworkin and MacKinnon.

Dworkin and MacKinnon did not plan to write a new municipal law against pornography. In the fall of 1983, they were teaching a class at the University of Minnesota, presenting and developing their analysis of the role of pornography in the oppression of women. Each woman is known for her advocacy of one of the more extreme forms of antipornography feminism—the belief that sexually explicit images that subordinate or degrade women are singularly dangerous, more dangerous than nonsexual images of gross violence against women, more dangerous than advertising images of housewives as dingbats obsessed with getting men's shirt collars clean. In fact, Dworkin and MacKinnon argue that pornography is at the root of virtually every form of exploitation and discrimination known to woman. Given these views, it is not surprising that they would turn eventually to censorship—not censorship of violent and misogynistic images generally, but only of the sexually explicit images that cultural reactionaries have tried to outlaw for more than a century.

Dworkin and MacKinnon were invited to testify at a public hearing on a new zoning law (Minneapolis's "adult business" zoning law had been stricken in the courts also). When they appeared, they testified *against* the zoning strategy, and offered a surprising new idea instead. Dworkin railed at the City Council, calling its members "cats and dogs" for tolerating pornography; MacKinnon suggested a civil rights approach to eliminate, rather than merely regulate, pornography. City officials must have enjoyed the verbal abuse—they hired the women to write a new law and to conduct public hearings on its merits.

In Minneapolis, Dworkin/MacKinnon were an effective duo. Dworkin, a remarkably effective public speaker, whipped up emotion with sensational rhetoric. At one rally, she encouraged her followers to "swallow the vomit you feel at the thought of dealing with the city council and get this law in place. See that the silence of women is over, that we're not down on our backs with our legs spread anymore." In contrast, MacKinnon, a professor of law, offered legalistic, seemingly rational, solutions to the sense of panic and doom evoked by Dworkin. In such a charged atmosphere, amid public demonstrations by antiporn feminists—one young woman later set herself on fire to protest pornography—the law passed. It was vetoed by the mayor on constitutional grounds.

Indianapolis, though, is not Minneapolis. When Mayor Hudnut heard of the Dworkin/MacKinnon bill at a Republican conference, he did not think of it as a measure to promote feminism, but as a weapon in the war on smut. He recruited City-County Councilmember Beulah Coughenour—an activist in the Stop ERA movement—to introduce the law locally. A Republican conservative, she is a member of the lobbying group Pro-America; she sent her children to Reverend Dixon's Baptist Temple schools. Although Coughenour has much in common with Phyllis Schlafly, she does not share her flamboyance—she does not challenge or antagonize. Instead, she emphasizes her listeners' points of agreement, smoothing over any possible conflict. A city councilmember for nine years, Coughenour had been considered a minor figure in Indianapolis politics, but she displayed unexpected skill in overseeing the passage of the antiporn bill. How else could she have gotten radical feminist Catharine MacKinnon and right-wing preacher Greg Dixon to work together to pass legislation she sponsored, without ever running into one another?

Coughenour's first smart move was to hire MacKinnon but not Dworkin as a consultant to the city in developing the legislation. MacKinnon was the legal brains behind the law, after all (and is probably still the only person to fully understand the legal theory behind it). MacKinnon is also "respectable." She wears tailored suits and gold jewelry; her hair is neatly pulled back in a bun. She looks like a well-heeled professional, and sounds like an academic. Of the law's coauthors, she was most likely to be accepted by Indianapolis's conservative city officials. Dworkin's style would not have gone over in Indianapolis—there are no crowds of antiporn feminists to galvanize into action, while there are innumerable tight-laced conservatives to be alarmed by the feverish pitch of Dworkin's revival-style speeches, not to mention her overalls and unruly appearance.

MacKinnon worked closely with Coughenour from the start. She advised city officials in the drafting of the law, but by her own admission she made no contacts with local feminists. In addition, she accepted Coughenour's claim that right-wing fundamentalists were not involved with the law and its progress through the council. In talking to MacKinnon, one gets the impression of someone so immersed in the theory of the law that she never noticed the local politics behind it. When she gave her testimony at the public hearing on the antiporn bill, she went so far as to describe Indianapolis as "a place that takes seriously the rights of women and the rights of all people...." Apparently, she did not know that her supporters in the police department had been involved in the videotaping and beating of gay men in the city's downtown only weeks before.

Many local feminists were surprised to discover that Indianapolis was a place that took "seriously the rights of women," and they responded angrily to MacKinnon's distortion of their situation. An outsider had been brought in to represent "the" feminist position, and this had been done by their political adversaries. Sheila Suess Kennedy, a Republican feminist attorney, submitted written testimony to the council in which she said:

> As a woman who has been publicly supportive of equal rights for women, I frankly find it offensive when an attempt to regulate expression is cloaked in the rhetoric of feminism. Many supporters of this proposal have been conspicuously indifferent to previous attempts to gain equal rights for women.

In 1980 Coughenour had attacked Kennedy in a local political race because of her feminism. Kathy Sarris, president of Justice, Inc., an Indiana statewide lesbian and gay rights organization, and another feminist opponent of the measure, commented, "It has not occurred to Mayor Hudnut to put women in leadership positions in city-county government; why is he now so concerned with the subordination of women in pornography?" During his tenure, Hudnut has refused to meet with lesbian and gay rights advocates. Even a local feminist attorney sympathetic with the law expressed surprise that she had not been informed about the public hearing, given that she has been contacted in connection with nearly every other women's issue that has come up in the city council.

In organizing the public hearing on the law, Coughenour was careful to make sure it would not turn into a circus, but rather be a forum for rational exchange and sympathetic testimony. This was in direct contrast to how she would stage-manage the final vote. At the public hearing, MacKinnon explained the legal theory of the bill for more than an hour, in academic terms that seemed to pass right by the council members. The remaining proponents did not speak about the law at all, but about the pain of rape and abuse, or about the terrors of "unnatural acts" and "sodomy." A woman from the prosecutor's office introduced the psychological studies that antipornography activists claim prove that porn causes sexual violence. Social psychologist Edward Donnerstein, one of the experts cited, appeared before the full council two weeks later to stress that his studies showed the effects of violent images on attitudes, not the effects of sexually explicit materials on behavior. Donnerstein has since complained that his studies are being misused in antipornography campaigns.

Opposition to the law was organized by Michael Gradison in the Indiana Civil Liberties Union office. Predictably, civil liberties attorneys were appalled by the bill's breadth and vagueness. In addition, many members of the city's black community were upset that complaints about porn, under the law's provision, would be screened by the city's Equal Opportunity Board, a body already overloaded with complaints about racial and sex discrimination. A representative of the Urban League asked that council members consider what would happen to antidiscrimination efforts in the city once the Office of Equal Opportunity was swamped with examples of pornography to rule upon. Two members of the gay community suggested to the council that it consider strengthening antiviolence, antiabuse laws or provide additional services for victims, rather than support censorship.

Oddly, there were no right-wing fundamentalists present at the public hearing. This, no doubt, contributed to MacKinnon's belief that they were not directly involved. It was only after the hearing that Coughenour called

Reverend Dixon and asked for his help. The law was in trouble. Although it had been passed out of committee, many council members had serious doubts about its constitutionality, its practicality, the cost of litigating it in federal court. Dixon called a meeting of the Coalition for a Clean Community and got to work, phoning council members to assure them that this law was not a "backdoor" attempt to legitimate feminism: a vote for this law would be a vote against smut. Dixon turned out nearly three hundred of his supporters for the final vote on the measure—a vote at which MacKinnon was not present.

Dixon was not fully informed by Coughenour. When asked why he did not appear at the public hearing, he replied, "Public hearing? What public hearing?" When supplied with the date, he looked at his calendar. After a long silence he said, "I was in town on that day." Then the light went on in his eyes, and he explained that his absence was probably a tactical maneuver on Coughenour's part. "Mrs. Coughenour," he said, "was probably engineering that...."

Dixon spoke to me from behind his large desk in a comfortable office at his Baptist Temple complex—which includes the church, day care facilities, schools and offices. A smooth, articulate speaker, he revealed the depths of his paranoia only when we were well into our conversation. He believes abortion is murder, ERA would destroy the family and the free enterprise system, homosexuality ought to be a felony. But his fears go deeper. He is convinced that there is a conspiracy of "elitists" to control the world's population through advocacy of a "six-pronged program" of contraception, abortion, homosexuality, euthanasia, suicide, and even war and terrorism. This program, called "globalism," is, in Reverend Dixon's view, the agenda of public schools. Political activism, in his mind, is a sacred duty, necessary to avert physical as well as moral destruction.

Reverend Dixon's political activism played a decisive role in passing the antiporn law in Indianapolis. During the final discussion before the vote, many council members were equivocating. But every time a doubt was voiced, Dixon's supporters, crowded into council chambers, grumbled; every time praise was uttered, they broke out in applause. In the end, it was the most conservative councillors who felt the pressure and passed the law—overwhelmingly. All the Republicans on the council voted yes. All the Democrats, including those black councillors concerned with strengthening civil rights enforcement in the city, voted no. The total was twenty-four to five.

Now that the passage of the law is a *fait accompli* and cities around the country await Judge Barker's decision on its constitutionality, it is worth asking the obvious question: what the hell happened in Indianapolis?

Radical feminists allied with the Moral Majority? A censorship law as a means to gain equality between the sexes? It is confusing, and of course the principals involved have different interpretations of what occurred.

Reverend Dixon believes that he helped galvanize the war on smut by supporting a new weapon in the public arsenal. Ron Hackler of the Citizens for Decency has more modest hopes. He has tried to raise public awareness of the problem posed by pornography, so that obscenity laws (which he actually prefers to antiporn legislation) can be more vigorously enforced. Obscenity laws, he thinks, could eliminate a wide variety of sexual materials, including: "The explicit depiction of sexual acts ... fellatio and cunnilingus close up in living color, the erect penis in sex acts, and things that are of no particular value. They're offensive to most people, they lead to an unrealistic expectation of people as they view sex...." He also added, "We saw movies of men taking artificial penises and shoving them up the rear end of other men, tying up a man and one man banging his penis against another man's penis. Maybe that's not obscene, I don't know—it's kind of stupid."

MacKinnon sees events in Indianapolis quite differently from Dixon and Hackler. She told me the coalition that supported and passed the law represented:

> Women who understand what pornography does and means for women in this culture, and therefore think that we should be able to do something about it, and men who do not want to live in a society in which the subordination of women is enjoyed, profited from, and is a standard for masculinity.

This is undoubtedly the coalition MacKinnon would like to have seen, but as a description of events in Indianapolis, her statement is profoundly out of touch with political reality. She acknowledges that supporters came from "diverse points on the political spectrum," but she believes that the Indianapolis coalition reconstituted alignment "on a feminist basis"—an assessment that ignores the explicitly *antifeminist* politics of the law's right-wing supporters.

MacKinnon is also convinced that, if some supporters of the law are really after "obscene" materials rather than "subordinating" ones, they're "doing something stupid." The civil rights approach, she says, will not meet their demands. But supporters of the law such as Reverend Dixon and Ron Hackler understand the limitations of the civil rights ordinance. Dixon, in fact, hopes that the law will be combined with obscenity and prostitution busts and the recriminalization of homosexuality. MacKinnon to the contrary, these antipornography campaigners are not doing something stupid. They are working to organize a public morality crusade, and they believe that the attention focused on this law has helped them.

Still the question persists—how have feminists managed to ally themselves with right-wing moralists on this issue? What is it about pornography that attracts such energy from such disparate places? If one looks closely at the Indianapolis "coalition," one sees first the great advantage to the politicians who managed to hold it together. The names of Mayor William Hudnut and Beulah Coughenour have appeared in the national press for the first time in their political careers. There is nothing like the combination of sex and violence to generate public interest and media attention. But another look reveals the outlines of a symbolic campaign on the part of various antipornography "true believers."

Right-wing moralists see pornography as representative of social disorder. Its depictions of nonmarital, nonreproductive sex invoke the threatening social changes associated, for them, with divorce, birth control, abortion, miscegenation, and homosexuality. Pornography is understood as a threat to the sanctity and authority of the patriarchal family, and it is made to stand for gender confusion and sexual chaos. In this context, right-wing moralists can agree with feminists that "pornography degrades women," because women's sexuality outside the family is itself seen as cheapened and degraded. Reverend Dixon and Phyllis Schlafly agree that it is women, as upholders of morality and the home, who should lead the fight against pornography.

Neighborhood groups do not necessarily share the cosmology of right-wingers when they set out to fight pornography. In part they are responding to the real-world association of porn shops with organized crime in cities throughout America. But neighborhood groups in Indianapolis also see porn shops and pornography as symbolic substitutes for social change in the community. Economic decline and increased crime are blamed on the porn shop—as are the fears of some white residents about racial integration. It is imagined that if the porn shop were closed, all would be well again; the happy secure neighborhoods of the nostalgia-laden past could be restored.

The radical feminist antipornography campaign, represented in Indianapolis by MacKinnon (and only MacKinnon), is also engaged in symbolic politics. Pornography is made to stand in for all misogyny, all discrimination, all exploitation of women—in their view, it not only causes but constitutes the subordination of women. The commodification and objectification of women's bodies is believed to reside more centrally in pornography than in mainstream media; this society's culture of violence against women is said to radiate from, rather than be reflected in, pornography.

The campaign against porn is thus a symbolic substitute for a more diffuse, but more necessary, campaign against the myriad forms of male domination in economic life, in political life, in sexual life. Pornography serves as a condensed metaphor for female degradation. It is also far easier to fight, politically, in the conservative climate of the Reagan years—far easier now to gain support for an antiporn campaign than for affirmative action, abortion, lesbian rights.

What all these antiporn zealots have in common is a conviction of the special power of sexual representation to endanger. For some it endangers the family, for some community, for others the well-being of women. All are agreed that sexually explicit images must be controlled—though each group would differ as to *which* images are most in need of control—in order to control the perceived social danger, in order to prevent ruin, decay, obliteration. The groups allied against porn in Indianapolis also share a vision of sexuality as a terrain of female victimization and degradation; none of them offers a vision of female sexual subjectivity, of female power and joy in the sexual arena.

Feminists have engaged in such symbolic campaigns before. In the nineteenth and early twentieth centuries, for instance, some British and American feminists waged campaigns against prostitution and for "social purity," and they achieved legislative success with the help of conservative allies. However, the strengthening of laws against prostitution had the effect of worsening the condition of prostitutes, making them yet more vulnerable to victimization at the hands of law enforcement officials, as well as pimps and johns. The raising of the age of consent in the early twentieth century, also accomplished with feminist support in the United States, had the result of empowering institutions of juvenile justice to persecute and incarcerate adolescent girls for the "offense" of sexual activity. In all these cases, conservatives ultimately exercised more power in determining how laws, once enacted, would finally affect women's lives—more power than feminists then imagined.

One of the insights gained by feminist historians, who have examined such social legislation, is that a "feminist issue" or "feminist law" does not exist in the abstract: it is the alignment of political and cultural forces that gives meaning to issues and laws. In Indianapolis, local feminists were invisible except for the handful who opposed the antiporn law. *No* effort was made to distinguish clearly the feminist from the conservative position. As a result the visibility of reactionary, antifeminist forces was enhanced—exactly the opposite of what MacKinnon intended.

And it is not only in Indianapolis that the reactionary, antifeminist position has been enhanced. The MacKinnon/Dworkin bill has contributed to a moral crusade that is threatening to expand to other places on a wider scale. In Suffolk County, Republican legislator Michael D'Andre has recently introduced a version of the antiporn law that emphasizes the repressive potential of the MacKinnon/Dworkin approach by asserting that pornography causes "sodomy" and "destruction of the family unit," as well as crimes and immorality "inimical to the public good." In Washington, Pennsylvania senator Arlen Specter is broadening his congressional hearings on child pornography to investigate the effects of adult porn on women. President Reagan has also announced his intention to establish a federal commission to study pornography and offer legislative action. Imagine the administration that brought you the Family Protection Act introducing measures to control pornography. Imagine antipornography feminists helping to legitimate such a nightmare.

In Canada, the conservative Fraser Committee on Pornography and Prostitution has been holding hearings across the country, while some city governments have already been prosecuting prostitutes, rounding up gay men in bathhouses, and bringing charges against gay publications for obscenity. Canadian antiporn feminists, joined by some American sympathizers, have testified in favor of more restrictions on sexual representation.

If the discussion of sexuality surrounding the antiporn law in Indianapolis had resulted in increased awareness of feminist issues, in the increased visibility and social/political power of feminists, in the enhanced ability of feminists on both sides of the issue to define and control the terms of debate, perhaps it could have been useful. But it did not. Instead, Catharine MacKinnon joined with the right wing in invoking the power of the state against sexual representation. In so doing she and her supporters have helped spur a moral crusade that is already beyond the control of feminists—antiporn or otherwise. And that moral crusade can only be dangerous to the interests of feminists everywhere, and to the future of women's rights to free expression.

Sexual Dissent and Representation

CHAPTER 3

False Promises

Feminist Antipornography Legislation

LISA DUGGAN, NAN D. HUNTER AND CAROLE S. VANCE (1985)

In the United States, after two decades of increasing community tolerance for dissenting or disturbing sexual or political materials, the 1980s have produced a momentum for retrenchment. In an atmosphere of increased conservatism, support for new repressive legislation of various kinds—from an Oklahoma law forbidding schoolteachers from advocating homosexuality to new antipornography laws passed in Minneapolis and Indianapolis—has emerged as a powerful force.

The antipornography laws have mixed roots of support, however. Though they are popular with the conservative constituencies that traditionally favor legal restrictions on sexual expression of all kinds, they were drafted and are endorsed by antipornography feminists who oppose traditional obscenity and censorship laws. The model law of this type was drawn up in the politically progressive city of Minneapolis by two radical feminists, author Andrea Dworkin and attorney Catharine MacKinnon. It was passed by the city council but vetoed by the mayor. A similar law was enacted in Indianapolis, and then ruled unconstitutional by the Supreme Court in 1986.

Dworkin, MacKinnon and their feminist supporters believe that these proposed antipornography ordinances are not censorship laws. They also claim that the legislative effort behind them is based on feminist support.

Both of these claims are dubious at best. Though the new laws are civil laws that allow individuals to sue the makers, sellers, distributors or exhibitors of pornography, and not criminal laws leading to arrest and imprisonment, their censoring impact would be substantially as severe as criminal obscenity laws. Materials could be removed from public availability by court injunction, and publishers and booksellers could be subject to potentially endless legal harassment. Passage of the laws was achieved with the support of right-wing elements who expect the new laws to accomplish what censorship efforts are meant to accomplish. Ironically, many anti-feminist conservatives backed these laws, while many feminists opposed them. In Indianapolis, the law was supported by extreme right-wing religious fundamentalists, including members of the Moral Majority, while there was *no* local feminist support. In other cities, traditional pro-censorship forces expressed interest in the new approach to banning sexually explicit materials. Meanwhile, anti-censorship feminists became alarmed at these new developments and are seeking to galvanize feminist opposition to the new antipornography legislative strategy pioneered in Minneapolis.

One is tempted to ask in astonishment; How can this be happening? How can feminists be entrusting the patriarchal state with the task of legally distinguishing between permissible and impermissible sexual images? But in fact this new development is not as surprising as it seems at first. Pornography has come to be seen as a central cause of women's oppression by a significant number of feminists. Andrea Dworkin argues that pornography is the root of virtually all forms of exploitation and discrimination against women. It is a short step from such a belief to the conviction that laws against pornography can end the inequality of the sexes. But this analysis takes feminists very close—indeed far too close—to measures that will ultimately support conservative, antisex, pro-censorship forces in American society, for it is with these forces that women have forged alliances in passing such legislation.

The first feminist-inspired antipornography law was passed in Minneapolis in 1983. Local legislators had been frustrated when their zoning restrictions on porn shops were struck down in the courts. Public hearings were held to discuss a new zoning ordinance. The Neighborhood Pornography Task Force of South and South Central Minneapolis invited Andrea Dworkin and Catharine MacKinnon, who were teaching a course on pornography at the University of Minnesota, to testify. They proposed an alternative that, they claimed, would completely eliminate, rather than merely regulate, pornography. They suggested that pornography be defined as a form of sex discrimination, and that an amendment to the city's civil rights law be passed to proscribe it. City officials hired Dworkin and MacKinnon to develop their new approach and to organize another series of public hearings.

The initial debate over the legislation in Minneapolis was intense, and opinion was divided within nearly every political grouping. By contrast, the public hearings held before the city council were tightly controlled and carefully orchestrated; speakers invited by Dworkin and MacKinnon—sexual abuse victims, counselors, educators and social scientists—testified about the harm pornography does to women. (Dworkin's and MacKinnon's goal was to compile a legislative record that would help the law stand up to court challenges.) The legislation passed, supported by antipornography feminists, neighborhood groups concerned about the effects of porn shops on residential areas, and conservatives opposed to the availability of sexually explicit materials for "moral" reasons.

In Indianapolis, the alignment of forces was different. For the previous two years, conservative antipornography groups had grown in strength and public visibility, but they had been frustrated in their efforts. The police department could not convert its obscenity arrests into convictions; the city's zoning law was also tied up in court challenges. Then Mayor William Hudnut III, a Republican and a Presbyterian minister, learned of the Minneapolis law. Mayor Hudnut thought Minneapolis's approach might be the solution to the Indianapolis problems. Beulah Coughenour, a conservative, Republican Stop ERA activist, was recruited to sponsor the legislation in the City-County Council.

Coughenour engaged MacKinnon as consultant to the city. MacKinnon worked on the legislation with the Indianapolis city prosecutor (a well-known antivice zealot), the city's legal department and Coughenour. The law received the support of neighborhood groups, the Citizens for Decency and the Coalition for a Clean Community. There were no crowds of feminist supporters—in fact, there were no feminist supporters at all. The only feminists to make public statements opposed the legislation, which was nevertheless passed in a council meeting packed with three hundred religious fundamentalists. All twenty-four Republicans voted for its passage; all five Democrats opposed it, to no avail.

Before the Supreme Court ruled it unconstitutional, mutated versions of the Dworkin-MacKinnon bill began to appear. A version of the law introduced in Suffolk County on Long Island in New York emphasized its conservative potential—pornography was said to cause "sodomy" and "disruption" of the family unit, in addition to rape, incest, exploitation and other acts "inimical to the public good." In Suffolk, the law was advanced by a conservative, anti-ERA, male legislator who wished to "restore ladies to what they used to be." The Suffolk County bill clearly illustrates the repressive, antifeminist potential of the new antipornography legislation.

The support of such legislation by antipornography feminists marks a critical moment in the feminist debate over sexual politics. We need to examine carefully these proposals for new laws and expose their underlying assumptions. We need to know why these proposals, for all their apparent feminist rhetoric, actually appeal to conservative antifeminist forces, and why feminists should move in a different direction.

Definitions: The Central Flaw

The antipornography ordinances in Minneapolis and Indianapolis were framed as amendments to municipal civil rights laws. They provide for complaints to be filed against pornography in the same manner that complaints are filed against employment discrimination. If enforced, the laws would make illegal public or private availability (except in libraries) of any materials deemed pornographic.

Such material could be the object of a lawsuit on several grounds. The ordinance would penalize four kinds of behavior associated with pornography: its production, sale, exhibition or distribution ("trafficking"); coercion into pornographic performance; forcing pornography on a person; and assault or physical attack due to pornography.

Under such a law, a woman "acting as a woman against the subordination of women" could file a complaint; men could also file complaints if they could "prove injury in the same way that a woman is injured." The procedural steps in the two ordinances differ, but they generally allow the complainant either to file an administrative complaint with the city's Equal Opportunity Commission (Minneapolis or Indianapolis), or to file a lawsuit directly in court (Minneapolis). If the local commission found the law had been violated, it would file a lawsuit. By either procedure, the court—not "women"—would have the final say on whether the materials fit the definition of pornography, and would have the authority to award monetary damages and issue an injunction (or court order) preventing further distribution of the material in question.

The Minneapolis ordinance defines pornography as "the sexually explicit subordination of women, graphically depicted, whether in pictures or words." To be actionable, materials would also have to fall within one of a number of categories: nine in the Minneapolis ordinance, six in the Indianapolis version. (The text of the original Minneapolis ordinance, from which the excerpts from the legislation quoted here are taken, is appended to the end of this chapter.)

Although proponents claim that the Minneapolis and Indianapolis ordinances represent a new way to regulate pornography, the strategy is still laden with our culture's old, repressive approach to sexuality. The implementation of such laws hinges on the definition of pornography as interpreted by a court. The definition provided in the Minneapolis legislation is vague, leaving critical phrases such as "the sexually explicit subordination of women," "postures of sexual submission" and "whores by nature" to the interpretation of the citizen who files a complaint and to the judge who hears the case. The legislation does not prohibit only the images of rape and abusive sexual violence that most supporters claim to be its target, but instead drifts toward covering an increasingly wide range of sexually explicit material.

The most problematic feature of this approach is a conceptual flaw embedded in the law itself. Supporters of this type of legislation say that the target of their efforts is misogynist, sexually explicit and violent representation, whether in pictures or words. Indeed, the feminist antipornography movement is fueled by women's anger at the most repugnant examples of pornography. But a close examination of the wording of the model legislative text and examples of purportedly actionable material offered by proponents of the legislation in court briefs suggest that the law is actually aimed at a range of material considerably broader than that which proponents claim is their target. The discrepancies between the law's explicit and implicit aims have been almost invisible to us, because these distortions are very similar to distortions about sexuality in the culture as a whole. The legislation and supporting texts deserve close reading. Hidden beneath illogical transformations, *non sequiturs*, and highly permeable definitions are familiar sexual scripts drawn from mainstream, sexist culture, that potentially could have very negative consequences for women.

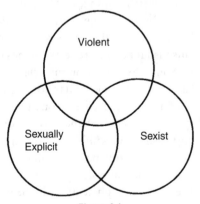

Figure 2.1

The Venn diagram illustrates the three areas targeted by the law, and represents a scheme that classifies words or images that have any of three characteristics: violence, sexual explicitness or sexism.

Clearly, a text or an image might have only one characteristic. Material can be violent but not sexually explicit or sexist: for example, a war movie in which both men and women suffer injury or death without regard to or because of their gender. Material can be sexist but not sexually explicit or violent. A vast number of materials from mainstream media—television, popular novels, magazines, newspapers—comes to mind, depicting, for example, either distraught housewives or the "happy sexism" of the idealized family, with mom self-sacrificing, other-directed and content. Finally, material can be sexually explicit but not violent or sexist: for example, the freely chosen sexual behavior depicted in some sex education films or women's own explicit writing about sexuality.

As the diagram illustrates, areas can also intersect, reflecting a range of combinations of the three characteristics. Images can be violent and sexually explicit without being sexist—for example, a narrative about a rape in a men's prison, or a documentary about the effect of a rape on a woman. The latter example illustrates the importance of context in evaluating whether material that is sexually explicit and violent is also sexist. The intent of the maker, the context of the film and the perception of the viewer together render a depiction of a rape sympathetic, harrowing, even educational, rather than sensational, victim-blaming and laudatory.

Another possible overlap is between material that is violent and sexist but not sexually explicit. Films or books that describe violence directed against women by men in a way that clearly shows gender antagonism and inequality, and sometimes strong sexual tension, but no sexual explicitness fall into this category—for example, the popular genre of slasher films in which women are stalked, terrified and killed by men, or accounts of mass murder of women, fueled by male rage. Finally, a third point of overlap arises when material is sexually explicit and sexist without being violent— that is, when sex is consensual but still reflects themes of male superiority and female abjectness. Some sex education materials could be included in this category, as well as a great deal of regular pornography.

The remaining domain, the inner core, is one in which the material is simultaneously violent, sexually explicit and sexist—for example, an image of a naked woman being slashed by a knife-wielding rapist. The Minneapolis ordinance, however, does not by any means confine itself to this material.

To be actionable under the law as pornography, material must be judged by the courts to be "the sexually explicit subordination of women, graphically depicted whether in pictures or in words that also includes at least one or more" of nine criteria. Of these, only four involve the intersection of violence, sexual explicitness and sexism, and then only arguably. Even in these cases, many questions remain about whether images with all three characteristics do in fact cause violence against women. And the task of evaluating material that is ostensibly the target of these criteria becomes complicated—indeed, hopeless—because most of the clauses that contain these criteria mix actions or qualities of violence with those that are not particularly associated with violence.

The section that comes closest to the stated purpose of the legislation is clause (iii): "women are presented as sexual objects who experience sexual pleasure in being raped." This clause is intended to cover depictions of rape that are sexually explicit and sexist; the act of rape itself signifies the violence. But other clauses are not so clear-cut, because the list of characteristics often mixes signs or by-products of violence with phenomena that are unrelated or irrelevant to judging violence.

Such a problem occurs with clause (iv): "women are presented as sexual objects tied up or cut up or mutilated or bruised or physically hurt." All these except the first, "tied up," generally occur as a result of violence. "Tied up," if part of consensual sex, is not violent and, for some practitioners, not particularly sexist. Women who are tied up may be participants in nonviolent sex play involving bondage, a theme in both heterosexual and lesbian pornography. (See, for example, *The Joy of Sex* and *Coming to Power*.) Clause (ix) contains another mixed list, in which "injury," "torture," "bleeding," "bruised" and "hurt" are combined with phrases such as "degradation" and "shown as filthy and inferior," neither of which is violent. Depending on the presentation, "filthy" and "inferior" may constitute sexually explicit sexism, although not violence. "Degradation" is a sufficiently inclusive term to cover most acts of which a viewer disapproves.

Several other clauses have little to do with violence at all; they refer to material that is sexually explicit and sexist, thus falling outside the triad of characteristics at which the legislation is supposedly aimed. For example, movies in which "women are presented as dehumanized sexual objects, things, or commodities" may be infuriating and offensive to feminists, but they are not violent.

Finally, some clauses describe material that is neither violent nor necessarily sexist. Clause (v), "women ... in postures of sexual submission or sexual servility, including by inviting penetration," and clause (viii), "women ... being penetrated by objects or animals," are sexually explicit, but not violent and not obviously sexist unless one believes that penetration—whether heterosexual, lesbian, or autoerotic masturbation—is indicative of gender inequality and female oppression. Similarly problematic are clauses that invoke representations of "women … as whores by nature" and "women's body parts … such that women are reduced to those parts."

Texts cited in support of the Indianapolis law show how broadly it could be applied. In the amicus brief filed on behalf of Linda Marchiano ("Linda Lovelace," the female lead in *Deep Throat*) in Indianapolis, Catharine MacKinnon offered *Deep Throat* as an example of the kind of pornography covered by the law. *Deep Throat* served a complicated function in this brief, because the movie, supporters of the ordinance argue, would be actionable on two counts: coercion into pornographic performance, because Marchiano alleges that she was coerced into making the movie; and trafficking in pornography, because the content of the film falls within one of the categories in the Indianapolis ordinance's definition—that which prohibits presenting women as sexual objects "through postures or positions of servility or submission or display." Proponents of the law have counted on women's repugnance at allegations of coerced sexual acts to spill over and discredit the sexual acts themselves in this movie.

The aspects of *Deep Throat* that MacKinnon considered to be indicative of "sexual subordination" are of particular interest, because any movie that depicted similar acts could be banned under the law. MacKinnon explained in her brief that the film "subordinates women by using women … sexually, specifically as eager servicing receptacles for male genitalia and ejaculate. The majority of the film represents 'Linda Lovelace' in, minimally, postures of sexual submission and/or servility." In its brief, the City of Indianapolis concurred: "In the film *Deep Throat* a woman is being shown as being ever eager for oral penetration by a series of men's penises, often on her hands and knees. There are repeated scenes in which her genitalia are graphically displayed and she is shown as enjoying men ejaculating on her face."

These descriptions are very revealing, since they suggest that multiple partners, group sex and oral sex subordinate women and hence are sexist. The notion that the female character is "used" by men suggests that it is improbable that a woman would engage in fellatio of her own accord. *Deep Throat* does draw on several sexist conventions common in advertising and the entire visual culture—the woman as object of the male gaze, and the assumption of heterosexuality, for example. But it is hardly an unending paean to male dominance, since the movie contains many contrary themes. In it, the main female character is shown as both actively seeking her own pleasure and as trying to please men; a secondary female character is shown directing encounters with multiple male partners. The briefs described a movie quite different from the one viewers see.

At its heart, this analysis implies that heterosexual sex itself is sexist; that women do not engage in it of their own volition; and that behavior pleasurable to men is intrinsically repugnant to women. In some contexts, for example, the representation of fellatio and multiple partners can be sexist, but are we willing to concede that they always are? If not, then what is proposed as actionable under the Indianapolis law includes merely sexually explicit representation (the traditional target of obscenity laws), which proponents of the legislation vociferously insist they are not interested in attacking.

Exhibits submitted with the City of Indianapolis brief and also introduced in the public hearing further illustrate this point. Many of the exhibits are depictions of sadomasochism. The court briefs treat S/M material as depicting violence and aggression, not consensual sex, in spite of avowals to the contrary by many S/M practitioners. With this legislation, then, a major question for feminists that has only begun to develop would be closed for discussion. Instead, a simplistic reduction has been advanced as the definitive feminist position. The description of the material in the briefs focused on submissive women and implied male domination, highlighting the similarity proponents would like to find between all S/M narratives and male/female inequality. The actual exhibits, however, illustrated plots and power relations far more diverse than the descriptions provided by MacKinnon and the City of Indianapolis would suggest, including S/M between women and female dominant/male submissive S/M. For example, the Indianapolis brief stated that in the magazine *The Bitch Goddesses*, "women are shown in torture chambers with their nude body parts being tortured by their 'master' for 'even the slightest offense'…. The magazine shows a woman in a scenario of torture." But the brief failed to mention that the dominants in this magazine are all female, with one exception. This kind of discrepancy characterized many examples offered in the briefs.

This is not to say that such representations do not raise questions for feminists. The current lively discussion about lesbian S/M demonstrates that this issue is still unresolved. But in the Indianapolis briefs, all S/M material was assumed to be male dominant/female submissive, thereby squeezing a nonconforming reality into prepackaged, inadequate—and therefore dangerous—categories. This legislation would virtually eliminate all S/M pornography by recasting it as violent, thereby attacking a sexual minority while masquerading as an attempt to end violence against women.

Analysis of clauses in the Minneapolis ordinance and several examples offered in court briefs filed in connection with the Indianapolis ordinance show that the law targets material that is sexually explicit and sexist, but ignores material that is violent and sexist, violent and sexually explicit, only violent, or only sexist.

Certain troubling questions arise here, for if one claims, as some anti-pornography activists do, that there is a direct relationship between images and behavior, why should images of violence against women or scenarios of sexism in general not be similarly proscribed? Why is sexual explicitness singled out as the cause of women's oppression? For proponents to exempt violent and sexist images, or even sexist images, from regulation is inconsistent, especially since they are so pervasive.

Even more difficulties arise from the vagueness of certain terms crucial in interpreting the ordinances. The term "subordination" is especially important, since pornography is defined as the "sexually explicit subordination of women." The authors of this legislation intend it to modify each of the clauses, and they appear to believe that it provides a definition of sexism that each example must meet. The term is never defined in the legislation, yet the Indianapolis brief, for example, suggests that the average viewer, on the basis of "his or her common understanding of what it means for one person to subordinate another" should be able to decide what is pornographic. But what kind of sexually explicit acts place a woman in an inferior status? To some, *any* graphic sexual act violates women's dignity and therefore subordinates them. To others, consensual heterosexual lovemaking within the boundaries of procreation and marriage is acceptable, but heterosexual acts that do not have reproduction as their aim lower women's status and hence subordinate them. Still others accept a wide range of nonprocreative, perhaps even nonmarital, heterosexuality, but draw the line at lesbian sex, which they view as degrading.

The term "sex object" is also problematic. The city of Indianapolis's brief maintains that "the term sexual object, often shortened to sex object, has enjoyed a wide popularity in mainstream American culture in the past fifteen years, and is used to denote the objectification of a person on the basis of their sex or sex appeal.... People know what it means to disregard all aspects of personhood but sex, to reduce a person to a thing used for sex." But, indeed, people do not agree on this point. The definition of "sex object" is far from clear or uniform. For example, some feminist and liberal cultural critics have used the term to mean sex that occurs without strong emotional ties and experience. More conservative critics maintain that any detachment of women's sexuality from procreation, marriage and family objectifies it, removing it from its "natural" web of associations and context. Unredeemed and unprotected by domesticity and family, women—and their sexuality—become things used by men. In both these views, women are never sexually autonomous agents who direct and enjoy their sexuality for their own purposes, but rather are victims. In the same vein, other problematic terms include "inviting penetration," "whores by nature" and "positions of display."

Through close analysis of the proposed legislation one sees how vague the boundaries of the definitions that contain the inner core of the Venn diagram really are. Their dissolution does not happen equally at all points, but only at some: the inner core begins to include sexually explicit and sexist material, and finally expands to include purely sexually explicit material. Thus "sexually explicit" becomes identified and equated with "violent" with no further definition or explanation.

It is also striking that so many feminists have failed to notice that the proposed laws (as well as examples of actionable material) cover so much diverse work, not just that small and symbolic epicenter where many forms of opposition to women converge. It suggests that for us, as well as for others, sexuality remains a difficult area. We have no clearly developed framework in which to think about sex equivalent to the frameworks that are available for thinking about race, gender and class issues. Consequently, in sex, as in few other areas of human behavior, unexamined and unjustifiable prejudice passes itself off as considered opinion about what is desirable and normal. And finally, sex arouses considerable anxiety, stemming from both the meeting with individual difference and from the prospect—suggested by feminists themselves—that sexual behavior is constructed socially and is not simply natural.

The proposed law takes advantage of everyone's relative ignorance and anxious ambivalence about sex, distorting and oversimplifying what confronts us in building a sexual politic. For example, antipornography feminists draw on several feminist theories about the role of violent, aggressive or sexist representations. The first is relatively straightforward: that these images trigger men into action. The second suggests that violent images act more subtly, to socialize men to act in sexist or violent ways by making this behavior seem commonplace and more acceptable, if not expected. The third assumption is that violent, sexually explicit or even sexist images are offensive to women, assaulting their sensibilities and sense of self. Although we have all used metaphor to exhort women to action or illustrate a point, antipornography proponents have frequently used these conventions of speech as if they were literal statements of fact. But these metaphors have gotten out of hand, as Julie Abraham has noted, for they fail to recognize that the assault committed by a wife-beater is quite different from the visual "assault" of a sexist ad on TV. The nature of that difference is still being clarified in a complex debate within feminism that must continue; this law cuts off speculation, settling on a causal relationship between image and action that is starkly simple, if unpersuasive.

This metaphor also paves the way for reclassifying images that are merely sexist as also violent and aggressive. Thus, it is no accident that the briefs supporting the legislation first invoke violent images and rapidly move to include sexist and sexually explicit images without noting that they are different. The equation is made easier by the constant shifts back to examples of depictions of real violence, almost to draw attention away from the sexually explicit or sexist material that in fact would be affected by the laws.

Most important, what underlies this legislation and the success of its analysis in blurring and exceeding boundaries, is an appeal to a very traditional view of sex: sex is degrading to women. By this logic, any illustrations or descriptions of explicit sexual acts that involve women are in themselves affronts to women's dignity. In its brief, the city of Indianapolis was quite specific about this point: "The harms caused by pornography are by no means limited to acts of physical aggression. The mere existence of pornography in society degrades and demeans all women." Embedded in this view are several other familiar themes: that sex is degrading to women, but not to men; that men are raving beasts; that sex is dangerous for women; that sexuality is male, not female; that women are victims, not sexual actors; that men inflict "it" on women; that penetration is submission; that heterosexual sexuality, rather than the institution of heterosexuality, is sexist.

These assumptions, in part intended, in part unintended, lead us back to the traditional target of obscenity law: sexually explicit material. What initially appeared novel, then, is really the reappearance of a traditional theme. It is ironic that a feminist position on pornography incorporates most of the myths about sexuality that feminism has struggled to displace.

The Dangers of Application

The Minneapolis and Indianapolis ordinances embody a political view that holds pornography to be a central force in "creating and maintaining" the oppression of women. This view appears in summary form in the legislative findings section at the beginning of the Minneapolis bill, which describes a chain reaction of misogynistic acts generated by pornography. The legislation is based on the interweaving of several themes: that pornography constructs the meaning of sexuality for women and, as well, leads to discrete acts of violence against women; that sexuality is the primary cause of women's oppression; that explicitly sexual images, even if not violent or coerced, have the power to subordinate women; and that women's own accounts of force have been silenced because, as a universal and timeless rule, society credits pornographic constructions rather than women's experiences. Taking the silencing contention a step further, advocates of the ordinance effectively assume that women have been so conditioned by the pornographic world view that if their own experiences of the sexual acts identified in the definition are not subordinating, then they must simply be victims of false consciousness.

The heart of the ordinance is the "trafficking" section, which would allow almost anyone to seek the removal of any materials falling within the law's definition of pornography. Ordinance defenders strenuously protest that the issue is not censorship because the state, as such, is not authorized to initiate criminal prosecutions. But the prospect of having to defend a potentially infinite number of privately filed complaints creates at least as much of a chilling effect against pornographic or sexual speech as does a criminal law. And as long as representatives of the state—in this case, judges—have the ultimate say over the interpretation, the distinction between this ordinance and "real" censorship will not hold.

In addition, three major problems should dissuade feminists from supporting this kind of law: First, the sexual images in question do not cause more harm than other aspects of misogynist culture; second, sexually explicit speech, even in male-dominated society, serves positive social functions for women; and third, the passage and enforcement of antipornography laws such as those supported in Minneapolis and Indianapolis are more likely to impede, rather than advance, feminist goals.

Ordinance proponents contend that pornography does cause violence because it conditions male sexual response to images of violence, and thus provokes violence against women. The strongest research they offer is based on psychology experiments that employ films depicting a rape scene, toward the end of which the woman is shown to be enjoying the attack. The proposed ordinances, by contrast, cover a much broader range of materials than this one specific heterosexual rape scenario. Further, the studies cited by ordinance supporters do not support the theory that pornography causes violence against women.

In addition, the argument that pornography itself plays a major role in the general oppression of women contradicts the evidence of history. It need hardly be said that pornography did not lead to the burning of witches or the English common law treatment of women as chattel property. If anything functioned then as the prime communication medium for woman-hating, it was probably religion. Nor can pornography be blamed for the enactment of laws from at least the eighteenth century that allowed a husband to rape or beat his wife with impunity. In any period, the causes of women's oppression have been many and complex, drawing on the fundamental social and economic structures of society. Ordinance proponents offer little evidence to explain how the mass production of pornography—a relatively recent phenomenon—could have become so potent a causative agent so quickly.

The silencing of women is another example of the harm attributed to pornography. Yet if this argument were correct, one would expect that as the social visibility of pornography has increased the tendency to credit women's accounts of rape would have decreased. In fact, although the treatment of women complainants in rape cases is far from perfect, efforts by the women's movement have resulted in marked improvements. In many places, the corroboration requirement has now been abolished; evidence of a victim's past sexual experiences has been prohibited; and a number of police forces have developed specially trained units and procedures to improve the handling of sexual assault cases. The presence of rape fantasies in pornography may in part reflect a backlash against these women's movement advances, but to argue that most people routinely disbelieve women who file charges of rape belittles the real improvements made in social consciousness and law.

The third type of harm is a kind of libel: the maliciously false characterization of women as a group of sexual masochists. To claim that all pornography is a lie is a false analogy. If truth is a defense to charges of libel, then surely depictions of consensual sex cannot be thought of as equivalent to a falsehood. For example, some women (and men) do enjoy being tied up or displaying themselves. The declaration by fiat that sadomasochism is a "lie" about sexuality reflects an arrogance and moralism that feminists should combat, not engage in. When mutually desired sexual experiences are depicted, pornography is not "libelous."

Not only does pornography not cause the kind and degree of harm that can justify the restraint of speech, but its existence serves some social functions which benefit women. Pornographic speech has many, often anomalous, characteristics. One is certainly that it magnifies the misogyny present in the culture and exaggerates the fantasy of male power. Another, however, is that the existence of pornography has served to flout conventional sexual mores, to ridicule sexual hypocrisy and to underscore the importance of sexual needs. Pornography carries many messages other than woman-hating; it advocates sexual adventure, sex outside marriage, sex for no reason other than pleasure, casual sex, anonymous sex, group sex, voyeuristic sex, illegal sex, public sex. Some of these ideas appeal to women reading or seeing pornography, who may interpret some images as legitimating their own sense of sexual urgency or desire to be sexually aggressive. Women's experience of pornography is not as universally victimizing as the ordinance would have it.

Antipornography laws, as restrictions on sexual speech, in many ways echo and expand upon the traditional legal analysis of sexually explicit speech under the rubric of obscenity. The Supreme Court has consistently ruled that sexual speech defined as "obscenity" does not belong in the system of public discourse, and is therefore an exception to the First Amendment and hence not entitled to protection under the free speech guarantee. The definition of obscenity has shifted over the years and remains imprecise. In 1957 the Supreme Court ruled that obscenity could be suppressed regardless of whether it presented an imminent threat of illegal activity. In the opinion of the Supreme Court, graphic sexual images do not communicate "real" ideas. These, it would seem, are found only in the traditionally defined public arena. Sexual themes can qualify as ideas if they use sexuality for argument's sake, but not if they speak in the words and images of "private" life—that is, if they graphically depict sex itself. At least theoretically, and insofar as the law functions as a pronouncement of moral judgment, sex is consigned to remain unexpressed and in the private realm.

The fallacies in this distinction are obvious. Under the U.S. Constitution, for example, it is acceptable to write: "I am a sadomasochist," or even: "Everyone should experiment with sadomasochism in order to increase sexual pleasure." But to write a graphic fantasy about sadomasochism that arouses and excites readers is not protected unless a court finds it to have serious literary, artistic or political value, despite the expressive nature of the content. Indeed, the fantasy depiction may communicate identity in a more compelling way than the "I am" statement. For sexual minorities, sexual representation can be self-identifying and affirming in a hostile world. Images of those acts should be protected for that reason, for they do have political content. Just as the personal can be political, so can the specifically and graphically sexual.

Supporters of the antipornography ordinances both endorse the concept that pornographic speech contains no ideas or expressive interest, and at the same time attribute to pornography the capacity to trigger violent acts by the power of its misogyny. The city's brief in defense of the Indianapolis ordinance expanded this point by arguing that all sexually explicit speech is entitled to less constitutional protection than other speech. The antipornography groups have cleverly capitalized on this approach—a product of a totally non-feminist legal system—to attempt, through the mechanism of the ordinances, to legitimate a new crusade for protectionism and sexual conservatism.

The consequences of enforcing such a law, however, are much more likely to obstruct than advance feminist political goals. On the level of ideas, further narrowing of the public realm of sexual speech coincides all too well with the privatization of sexual, reproductive and family issues sought by the far right. Practically speaking, the ordinances could result in attempts to eliminate the images associated with homosexuality. Doubtless there are heterosexual women who believe that lesbianism is a "degrading" form of "subordination." Since the ordinances allow for suits against materials in which men appear "in place of women," far-right antipornography crusaders could use these laws to suppress gay male pornography. Imagine a Jerry-Falwell-style conservative filing a complaint against a gay bookstore for selling sexually explicit materials showing men with other men in "degrading" or "submissive" or "objectified" postures—all in the name of protecting women.

And most ironically, while the ordinances would do nothing to improve the material conditions of most women's lives, their high visibility might well divert energy from the drive to enact other, less popular laws that would genuinely empower women—comparable worth legislation, for example, or affirmative action requirements or fairer property and support principles in divorce laws.

Other provisions of the ordinances concern coercive behavior: physical assault which is imitative of pornographic images, coercion into pornographic performance, and forcing pornography on others. On close examination, however, even most of these provisions are problematic.

Existing law already penalizes physical assault, including when it is associated with pornography. Defenders of the proposed legislation often cite the example of models who have been raped or otherwise harmed while in the process of making pornographic images. But victims of this type of attack can already sue or prosecute those responsible. (Linda Marchiano, the actress who appeared in the film *Deep Throat*, has not recovered damages for the physical assaults she describes in her book *Ordeal* because the events happened several years before she decided to try to file a suit. A lawsuit was thus precluded by the statute of limitations.) Indeed, the ordinances do not cover assault or other harm incurred while producing pornography, presumably because other laws already achieve that end.

The ordinances would penalize coercing, intimidating or fraudulently inducing anyone into performing for pornography. Although existing law already provides remedies for fraud or contracts of duress, this section of the proposed ordinance seeks to facilitate recovery of damages by, for example, pornography models who might otherwise encounter substantial prejudice against their claims. Supporters of this section have suggested that it is comparable to the Supreme Court's ban on child pornography. The analogy has been stretched to the point where the City of Indianapolis brief argued that women, like children, need "special protection." "Children are incapable of consenting to engage in pornographic conduct, even absent physical coercion and therefore require special protection," the brief stated. "By the same token, the physical and psychological well-being of women ought to be afforded comparable protection, for the coercive environment in which most pornographic models work vitiates any notion that they consent or 'choose' to perform in pornography."

The reality of women's lives is far more complicated. Women do not become pornography models because society is egalitarian and they exercise a "free choice," but neither do they "choose" this work because they have lost all power for deliberate, volitional behavior. Modeling or acting for pornography, like prostitution, can be a means of survival for those with limited options. For some women, at some points in their lives, it is a rational economic decision. Not every woman regrets having made it, although no woman should have to settle for it. The fight should be to expand the options as well as to insure job safety for women who do become pornography models. By contrast, the impact of the proposed ordinance as a whole would be to drive the pornography industry further underground.

One of the vaguest provisions in the ordinance prohibits "forcing" pornography on a person. "Forcing" is not defined in the law, and one is left to speculate whether it means forced to respond to pornography, forced to read it or forced to glance at it before turning away. Also unclear is whether the perpetrator must in fact have some superior power over the person being forced—that is, whether there is a meaningful threat that makes the concept of force real.

Again, widely varying situations are muddled, and a consideration of context is absent. "Forcing" pornography on a person "in any public space" is treated identically to using it as a method of sexual harassment in the workplace. The scope of "forcing" could include walking past a newsstand or browsing in a bookstore that had pornography on display. The force involved in such a situation seems mild when compared, for example, to the incessant sexist advertising on television.

The concept behind the "forcing" provision is appropriate, however, in the case of workplace harassment. A worker should not have to endure, especially on pain of losing her job, harassment based on sex, race, religion, nationality or any other factor. This general policy was established by the U.S. courts as part of the guarantees of Title VII of the 1964 Civil Rights Act. Pornography used as a means of harassing women workers is already legally actionable, just as harassment in the workplace by racial slurs is actionable. Any literature endorsing the oppression of women—whether pornography or the Bible—could be employed as an harassment device to impede a woman's access to a job, or to education, public accommodations or other social benefits. It is the usage of pornography in this situation, not the image itself, that is discriminatory. Appropriately, this section of the ordinances provides that only perpetrators of the forcing, not makers and distributors of the images, could be held liable.

Forcing of pornography on a person is also specifically forbidden "in the home." In her testimony before the Indianapolis City Council, Catharine MacKinnon referred to the problem of pornography being "forced on wives in preparation for later sexual scenes." Since only the person who forces the pornography on another can be sued, this provision becomes a kind of protection against domestic harassment. It would allow wives to seek court orders or damages against husbands for some usages of pornography. Although a fascinating attempt to subvert male power in the domestic realm, it nonetheless has problems. "Forcing" is not an easy concept to define in this context. It is hard to know what degree of intrusion would amount to forcing images onto a person who shares the same private space.

More important, the focus on pornography seems a displacement of the more fundamental issues involved in the conflicts that occur between husbands and wives or lovers over sex. Some men may invoke images that reflect their greater power to pressure women into performing the supposedly traditional role of acceding to male desires. Pornography may facilitate or enhance this dynamic of male dominance, but it is hardly the causative agent. Nor would removing the pornography do much to solve the problem. If the man invokes instead his friends' stories about sexual encounters or his experience with other women, is the resulting interaction with his wife substantially different? Focusing on the pornography, rather than on the relationship and its social context, may serve only to channel heterosexual women's recognition of their own intimate oppression toward a movement hailed by the far right as being antiperversion rather than toward a feminist analysis of sexual politics.

The last of the sections that deal with actual coercive conduct is one that attempts to deal with the assault, physical injury or attack of any person in a way that is directly caused by specific pornography. The ordinances would allow a lawsuit against the makers and distributors of pornographic materials that were imitated by an attacker—the only provision of the ordinance that requires proof of causation. Presenting such proof would be extremely difficult. If the viewer's willful decision to imitate the image were found to be an intervening, superseding cause of the harm, the plaintiff would lose.

The policy issues here are no different from those concerning violent media images that are nonsexual: Is showing an image sufficient to cause an act of violence? Even if an image could be found to cause a viewer's behavior, was that behavior reasonably foreseeable? So far, those who have produced violent films have not been found liable under the law when third persons acted out the violence depicted. If this were to change, it would mean, for example, that the producer of the TV movie *The Burning Bed*, which told the true story of a battered wife who set fire to her sleeping husband, could be sued if a woman who saw the film killed her husband in a similar way. The result, of course, would be the end of films depicting real violence in the lives of women.

The ordinances' supporters offer no justification for singling out sexual assault from other kinds of violence. Certainly the experience of sexual assault is not always worse than that of being shot or stabbed or suffering other kinds of nonsexual assault. Nor is sexual assault the only form of violence that is fueled by sexism. If there were evidence that sexual images are more likely to be imitated, there might be some arguable justification for treating them differently. But there is no support for this contention.

Laws which would increase the state's regulation of sexual images present many dangers for women. Although they draw much of their feminist support from women's anger at the strength of the market for images of sexual violence, these proposals are aimed not at violence, but at sexual explicitness. Far-right elements recognize the possibility of using the full potential of the ordinances to enforce their sexually conservative worldview, and have supported them for that reason. Feminists should therefore look carefully at the text of these "model" laws in order to understand why many believe them to be a useful tool in *anti*feminist moral crusades.

The proposed ordinances are dangerous because they seek to embody in law an analysis of the role of sexuality and sexual images in the oppression of women with which even all feminists do not agree. Underlying virtually every section of the proposed laws there is an assumption that sexuality is a realm of unremitting, unequaled victimization for women. Pornography appears as the monster that made this so. The ordinances' authors seek to impose their analysis by putting state power behind it. But this analysis is not the only feminist perspective on sexuality. Feminist theorists have also argued that the sexual terrain, however power-laden, is actively contested. Women are agents, and not merely victims, who make decisions and act on them, and who desire, seek out and enjoy sexuality.

Appendix

Excerpts from the Minneapolis Ordinance*

The key provisions of the original Minneapolis ordinance are reprinted below:

(1) Special Findings on Pornography: The council finds that pornography is central in creating and maintaining the civil inequality of the sexes. Pornography is a systematic practice of exploitation and subordination based on sex which differentially harms women. The bigotry and contempt it promotes, with the acts of aggression it fosters, harm women's opportunities for equality of rights in employment, education, property rights, public accommodations and public services; create public harassment and private denigration; promote injury and degradation such as rape, battery and prostitution and inhibit just enforcement of laws against these acts; contribute significantly to restricting women from full exercise of citizenship and participation in public life, including in neighborhoods; damage relations between the sexes; and undermine women's equal exercise of rights to speech and action guaranteed to all citizens under the constitutions and laws of the United States and the State of Minnesota.

(gg) *Pornography.* Pornography is a form of discrimination on the basis of sex.

(1) Pornography is the sexually explicit subordination of women, graphically depicted, whether in pictures or in words, that also includes one or more of the following:

(i) women are presented as dehumanized sexual objects, things or commodities; or

(ii) women are presented as sexual objects who enjoy pain or humiliation; or

(iii) women are presented as sexual objects who experience sexual pleasure in being raped; or

(iv) women are presented as sexual objects tied up or cut up or mutilated or bruised or physically hurt; or

(v) women are presented in postures of sexual submission; [or sexual servility, including by inviting penetration;][1] or

(vi) women's body parts—including but not limited to vaginas, breasts, and buttocks—are exhibited, such that women are reduced to those parts; or

(vii) women are presented as whores by nature; or

(viii) women are presented being penetrated by objects or animals; or

---

* Revised and reprinted from *Women Against Censorship*, Varda Burstyn, editor. Douglas and McIntyre, Ltd. © 1985.

(ix) women are presented in scenarios of degradation, injury, abasement, torture, shown as filthy or inferior, bleeding, bruised, or hurt in a context that makes these conditions sexual.

(2) The use of men, children, or transsexuals in the place of women ... is pornography for purposes of ... this statute.

(1) Discrimination by trafficking in pornography.

The production, sale, exhibition, or distribution of pornography is discrimination against women by means of trafficking in pornography:

(1) City, state, and federally funded public libraries or private and public university and college libraries in which pornography is available for study, including on open shelves, shall not be construed to be trafficking in pornography, but special display presentations of pornography in said places is sex discrimination.

(2) The formation of private clubs or associations for purposes of trafficking in pornography is illegal and shall be considered a conspiracy to violate the civil rights of women.

(3) Any woman has a cause of action hereunder as a woman acting against the subordination of women. Any man or transsexual who alleges injury by pornography in the way women are injured by it shall also have a cause of action.

(m) *Coercion into pornographic performances.* Any person, including a transsexual, who is coerced, intimidated, or fraudulently induced (hereafter, "coerced") into performing for pornography shall have a cause of action against the maker(s), seller(s), exhibitor(s) or distributor(s) of said pornography for damages and for the elimination of the products of the performance(s) from the public view.

(1) Limitation of action. This claim shall not expire before five years have elapsed from the date of the coerced performance(s) or from the last appearance or sale of any product of the performance(s); whichever date is later;

(2) Proof of one or more of the following facts or conditions shall not, without more, negate a finding of coercion:

(aa) that the person is a woman; or

(bb) that the person is or has been a prostitute; or

(cc) that the person has attained the age of majority; or

(dd) that the person is connected by blood or marriage to anyone involved in or related to the making of the pornography; or

(ee) that the person has previously had, or been thought to have had, sexual relations with anyone including anyone involved in or related to the making of the pornography; or (ff) that the person has previously posed for sexually explicit pictures for or with anyone, including anyone involved in or related to the making of the pornography at issue; or

(gg) that anyone else, including a spouse or other relative, has given permission on the person's behalf; or

(hh) that the person actually consented to a use of the performance that is changed into pornography; or

(ii) that the person knew that the purpose of the acts or events in question was to make pornography; or

(jj) that the person showed no resistance or appeared to cooperate actively in the photographic sessions or in the sexual events that produced the pornography; or

(kk) that the person signed a contract, or made statements affirming a willingness to cooperate; or

(ll) that no physical force, threats, or weapons were used in the making of the pornography; or

(mm) that the person was paid or otherwise compensated.

(n) *Forcing pornography on a person.* Any woman, man, child, or transsexual who has pornography forced on them in any place of employment, in education, in a home, or in any public place has a cause of action against the perpetrator and/or institution.

(o) *Assault or physical attack due to pornography.* Any woman, man, child, or transsexual who is assaulted, physically attacked or injured in a way that is directly caused by specific pornography has a claim for damages against the perpetrator, the maker(s), distributor(s), seller(s), and/or exhibitor(s), and for an injunction against the specific pornography's further exhibition, distribution, or sale. No damages shall be assessed (A) against maker(s) for pornography made, (B) against distributor(s) for pornography distributed, (C) against seller(s) for pornography sold, or (D) against exhibitors for pornography exhibited prior to the effective date of this act.

(p) *Defenses.* Where the materials which are the subject matter of a cause of action under subsections (l), (m), (n), or (o) of this section are pornography, it shall not be a defense that the defendant did not know or intend that the materials are pornography or sex discrimination.

CHAPTER 4

Feminist Historians and Antipornography Campaigns

An Overview

LISA DUGGAN (1993)

I am not going to give you a standard history lesson this morning. Instead, I want to talk about why feminist historians, as a group, have been highly critical of antipornography legislation and the politics underlying it.

In the mid-1980s, an acrimonious split developed in the feminist movement after antipornography feminists began drafting and campaigning for legislation directed at regulating pornographic expression. This faction, which had until then often stated that its members opposed censorship as a remedy for pornography's misogyny,[1] proposed ordinances in Cambridge,[2] Los Angeles,[3] Minneapolis,[4] and in Indianapolis,[5] where the proposal was enacted. This split was found among all different kinds of feminists and in all different kinds of locations. Within the National Organization for Women, among lesbian-feminists, and among various feminist scholars, a heated, intense and rancorous debate ensued, lasting until about 1986 or 1987, when most feminist opinion came to oppose the use of this kind of legislation in antipornography campaigns.[6]

But even during this period—often referred to as "the Sex Wars," which is the casual, although bitter reference people use for this time[7]— there was no debate among feminist historians. Feminist historians, almost completely to a woman, almost without exception, opposed this legislative strategy and criticized the political analysis underlying it. Almost immediately, well-known historians, such as Judith Walkowitz,[8] Ellen DuBois and Linda Gordon,[9] wrote to explain why this was a problematic strategy for feminism. Given the magnitude and bitterness of the debate, the question arises: why was there no debate among feminist historians? Why was there such widespread agreement that this was a bad course of action?

Given that the legislation was presented as an historical achievement in the campaign against violence against women[10] and as a legal breakthrough for feminists,[11] you would think that feminist historians would at least have had some two-sided conversation about this. Feminist historians had been working very hard for several decades to reevaluate women's reform campaigns, such as the nineteenth- and early twentieth-century temperance and social-purity campaigns;[12] they had treated those campaigns seriously to counter the way in which mainstream historians and even progressive male historians had treated them as trivial, comic or simply puritanical.[13] Feminists had worked to show that there were serious issues at stake and real feminist angers underlying these campaigns. So, given the similarity between the 1980s' antipornography campaign and these earlier campaigns, and the vigorous attempts by feminist historians to get people to take these kinds of reforms seriously, why then would feminist historians be so uniformly critical of the campaigns in the 1980s?

The answer has four parts. Four major issues motivated feminist historians to mobilize opposition to this strategy and this political analysis.

The first reason comes under the rubric of displacement. I will give you an historical example and then a current example of what I mean. Much of the rhetoric of the temperance movement in the late nineteenth and early twentieth centuries addressed the problems of domestic violence and all-male social spaces such as saloons.[14] But the temperance campaign focused its efforts on *banning* alcohol. Although there were serious problems related to the consumption of alcohol, the notion that the banning of alcohol would address the problem of domestic violence or do anything about all-male social spaces was a very mistaken, displaced strategy. The real issues were not attacked directly because of social and cultural taboos.[15] Instead, energy was displaced onto a campaign to ban alcohol, a campaign that ultimately was a fruitless, counterproductive political strategy. And because feminist historians have looked at these campaigns so closely, they immediately recognized the same kind of displacement when they looked at the antipornography campaign.

For a more recent example, let me take you to Suffolk County, New York, in 1984, where a hearing was conducted on whether an antipornography ordinance modeled on the MacKinnon-Dworkin ordinance should be passed.[16] The initiative had been organized by a right-wing person and had a lot of right-wing support.[17] I went to these hearings, where there were mobs of people lined up to speak—and close to fifty percent of those who spoke were men. It seemed that they had come to confess. They would come to the microphone and confess that they had battered their wives, had raped their daughters, but that pornography had made them do it. They would use language like, "pornography came into my home and made me do it." And so, the remedy for these problems was not battered women's shelters. The remedy for these problems was not more aggressive prosecution of rape and sexual assault. Their remedy was an antipornography law. They confessed their acts of violence, but did not hold themselves accountable. Instead, they displaced responsibility for their acts onto pornography in exactly the way that is so familiar to people who have looked closely at the temperance campaign. Feminist anger, women's anger at the conditions in their households was displaced onto a campaign for an antipornography law.

The second reason feminist historians object to antipornography campaigns comes under the rubric of alliances and how alliances work. An historical example is the social-purity campaigns in the United States and England, which worked to strengthen antiprostitution laws at the turn of the century.[18] The feminists who were engaged in the campaign to strengthen antiprostitution laws were concerned about the economic and sexual vulnerability of young women in the cities.[19] But these feminist campaigners allied themselves with conservatives whose goal was to enforce morality—not to protect women.[20] Because conservatives had more social, cultural and political clout than the feminists involved in these campaigns, it was the conservatives who ultimately shaped the laws and the ways the laws were enforced.[21] So the alliance of feminists with conservatives in social-purity campaigns (which is something that Judith Walkowitz has written quite extensively about[22]) displaced energy onto campaigns to suppress prostitution, rather than to do things that actually would work to give women more economic and social resources.

The contemporary example of how forming an alliance can misdirect efforts can be seen in Indianapolis in 1984, where Catharine MacKinnon, who drafted the original antipornography ordinance with Andrea Dworkin, worked with Beulah Coughenour, a Stop-ERA activist, to pass the ordinance. MacKinnon also worked with the Rev. Greg Dixon, who was the national secretary of the Moral Majority. So, this "feminist law" was passed by the overwhelmingly Republican city council. It was opposed locally by feminists, by black politicians, by the gay community and by the few Democrats on the city council. But in their accounts of the events in Indianapolis, MacKinnon and others insist that there was no intent to form a coalition with conservatives. They say this was a feminist law, that this was a feminist campaign. But the statement that the feminist antipornography movement has never collaborated with the right wing is possible only by reinterpreting Beulah Coughenour's motives as feminist, which is—to put it mildly—a stretch. So, the same problem of collaboration with conservatives, whose agenda is explicitly antifeminist and misogynist, reappears. The problem has to do with the shaping of the law, the meaning of the law, and the understanding people give the law, as well as how the law is enforced and how it is interpreted by judges.[23]

This problem leads us to the third reason why feminist historians think critically about antipornography campaigns and other similar legislative strategies: they so often harm women. Among the more appalling examples are the practical applications of the antiprostitution laws that I just mentioned. Those laws operated to penalize primarily women. Women were arrested under those laws.[24] Women, not men, were harassed under those laws. And those laws ended up making the lives of women in cities more dangerous, more difficult. A recent example is the help that MacKinnon has given to the Canadian judiciary in interpreting their obscenity law.[25] Under this "feminist" interpretation, the first prosecution was of a lesbian publication.[26] An earlier example is the collaboration of the social-purity movement with figures such as Anthony Comstock to produce laws that resulted in the persecution of Margaret Sanger.[27] The antipornography campaigns in some sense helped to motivate and legitimate the notion that obscenity was dangerous. Most recently, such notions led the National Endowment for the Arts to discontinue funding several lesbian and gay and feminist artists.[28]

The fourth reason why feminist historians uniformly criticize this strategy concerns the historical analysis underlying it: pornography causes misogyny and violence against women.[29] That argument has absolutely no basis as an historical claim because the mass availability of pornography since World War II certainly cannot have caused violence and misogyny; they have existed for centuries. This argument has no merit as a cross-cultural claim because the status of women does not increase in societies that suppress sexually explicit materials[30]—whether it is the State of Utah or Saudi Arabia.[31] There is simply no direct correlation between suppressing sexually explicit material and improving the status of women.

So, on a very mechanical level, as a cross-cultural and historical claim, this causal analysis is much too simple.

This is not to say that misogyny and pornography or sexually explicit materials have no importance, or that we should not criticize them. Certainly we should, in the same way we criticize and organize against misogyny in television, in novels, in advertising. But it makes as much sense to organize a group called Women Against the Novel as it does to organize Women Against Porn. We are against *misogyny* in sexually explicit materials. We are not against sexually explicit materials *per se*.

In conclusion, I want to say that this is still very relevant; it is not just about the 1980s or the turn of the century. Renewed efforts—from the Pornography Victims' Compensation Act[32] to local initiatives—are constantly popping up, attempting to regulate and suppress sexually explicit images and sexually explicit speech. In our strategies we need to carefully separate the question of sexual explicitness from the question of misogyny and the question of violence. We also need to think about what we mean when we casually throw around the word *violence*, because much consensual sadomasochistic imagery is referred to as "*violence*," and distinctions need to be made. We do not always agree about what is or is not sexist, and we need to talk about that as well. We need to very carefully make these distinctions in our political analysis and in our legislative efforts because if we do not, we will end up being co-opted into and collaborating with right-wing efforts that are not now—and have never been—in the interests of women or of feminists.

CHAPTER 5

Sex Panics

LISA DUGGAN (1989)

What is to be done? This summer's escalating attacks on the autonomy of the National Endowment for the Arts (NEA) have sent artists, arts administrators and arts advocates reeling. The scramble is on to mount an effective line of defense. But the methods of attack have made defense uncommonly difficult—they are one part apparently rational circumspection about the use of taxpayers' dollars to support "offensive" art, and one part irrational panic and hate-filled attack on "deviant" sexuality.

The arts community has responded directly to the "rational" part, but has generally avoided the underlying, and far more destructive, panic and hate. Arts supporters have been on familiar ground when confronted with arguments about the need to restrict funding for unpopular art. Everyone knows what to say: art is not supposed to be tamely popular, it *should* provoke, question, enlighten; the public purse is best served by the peer review process, which places evaluation of art where it belongs, in the hands of artists, not crudely partisan politicians. But nearly everyone goes strangely mute when faced with completely unhinged hysterics over images of interracial homoeroticism, sadomasochism, and nude children.

This muteness is expected; it is enforced by the logic of a sex panic. Sex panics, witch-hunts, and red scares are staples of American history. While often promoted by relatively powerless but vocal minorities hostile to cultural difference, they have been enthusiastically taken up by powerful groups in an effort to impose a rigid orthodoxy on the majority. In this context, "moral reforms" and the like have been the public-relations mask for what is in fact an abnegation of any responsibility to confront and address very real problems, that is, poverty, militarism, sexism, racism. Often in these PR campaigns, words assume the reverse of their common meaning: liberation becomes chaos, desire becomes deviance, and dissent becomes the work of the devil.

In the grip of a sex panic, if you are accused of sexual "deviance," your defensive strategies are limited to either confession and repentance, or denials of personal "guilt," both of which only reinforce the legitimacy of the attack ("I am not now, nor have I ever been …"). If you refuse to deny or apologize, you are isolated and calumnies are heaped upon you. No one will defend your actions, only your right to due process and a good lawyer.

In the case of Congress and the NEA, sex-panic attacks on photographer Robert Mapplethorpe had the predictable effect. The Corcoran canceled its scheduled exhibition of his photographs (denial), arts supporters in the House accepted a symbolic NEA funding cut as "punishment" for its support for the Mapplethorpe exhibition (apology), and members of the Senate voted overwhelmingly to restrict funding for sexualized imagery (the sex panic grows unchallenged). Volumes have been spoken about the value of the peer review process, about the importance of the abstract right to artistic freedom. But very few arts supporters have been willing to say much to defend sexual images *per se*, and this muteness about bodies and sexuality implicitly concedes that the particular images at issue are indefensible.

Initially, the art world was collectively flabbergasted at attacks on the NEA. After all, most Americans at least give lip service to the idea that the arts should be free from government restrictions. But this cultural consensus is relatively recent and, as we all have now been reminded, relatively fragile, especially with regard to sexual content.

From the nineteenth to the mid-twentieth century, conflicts over the regulation of sexual behavior and sexual representations intensified in legislatures and courtrooms. Social- and sexual-purity crusaders managed to pass layer after layer of repressive legislation penalizing prostitution, homosexuality, and pornography, and severely restricting child and adolescent sexuality. (For instance, juvenile detention homes established during the early twentieth century were used to incarcerate teenage girls almost exclusively for sexual activity.) They were opposed with increasing effectiveness over time by civil libertarians and other advocates of cultural openness and sexual freedom. In the post-World War II period, a partial truce was achieved in the continuing conflicts through a slowly developed, contradictory and hypocritical compromise consensus. In the arena of sexual behavior, antiprostitution and sodomy laws would remain on the books, but they would be only selectively enforced. (For example, prostitutes are usually arrested, not johns; and conservative politicians have been known to fuel their reelection campaigns by periodic sweeps of prostitute hangouts and gay bars, which are normally left alone. In Indianapolis, for instance, during an election year in the early eighties, police used hidden video cameras to monitor gay public spaces and made arrests based on the "evidence" collected.) In the arena of sexual representation, "obscenity" laws would be enforced, but works of "serious" artistic or literary merit would be exempted.

This precarious consensus has been periodically disrupted by both repressive panics (the persecution of gay people in the military and the government, the passage of "sexual psychopath" laws in the 1950s) and moves toward greater openness (the repeal of some sodomy laws, the formation of prostitutes' rights groups in the sixties and seventies). But the consensus remained substantially intact right up to the 1980s, when conflict broke out all over the place. Early eighties right-wing hysteria over pornography was fanned, ironically, by a feminist antipornography crusade (which transmuted the necessary critique of sexism in pornography into a campaign for the legal suppression of sexual imagery). But such efforts at censorship energized civil libertarian and feminist oppositions, which managed to defuse the repressive agenda of the Attorney General's Commission on Pornography in the mid-eighties. Antigay hysteria fanned by fear of AIDS resulted in an indefensible indifference to human suffering during the latter part of the decade, but also fueled a revitalized activism among gay people and advocates of humane health care.

The result of all the renewed conflict is that the postwar consensus is closer than ever before to a complete breakdown. And so the moral conservatives have felt free to do what the art world thought they would not dare to do. They have directed their antiporn, antigay fervor at the "high," the "respectable" arts—the stuff shown in museums rather than adult bookstores. They do not have the power successfully to advocate the outright banning of art work or the prosecution of artists, but they have hit upon a strategy used with some success by antiabortion activists: the defunding of materials they object to and the intimidation of arts institutions into self-censorship to protect their bottom lines. Their tactic is to inaugurate a sex panic, and arts advocates are learning quickly how the logic plays itself out. The restrictions do not even have to pass into law to have the desired effect—the Corcoran cancellation was a *preemptive* measure.

Of course, it is not purely accidental that the conservatives hit upon Robert Mapplethorpe as a primary target for a sex panic. Mapplethorpe's work exposes the contradiction and hypocrisy at the heart of the post-war consensus. His images cross the designated boundaries, appropriating images from the stigmatized zone of "pornography" and carting them across the lines into the free zone of "art." Mapplethorpe's strategy was radically to disrupt the belief that images of some bodies and practices are fit only for squalid, hidden or persecuted surroundings.

Mapplethorpe is certainly not the only artist to have created sexually explicit imagery, or appropriated "pornographic" conventions. But he has moved much further than most others into the mainstream institutions of culture, partly because his images are of such high formal quality and conventional presentation, and partly because he was a well-connected white male. He got far enough into the mainstream to cause conservatives to fear that he was posthumously succeeding in a strategy of legitimation of the practices he represented. Or, as Walter Annenberg put it in *The New York Times*, "[He] went too far, trying to justify his own inclinations." He went far enough, anyway, to elicit the sort of hysterical attacks that had been confined, earlier in the decade, to less artistically respectable representations. Judith Reisman, a former feminist but now a right-wing anti-porn campaigner associated with the American Family Association, put it all rather starkly in the *Washington Times*. She describes Mapplethorpe's photographs of nude and partially nude children, not engaged in any sexual activity (for example, *Honey*, 1976), as "child pornography" and "photographic assault and rape." She claims that his representation of his own rectum with bullwhip inserted "encourages" the "sadistic acts, which, on the evidence, facilitate AIDS."

Reisman's charges neatly illustrate the favored tactics of 1980s antiporn attacks. Consensual sadomasochism is equated with violence, anal eroticism is damned as the cause of AIDS, and any depiction of the bodies of children is blasted as child abuse. Public outrage at real violence, real suffering and widespread abuse is diverted away from substantive analysis and action into a censorship campaign.

The charge of child pornography has been the most successful of all these tactics. The widely respected sex education book *Show Me* was suppressed under child pornography laws by the early eighties. In 1988, Virginia artist Alice Sims was arrested and her children removed to a foster home—police considered her personal snapshots of her naked daughter, studies for a series of drawings called *Water Babies*, to be evidence of child abuse. And when Broadway actress Colleen Dewhurst testified in opposition to censorship before the Meese Commission on Pornography, she was asked if she or her theater organization therefore supported child pornography.

Attacks like these cannot be fended off by reasoned appeals to the First Amendment or the NEA's peer review process. Moral conservatives will push their opportunity to erode the postwar consensus on the regulation of sexuality in a rightward direction, extending content restrictions on images from the adult bookstores into the museums. If they can frighten arts supporters into silence about sex, they will be encouraged to continue. To secure creative freedom against the onslaught, arts activists must seize the opportunity to push back in the other direction. The time has come to argue forcefully for the complete deregulation of consensual sexuality and its representations. Nothing less will move us forward.

CHAPTER 6

Banned in the U.S.A.

What the Hardwick Ruling Will Mean

NAN D. HUNTER (1986)

The Supreme Court's decision in *Bowers v. Hardwick* demonstrates that in the McCarthysim of the eighties, sexuality is a primary form of deviancy. Gay men and lesbians are no more of a real threat to the republic or Western civilization than the American Communist Party was in 1952. But just as the Supreme Court virtually suspended the First Amendment in order to silence Communists 35 years ago, it has now rendered homosexuals, as a class, outlaws in the eyes of America.

There is no dispelling the bitterness of this defeat.

Winning *Hardwick* was to have been the first giant step toward dismantling the legal apparatus of homophobia. Sodomy laws have functioned as the linchpin for denial of employment, housing and custody or visitation rights; even when we have proved that there was no nexus between homosexuality and job skills or parenting ability, we have had the courts throw the "habitual criminal" label at us as a reason to deny relief. What brought us within striking distance on this case was the essential conservatism of the claim—a privacy argument based on the intersection of core values of individual identity and a-man's-home-is-his-castle locational sanctity. Almost none of the lawyers who worked on the case believed that the Court would, when the chips were down, give Big Brother free rein to police the bedroom—even gay bedrooms. Were we ever wrong.

There are strong hints that a bare majority could be achieved for the proposition that prison sentences for lovemaking might, just might, be found impermissible under the Eighth Amendment's prohibition of cruel and unusual punishment. The ACLU and the gay civil rights groups certainly will not stop trying to eradicate sodomy laws. But for the moment we are left to sort out the ramifications of this ruling, and to decide what to do next.

First it is important to note what *Hardwick* is not. It is not a setback in the same way that a reversal of *Roe v. Wade* or *Miranda* or *Brown v. Board of Education* would be—we have not lost ground that we once occupied. It is not the death knell to every kind of gay rights case in every context—we have been winning increasing numbers of these cases for years, despite the sodomy laws, and we will continue to win them. Nor will it have a direct, immediate impact on day-to-day life—again, unlike a decision eliminating legal abortion, or inviting coercion of confessions, or ending desegregation plans.

But in its language and its social meaning as a symbol, *Hardwick* is overpowering. It is a statement of unmasked contempt. The argument that the private, intimate lives of gay men and lesbians might be entitled to some protection from police intrusion was, Justice White wrote for the Court, "facetious." Arrogance flavors the opinion. The Court accepts the right of privacy relating to marriage, family and procreation, but concludes, "we think it is evident that none of [those] rights ... bears any resemblance" to a sexual privacy right—at least for homosexuals. (The Court declined to rule on whether states may ban heterosexual sodomy, but no argument supporting that right survives the rationale of this decision.) That's it. No reasoning, no attempt to build an intellectually defensible principle or grounding for this distinction—as if gay people do not create families, belong in families, raise children, or have the staying power for those nine-point-four-year-long average marriages that are the bedrock of civilized society.

Once, long ago, when I was locked in a screaming argument over race with a relative of mine in the Southern town where we both grew up, I got to a point where, I thought, I had him. He had just conceded that his position was based on some bizarre double standard for black as opposed to white public drunkenness, or military service, or restaurant seating or whatever. "There," I said, pouncing, "can't you see, there is no real distinction—it's not rational!" "Rationality," he shot back, "doesn't matter when you're talking about niggers."

Hardwick feels that way to me. The ordinary processes of the law—identification of governing principles, extrapolation to newly presented sets of facts, and logical application and extension to build a rational continuity of principle—just didn't seem to matter, to even merit a full explanation.

What was before the Court in *Hardwick* was not even whether to rule the sodomy law unconstitutional, but whether to affirm a lower court ruling that Georgia would have to demonstrate a compelling state interest for the statute in order to save it. Although such a standard is extremely difficult to satisfy, the next round would have given Georgia another chance to invoke whatever rationale—morality, public health—it chose to try to meet the test.

That this decision comes during the thick of the AIDS crisis can only make its impact worse. Although the Court did not mention AIDS, it vitiates the legal premise which has been invoked most often in challenging AIDS-based restrictions aimed at penalizing gay men. If the sexual conduct in question can be prohibited by the state, then the state can more easily defend a range of restrictions designed to deter it, even if the restrictions fail to narrowly target only unsafe sex practices.

The Court's obvious homophobia, however, only partly explains the outcome. There is a broader agenda behind this decision. As Justice White wrote for the majority: "The Court is most vulnerable and comes nearest to illegitimacy when it deals with judge-made law having little or no cognizable roots in the language or design of the Constitution." *Hardwick* was the case the Court picked to quiet its Meesian critics.

The Court has been burned politically by the reaction to *Roe v. Wade*, and busing and the other desegregation decisions. The liberal fallacy of law as the nonpartisan application of neutral principles fell apart, as the Warren Court's consensus disintegrated into the Burger Court's factionalism, and the swing votes became the only votes for either side. Now the entire society counts votes on the Court like tallies on some huge constitutional scoreboard. We have still got five for affirmative action, but we are one down on municipal creches. Everyone knew that Justice Powell alone could decide *Hardwick*, for example, because his seemed to be the only vote not already unambiguously aligned with one of the polar wings of the Court. The secret to litigating in the Supreme Court, former solicitor general Rex Lee remarked, is learning to count to five. Horrified liberals and expectant conservatives alike give mortality odds on individual justices, and everyone knows that losing the right to abortion is only a heartbeat away.

The pressure on the Court to cut back on social justice has been building for twenty years. The Burger Court has already moderated the pace and the reach of the Warren Court's efforts to give meaning to individual liberties which had been buried under the weight of racist and sexist social structures since the nation's inception. The Warren Court was willing to put government to the test of justifying state practices which had become cultural customs, whether of racial segregation, police abusiveness or male exclusivity. The Burger Court slowed this process. But the rationale of *Hardwick*, if relied on in future cases and extended, would reverse it.

The basis for *Hardwick* is the very antithesis of the precept that animated the Warren Court. The *Hardwick* opinion's recitation of the long history of sodomy laws, and Chief Justice Burger's pontifical concluding reference to "millennia of moral teaching" invoke a history of invidious treatment as a reason for continuing it. Indeed, it was this proposition that seems to have moved Powell into the conservative column. "I cannot say," he said, "that conduct condemned for hundreds of years has now become a fundamental right."

That gay people were the group on whose backs the Court's right wing finally won majority acceptance of this argument is no shocker. We have known we were expendable for a long time. But the crudeness of the ruling may provoke its own backlash. Few voices outside the Moral Majority fringe have defended the decision, and liberal criticism—as in *The Times'* "Crime in the Bedroom" editorial—has been strong and pointed. The Court may find out that the perception that it openly parcels out fundamental rights based on the perceived political power of the group in question does not do wonders for its institutional legitimacy either.

Whatever the future directions of the Court, however, the lesson for the gay community is an old one. As the phone message I got from an old friend on the day of the decision said, "solution is political, not legal." Our greatest weakness is that we lack the organizations necessary to implement a sustained program of political action. Legal rights and AIDS service groups are our strong point, and they are essential and must be supported, but they do not a movement make. Whether it is some struggling group already in existence, or a network of independent local groups, or an entirely new organization, our community has got to build a functioning national political infrastructure, and find and pay top-quality organizers. If we are ever to achieve the threshold of legal equality won by blacks, we must rededicate ourselves to waging the same kind of long-term war. And if we ever want to see a sexual orientation clause added to the federal Civil Rights Act, we had better start planning where to make our Selma.

Demographics, if nothing else, are on our side. Millions of Americans are experimenting with sex *sans* labels, and marrying and remarrying in the serial monogamy pattern our community knows so well. Household size is shrinking, and there are more never-married adults in the United States today than ever before. Someday, someone besides the marketing industry is going to notice the similarities and common interests.

And, who knows, maybe even simple justice will have an impact. Eight years ago, Justice Blackmun *joined* Justice Rehnquist in voting to review and reverse a decision ordering a public university to grant official recognition to a gay student group. Blackmun and Rehnquist together wrote: "From the point of view of the University ... the question is ... akin to whether those suffering from measles have a constitutional right, in violation of quarantine regulations, to associate together and with others who do not presently have measles, in order to urge repeal of a state law providing that measles sufferers be quarantined."

Last Monday, Justice Blackmun dissented. "Only the most willful blindness," he wrote, "could obscure the fact that sexual intimacy is a sensitive, key relationship of human existence, central to family life, community welfare and the development of human personality .... There may be many 'right' ways of conducting those relationships, and ... much of the richness of a relationship will come from the freedom of an individual to choose the form and nature of these intensely personal bonds."

Some person, some argument, some experience reached this man. He saw the discrepancy in liberal principles; perhaps he was simply offended by the sheer callousness of the majority. For whatever reason, he changed.

Perhaps we can use *Hardwick* to change others as well.

Sexual Dissent and the Law

CHAPTER 7

Life After Hardwick

NAN D. HUNTER (1992)

Unless or until it is narrowed or overruled, *Bowers v. Hardwick*[1] will dominate the law concerning government regulation of sexuality. In *Hardwick*, the Supreme Court upheld as constitutional a Georgia sodomy statute that made oral or anal intercourse a felony punishable by up to twenty years in prison.[2] The Court ended its long reluctance to assess the constitutionality of limitations on sexuality as distinct from contraception[3] by ruling that the protected zone created by the privacy right stops short of covering private consensual sexual relations between adults. In so ruling, the Court left in place a patchwork of prohibitory laws in which identical acts are immunized or criminalized as one traverses state borders.[4]

Although *Hardwick* was litigated as a sexual privacy case, and despite the fact that the Georgia statute drew no distinctions based on sexual orientation, the case has been interpreted primarily as a ruling on homosexuality. The Court explicitly limited its holding to the legitimacy of laws criminalizing sexual acts between persons of the same sex, refusing to indicate whether the same standard of deference to legislative determinations of morality would apply if pairs of the opposite sex engaged in the prohibited behavior.[5] Since *Hardwick* was decided, the threshold question in the litigation of lesbian and gay rights cases has become whether *Hardwick* only extinguishes the claim to a substantive due process privacy right, or whether it also predetermines challenges under the Equal Protection

Clause. The courts must still decide whether the decision in *Hardwick* was a ruling on conduct or a ruling on a class of people.

The result is an extraordinary new judicial discourse about the social meaning of homosexuality and the determinants of sexual behavior and sexual identity. It is driven by the needs both of those who seek repressive measures and of those who seek group-based civil rights. Both interests require a reliable definitional structure on which to ground their arguments and a coherent system for identifying homosexuality. Both camps accept the idea of sexual identity as a central aspect of the human condition, but sharply dispute the definition, expression and regulation of such identity. Implicit in each adjudication is the threat of reinforcing or increasing the social penalty accruing to disfavored sexualities, yet at the same time the very debate itself creates opportunities to contest hegemonic categories.

The context for the post-*Hardwick* debate is deeply paradoxical. The law is dominated by the emergence of the Rehnquist Court, well advanced in what has become a liberty demolition project. At the same time, the investigation of homosexuality has blossomed in scientific and academic circles.[6] Popular movements seeking greater political and social freedom for lesbians and gay men have also mushroomed.[7] These factors ensure that the issues raised in the post-*Hardwick* litigation are not transitory.

This article argues that the term sodomy is a cultural chameleon, which has shifted in meaning from its original delineations based primarily on non-procreative sex to a contemporary view that reflects social anxiety over sexual orientation. Despite its ideals of constancy and clarity, the law has collaborated in that shift, as the Supreme Court did, *sub silentio*, in *Hardwick*, and as the majority of the federal judiciary continues to do. This phenomenon is now confusing Equal Protection doctrine, and it necessitates a deconstruction of the new sexual orientation categories.

I. The "Utterly Confused Category"[8]

The core of the debate over the ramifications of Hardwick grows out of the disjuncture between the legal definition of sodomy and its social and cultural meanings. The crime of sodomy originated in ecclesiastical regulation of a range of nonmarital, nonprocreative sexual practices. Nonprocreation was the central offense and the core of the crime.[9] Homosexual conduct fell within the cluster of activities that were regulated, but most early American statutes defined sodomy in terms of anal intercourse, whether between men or between a man and a woman.[10] The "crime against nature" to which that phrase refers was not, as is often assumed today, a crime against heterosexuality, but a crime against procreation.

Confusion as to the meaning of sodomy is not new. It was evident in the first recorded debate in American law over the scope of its definition. In the winter of 1641 to 1642, a sodomy case arose in the Massachusetts Bay Colony. Three men were discovered to have had sexual contact with two female children. John Winthrop's account of the case described the act as "agitation and effusion of seed." Vaginal penetration was also alleged, but was denied by the defendants.[11] The Massachusetts Bay Colony at that time had not yet adopted a formal body of laws, and the colony's leadership was unsure with which violation of criminal law to charge these men, and whether their offense merited capital punishment.[12] As a result, the governor asked jurists and church elders in that colony and in Plymouth whether the defendants' behavior constituted a "sodomitical act," punishable by death.[13]

As these colonists understood sodomy and rape,[14] the primary legal question at issue was whether proof of penetration was necessary to sustain an offense meriting the death penalty. Bradford and one of the Plymouth clergymen contended that proof of penetration was required. The two others argued that nonpenetrative acts which led to ejaculation and the "spilling of seed" were comparable in infamy to penetrative crimes and should be equally punished. As one minister put it, the spilling of seed "is equivalent to killing the man who could have been born out of it."[15]

Apparently, none of the disputants suggested that the same-sex phrasing of the Biblical injunction that a "man shall not lie with a man as with a woman" precluded a sodomy charge in a case involving male-female conduct, even though that command was cited repeatedly as the original source of the law and as the basis for an analogy to the case before them.[16] As Jonathan Ned Katz notes in his summary of the incident, "[t]hat this discussion of 'sodomy' was motivated by a crime of male against female illustrates the colonists' relative lack of preoccupation with gender in their categorizing of sexual acts and their relative emphasis on other characteristics of those acts."[17] The willingness to consider sodomy as meaning something more than same-sex conduct in this instance is all the more notable since it was only the New England states—including Massachusetts—that later used a same-sex definition in their early statutes.[18]

This seventeenth-century debate illustrates fundamental problems that continue to muddle the law of sexuality. First, the Massachusetts Bay Colony debate exemplifies the indeterminacy at the very core of the concept of sodomy. Lacking a statutory definition, the Massachusetts Colony elites drew on their understanding of English law and Biblical prohibitions in an attempt to reach a jointly acceptable interpretation. Their difficulty in doing so signified that then, as now, the term sodomy lacked a fixed cultural or social meaning. Although same-sex conduct was included as part of the meaning of sodomy, its boundaries were drawn by the requirements of penetration and nonprocreative acts.

Most colonial sodomy laws regulated sexual acts solely by men, whether with other men or with women. Proof of phallic penetration was needed to sustain a conviction for sodomy, not because the crime focused on same-sex conduct, but because its prohibitions were directed at men. Official acknowledgment of sexual acts between women within the statutory text was rare, although enforcement of some statutes against women was initiated under colonial laws.[19] Later codifications of or amendments to sodomy laws encompassed sexual acts between women.[20]

If the direct prohibitory effect was on men, however, the indirect and obligatory effect fell heavily on women, because the law sought to force all sexual activities to be at least potentially procreative. The repulsion expressed by the two Plymouth clergymen for the "spilling of seed" was triggered by the nonprocreative nature of the defendants' acts. This same aim of the law—discouragement of nonprocreative sex—underlay the statutes prohibiting the use of birth control devices which were stricken as unconstitutional by the Supreme Court in the 1960s.[21] Ironically, in *Hardwick*, the Court concluded that a privacy claim on behalf of "homosexual sodomy" bore no relationship to those earlier decisions: "[n]o connection between … procreation on the one hand and homosexual activity on the other has been demonstrated. …"[22] In fact, the exact opposite was the case. Michael Hardwick, as a person engaged in sodomy, had the same relationship to procreation as persons using birth control during heterosexual intercourse: none, which was precisely the point. The issue in *Hardwick* should have been controlled by *Griswold* and *Eisenstadt*.

Illustrated by a comparison of the Massachusetts Bay Colony debate to *Hardwick*, the second major shift in the law of sexuality is the role ascribed to "identity." The debate 350 years ago was clearly a dispute about acts and about which acts, in some specific detail, constituted a particular crime. It could easily be analogized to a debate about the elements necessary for burglary or robbery; about, for example, what the charge should be if property is stolen from a person or removed from a home. It is not a debate about a type of person, any more than one discusses theft in terms of two distinct types of human beings—the robbers and the burglars. The law does not assume that a certain personality type will commit theft one way, and another personality type, another way. Anyone could be guilty of either kind of conduct, depending on the facts of the particular incident.

The difference illustrates one of the central arguments of French philosopher Michel Foucault, who wrote that social regulation of sexuality was transformed during the eighteenth and nineteenth centuries in part by:

> ... a new *specification of individuals*. As defined by the ancient civil or canonical codes, sodomy was a category of forbidden acts; their perpetrator was nothing more than the juridical subject of them. The nineteenth-century homosexual became a personage, a past, a case history, and a childhood, in addition to being a type of life, a life form, and a morphology.[23]

Sex between two women or between two men has been recorded for centuries, but understanding of what those acts signifies about the persons participating in them has shifted radically. "[I]t never occurred to pre-modern cultures to ascribe a person's sexual tastes to some positive, structural, or constitutive feature of his or her personality."[24]

A rich new vein of historical analysis has begun to trace the evolutionary changes in the social meaning of sexual practices, including sodomy.[25] One British historian has argued that the shift in popular meaning of the term "sodomite"—from that of a libertine male sexually active with both women and men to that of an effeminate male interested only in other men—can be pinpointed to the first half of the eighteenth century.[26] The word "homosexual" and the idea that the homosexual was a different kind of person were developed by late nineteenth-century sexologists proposing medicalized causation theories for sexual behavior.[27]

Both the indeterminacy of sodomy's meaning and Foucault's theory on the specification of individuals are borne out in the modern history of sodomy law. Indeed, one of the first bases on which such laws were challenged was the very question of confusion. A number of statutes that prohibited the "crime against nature" without defining it were challenged on grounds of vagueness, although most were upheld with limiting constructions.[28]

In the last twenty years, however, the dominant legislative trend has been specification. The first state to decriminalize sodomy was Illinois in 1961; in the next twenty years, nearly half the states decriminalized all sodomy, usually by adoption of Model Penal Code recommendations that included repeal of sodomy statutes.[29] The last repeal of a sodomy law occurred in Wisconsin in 1983. Starting in the 1970s, however, a countertrend began, in which specification has replaced repeal. Since 1973, eight states have amended their laws to specify that oral or anal sex is prohibited only between persons of the same sex.[30] In one state, Oklahoma, a state appellate court ruled on constitutional grounds that the sodomy statute's gender-neutral prohibition could not be enforced against opposite-sex partners.[31] Even in the majority of states that retain gender-neutral language, the ancillary effects of the sodomy prohibition are directed against lesbian and gay citizens.[32]

It is intriguing to speculate about why state legislatures stopped repealing sodomy statutes and began to single out homosexual acts as crimes. The specification trend coincided with the emergence of the contemporary versions of both the lesbian and gay rights movement and a renewed movement for religious fundamentalism in American politics. In 1973, the year in which specification amendments began, two critical events occurred: the American Psychiatric Association removed homosexuality from its list of mental diseases,[33] and the United States Civil Service Commission forbade federal personnel supervisers from finding a person unsuitable for a federal government job based solely on homosexuality.[34] By 1975, anti-discrimination laws had been adopted by the District of Columbia, San Francisco, Los Angeles, Minneapolis, Philadelphia and several smaller cities.[35] Antiequality forces mobilized during the 1970s also, however, securing repeal of a civil rights law in Dade County, Florida, and conducting two electoral campaigns to enact laws mandating the firing of state school system employees who advocated homosexuality: one unsuccessfully (California), the other successfully (Oklahoma).[36] For states revising their criminal codes, the specification of homosexual acts as a crime marked both the greater visibility of homosexuality in a positive sense, and the tremendous social anxiety which that visibility generated.

The *Hardwick* litigation was an attempt to complete the repeal process, but it ran headlong into the shift toward specification. The case was based at the outset primarily on a sexual privacy theory, encompassing the full scope of Georgia's law, which prohibits oral and anal sex between any two partners, heterosexual or homosexual, married or unmarried. Along with Michael Hardwick, a husband and wife couple joined as plaintiffs. They were dismissed for lack of standing, however, in part because the district and appellate courts concluded that because they were heterosexual, they had less at stake.[37]

John and Mary Doe asserted that they desired to engage in sodomy but had been "chilled" and "deterred" by the statute. Hardwick, by contrast, asserted that he regularly engaged in sodomy. The Court of Appeals viewed each of them as claiming "that their normal course of activity will lead them to violate the statute, completely apart from their desire to invalidate it."[38] Yet, the court ruled:

> Hardwick's status as a homosexual adds special credence to his claim.... While a plaintiff hoping only to challenge a statute might overestimate his or her willingness to risk actual prosecution, a

plaintiff who genuinely desires to engage in conduct regardless of its legal status presents a court with a more plausible threat of future prosecution.[39]

This contributed to what the court referred to as "the authenticity of Hardwick's desire to engage in the proscribed activity in the future,"[40] necessarily imputing less authenticity or desire to the married couple.

The Court of Appeals' application of standing doctrine prefigured the Supreme Court's conflation of homosexuality with sodomy. The Court of Appeals could have limited its rationale for the standing ruling only to incidents of past enforcement or to claims of current illegal activity. Instead, however, it suggested that only a homosexual could be genuinely interested in engaging in oral sex, the act for which Michael Hardwick was arrested. The language of the standing ruling reflects a belief that the categories "homosexual" and "heterosexual" denote radically different experiences of the same behavior.

The denial of standing to the husband and wife plaintiffs so undermined a general theory of sexual privacy that, in some respects, the whole story of *Hardwick* is revealed in the ruling on standing. It removed the two plaintiffs who represented the full scope of the sodomy law from the litigation, and set up a factual context in which the Supreme Court could adjudicate the statute's constitutionality solely "as applied to consensual homosexual sodomy."[41]

From there, the Court's opinion embarks on a series of slippery substitutions between generally prohibited conduct and the civic status of a class of people. The Court moves back and forth from discussion of "homosexual sodomy"[42] to "the fundamental rights of homosexuals"[43] to "the claimed constitutional right of homosexuals to engage in acts of sodomy"[44] to "the morality of homosexuality."[45] The Court equates a subset of acts with the rights of a class.

In so doing, the Court rewrote history to reflect a contemporary preoccupation with homosexuality. The majority ignored what Justice Stevens, in dissent, accurately described as "the traditional view that sodomy is an immoral kind of conduct regardless of the identity of the persons who engage in it."[46] Instead, having framed the scope of the case as "homosexual sodomy," the Court recapitulated the history of sodomy law as though it, too, were limited to homosexuality.

The difference here is important for reasons of more than historical accuracy. The Court used its version of history to claim a kind of moral authority as much as, or more than, to discern the views of the framers. Although homosexual sexual conduct had been the subject of legal proscription under colonial statutes, it was no more prohibited than some consensual heterosexual sexual behaviors often subject to the same penalties.[47] The majority used its misreading of history to justify a distinct condemnation of homosexuality, a condemnation that has been transformed by subsequent courts into the holding of the case.

The result is a paradoxical configuration of opinions. Because the dissenters endorse a more liberal or tolerant interpretation of the meaning of privacy, they may be thought also to represent a more progressive, more forward-looking, less history-bound approach than the majority. By contrast, the majority builds on a history of censure as the primary foundation for continuing that censure. Yet, it was the dissents, especially that of Justice Stevens, which got the history right, refusing to distort previous meanings of sodomy by reading into them a contemporary obsession with homosexuality. The irony is that the dissent, rather than the majority, has history on its side.

Concomitantly, the conservative majority could claim modernity in support of its focus on homosexuality. Contemporary social norms—as distinct from the history of sodomy laws—do include a remaking of the understanding of which sexual practices are condemned. New social understandings have converted sodomy into a code word for homosexuality, regardless of the statutory definition.[48] Thus, ironically, the viewpoint of a majority that believed its decision to be anchored in "millennia of moral teaching"[49] was actually quite contemporary in its fundamental approach, and totally dependent on recent social trends. The source of authority that the majority claimed most fervently, however—a strict adherence to the world view of the framers—was an historical forgery.

II. The Current Debate

The decision in *Hardwick* now bedevils virtually all litigation concerning lesbian and gay rights claims. A series of federal court decisions have concluded that *Hardwick* precludes any heightened review under the Equal Protection Clause of the Fifth and Fourteenth Amendments for classifications based on sexual orientation. A minority of judges have written that the equal protection question is still open. In effect, American jurists are still asking, 350 years after the Massachusetts Bay Colony debate, what does sodomy *mean*? As Judge Stephen Reinhardt of the Ninth Circuit has written, "either *Hardwick* is about 'sodomy' ... or it is about 'homosexuality'."[50]

The emerging majority position, adopted by the Seventh, Ninth, D.C. and Federal Circuits, is that *Hardwick* is about homosexuality. The opinions constituting this position share in common a conclusion that, because homosexual sodomy can be made criminal, and because that "conduct defines the class," homosexuals as a group can be regulated by the state with no greater justification than is required under the traditional rational basis test.[51]

This conduct-centered view is premised on a radical imbalance. The act of homosexual sodomy "defines the class" of gay men and lesbians, but the same act of sodomy between opposite-sex partners does not "define the class" of heterosexuals. Heterosexuality discreetly disappears as a category of persons defined by sex. Homosexual sodomy, on the other hand, not only becomes the totality of sodomy, it also becomes the totality of homosexuality.

Only Judge Reinhardt among the proponents of the conduct-centered approach has sought fully to engage with this contradiction. He acknowledges that the behavior in question, oral or anal sex, is practiced by "a substantial majority" of both heterosexual and homosexual persons. Indeed, the frequency of this conduct is quite similar for the two groups.[52] Reinhardt justifies the differential that he reads *Hardwick* to establish (but which he does not endorse) as based on the difference that, for homosexuals alone, such behavior "is fundamental to their very nature."[53]

The illogic of the Reinhardt view, and also of the rationale for the standing decision in *Hardwick*, inheres in the effort to base a finding of intrinsic difference on precisely that which is similar. The acts at issue in *Hardwick*—that is, sodomy as defined by the Georgia statute—are the very acts that the two groups share in common. If there are specific sexual practices that explain the difference between the two groups, it must be those practices that are missing from one group and present for the other. *That* conduct is procreative sexuality.

Although the distinction based on procreation has been ignored in the sodomy cases, where its recognition would lead to an extension of the *Griswold-Eisenstadt* principle to homosexual acts, and a rights-positive result, it has been relied on in other contexts to defeat lesbian and gay rights claims. In *Singer v. Hara*, gay plaintiffs invoked a state equal rights amendment that prohibited any differential treatment based on sex, arguing that the marriage law could not bar a man from marrying a man if he could marry a woman. The Washington Court of Appeals rejected this argument, reasoning that the controlling difference was the "impossibility of reproduction." There, the court did focus on reproductive conduct as the distinction, and found it sufficient to constitute a unique physical characteristic of the sexes, and thus a defense to an ERA claim.[54]

The other view asserts that homosexuals are defined by their status, not by their conduct. The status-centered view has the better legal argument; it is more true to the actual, limited holding of *Hardwick*. It insists that the power of the state to prohibit certain conduct must be applied evenhandedly.[55] It is more intellectually honest. If one imagines, for example, that *Hardwick* had been decided the other way, such that the privacy right covered acts including homosexual sodomy, there would not be automatic invalidation of sexual orientation classifications under an equal protection test. If we had won *Hardwick*, we would not automatically, *ipso facto*, win a challenge to the military's exclusion of lesbian and gay service members. The government would still be able to argue (I believe incorrectly) that it should be entitled to create a sexual orientation classification based on factors unrelated to whether particular conduct was criminal.[56] The same distinction between privacy and equality holds in the opposite direction: although we lost *Hardwick*, our claims under the Equal Protection Clause should not, *ipso facto*, be foreclosed.[57]

The weakness of the status-centered view is its erasure of all conduct and its focus solely on identity. Judges Canby and Norris insist that the class of persons who consider themselves homosexual is not the same as those who engage in homosexual sodomy.[58] They are boxed into this position by a need to distinguish both *Hardwick* and Ninth Circuit precedent that held that there was no equal protection violation from the government selecting homosexual sodomy charges for heightened prosecution, even under a neutral sodomy law.[59] Although lesbian and gay sexual expression does encompass many more acts than oral or anal sex alone, the Canby-Norris argument is unpersuasive in its refusal to acknowledge the substantial overlap.

What the status-centered view substitutes for sexual acts as the core meaning of homosexuality is a concept of identity that is just as "fundamental" and essentializing as conduct is in the Reinhardt approach. Under the status-centered view, sexual orientation is "a central character of individual and group identity,"[60] "a central and defining aspect" of every individual's personality.[61] Citing the amicus brief filed by a gay rights advocacy group, Judges Canby and Norris assert that "one is a homosexual or a heterosexual while playing bridge just as much as while engaging in sexual activity."[62]

Both the conduct-centered and the status-centered views illustrate the ascendancy of an identity definition in the debate over the parameters of constitutional rights. The conduct-centered view holds that what a person does determines what she is; the status-centered view argues that her sexuality is so central to her identity that what she is exists independently of what she does. Both approaches would have the law institutionalize the category of sexual orientation, albeit with radically different rationales and opposite outcomes. The former would permit the state to use homosexual identity as a bull's-eye at which to aim repressive measures, while the latter would legitimate the same identity as the basis for an egalitarian demand.

III. Problems for the Future

In lesbian and gay rights litigation that lies in the immediate future, correcting the misreading of *Hardwick* is only the first barrier to be overcome. Successfully distinguishing the question of governmental power to penalize sexual acts from the independent question of whether classifications based on sexuality are impermissibly invidious merely sets the stage for further complex questions. Many of the thorniest challenges will come in trying to subvert categorical modes of thinking about sexuality and sexual orientation, while still taking advantage of a civil rights heritage that is grounded on identity politics.

Breaking the gridlock of identity politics is no easy task. The civil rights claim remains the most powerful device for securing equality in American society, yet it is premised on recognition of a coherent group identity. What often goes unspoken in the assertion of such a claim is the tension between the desire to deconstruct the imprisoning category itself and the need to defend those persons who are disadvantaged because they bear the group label.[63]

This tension is particularly acute for lesbian and gay rights advocates, and will grow more so, for two reasons. First, the constructionist-essentialist dispute currently dominates intellectual debates on issues of sexuality.[64] These debates have only begun to surface in the discourse of law, but they will inevitably spread from the nonlegal activists and academics now most engaged in them to the courts. Second, much future litigation in this area will be grounded on equal protection doctrine, which directs judicial attention to a history of group discrimination, a status of relative political disempowerment and the indicia of identifiable group status itself.[65] Each of these criteria raises problems that are unique to lesbian and gay rights claims and that exemplify the strategic questions inherent in those claims.

Although a history of discrimination is perhaps the least contested of these criteria,[66] the view among lesbian and gay historians that homosexuality did not exist as a concept distinct in kind from other sexual behaviors until near the end of the last century calls into question at least some of the more sweeping invocations of oppression found in decisions that grant equal protection claims.[67] The district judge in *Jantz v. Muci*, for example, wrote that "stigmatization of homosexuals has 'persisted throughout history, across cultures'."[68] Hyperbole should not be necessary, however. A century of animosity has in fact created the kind of failure in the political system that "footnote four" principles[69] are permitted to remedy.

The second of the criteria for heightened scrutiny, powerlessness in the legislative process, has become, surprisingly, a point of disagreement in judicial assessments of classifications based on sexual orientation. Several courts

have found that the election of a handful of openly lesbian and gay officehold-
ers, together with the enactment of primarily municipal antidiscrimination
laws, demonstrate that judicial intervention is unnecessary.[70] These decisions
raise the threshold for heightened scrutiny to the point that past determinations could not stand if the new standard were applied retroactively.[71]

A more fair-minded approach to the question of political powerlessness, however, will not necessarily be simple. Lesbian and gay Americans
present the unique problem of a minority that is both anonymous and diffuse *and* insular and discrete. As a population group, homosexually active
persons live throughout the nation, but the combination of social penalty
and lack of a visible marker leads to public anonymity. In many urban
areas, on the other hand, self-conscious communities have formed that
have generated a kind of ethnic politics founded on sexuality. As Bruce
Ackerman has described, equal protection doctrine to date has not ven-
tured beyond the surface in analyzing whether insular groups are more
or less disadvantaged in pluralist negotiations than diffuse groups, or
whether pariah status (a minority so stigmatized that others are unwilling to work with them on any terms)[72] or some lesser showing of prejudice
is required for judicial intervention.[73] Lesbian and gay rights claims may
well be one of the vehicles that forces a closer, more refined examination
of these questions.

It is the last of these three criteria, however—often described as an
immutability requirement—that poses the most troublesome challenges.
The immutability criterion forces into the forefront the question of what
causes differing sexual orientations, a question that is by no means settled.
Advocates of a rights claim for lesbians and gay men typically have invoked
an essentialist position, arguing that even the most literal interpretation of
immutability is satisfied if the origins of sexual orientation lie in genes or
genetic codes, hormones or brain structure.[74] Opponents of the rights claim
have focused on the volitional nature of sexual conduct.[75] Judges Canby and
Norris have framed the issue as one of state coercion, rather than absolute
physical inability to change or disguise a trait.[76] Janet Halley argues that
it is the very mutability of sexual identity, and its creation by the process
of a social and political discourse, which should entitle it to heightened
protection; otherwise the political process is skewed and delegitimized by
the systematic silencing of one voice in that discussion.[77] Halley's approach
helpfully lifts the question out of the realm of physiological determinism, a
realm where, at least at present, it is factually unresolvable.

Eschewing an essentialist claim need not be a tactical weakness for equal
rights advocates. Biological immutability is not an absolute prerequisite to
invalidating classifications on the basis of that trait.[78] Aliens can and do

become citizens; persons can and do alter their religious faith group affiliations.[79] Neither group is penalized for the refusal to change, even though change is possible.

Most courts in equal protection cases have simply listed immutability as a component of the heightened scrutiny test without considering its ramifications. Implicit and largely unexamined in the immutability doctrine is a political choice about the social value of the trait in question. Here too, lesbian and gay rights claims have a potential to reshape equal protection jurisprudence by shifting the focus from whether a particular trait is inherited and/or impossible to alter, to whether individuals are being coerced into conforming to a certain set of behaviors.

Although equal protection cases may be the most frequent context for lesbian and gay rights litigants, the conceptual and political problems that lie ahead transcend equal protection doctrine. Whichever doctrinal cards advocates play, they will be countered with arguments born of deep cultural anxiety about sexuality. In the hope of furthering the deconstructionist project without torpedoing the necessary work of defense, I offer three general suggestions for framing interventions in this discourse.

First, whatever the history of the meaning of homosexuality, it now cannot be divorced from social conflicts over the meanings of masculinity and femininity. It is not acts alone, but those acts in conjunction with same-gender desire that marks homosexuality. Gender is central to sexual orientation,[80] and much of the positive social value of homosexuality lies in its creation of a zone of antiorthodoxy for men and women, of whatever sexual orientation.[81]

Second, to paraphrase the issue of *Hardwick's* meaning as posed by Judge Reinhardt, sodomy may be about privacy, but homosexuality is not. The primary rationales for discrimination, as well as the arenas in which it occurs and is experienced, concern public perceptions, not private events. The issue that has generated most of the current judicial debate—the military's personnel policy declaring homosexuality to be incompatible with military service—is about secret versus public identity rather than about status versus conduct. The military does not seek to justify its policy on the ground that private sexual acts render gay and lesbian personnel unfit for service, but on the grounds that public opprobrium toward homosexuals would imperil morale, discipline and recruitment if homosexuals were openly part of the armed forces. In numerous other cases, the asserted state interest used to justify discrimination was a fear that equal treatment would be perceived by the public as an endorsement of homosexuality.[82] It is the public process of creation, assignment and use of sexual identity—

not the right to keep private conduct secret—on which future litigation will focus.

Lastly, lesbian and gay rights advocates must recast the terms of the debate as to the state's interest in morality—an interest that has been found sufficient to justify both gender-neutral[83] and same-sex-only[84] sodomy statutes, as well as the military's antigay personnel policy.[85] In each of these opinions, the court interpreted "morality" to mean the suppression of homosexuality, a goal accepted as a public good.[86] So long as discouragement of homosexuality is treated as a legitimate state interest, resolving such disputes as the immutability debate is likely to be pointless. Even if a predisposition to homoeroticism is substantially inborn, the government still can determine to seek a cure, or justify laws that impose a social cost on its expression as a means to diminish its public visibility, if not its private manifestations.

Whatever the merits of the argument that the government should not be permitted to enforce a public morality because of principles of limited government, it is likely to be largely unavailable to litigators—at least in the federal courts—in the immediate post-*Hardwick* era.[87] In addition to arguing that "morality" is impermissibly subjective, lesbian and gay rights advocates must reinvoke the positive moral dimension of equality, a principle that helped inspire the movement for racial civil rights. In 1963, Robert Bork, then a law professor, argued against enactment of a federal civil rights statute on the grounds that the moral view it embodied—that segregation was wrong—should not be enforced by the power of the state.[88] In the *Dronenburg* decision, two decades later, Judge Bork not only abandoned that position, but also ridiculed the argument made by the gay plaintiff that law should not be based on morality.[89] Whatever change of heart Judge Bork may have had as to the role of government, it is also true that, during that interval, the rhetoric of morality adopted by those seeking equality was appropriated by those defending the hierarchy. Perhaps the biggest challenge lesbian and gay rights advocates face is the need to shift that rhetoric once again.

CHAPTER 8

Sexual Dissent and the Family

The Sharon Kowalski Case

NAN D. HUNTER (1991)

No connection between family, marriage, or procreation on the one hand and homosexual activity on the other has been demonstrated.

—**Supreme Court,** *Bowers v. Hardwick,* 1986

Sharon Kowalski is the child of a divorce between her consanguineous family and her family of affinity, the petitioner Karen Thompson. ... That Sharon's family of affinity has not enjoyed societal recognition in the past is unfortunate.

—**Minnesota State District Court**
In re: Guardianship of Sharon Kowalski, Ward, 1991

In the effort to end second-class citizenship for lesbian and gay Americans, no obstacle has proved tougher to surmount than the cluster of issues surrounding "the family." The concept of family functions as a giant cultural screen. Projected onto it, contests over race, gender, sexuality and a range of other "domestic" issues from crime to taxes constantly create and recreate a newly identified zone of social combat, the politics of the family. Activists of all persuasions eagerly seek to enter the discursive field, ever ready to debate and discuss: Who counts as a family? Which "family values" are the authentic ones? Is there a place in the family for queers? As battles are won and lost in this cultural war, progressives and conservatives agree on at least one thing—the family is highly politicized terrain.

For lesbians and gays, these debates have dramatic real-life consequences, probably more so than with any other legal issue. Relationship questions touch almost every person's life at some point, in a way that military issues, for example, do not. Further, the unequal treatment is blatant, *de jure* and universal, as compared with the employment arena, where discrimination may be more subtle and variable. No state allows a lesbian or gay couple to marry. No state recognizes (although a number of countries and cities do) domestic partnership systems under which unmarried couples (gay or straight) can become eligible for certain benefits usually available only to spouses. The fundamental inequity is that, barring mental incompetence or consanguinity, virtually any straight couple has the option to marry and thus establish a next-of-kin relationship that the state will enforce. No lesbian or gay couple can. Under the law, two women or two men are forever strangers, regardless of their relationship.

One result is that every lesbian or gay man's nightmare is to be cut off from one's primary other, physically incapacitated, stranded, unable to make contact, without legal recourse. It is a nightmare that could not happen to a married couple. But it did happen to two Minnesota women, Sharon Kowalski and Karen Thompson, in a remarkable case that thread its way through the courts for seven years.

Sharon Kowalski, notwithstanding the Minnesota State District Court's characterization of her as a "child of divorce," is an adult with both a committed life partner and parents who bitterly refuse to acknowledge either her lesbianism or her lover. Kowalski is a former physical education teacher and amateur athlete, whose Minnesota women's high school shot-put record still stands. In 1983, she was living with her lover, Thompson, in the home they had jointly purchased in St. Cloud. Both women were deeply closeted; they exchanged rings with each other but told virtually no one of their relationship. That November, Kowalski suffered devastating injuries in a car accident, which left her unable to speak or walk, with arms deformed and with major brain damage, including seriously impaired short-term memory.

After the accident, both Thompson and Kowalski's father petitioned to be appointed Sharon's guardian; initially, an agreement was entered that the father would become guardian on the condition that Thompson retain equal rights to visit and consult with doctors. By the summer of 1985, after growing hostilities, the father refused to continue the arrangement, and persuaded a local court that Thompson's visits caused Kowalski to feel depressed. One doctor hired by the father wrote a letter stating that Kowalski was in danger of sexual abuse. Within twenty-four hours after being named sole guardian, the father cut off all contact between Thompson and Kowalski, including mail. By this time, Kowalski had been moved to a nursing home near the small town where she grew up in the Iron Range, a rural mining area in northern Minnesota.

Surely one reason the Kowalski case is so compelling is that, for millions of parents, learning that one's son is gay or daughter is lesbian would be *their* worst nightmare. That is all the more true in small-town America, among people who are religiously observant and whose expectations for a daughter are primarily marriage and motherhood. "The good Lord put us here for reproduction, not that kind of way," Donald Kowalski told the *Los Angeles Times* in 1988. "It's just not a normal life style. The Bible will tell you that." Karen Thompson, he told other reporters, was "an animal" and was lying about his daughter's life. "I've never seen anything that would make me believe" that his daughter is lesbian, he said to *The New York Times* in 1989. How much less painful it must be to explain a lesbian daughter's life as seduction, rather than to experience it as betrayal.

In 1988, Thompson's stubborn struggle to "bring Sharon home" entered a new stage. A different judge, sitting in Duluth, ordered Kowalski moved to a new facility for medical evaluation. Soon thereafter, based on staff recommendations from the second nursing facility, the court ordered that Thompson be allowed to visit. The two women saw each other again in the spring of 1989, after three and a half years of forced separation. Kowalski, who can communicate by typing on a special keyboard, said that she wanted to live in "St. Cloud with Karen."

In May 1990, citing a heart condition for which he had been hospitalized, Donald Kowalski resigned as his daughter's guardian. This resignation set the stage for Thompson to file a renewed petition for appointment as guardian, which she did. But in an April 1991 ruling, Minnesota State District Court Judge Robert Campbell selected as guardian Karen Tomberlin—a friend of both Kowalski and her parents, who supported Tomberlin's request. On the surface, the court sought balance. The judge characterized the Kowalski parents and Karen Thompson as the "two wings" of Sharon Kowalski's family. He repeatedly asserted that both must have ample access to visitation with Kowalski. He described Tomberlin as a neutral third party who would not exclude either side. But the biggest single reason behind the decision, the one that he characterized as "instrumental," seemed to be the judge's anger at Thompson for ever telling Kowalski's parents (in a private letter), and then the world at large, that she and Kowalski were lovers.

The court condemned Thompson's revelation of her own relationship as the "outing" of Sharon Kowalski. Thompson did write the letter to Kowalski's parents without telling Kowalski (who was at the time just emerging from a three-month coma after the accident) and did build on her own an active political organization around the case, composed chiefly of disability and lesbian and gay rights groups. Of course, for most of that period, she could not have consulted Kowalski because the two were cut off from each other.

In truth, though, the judge's concern seemed to be more for the outing of Kowalski's parents. He describes the Kowalskis as "outraged and hurt by the public invasion of Sharon's privacy and their privacy," and he blames this outing for the bitterness between Thompson and the parents. Had Thompson simply kept this to herself, the court implies, none of these nasty facts would ever have had to be discussed. The cost, of course, would have been Thompson's surrender of a spousal relationship with Kowalski.

An openly stated preference for ignorance over knowledge is remarkable in a judicial opinion. One imagines the judge silently cursing Thompson for her arrogance in claiming the role of spouse, and for her insistence on shattering the polite fiction of two gym teachers living and buying a house together as just good friends. Women, especially, aren't supposed to be so stubborn or uppity. One can sense the court's empathetic response of shared embarrassment with the parents, of the desire not to be told and thus not to be forced to speak on this subject.

The final chapter in the Kowalski case vindicated Karen Thompson's long struggle. The Minnesota Court of Appeals granted Thompson's guardianship petition in December, 1991, reversing the trial judge on every point.

The conflict in the Kowalski case illustrates one of the prime contradictions underlying all the cases seeking legal protection for lesbian and gay couples. This culture is deeply invested with a notion of the ideal family as not only a zone of privacy and a structure of authority (preferably male in the conservative view) but also as a barrier against sexuality unlicensed by the state. Even many leftists and progressives, who actively contest male authority and at least some of the assumptions behind privacy, are queasy about constructing a family politics with queerness on the inside rather than the outside.

When such sexuality is culturally recognized *within* family bounds, "the family" ceases to function as an enforcer of sexual norms. That is why the moms and dads in groups like P-FLAG, an organization primarily of parents supportive of their lesbian and gay children, make such emotionally powerful spokespersons for the cause of civil rights. Parents who welcome sexual dissenters within the family undermine the notion that such dissent is intrinsically antithetical to deep human connection.

The theme of cultural anxiety about forms of sexuality not bounded and controlled by the family runs through a series of recent judicial decisions. In each case, the threat to norms did not come from an assault on the prerogatives of family by libertarian outsiders, a prospect often cited by the right wing to trigger social anxieties. Instead, each court faced the dilemma of how to repress, at least in the law, the anomaly of unsanctioned sexuality within the family.

§In a stunning decision in 1989, the Supreme Court ruled in *Michael H. v. Gerald D.* that a biological father had no constitutionally protected right to a relationship with his daughter, despite both paternity (which was not disputed) and a psychological bond that the two had formed. Instead, the Court upheld the rule that because the child's mother—who had had an affair with the child's biological father—was married to another man, the girl would be presumed to be the husband's child. It was more important, the Court declared, to protect the "unitary family," that is, the marriage, than to subject anyone to "embarrassment" by letting the child and her father continue to see each other. The Court ruled that a state could properly force the termination of that bond rather than "disrupt an otherwise harmonious and apparently exclusive marital relationship." We are not bound, the Court said, to protect what it repeatedly described as "adulterous fathers."

§In *Hodgson v. Minnesota*, the Supreme Court upheld a Minnesota requirement that a pregnant teenager had to notify both of her parents— even if they were divorced or if there was a threat of violence from her family—prior to obtaining an abortion, so long as she had the alternative option to petition a court. The decision was read primarily as an abortion decision and a ruling on the extent of privacy protection that will be accorded a minor who decides to have an abortion. But the case was also, at its core, about sex in the family and specifically about whether parents could rely on the state for assistance in learning whether a daughter is sexually active.

§In two very similar cases in 1991, appellate courts in New York and California ruled that a lesbian partner who had coparented a child with the biological mother for some years had no standing to seek visitation after the couple split up. Both courts acknowledged that the best interests of the child would be served by allowing a parental relationship to continue, but both also ruled that the law would not recognize what the New

York court called "a biological stranger." Such a person could be a parent only if there had been a marriage or an adoption.

Indeed, perhaps the most important point in either decision was the footnote in the California ruling that invited lesbian and gay couples to adopt children jointly: "We see nothing in these [statutory] provisions that would preclude a child from being jointly adopted by someone of the same sex as the natural parent." This opens the door for many more such adoptions, at least in California, which is one of six states where lesbian- or gay-couple adoption has occurred, although rarely. The New York court made no such overture.

The effort to legalize gay marriage will almost certainly emerge as a major issue in the next decade. Lawsuits seeking a right to marry have been filed in the District of Columbia and Hawaii, and activists in other states are contemplating litigation. In 1989, the Conference of Delegates of the State Bar of California endorsed an amendment of that state's law to permit lesbian and gay couples to marry.

The law's changes to protect sexual dissent within the family will occur at different speeds in different places, which might be useful. Family law has always been a province primarily of state rather than federal regulation, and often has varied from state to state; grounds for divorce, for example, used to differ dramatically depending on geography. What seems likely to occur in the next wave of family cases is the same kind of variability in the legal definition of the family itself. Those very discrepancies may help to denaturalize concepts like "marriage" and "parent," and to expose the utter contingency of the sexual conventions that, in part, construct the family.

CHAPTER 9

Marriage, Law and Gender

A Feminist Inquiry

NAN D. HUNTER (1991)

Reflecting on the problems and possibilities inherent in the concept of same-sex marriage is especially intriguing as we approach the turn of the century.[1] That is not because the idea is new. A series of constitutional challenges to the exclusion of gay male and lesbian couples from the matrix of rights and responsibilities which comprise marriage were brought and failed twenty years ago.[2] Nor is it because there is a substantial body of newly developed constitutional doctrine which would undergird litigation to establish such a claim.[3] It is because there is a rapidly developing sense that the legalization of marriage for gay and lesbian Americans is politically possible at some unknown but not unreachable point in the future, that it shimmers or lurks—depending on one's point of view—on the horizon of the law.

The most dramatic development to date in the campaign to establish a right to gay marriage occurred in May 1993, when the Hawaii Supreme Court ruled that, under the state constitution, marriage could not be limited to opposite-sex couples unless the state could demonstrate a compelling interest in doing so.[4] The outcome of the case on remand is not yet known. If the statute falls, however, the stage will be set for a series of challenges in other states that would inevitably result from gay and lesbian couples legally married in Hawaii seeking recognition elsewhere.

Whatever the outcome, it seems inevitable that lesbians and gay men will continue to press a second wave of litigation challenges to marriage laws, forcing courts across America to engage with the issue in a political context that has changed significantly from that of the 1970s.

A series of events prior to the 1993 Hawaii decision helped to propel the issue of legal recognition of gay relationships into widespread public consciousness. A 1989 decision by New York's highest court held that gay couples whose relationship exhibited the indicia of long-term commitment qualified as "members of the family" for purposes of a rent control law.[5] A number of municipalities have adopted domestic partnership laws granting recognition for limited purposes to unmarried couples (usually both heterosexual and homosexual) who met certain functional criteria roughly comparable to marriage.[6] The most widely publicized of the campaigns associated with such laws occurred in San Francisco. The San Francisco Board of Supervisors first enacted a domestic partners ordinance in 1989.[7] Voters in a referendum election repealed it later that year, but then adopted a revised version in November 1990.[8] Denmark adopted the "partnership" statute that comes the closest to marriage. The provision amended Danish marriage law to permit lesbian and gay couples to join in "registered partnerships" carrying most of the rights of marriage, the primary exception being for eligibility to adopt children.[9]

The sense that legalization of gay marriage is a real possibility has in turn triggered multiple debates. The mainstream public debate centers on whether the current exclusionary laws promote a moral good in preserving "traditionalism" in family relationships, or whether they perpetuate the moral evil of injustice.[10] Within the lesbian and gay community, an intense debate has also arisen, not about whether the exclusionary laws are good, but about whether seeking the right to marry should be a priority.[11] Proponents of a campaign for marriage rights have framed their arguments largely in terms of equality for lesbians and gay men,[12] and have employed a body of rights discourse which has animated the major civil rights struggles of this century.[13] Opponents have relied on two primary arguments. First, they invoked a feminist critique of marriage as an oppressive institution[14] which lesbians and gay men should condemn, not join. Second, these activists have drawn on the politics of validating difference, both the difference of an asserted gay identity and culture which resist assimilation, and the differences between persons who would marry and those (homosexual or heterosexual) who would elect to forgo marriage and thereby, it is argued, become even more stigmatized.[15] Analogous tensions between equality-based strategies and difference-based strategies buffeted feminist theory throughout the 1980s.[16]

The question of whether the law should recognize same-sex marriage has its own intrinsic importance, both as a matter of law and as a liberationist goal. This essay, however, seeks to position that issue in a different theoretical context. Section I frames the question primarily as one of gender systems, rather than of minority rights. I argue that same-sex marriage would move beyond the formalistic equality in marriage law that has been achieved to date, and would radically denaturalize the social construction of male/female differentness, once expressed as authority/dependence relationships, that courts have deemed essential to the definition of marriage. Section II analyzes the major doctrinal debates in law concerning proposals to reform regulatory schemes applicable to conventional family structures, and suggests the need to synthesize those with proposals for the legal recognition of lesbian and gay relationships. Section III analyzes efforts to secure legal protection for lesbian and gay relationships as examples of the problematics of rights discourse, and proposes a political and rhetorical strategy distinct from a legal strategy as a means to minimize the intrinsic limitations of rights claims.

I. Marriage As Nature

Decisional law on the issue of gay marriage is most striking for its brevity and tautological jurisprudence. In each of the pre-Hawaii cases, the justices of the respective courts (not one of whom dissented) seem somewhat astonished at even having to consider the question of whether the limitation of marriage to opposite-sex couples is constitutionally flawed.[17] These cases tell us nothing about equality or privacy doctrine. Instead, their holdings are grounded in statements about what the courts believe marriage *is*. Their significance lies in their thorough conflation of gender, nature and law.

Marriage is, after all, a complete creation of the law, secular or ecclesiastical. Like the derivative concept of illegitimacy, for example, and unlike parenthood, it did not and does not exist without the power of the state (or some comparable social authority) to establish, define, regulate and restrict it. Beyond such social constructs, individuals may couple, but they do not "marry." Moreover, although marriage may have ancient roots, its form has not been unchanging. It is an historically contingent institution, having existed with widely differing indicia and serving shifting social functions in various cultures.[18] Marriage can be defined empirically as "a socially approved union between unrelated parties that gives rise to new families and, by implication, to socially approved sexual relations. But beyond that minimal definition, there is no linguistically valid explanation of what marriage entails."[19] Yet in each of the rulings in a lesbian or gay marriage challenge, the courts have essentialized as "nature" the gendered definitional boundaries of marriage.[20]

It was the assumption that gender is an essential aspect of marriage that enabled these courts to so easily rebuff the analogy to *Loving v. Virginia*,[21] which held that the equal protection clause forbade the criminalization of marriage between persons of different races. The Minnesota Supreme Court drew "a clear distinction between a marital restriction based *merely* upon race and one based upon the *fundamental* difference in sex."[22] The Washington court in *Singer* similarly dismissed *Loving* as inapposite because irrelevant to the definition of marriage.[23] Having done so, it was then free, in its analysis of the plaintiffs' sex discrimination claim, to reason that, because neither men nor women could marry a person of the same sex, there was no sex discrimination, thus repeating the identical separate-but-equal logic rejected by the Supreme Court in *Loving*.[24] By so casually distinguishing *Loving*, both courts simultaneously essentialized gender and ignored the history of the essentialization of race in marriage law.

The constructed basis of this essentialized definition is illustrated by the fact that, for most of American history, race also defined who could marry. Under the slave codes, African-American slaves could not lawfully marry, either other slaves or any other person, of any race.[25] After slavery was abolished, laws establishing race as a defining element of marriage did not disappear, nor were they limited to a handful of states. Not until 1948 did the California Supreme Court declare that state's antimiscegenation law unconstitutional, the first such ruling in the nation.[26] Statutes prohibiting miscegenation, carrying penalties of up to ten years in prison, were in effect in twenty-nine states in 1953.[27] The Motion Picture Production Code, a voluntary but effective self-regulator of the content of Hollywood films, forbade depiction of interracial sex or marriage until 1956.[28] *Loving* was not decided until 1967, nearly twenty years after the California ruling.

Race is often understood to be a biological fact of nature. But in social organization and in law, it is a cultural category with multiple, shifting historical meanings onto which power relationships are inscribed. What changed in *Loving* were not biological facts, but social relations. Today, the state formally defines eligibility for marriage on the basis of sex, understood as a biological category. In reality, however, the definition of marriage is grounded on the social category of gender. The key to this distinction lies in how gender-determined *roles* were once invoked, with equal assurance, as the "nature" of marriage.

For many decades, courts proclaimed and enforced the precept that marriage necessitated not only an authority and dependence relationship, but one that was gendered. One's status as either husband or wife determined all duties and obligations, as well as one's right to name, domicile, physical integrity, property, and other attributes of personhood.[29] When faced with nonconforming individuals, courts struck down their attempts to alter these gender-determined aspects of marriage in terms that underscored the perceived fixedness of the male authority/female dependence "nature" of marriage.[30]

The legal landscape on which the possibility of lesbian and gay marriage is being debated now may not differ greatly from that of twenty years ago in its treatment of homosexuality, but it is a different world as to regulation of the terms and conditions of marriage. Two decades of feminist litigation efforts have established virtual equality in formal legal doctrine.[31] The Supreme Court has repeatedly stricken sex-based classifications in family law, whether of the male as the economic provider for women and children,[32] or of the female as solely the wife and mother.[33]

What feminist litigation has not been able to do is achieve social and economic equality. In such areas as no-fault divorce, alimony and child support, the enforcement by law of a presumed equality that usually does not exist has, in fact, operated to the detriment of many women.[34] The terms of marriage as a legal institution (as in, for example, the right to a separate name or domicile) have changed dramatically. But the social power relations between men and women, inside or outside marriage, have changed much less significantly.

The legalization of lesbian and gay marriage would not, of course, directly shift the balance of power in heterosexual relations. Gay marriage is no panacea. It could, however, alter the social meaning of marriage. Its potential is to disrupt both the gendered definition of marriage and the assumption that marriage is a form of socially, if not legally, prescribed hierarchy.[35]

With the erosion of legally enforceable authority and dependence statuses as a central defining element of marriage, all that remains of gender as the formal structural element of marriage are the foundational constructs of "husband" and "wife." The once elaborate *de jure* assignations of gender status in marriage have now been reduced to their most minimal physical manifestation, the gendered pair of spouses. Claims for the legalization of lesbian and gay marriage raise the question of what, without gendered content, could the social categories of "husband" and "wife" mean.

Seizing on the same definitional concerns as those expressed by the courts, conservatives have ridiculed the challenge to husband and wife constructs posed by the idea of lesbian and gay marriage in order to mobilize the social anxiety that that possibility precipitates. Taunts such as "Who would be the husband?" have a double edge, however, if one's project is the subversion of gender. Who, indeed, would be the "husband" and who the "wife" in a marriage of two men or of two women? Marriage enforces and reinforces the linkage of gender with power by husband/wife categories that are synonymous with the social power imbalance between men and women. Whatever the impact that legalization of lesbian and gay marriage would have on the lives of lesbians and gay men, it has fascinating potential for denaturalizing the gender structure of marriage law for heterosexual couples.

Marriage between men or between women would create for the first time the possibility of marriage as a relationship between members of the same social status categories. However valiantly individuals try to build marriages grounded on genuine equality, no person can erase his or her status in the world as male or female, or create a home life apart from culture. Same-sex marriage could create the model in law for an egalitarian kind of interpersonal relation, outside the gendered terms of power, for many marriages.[36] At the least, it would radically strengthen and dramatically illuminate the claim that marriage partners are presumptively equal.

Beyond "nature," the other most likely argument in defense of exclusionary marriage laws is also, at bottom, gender-based. The *Singer* court found that, even if the denial of same-sex marriage did constitute sex discrimination, it fell within the exception to Washington State's Equal Rights Amendment, which permits differential treatment based on the unique physical characteristics of the sexes. The court reasoned that "marriage exists as a protected legal institution primarily because of societal values associated with the propagation of the human race," and that "it is apparent that no same-sex couple offers the possibility of the birth of children by their union."[37] Inability to bear children, however, has never been a bar to marriage, nor is it a ground for divorce.[38] Persons who lack the ability or the intent to procreate are nonetheless allowed to marry. The real interest behind the procreation argument probably lies in discouraging child*rearing* by homosexual couples. That concern stems from the fear that the children will be exposed, not to negligent or inept parenting, but to the wrong models of gender.[39]

To date, the debate about whether the marriage law should change to include lesbian and gay couples has been almost universally framed, both in the larger public and within the lesbian and gay community, as revolving around a claim of rights for particular persons now excluded from marriage. The implicit corollary is that this issue affects only lesbians and gay men. That is much too restricted a focus. The extent of the opposition to the legalization of lesbian and gay marriage indicates not mere silliness or stupidity, as it would if the change were of little consequence to the larger world, nor is it solely a manifestation of irrational prejudice.[40] Legalization of lesbian and gay marriage poses a threat to gender systems, not simply to antilesbian and antigay bigotry.[41]

What is most unsetting to the status quo about the legalization of lesbian and gay marriage is its potential to expose and denaturalize the construction of gender at the heart of marriage. On the other side, those who argue that marriage has always been patriarchal, and thus always will be, make the same historical mistake, in mirror image, as the courts that have essentialized the "nature" of marriage.[42] There is no "always has been and ever shall be" truth of marriage. Nor is the experience of marriage and family life problematic to all women in identical ways.[43] Certainly marriage is a powerful institution, and the inertial force of tradition should not be underestimated. But it is also a social construct. Powerful social forces have changed it before and will continue to do so.[44]

Legalizing lesbian and gay marriage is often thought of as the next frontier for gay rights law. It could also be the next frontier in democratizing marriage. I do not claim that gay marriage alone necessarily would reshape marriage law. But it is difficult to imagine any other change in the law of marriage that feminists could achieve today that would have even remotely as significant an effect. Although the theory used in future litigation to secure legalization of lesbian and gay marriage will likely be grounded on an equality or a due process privacy or associational claim for lesbians and gay men, the impact, if such a challenge prevails, will be to dismantle the legal structure of gender in every marriage. Whether and to what extent the social structure of gender will change is the big question.

II. Marriage As Function and Contract

During the same period of the last twenty years, when legalization of lesbian and gay marriage has been attempted and so far has failed, various other proposals for pluralizing the law of intimate relationships have been advanced. An enormous body of law and commentary has developed in contemporary family law to address the range of issues posed by the formation and dissolution of cohabiting, unmarried, heterosexual unions. Yet despite the obvious similarities between those issues and the efforts to secure benefits (short of marriage) for lesbian and gay couples, there have been virtually no linkages between the family law theorists (mostly feminists) and the lesbian and gay rights advocates.

New family law models for heterosexuals have emerged in response to profound demographic changes that have reshaped the social experience of marriage. Marriage is still central to the adult life experience of a large majority of Americans, but there has been a dramatic alteration in its role and timing. A majority of Americans will spend more of their lifetimes outside, rather than as part of, married-couple households.[45] Cohabitation, often for a significant period of time, frequently precedes marriage and/or remarriage.[46] The number of unmarried, cohabiting, heterosexual couples increased by more than five hundred percent from 1970 to 1989.[47] The average American marriage does not last a lifetime, but a much more modest 9.6 years.[48] The American divorce rate doubled between 1966 and 1976, peaked in 1981, and has dropped somewhat since, but remains much higher than it was before 1970.[49] Concomitant with that shift, there has been an enormous growth in the remarriage rate, so much so that one-third of all marriages are remarriages.[50] As of 1989, the number of Americans who had never married by the age of forty-five remained low: six percent for women and eight percent for men.[51] The rate of nonmarriage differed significantly by race. Of all Americans at age forty-five, 7.3 percent had never married; for African-Americans, the comparable figure was 14.4 percent.[52]

For many Americans, then, the formation of couples and coupled households will, over the course of a lifetime, include both nonmarital cohabitant unions as well as marriages, often multiple times. The response of the law has been contradictory. The law still penalizes cohabiting couples, both directly, by criminalizing cohabitation outside of marriage,[53] and indirectly, by upholding sanctions such as firing.[54] The courts also, however, have undertaken the adjudication of increasing numbers of civil disputes initiated by persons in relationships comparable to marriage. In that context, two distinct lines of doctrine have emerged.[55]

In situations involving the dissolution of the relationship and disputes between the two partners, many courts have followed the lead of *Marvin v. Marvin*, and adopted contract law principles to decide the allocation of economic assets and responsibilities based on the terms of the agreement expressed or implied between the parties.[56] The focus of such an analysis is on the intent of the parties. In opting for a contract measure, virtually all of these courts have explicitly rejected the possibility of declaring a constructive marriage and applying a jurisdiction's divorce law.[57] To do so, they have reasoned, would be to frustrate a presumed desire of the parties not to marry and to subvert the interest of the state in preserving a clear boundary between marriage and nonmarriage.

In situations involving the eligibility of the nonmarital family unit or its members for benefits from the state or from third parties, courts have developed a different approach, a jurisprudence of functionalism. In the functionalist approach, courts seek to identify by objective criteria those relationships that are the "functional and factual equivalent"[58] of marriage.

A functionalist approach to family law underlay the recognition of common-law marriage, which was widespread in the nineteenth century,[59] and was used to mitigate the effects of a race-bound definition of marriage in cases involving slaves.[60] The leading functionalist case to have reached the U.S. Supreme Court involved an extended multigenerational household, which the Court ruled had to be considered as one family to determine eligibility to live in a neighborhood zoned for single-family units.[61] Functionalism can also operate to the detriment of nonmarital couples, as when governmental benefits are denied on the grounds that the couple should be treated as married, even when they are not, because they are presumed to be enjoying the same economies of shared expenses.[62]

The high-water mark of functionalism to date with regard to homosexual couples was the ruling of the New York Court of Appeals, in *Braschi v. Stahl Associates*,[63] that a gay couple must be treated as a family for purposes of the provision in New York's rent control law that protected surviving "members of the family" from eviction in the event of the death of the named tenant. In interpreting the rent control law, the court reasoned that:

> [It] should not be rigidly restricted to those people who have formalized their relationship by obtaining, for instance, a marriage certificate or an adoption order. The intended protection against sudden eviction should not rest on fictitious legal distinctions or genetic history, but instead should find its foundation in the reality of family life.[64]

The court went on to articulate a set of criteria for determining whether a "family" existed:

> [T]he exclusivity and longevity of the relationship, the level of emotional and financial commitment, the manner in which the parties have conducted their everyday lives and held themselves out to society, and the reliance placed upon one another for daily family services.... [I]t is the totality of the relationship as evidenced by the dedication, caring and self-sacrifice of the parties [that] should, in the final analysis, control.[65]

Domestic partnership laws represent the most successful attempt to date to merge the two lines of doctrine into codified rights and benefits laws.[66] The status of domestic partner is not necessarily limited by sexual orientation; in many systems, both lesbian and gay as well as straight couples may register.[67] Politically, domestic partnerships serve as a mechanism for achieving legal protection for lesbian and gay couples without seeking legalization of lesbian and gay marriage.[68] Such provisions have been adopted in ten municipalities.[69] Domestic partnership laws present a way of solving, by legislation, two problems that arose in the case-by-case development of functionalist and contract principles: the uncertainty of definitional boundaries for a nonmarital relationship, and the risk of fraudulent claims.[70] The statutes set out objective definitions that specify which relationships can qualify for domestic partner status and that establish a mechanism, usually a registration system, for verifying whether a particular couple has self-declared as a partnership.[71] The procedure for terminating a partnership involves filing a notice with the registry.[72]

The domestic partnership laws enacted to date have established benefits primarily in the areas of bereavement and sick leave for municipal employees based on the illness or death of a partner; tenancy succession and other housing-related benefits; and health insurance benefits for partners of municipal employees.[73] All have been enacted by municipal, rather than state or federal jurisdictions, and so cannot alter provisions of the state or federal laws that accord benefits based on marriage in areas such as tax, inheritance or most public benefits.

Moreover, most domestic partnership laws emphasize their functionalist, rather than their contractual, aspects. Their focus, and the bulk of the political support for them, concerns the creation of a claim for entitlement by the nonmarried couple to rights or benefits offered by a third party to married couples. Most also, however, contain language that at least arguably establishes a contract between the two persons themselves.[74] The most recent of the laws, adopted by San Francisco voters, is the most explicit in this regard.[75]

The terms of the implied contract provisions of domestic partnership laws are far more libertarian than the state-imposed terms of marriage, however, and more limited than the scope of implied contracts potentially recognizable under *Marvin* and its progeny. Domestic partnerships cover only reciprocal obligations for basic support while the two individuals remain in the partnership. There is no implied agreement as to the ownership or division of property acquired during the term of the partnership, nor is there any basis for compelling one partner to support the other for any length of time, however short, after the partnership is dissolved.

These laws thus go the furthest toward removing the state from regulation of intimate relationships. The issue of whether the state should be expelled raises an old and continuing debate. Feminists have exposed the law's long-professed tradition of noninterference in certain aspects of family life as a mask for the ceding of control to those who wield greater power in the domestic sphere.[76] Some feminists have attacked the contract doctrine embodied in *Marvin*[77] for applying a market ideology that will inevitably disfavor those with less power in the market. These writers favor the imposition of constructive marriage as to certain terms, especially regarding support and property, when unmarried couples end a relationship. They argue that permitting judges to infer that a marriage exists, rather than simply attempting to discern the intent of the parties, operates as a necessary guarantor of balance between socially unequal parties.[78]

The feminist debates on regulation by the state have assumed, however, that only heterosexual unions were at issue.[79] Conversely, the debates about domestic partnerships have generally been based on the model of a lesbian or gay couple.[80] It is true that the terms of a domestic partnership would serve as a floor, rather than a ceiling, for establishing the mutual obligations between partners. Nothing in these statutes would preclude a partner from also asserting an implied contract for an equitable division of property, for example, when the partnership dissolves. But that possibility does not address—much less solve—the underlying problem of whether an imbalance in power led to which terms, if any, were agreed to between the couple. On the other hand, imposing marriage or marriage-like terms on all long-term relationships either ignores the ways that same-sex couples cannot be assumed to pose the same issues of imbalance of power, or it lends the imprimatur of the state once again to a classification that renders lesbian and gay Americans invisible.

These two conversations about reformulating the law of relationships— one among feminists critical of neutral forms that ignore power differentials, and the other among lesbian and gay rights advocates critical of *de jure* exclusions of a minority—need to be joined. And each needs to be reconstituted to incorporate the concerns and experiences of marriage and family, including the ways in which those experiences are shaped by race as powerfully as by gender or sexual orientation.[81]

Careful analysis of who will be affected in precisely which ways by any given option, with a critical examination of both marriage reform and of partnership proposals, has only begun. The impact of economic class, for example, may be complicated. It is possible that less affluent persons in the lesbian and gay community will benefit less by legalization of marriage because they have less property, and much of marriage law concerns property. However, it is precisely persons with less property who are less likely to have the disposable income with which to obtain the wills, powers of attorney and other devices that serve as an alternative mechanism for controlling the allocation and devise of property. Domestic partnership laws, as currently drafted, would not supplant that function. Thus, marriage is by far the least expensive and most easily accessible device by which to ensure that one's partner is the individual who makes whatever decisions might be necessary as to treatment at time of illness or procedures at time of death, as well as to provide that whatever possessions one values pass to that person.

As between legalizing lesbian and gay marriage and seeking domestic partnership laws, neither strategy is complete without the other. Reforming marriage, alone, diversifies only by eliminating gender from the definition of marriage; creates no mechanism by which to reject, rather than to seek to refashion, the customs of marriage; and offers no choice except marriage for any couple seeking any of the benefits of legal recognition. Domestic partnership laws, without the degendering of marriage, create a second-class status rather than an alternative, leaving lesbian and gay couples still excluded from marriage by force of state law; in no sense, without a marriage option available, could they be assumed to be "choosing" partnership. What these and most other proposals for reform share is the goal of pluralizing marriage and family law. As the discussion in this section illustrates, however, strategies for pluralization cannot avoid questions of equality and power.

III. Rights and Beyond: Law As Discourse

A campaign by lesbian and gay Americans to assert a "right," either to marry, or to secure certain benefits through domestic partnership laws, can be situated not only in a matrix of legal doctrine relating to the family, but also within an ongoing dialogue about the politics of rights. The invocation of rights claims is one of the most powerful weapons available to a movement seeking justice for the excluded and disempowered. The very framing of one's assertions in terms of rights highlights one's membership in, and thus the justifiable reciprocity of one's claim upon, the larger polis. It evokes American cultural understandings of rights, a culture in which "the sense of legal rights as claims whose realization has intrinsic value can fairly be called rampant...."[82] And it signals connection with a specific historical tradition of rights-based movements, thereby invoking a universalized call for equality, as well as group-specific demands for elimination of invidious social rules.

Rights claims are hardly unambiguous strategic choices, however. Many writers, especially those associated with the Critical Legal Studies (CLS) movement, have argued at length about the inherent limitations of rights frameworks.[83] They point out that the American political system has enormous capacity to absorb and co-opt seemingly radical demands for change;[84] to truncate the range of political discourse to fit the boundaries of arguments for individualized, atomized entitlements,[85] and, ultimately, to legitimate hierarchies of power, which rights claims can amend but never overturn.[86] The political viability of rights-based movements depends on an acceptance—and thus strengthening—of the existing system, which in turn preserves patterns of dominance by some social groups over others. Thus, the reduction of radical demands into claims of "rights under the law" perpetuates belief systems that teach that other, more transformative modes of change are impossible, unnecessary, or both.[87] Rights claims thereby become at least self-crippling, these writers argue, if not self-defeating, to the very people who make them.

The body of scholarship critical of rights claims has provoked a series of responses that, in part, defend the role of rights claims in bringing about fundamental change. This more recent scholarship, recalling the history of movements for racial and gender equality, has accused the CLS critique itself of hyperabstraction, and has sought to contextualize rights discourse as part of a radical, effective, political strategy.[88] Writers have argued that the process of organizing and litigating empowers and emboldens those who make such claims. Indeed, the very act of asserting rights both signals and strengthens a refusal to continue to accept previously unchallenged systems of subordination. That refusal itself constitutes a major disruption in hegemonic discourses of power.[89] Organized movements to assert rights function as incubators, modifiers and regenerators of demands for far-reaching change.[90]

The political debate over whether to seek legalization of lesbian and gay marriage, or legal protection through domestic partnership statutes, or both, constitutes another venue for this larger debate over the strategic uses of rights claims. Advocates for some form of legal recognition of lesbian and gay relationships face the dilemma posed by Kimberlé Williams Crenshaw:

> Although it is the [system's] need to maintain legitimacy [by incorporating principles of nondiscrimination] that presents powerless groups with the opportunity to wrest concessions from the dominant order, it is the very accomplishment of legitimacy that forecloses greater possibilities. In sum, the potential for change is both created and limited by legitimation. The central issue that the [Critical Legal Studies writers] fail to address ... is how to avoid the "legitimating" effects of reform if engaging in reformist discourse is the only effective way to challenge the legitimacy of the social order.[91]

Solving that conundrum is beyond the reach of this article. But at least some part of a practical response to it may lie in seeking to more deliberately develop strategies that incorporate but do not necessarily privilege law, campaigns that seek legal reform as one ultimate goal, but which also, simultaneously and intentionally, deploy arguments not limited so severely by the bounds of "rights talk."

The impact of law often lies as much in the body of discourse created in the process of its adoption as in the final legal rule itself. What a new legal rule is popularly understood to signify may determine more of its potential for social change than the particulars of the change in the law. The social meaning of the legalization of lesbian and gay marriage, for example, would be enormously different if legalization resulted from political efforts framed as ending gendered roles between spouses, rather than if it were the outcome of a campaign valorizing the institution of marriage, even if the ultimate "holding" is the same. Similarly, the meaning of securing for lesbians and gay men the right to adopt or to raise children is vastly different if understood as reflecting the equal worth of lesbian, gay and heterosexual role models, rather than as justified by the view that a parent's sexual orientation has no impact on, and thus poses no danger to, the sexual orientation of a child.

For feminists both inside and outside the lesbian and gay rights movement, the current focus on the possibility of legalization for lesbian and gay marriage provides an opportunity to develop ways to address the issues of hierarchy and power that underlie this debate. The politics of both gender and sexuality are implicated. The social stigma that attaches to sexuality outside marriage produces another hierarchy, parallel to the hierarchy of gender. Simply democratizing or degendering marriage, without also dislodging that stigma, would be at best a partial reform.

Faced with such difficult issues, advocates for change should consider formulating specifically rhetorical strategies that can be utilized in long-term political efforts, in addition to the rights claims that ground litigation. A concept of "gender dissent" might form one such theme. In contrast to much of the equality rhetoric used in the lesbian and gay marriage debate, "gender dissent" does not imply a desire merely to become accepted on the same terms within an unchallenged structure of marriage. Nor does it connote identity based on sexual orientation; anyone can dissent from a hierarchy of power. Rather, it conveys an active intent to disconnect power from gender, and an adversarial relationship to dominance. Its specific expression could take a variety of forms, appropriate to differing contexts and communities. The goal of such a strategy would be enhancement of an openness to change and maximization of the potential for future and ever broader efforts to transform both the law and the reality of personal relationships.

CHAPTER 10

Identity, Speech and Equality

NAN D. HUNTER (1993)

My experience as a litigator tells me that the First Amendment has provided the most reliable path to success of any of the doctrinal claims utilized by lesbian and gay rights lawyers. Certainly no other block of cases
can rival the success rate of the cases seeking recognition and even funding of lesbian and gay student organizations, all of which were brought on
First Amendment grounds and ultimately won by plaintiffs.[1]

My experience as a lesbian teaches me that silence and denial have been
the linchpins of second-class status. In almost any context that a lesbian or
gay American faces, whether it be the workplace, the military, the courts
or the family, the bedrock question is usually, is it safe to be out? Because
of the centrality of "outness," the most important theme arising from the
gay rights legal movement has been the relationship between expression
and equality.

The growth in the lesbian and gay rights movement has generated more
speech about sexuality. My argument is that it also has created a different kind of speech. Lesbian and gay rights lawyers are fighting a battle in
both judicial and legislative arenas over the fundamental question of the
scope of public discourse. Our claims set forth the first serious demand
that speech about sexuality be treated as core political speech. This development marks a radical shift in First Amendment doctrine, provoking a
category crisis of whether to treat sexual speech as part of a shared social

dialogue or as second-tier quasi-obscenity. The change in legal doctrine has altered political thought as well. It signals the conceptualization of sexuality—and specifically homosexuality—as a political idea.

Lesbian and gay rights legal claims have further complicated the expression-equality dynamic. As it has emerged in lesbian and gay rights case law, "identity" is a multilayered concept. The idea of identity is more complicated and unstable than either simply status or conduct. It encompasses explanation and representation of the self. Self-representation of one's sexual identity necessarily includes a message that one has not merely come out, but that one intends to *be* out—to act on and live out that identity.

Notions of identity increasingly form the basis for gay and lesbian equality claims. Those claims merge not only status and conduct, but also viewpoint, into one whole. To be openly gay, when the closet is an option, is to function as an advocate as well as a symbol. The centrality of viewpoint to gay identity explains the logic behind what has become the primary strategy of antigay forces: the attempted penalization of those who "profess" homosexuality, in a series of "no promo homo" campaigns.

This essay analyzes the history of the relationship between expression, equality and privacy in the state's regulation of sexuality. It traces the development of identity concepts in law and the general shift from privacy to equality claims. Within this story, speech is a constant thread; in a changing context, however, First Amendment assertions have evolved into a new kind of claim. Identity politics has led to identity speech.

I. The Right to Remain Silent

One can date the first stage of the lesbian and gay civil rights movement as occurring from 1950 to 1975. The three strands of doctrine that still dominate the field—privacy, equality and expression—materialized during that period. Because the focus of the early cases and legislation was on sexual conduct, privacy became the primary intellectual bulwark of rights advocates. The Hart-Devlin debate about sodomy law, in which Millsian notions of liberty warred with invocations of communally defined morality, provided the paradigmatic text. By the end of this period, however, equality and expression claims had also emerged in gay rights litigation.

Beginning after World War II, homosexuals as a class of persons were demonized in U.S. politics as subversives capable of destroying society and the state. As a 1950 Senate report on sex perversion among federal workers warned, "[o]ne homosexual can pollute a Government office."[2] In response to a panic about "[t]he [h]omosexual [m]enace,"[3] the government sought to purge its military, its teaching corps, its workforce and its immigrants of *persons* who were homosexual. President Eisenhower issued Executive Order 10,450 in 1953, which declared "sexual pervasion" inconsistent with the national security and thus rendered lesbians and gay men presumptively unfit for government employment.[4]

During this postwar period, the state used homosexual identity[5] as a mechanism of repression. It was the government that sought to impose identity as a public classification onto private acts. The state's ascertainment and exposure of private conduct created a forced public status, often accompanied by a confession, or forced speech. Knowledge of sexual conduct provided the means for identifying individuals and expelling them from public institutions, or—in the words of the Senate report—"detecting and removing perverts."[6] In this framework, conduct defined homosexual identity.

Further, homosexuality became synonymous with a psychological type. The state treated the identity which it imposed as a mental illness. The military took the lead in this shift during World War II, changing its approach to homosexuality from a brain disease model to a developmental personality model.[7] In 1952, Congress followed suit by repealing a 1917 provision in the immigration laws that had excluded individuals from emigrating to the United States who were persons of "constitutional psychopathic inferiority."[8] This "constitutional inferiority" was explained in a Senate report as meaning persons with "tainted blood," or "medical traits" that would harm the populace of the United States.[9] In its place, Congress substituted a provision that emphasized not constituent defects, but a more inchoate psychological illness: "psychopathic personality."[10] This latter phrase broadened the focus of the law to include "disorders of the personality.... Individuals with such a disorder may manifest a disturbance of intrinsic personality patterns, exaggerated personality trends, or are persons ill primarily in terms of society and the prevailing culture."[11]

The new category was necessary because Congress believed that the previous approach had failed to identify homosexuals as a group to be excluded. The Senate report recommended that "the classes of mentally defectives ... be *enlarged* to include homosexuals and other sex perverts."[12] By classifying the homosexual as a psychological type of person because he committed certain acts, Congress, like the military, merged homosexual acts and homosexual identity.

As a defense against public exposure, individuals sought to preserve their anonymity. Paradoxically, this desire for secrecy helped to create a zone in which a more public and collective gay identity could grow. The litigation surrounding gay bars and early gay organizations illustrates how the idea of privacy as a shield against the state functioned both to perpetuate secrecy and to help generate a visible social community.

After courts started to resist attempts to close the bars entirely, the state relied on intermittent raids against lesbian and gay bars, ostensibly to monitor for unlawful conduct, as a tactic to repress the then-nascent lesbian and gay subculture.[13] Often these raids served primarily to expose the identities of bar patrons, sometimes by publication of names in local newspapers.[14] Fighting to end the police raids was necessary, at least in part, not only to preserve one's anonymity, but also to retain the opportunity to congregate in virtually the only gay- or lesbian-positive venues in existence at the time. Secrecy also figured prominently in concerns about joining homophile groups. The ability to maintain secrecy of membership strengthened organizations whose very existence undermined the closet. Secrecy furnished the precondition for its very opposite, expression.[15]

The success of privacy arguments also began the process of teasing acts and identity apart. Perhaps the most significant development in lesbian and gay rights law prior to the 1970s occurred neither in courts nor legislatures, when the American Law Institute, in publishing its Model Penal Code, dropped any prohibition of sodomy.[16] Beginning with Illinois in 1961, twenty-one states decriminalized sodomy by adopting the Model Penal Code.[17] Privacy concepts provided the philosophical basis for this legislative reform.[18] In federal employment, the privacy-grounded claim that adverse employment action could not be based on off-hours conduct led to first a United States Court of Appeals decision, *Norton v. Macy*,[19] establishing that principle, then a Civil Service directive,[20] and finally an amendment to the code governing federal workers.[21]

These reforms provided the legal shelter for conduct but not identity. The legislative repeals rendered sodomy a legally neutral act rather than a criminal one in a significant number of states. Federal workers gained protection for the same "act of perversion" that had rendered them unemployable under Eisenhower's executive order. Gradually, homosexual conduct became increasingly lawful, while the extreme stigma associated with the person of the homosexual remained.

Affirmative declarations of homosexuality lay beyond the shelter of tolerance for secret acts. Speech about homosexuality was just beginning to emerge during this period. Until 1958, under the tendency-to-corrupt-morals test, the test for obscenity that preceded the current standard,[22] courts treated the promotion or advocacy of homosexuality as obscene. Two milestone cases illustrate how the law judged homosexuality as subject matter under the First Amendment. In finding Radclyffe Hall's *The Well of Loneliness* obscene in 1929, a New York judge wrote that "[t]he book can have no moral value, since it seeks to justify the right of a pervert to prey upon normal members of a community, and to uphold such relationship as noble and lofty."[23] In a ruling nearly thirty years later, the Ninth Circuit found the Mattachine Society's monthly political and literary magazine "*One*" to be obscene and thus not mailable.[24] The court based its finding of obscenity on one short story described as "nothing more than cheap pornography calculated to promote lesbianism" and one poem about gay male sexual activities that "pertains to sexual matters of such a vulgar and indecent nature that it tends to arouse a feeling of disgust and revulsion."[25] The judicial equating of the affirmation of homosexuality with obscenity ended when, without opinion, the Supreme Court reversed the Ninth Circuit in early 1958, citing its then-new obscenity standard, which had dropped moral corruption as its touchstone.[26]

Claims involving an explicit combination of speech and due process grounds began in the 1970s. These cases arose when public employees challenged discriminatory treatment in their employment after having themselves made their homosexuality public information.[27] They brought hybrid claims based on due process and First Amendment rights, rather than equality, and the courts essentially treated speech as a form of off-duty conduct, subject to the same kind of nexus analysis as the D.C. Circuit had promulgated in *Norton*.[28] Their cases rose or fell on whether the courts found that their speech had been sufficiently disruptive of the workplace to justify their firing.[29]

The next stage in the developing interrelationship between expression and equality emerged in the student organization cases. Beginning in the 1970s, lesbian and gay student organizations formed and immediately encountered refusals by universities to recognize them as legitimate campus groups. The universities argued that official recognition would lead to criminal acts, relying primarily on the sodomy laws. Courts invariably ruled for the students, concluding that the *Brandenburg* test requiring intentional incitement to immediate lawless action[30] had not been met.[31] In the student organization cases, the judicial response quickly and comfortably drew on the preexisting framework for analysis of the advocacy of unlawful conduct, making these easy cases. Courts and litigators generally treated advocacy of homosexuality as advocacy of conduct.[32]

A focus on individual conduct dominated disputes about sexuality and law during the postwar period, both in efforts of repression and of defense. But its primacy had begun to weaken by the mid-1970s. The very successes of privacy claims set the stage for a focus on identity other than as defined by conduct. Declarations of homosexuality had started to complicate speech law and to intertwine with notions of equality. Identity only partially determined by conduct proved to be a much more precarious concept and a more diffuse and shifting target for state repression.

II. The Briggs Initiative: "No Promo Homo" Begins

By consensus, the Stonewall rebellion in June 1969 marks the beginning of the lesbian and gay political movement.[33] During the subsequent decade, municipal legislatures began to enact amendments to existing civil rights ordinances that extended coverage to sexual orientation as a protected class.[34] These breakthroughs in turn led to a series of repeal campaigns in 1977 in which voters eliminated civil rights protections in Dade County, Florida; St. Paul, Minnesota; Wichita, Kansas; and Eugene, Oregon, in rapid succession.[35] Speech of various sorts obviously facilitated these events, but did not function openly as a constituent part of what was at stake. It was nearly ten years after Stonewall, in 1978, in the first political debate about homosexuality outside urban centers or limited enclaves like universities, that expression rather than conduct formed the core of the issue.

The Briggs Initiative appeared on the November 1978 California state ballot as a referendum question that would have permitted the firing of any school employee who engaged in the "advocating, soliciting, impos-ing, encouraging or promoting of private or public homosexual activity directed at, or likely to come to the attention of, schoolchildren and/or other employees."[36] It was widely understood to be a vote on whether the state should fire gay teachers and thus purge that group from the schools and from contact with children.[37] This understanding of the meaning of Briggs was consistent with the older purge-the-homosexuals theme that had long dominated public discussion.

But the Briggs Initiative was configured to play a double role. It was framed in terms of banning a viewpoint, the "advocating" or "promoting" of homosexuality, rather than the exclusion of a group of persons. Lesbians and gay men easily fell within this proscription because to come out is to implicitly, or often explicitly, affirm the value of homosexuality. For that reason, a Briggs-style law could be used to target all lesbian and gay school employees who had expressed their sexual orientation, except in the most furtive contexts.

The viewpoint target made the initiative more complicated, however. It threatened anyone, gay or straight, who voiced the forbidden ideas. Thus it simultaneously discriminated against gay people while broadening its target to include everyone not gay who supported them.

The proposed law did not merely include the two distinct elements of viewpoint bias and group classification. It merged them into one new concept. This merger—what I would describe as the formation of a legal construct of identity that incorporates both viewpoint and status—would come to dominate both the right-wing strategy against gay rights and the claims of the lesbian and gay community for equality.

Early opinion polls indicated that the Briggs Initiative was likely to pass.[38] In efforts that became a model for the later response to AIDS, the California lesbian and gay community mobilized on a scale that it had never before attempted. Thousands of volunteers, many politically active for the first time, joined the anti-Briggs crusade, and massive fundraising supported a sophisticated advertising and public relations campaign.[39] These efforts contrasted with the ineptness and underfunding of the pro-Briggs campaign, and combined with statements opposing the initiative from a series of conservative political leaders, most famously Ronald Reagan.[40] The initiative was defeated by a fifty-eight percent to forty-two percent vote.[41]

The Briggs Initiative referendum campaign marked the moment when American politics began to treat homosexuality as something more than deviance, conduct or lifestyle; it marked the emergence of homosexuality as an openly political claim and as a viewpoint. That, in turn, laid the foundation for the emergence of a new analysis of speech about homosexuality. Instead of treating such speech as the advocacy of conduct, courts shifted to a consideration of gay speech as the advocacy of ideas. The once-bright boundary between sexual speech and political speech began to fade.

A year after the Briggs vote, the California Supreme Court ruled that statements of homosexual identity constituted political speech protected by the state's labor code.[42] In a conclusion still unique in judicial decisions, the court ruled that a complaint that the defendant discriminated against "manifest" homosexuals and homosexuals who make "an issue of their homosexuality" stated a cause of action that defendants violated the labor code by trying to pressure employees to "refrain from adopting [a] particular course or line of political ... activity."[43]

> Measured by these standards, the struggle of the homosexual community for equal rights, particularly in the field of employment, must be recognized as a political activity.... [O]ne important aspect of the struggle for equal rights is to induce homosexual individuals to "come out of the closet," acknowledge their sexual preferences, and to associate with others in working for equal rights.[44]

This was the first ruling treating self-affirming "identity speech" as explicitly political because of—rather than despite of—its expression regarding sexuality, and not as a surrogate for, or prediction of, conduct.[45]

By contrast, the federal courts, in adjudicating the constitutionality of language identical to the Briggs Initiative, relied on reasoning that avoided the question of whether promoting homosexuality could qualify as political expression. Legislators in Oklahoma enacted the same language rejected by voters in California, after Anita Bryant, a former Miss Oklahoma who had led the effort to repeal the Dade County civil rights provision, urged them to protect schoolchildren from persons who "profess homosexuality."[46] The Tenth Circuit found the Oklahoma statute overbroad because it had the potential to reach such core political speech as a school employee's opinions in favor of adopting a civil rights law or repealing a sodomy law.[47] The dissent attempted to create a new rule against incitement to sexual conduct, arguing that although advocacy of "violence, sabotage and terrorism" was protected under the Brandenburg test, advocacy of "a crime malum in se"—"a practice as universally condemned as the crime of sodomy"—should not qualify for First Amendment protection.[48] Bryant's own phrase had captured the paradox, however: one "professes" a belief, not an act.

III. HIV Testing As Speech

With the advent of the HIV epidemic in the early 1980s, gay male sexuality became a topic of widespread political discussion and debate. Although legal and social reaction ostensibly focused on the disease, the disease itself was so closely associated with gay men in the first years of the epidemic that much of the reaction seemed a euphemism for opinions of male homosexuality.

In a narrow sense, most of the case law generated by and about HIV falls outside the category of gay rights law. Litigators most often based antidiscrimination claims on disability, not sexual orientation.[49] Privacy claims were framed as protection against intrusive medical tests, not the threat of forced disclosure of homosexuality that many gay men anticipated from mandatory HIV testing.[50]

But in a broader and deeper sense, courts, Congress and state legislatures had begun a fight over which new social understanding about homosexuality would supersede silence. At issue was the question of which body of information would comprise public knowledge, and how the government would define and enforce the boundaries of public discourse. Framed in this way, many aspects of AIDS law that we think of as falling within the doctrinal category of privacy really center on speech.

A. Reexamining the Testing Debate

This contest over public knowledge and discourse was fought first, and most significantly, in the policy debate over education versus testing. It quickly became a commonplace in policy discussions to note that, in the absence of a cure, prevention was the only weapon against the spread of HIV.[51] The contest then became how to define "prevention": Would that term be interpreted to mean testing or education?[52] The question became, in effect, which form of knowledge would be available in and constitute the public realm.

Education efforts, including safe-sex education, required a public discourse that was nonjudgmental of the individual and agnostic toward sexual practices. It sought to promote greater knowledge about sexualities and incited public discussion about specific sexual acts. Testing campaigns, by contrast, emphasized a private procedure that led to identification of those who were HIV-infected, and often to reporting of that information to public health authorities.

Two competing "right-to-know" campaigns began. Conservatives argued that the public most urgently needed to know who was infected and thus who posed a danger. The gay community used public health arguments to justify opening public fora such as schools and broadcast media to an unprecedented discussion of male homosexuality.

The combination of these arguments led to a two-part discourse by each side. AIDS activists argued for widespread knowledge and openness at the collective level and anonymity at the individual level, especially in the context of the individual reporting information to the state. Conservatives countered with arguments for revelation of information about individuals to some state authority, together with silence about sexuality in the public, collective discourse.

At the level of individual knowledge, HIV testing in the mid-1980s, before treatments became available, (usually) functioned as exposure of homosexuality with little or no benefit to the persons being tested. As a result, gay rights groups shortsightedly attempted to dissuade the Food and Drug Administration from licensing the antibody test in 1985.[53] Luckily for them, they failed; the antibody test saved the nation's blood supply and, in the process, probably averted what would have been a far worse social panic had contaminated blood remained a real threat. But the test also began to be used in exactly the way that rights advocates feared—as a marker for identification and exclusion.[54]

The testing debate within the Reagan administration climaxed in 1987. In February of that year, the Centers for Disease Control ("CDC") held a massive conference on mandatory testing proposals for a variety of populations. Hundreds of persons attended the conference, and the major sessions were filmed and broadcast by video and television cameras from platforms in the middle of cavernous rooms. CNN reporters conducted interviews of public health leaders and activists from sets built outside the meeting halls, and the network billed its day-long coverage as the "national AIDS meeting." The outcome of the conference was a major setback to proponents of forced testing; the consensus recommendations emphasized voluntariness and confidentiality, and urged the adoption of antidiscrimination protections.[55]

The CDC toned down these recommendations before transmitting them upward in the Executive Branch chain of command, but retained the basic focus on consent and confidentiality.[56] The issue reached the Domestic Policy Council that spring. Then-Surgeon General C. Everett Koop won acceptance of a let-the-states-decide position on a number of testing proposals, but could not stop the administration from undertaking mandatory testing of federal prisoners and immigrants, groups more characterized by their vulnerability to government control rather than by any logical relationship to a risk of transmission.[57]

For both sides in the debate over testing, knowledge of individuals' status became an important fact in and of itself. For social conservatives, screening and identification of the HIV-infected became a kind of justified stigmata, a rite of expulsion, and a method of defining the boundary of community and politics to reject the alien. For AIDS activists, resistance to testing served as both a protective barrier against those expulsions and also as a bargaining chip. Public health officials desperately needed the cooperation of the gay community in order for any prevention programs to succeed, and activists tacitly or explicitly sought to trade cooperation in exchange for support of new laws banning discrimination based on HIV status or sexual orientation.

B. Public Discourse and the Legacy of Briggs

Although the debates over individual testing still continue and remain important, a noticeable change in focus has occurred. In 1987, the same year that the testing controversy peaked, a major shift occurred in the debate as a whole, as it evolved from a contest primarily about knowledge of individual status to one increasingly about the scope of public discourse.

In 1985, the CDC began funding educational programs aimed at behavior change, which included support for some innovative programs undertaken by the Gay Men's Health Crisis (GMHC), a New York City group that provides education and other services to people infected with HIV. GMHC and other AIDS service organizations had always used private funds to develop their most provocative materials, which sought to eroticize condom use and other safe-sex practices. Officials at CDC became alarmed, however, by the potential for conservative backlash against the agency for supporting a gay organization engaged in controversial work.[58] In January 1986, the CDC first promulgated restrictions on the content of federally funded programs, requiring that all such materials must use language that "would be judged by a reasonable person to be unoffensive to most educated adults."[59]

In 1987, this issue reached Congress. In October, Senator Jesse Helms introduced an amendment to the appropriations bill for the Department of Health and Human Services that forbade use of any CDC funds "to provide AIDS education, information, or prevention materials and activities that promote or encourage, directly or indirectly, homosexual sexual activities"[60]—language that closely tracked that of the Briggs Initiative. Unlike Briggs, however, the Helms bill was unstoppable. Opponents succeeded only in deleting the term "indirectly," thus arguably limiting its scope to the most graphic materials.

The Helms Amendment combined the Briggs Initiative's one-stroke targeting of both gay people and progay ideas with the most successful argument made by the antichoice movement in the abortion debate: that public funds should not be used to "subsidize" activity associated with what conservatives paint as sexual permissiveness. The only difference was that the target group was gay men rather than indigent women. And, unlike abortions, the funded activity, education, was public in its nature, raising the questions of how and on what terms the nation would discuss AIDS. In fact, gay-targeted educational campaigns were very unlikely to be seen outside gay venues, but conservatives launched an attack that spread from the safe sex comics and erotic videos distributed in gay bars to sex education and condom availability in the schools.

The debate on adoption of the Helms Amendment centered on objections raised by Senator Helms to AIDS education efforts within the gay male community, specifically those of the GMHC. Senator Helms made clear, repeatedly, that the purpose of his amendment was to insure that the content of AIDS education be made to conform to what he believed to be moral precepts of behavior, which for him meant absolute opposition to homosexuality or any tolerance for it.

Senator Helms paraphrased the GMHC proposal, noting that AIDS education sessions (all of which were specifically targeted for gay male participants) included discussions of "a positive sense of gay pride."[61] He continued:

> Then ... we get to session 5 and session 6.... This is entitled "Guidelines for Healthy Sex." ... The behavioral objectives of these two sessions included the ability to "list satisfying, erotic alternatives to high-risk sexual practices; identify erogenous areas of the body,"—and here is here [sic] I get embarrassed—"other than the genitals, that produce an erotic response."...

There is no mention of any moral code.... Good Lord, I may throw up.[62]

Senator Helms reiterated throughout the debate his intent that the amendment was designed to forbid publicly funded AIDS education materials from advocacy of homosexuality: "Yes, it will require us to make a moral judgment. I think it is about time we started making some moral judgments and stop playing around with all those esoteric things and saying 'Yes but.' I believe ... it is time to draw the line."[63] Senator Helms concluded by stating: "What the amendment does is to propose that we ensure that any money spent for such purposes is not spent in such a way that even comes close to condoning or encouraging or promoting intravenous drug use or sexual activity outside of a sexually monogamous marriage including homosexual activities."[64]

In the course of the debate, Senator Helms amended his original proposed language to focus its prohibitions specifically on materials which promoted *homosexual* activities only, and not all premarital or extramarital activities, thereby accentuating the invidiousness of the targeted suppression. Immediately before the final vote, Senator Helms summed up the provision:

Earlier ... on this floor, I read from grant presentation documents prepared by the Gay Men's Health Crisis of New York City. That is a corporation. It is unmistakably clear that those activities are being federally funded and are promoting and encouraging homosexuality.... Therefore ... it should be clear that in adopting this amendment, if in fact it is adopted, this Senate is prohibiting further funding for programs such as those sponsored, operated by the Gay Men's Health Crisis Corp. that promote or encourage homosexual sexual relations.[65]

Restrictions on content remained in place for several years. The Helms language was rejected in the next year's appropriations bill, in favor of a provision that neutralized its antigay focus while retaining some limitations on speech. The new language, known as the Kennedy-Cranston Amendment, limited funding only if AIDS educational materials were "designed" to encourage sexual activity, whether heterosexual or homosexual.[66] Under this intent requirement, materials that were designed to reduce HIV transmission, but were erotic as part of that design, were supposed to be exempt from the limitation because they were not "solely and specifically" intended to encourage sexual activity.[67] Senator Helms vehemently opposed the Kennedy-Cranston Amendment, accusing its supporters of attempting to render his own approach "nugatory."[68]

In fact, however, despite the Kennedy-Cranston Amendment, the CDC retained its own "offensiveness" restrictions until they were found invalid by a federal district court in 1992,[69] a ruling that the government declined to appeal. The court found the language of "offensive[ness]" to be void for vagueness[70] and also ruled that the CDC's standard violated an AIDS-related statute that prohibited federal funding only to materials that were found to be obscene.[71]

In sum, although few of the judicial opinions addressing AIDS-related issues focus on expression, the politics of speech profoundly shaped AIDS policy. AIDS policies, in turn, transformed public discourse on homosexuality, more so than any other event to that time, including Stonewall, Briggs, or the battles over municipal and state civil rights laws.

By the late 1980s, the angle of attack was clearly directed at homosexual ideas as embodied in the gay community and not simply at gay persons as such. Dozens of AIDS service organizations, many openly affiliated with gay community groups, received millions of dollars of CDC funding for education and other prevention efforts. Neither the Reagan Administration nor Senator Helms ever attempted to exclude all gay persons or groups as grantees. Even if there had been the desire for such an exclusion, the need to fight the disease rendered such an approach practically infeasible and politically implausible. The attack on gay identity had now centered on expression, and "no promo homo" was its theme song.

IV. Beyond AIDS: "No Promo Homo" Revisited

The "no promo homo" language that originated in the Briggs Initiative and was used to restrict AIDS education became the model for many antigay legislative initiatives, in the United States and beyond. Arizona enacted criteria for AIDS education materials in public schools that prohibited any local district from providing instruction that promoted a homosexual lifestyle, portrayed homosexuality as a positive alternative lifestyle, or suggested that some methods of sex are safe methods of homosexual sex.[72] Alabama adopted similar legislation.[73] In Britain, Clause 28 of the Local Government Act of 1988 stated that local governments could not "promote homosexuality or publish material with the intention of promoting of homosexuality" or "promote the teaching ... of the acceptability of homosexuality as a pretended family relationship."[74] Nor could government funding go to private entities engaged in those acts.[75]

Members of Congress also became fond of the "no promo homo" principle, reinvoking it when various issues pertaining to homosexuality surfaced. In 1988, Congress relied on it twice, once to restrict speech, and once to attempt to alter a civil rights statute.

That spring, a local family planning clinic in New Hampshire finished work on a federally funded sex education program for adolescents, especially males, who, researchers found, believed that impregnating their girlfriends and becoming fathers proved to peers that they were not homosexual.[76] The manual written for teachers stated that "[g]ay and lesbian adolescents are perfectly normal and their sexual attraction to members of the same sex is healthy."[77] Senator Gordon Humphrey introduced legislation that passed the Senate, but died in a conference committee, which would have prohibited federal funding of sexual education materials that promoted "homosexuality and homosexual activity" or contained "references to homosexuality as 'normal or natural activity'."[78]

Also in 1988, Congress attempted to force the District of Columbia to alter its municipal civil rights law, one of the first to include sexual orientation as a protected category, by exempting religious colleges from its scope. The District's highest court had ruled that Georgetown University violated the local law by refusing to extend benefits to a lesbian and gay student group.[79] Congress reacted by conditioning federal appropriations to the District on the City Council's allowing religious schools to deny benefits or recognition to "any person or persons that are organized for, or engaged in, promoting, encouraging, or condoning any homosexual act, lifestyle, orientation, or belief."[80] Congress never defined "homosexual belief," but its inclusion of that term signifies the recognition of and the desire to suppress something more than (and different from) either conduct ("act") or status ("orientation").

The following year, in response to public outcry over reports that National Endowment for the Arts (NEA) funds had supported an exhibit of homoerotic Robert Mapplethorpe photographs and other controversial art, Congress enacted legislation prohibiting the NEA from funding obscene materials "including but not limited to, depictions of sadomasochism, homoeroticism, the sexual exploitation of children, or individuals engaged in sex acts."[81] As anthropologist Carole S. Vance has pointed out, this linguistic construction collapses homoeroticism and obscenity, making the former appear to be a synonym for the latter.[82] Although homoerotic materials are simply one example of what might meet the legal test for obscenity, the NEA restriction comes full circle from 1950s obscenity case law by seeming to equate the two. Its message—like that of the pre-*Roth* obscenity cases—is that homoeroticism is obscene.

Subsequent developments in the arts funding controversy further conflated gay identity with speech about sexuality. In 1990, as congressional consideration of agency funding approached, then chairperson of the NEA John Frohnmayer denied grants recommended by the agency's internal peer review process to four performance artists. Three of the four were lesbian or gay. In challenging the denials, the artists did not claim that they lost funding because they were gay. Rather, they asserted a viewpoint bias claim, arguing that the NEA denied funding based on two common themes in their work, one of which was the endorsement of equal legitimacy for homosexual and heterosexual practices.[83]

Each of these post-Briggs "no promo homo" campaigns utilized a concept of homosexuality that incorporated viewpoint. Each centered on a fight to control some public venue—whether it be arts grants, schools, or health education materials. And each represented a step further away from the focus on conduct and privacy that had dominated earlier case law.

V. The Evolution of Identity

The legal doctrines most relevant to lesbian and gay civil rights litigation have evolved in tandem, not as the distinct lines of doctrine that they sometimes appear to be, but in a dynamic tension with each other. Expression, equality, and privacy coexist as components of rights claims that are mutually dependent. The ban on military service by lesbians, gay men, and bisexuals, for example, renders identical conduct such as kissing permissible or punishable based on the sexual orientation of the actor.[84] Moreover, the ban restricts self-identifying speech with the justification that homosexual "conduct" is antithetical to morale, good order and discipline.[85] The military ban is a rich example of the inextricability of the concepts of expression, equality and privacy.

The military ban also illustrates how the boundaries of legal doctrine shape political debates and decisions. In the aftermath of *Bowers v. Hardwick*,[86] the federal judiciary divided over what has become known as the status-conduct debate, with most courts of appeal ruling that discrimination based on sexual orientation could not be subject to heightened scrutiny under the equal protection clause because it was constitutionally permissible under *Hardwick* for a state to criminalize sodomy, and participation in sodomy defined the class homosexual.[87] Left without a privacy-based defense against criminalization of that conduct, advocates and some judges argued that sexual orientation was first and foremost a status, not contingent on conduct. This riddle—is homosexuality status or conduct—was an artifact of the categories of legal doctrine and the outcome of a single case. Yet it was picked up, replicated and amplified in the arguments over the military ban. President Clinton framed his position as opposition to discrimination "based solely on status," and, in response, congressional opponents such as Senator Sam Nunn responded in part by arguing that there was no status without conduct. That entire framework grew out of *Hardwick*.

The doctrinal categories themselves muddy up the law. Is the claim one of expression or of equality when a Irish gay and lesbian group is denied participation in a St. Patrick's Day parade? Is the exclusion of the group wanting to carry a self-identifying banner based on speech or based on status? Are they being shut out because of who they are or because of what they are saying? In social practices, these distinctions are artificial. In the law, they carry enormous weight. If the defendant is a private entity, the only recourse in law is to assert an equality claim if there is a civil rights statute that includes sexual orientation as a prohibited classification. No right to freedom of speech exists against private actors. The state action doctrine thus drives litigation and debate about St. Patrick's-type events into diminishing important aspects of the situation having to do specifically with endorsement of homosexuality. Conversely, if the defendant is a public entity, the more powerful tactic is often a speech claim, as the student organization cases demonstrate.[88]

Judges will have to confront the irrationality of these distinctions as advocates continue to press claims that require courts to consider the meaning of homosexuality. Both are hobbled by the lack of a clearly articulated conceptualization of the intrinsic role of expression at the very heart of equality.

Self-identifying speech does not merely reflect or communicate one's identity; it is a major factor in constructing identity. Identity cannot exist without it. That is even more true when the distinguishing group characteristics are not visible, as is typically true of sexual orientation. Therefore, in the field of lesbian and gay civil rights, much more so than for most other equality claims, expression is a component of the very identity itself. This is a paradox that current law cannot resolve.

State-imposed penalties on identity speech—on speech that promotes or professes homosexuality—have multiple consequences.

First, penalizing self-identifying expression effectively nullifies any protection under equality principles. As Justice William Brennan noted with respect to a plaintiff who had been fired after informing coworkers of her bisexuality, "it is realistically impossible to separate her spoken statements from her status."[89] Such penalties would make the promise of equality a sham for lesbian and gay citizens, comparable to denying religion-based protection to Jews who wear yarmulkes or Christians who wear crosses.

Second, suppression of identity speech leads to compelled expression, a violation of the principle that an individual has the right not to speak as well as to speak.[90] In the absence of identity speech, most persons are assumed to be heterosexual. To paraphrase the ACT UP slogan, silent equals straight. To compel silence, then, is to force persons who are not heterosexual not only to speak, but, in effect, to lie.

Lastly, like forced speech, the collective, communal impact of forced silence amounts to more than an accumulation of violations of individual integrity. It creates a form of state orthodoxy.[91] If speaking identity can communicate ideas and viewpoints that dissent from majoritarian norms, then the selective silencing of certain identities has the opposite, totalitarian effect of enforcing conformity. In that sense, homosexuality is not merely, or either, status or conduct. It is also, independently, an idea.

In the contemporary United States, campaigns to secure state suppression of sexual identity speech are a complex phenomenon. Although they seek to control both individuals and ideas, the target of the exclusion has shifted from the former to the latter. At stake is the role sexuality will have in the realm of public discourse.

CHAPTER 11

History's Gay Ghetto

*The Contradictions of Growth
in Lesbian and Gay History*

LISA DUGGAN (1986)

I want you to see that there is a passion in what we do.

**—Joan Nestle, Lesbian Herstory Archives Founder,
to Judith Schwarz, 1977**

In June 1975, the New York Lesbian Herstory Archives collective proclaimed in its first newsletter: "For us, there is excitement and joy in sharing the records of our lives, and our Archives will be as living as the material we can collect and you can send us."[1] This sense of the living intensity of historical work has been sustained over the past decade in the astonishing proliferation of lesbian and gay history archives, projects, slide shows and publications. The appearance of Jonathan Katz's pioneering *Gay American History* in 1976 inspired a bevy of researchers to dig out records of the lesbian and gay past in conventional libraries and manuscript collections, while institutions like the Lesbian Herstory Archives provided a model for subsequent efforts to collect materials from previously untapped sources.[2] Slide shows such as Allan Bérubé's "Lesbian Masquerade" (an account of the lives of women who "passed" as men in nineteenth-century

San Francisco, produced with the San Francisco Lesbian and Gay History Project) began to make the rounds of major U.S. cities in 1979, playing to large and enthusiastic audiences at community centers, churches, bars, and organizational meetings.[3] Long-term research projects requiring sustained energy and commitment were also undertaken by individuals and groups such as the Buffalo Oral History Project, which designed an ambitious, continuing study of that city's working-class lesbian community before 1970.[4]

News of this activity has been carried to the lesbian and gay communities via the gay press. Newspapers and periodicals, such as Boston's *Gay Community News* and Toronto's *Body Politic*, have promoted historical awareness as an integral part of the building of gay politics and community. In fact, the growth of lesbian and gay history overall has depended on the passionate energy generated by the gay liberation and lesbian-feminist movements. Lesbian and gay historical work thus has much in common with other community-based history movements generated by the social activism of the 1960s and 1970s—women's history, black history, labor history and social history more generally. In the context of vital political movements, the political meaning of historical understanding becomes suddenly manifest, and historical work is received with an enthusiasm very far indeed from the emotional pall of the deliberately depoliticized history classroom or museum hall.

Lesbian and gay historical work has also had a special history of its own. Its subject matter is to some extent taboo in most mainstream settings, and its practitioners are saddled with a pariah status even more constraining than the culturally marginal position of leftists and feminists. This unique situation has led to a series of contradictory effects. On the one hand, lesbian and gay historians have been crippled by exclusion from the funding sources and institutional supports available to other academic and community historians. The work itself has also suffered from this intense ghettoization—it has been confined almost entirely to lesbian and gay authors and audiences. On the other hand, the stigmatization of lesbian and gay history and historians has led, ironically, to some unusual strengths. Lesbian and gay history is strongly rooted in a political community upon which it is dependent for support. The practice of historical research fostered in this context is highly democratic and innovative. Necessity has been the source of invention—lesbian and gay historical researchers have exhibited a methodological imagination, material resourcefulness and social diversity that are rare in the practice of history.

The great bulk of work in lesbian and gay history has been undertaken outside the university, in community settings. This has remained true even as lesbian and gay historians and their work have gained a small foothold in academic institutions over the past few years. John Boswell of Yale, John D'Emilio of the University of North Carolina at Greensboro, and Lillian Faderman of the University of California at Fresno, among others, have made major contributions to the growing body of published work in lesbian and gay history.[5] Most lesbians and gay men employed on academic faculties are still closeted, however, and lesbian and gay subjects are still considered the kiss of death for an academic career. Therefore, by necessity, the primary locations for research have developed in the community, where two major institutions have been created—the independent archive and the history project.

Lesbian and gay archives have sprung up throughout North America and Europe since the mid-1970s. Though these institutions have a variety of structures and funding sources, most subsist on volunteer labor and individual contributions. Some collect only local materials; others have a national or even international scope. The range is from a few boxes of materials stored in someone's home to a large, structured organization like the Canadian Gay Archives in Toronto, which has organized international conferences and put out a number of publications, including a useful guide entitled *Organizing an Archives: The Canadian Gay Archives Experience*.[6] Archives collect a wider range of materials than more traditional repositories. The majority have a small library of published works, emphasizing materials likely to be missing from mainstream libraries, such as lesbian pulp novels of the 1950s. Most also collect letters, diaries and unpublished manuscripts, as well as political materials, including flyers, posters, buttons, tapes of conferences and speeches, and photographs of events. Some focus on special collections, such as the records of organizations (One Institute Library) or individuals (Harvey Milk Archives). Visitors to archives include browsers, serious researchers, and even occasional visitors hoping to make contact with the local lesbian or gay community.

The dependence of gay archives on volunteers and community fund-raising means that their continuing existence reflects, and in part creates, a high level of grassroots commitment to historical archiving. But most also suffer from chronic underfunding and a shortage of useful archival technology and trained personnel. Acquisitions also tend to be haphazard, and cataloguing incomplete. Coordination among archives is at present nonexistent.

History projects have popped up and dissolved, in recurring cycles of interest, in most urban areas in the United States. Some projects, such as the one in New York, have collected sources, fostered exchange of information among members, and supported individual researchers. The New York Lesbian and Gay Historical Society began in the late 1970s as a support circle for individuals engaged in lesbian or gay history research. Eventually, a smaller Lesbian History Project evolved out of the larger group and engaged in collective research about New York City's lesbian bars during the 1950s and lesbian-theme theater productions of the 1920s and 1930s. Eventually both groups disbanded, leaving behind at the Lesbian Herstory Archives voluminous files for possible successors.[7]

Other projects, such as those in San Francisco and Boston, have produced major presentations based on local, collective research. The slide show "Our Boston Heritage," which chronicles over a century of lesbian and gay history in that city, was produced and presented throughout the United States by a collective of women and men who met and shared their original research over a period of years. The slide show provides accounts of the lives of noted lesbian and gay Bostonians, such as the poet Amy Lowell, but it also chronicles collective experience. The growth of a gay subculture, the social organization of bar culture, the pattern of police persecution and the birth of gay liberation and lesbian feminism are presented through a text and visual images.[8] These projects, usually undertaken without outside funding, require extraordinary commitment, especially from those members who work full-time and are politically active in addition. Not surprisingly, many projects have short lives.

Archives and history projects involve both academic and community-based researchers—an integration of effort that is unusual in the historical profession. Both categories of researchers keep in touch informally as well as through a formal network, newsletters and conferences. A few years ago, the Lesbian and Gay Researchers Network, a nonacademic group composed primarily of independent historians, merged with the Committee on Lesbian and Gay History, an affiliate of the American Historical Association. This organization puts out a newsletter and provides a structure for the sharing of resources and information.[9] This integration of community and university researchers extends beyond the U.S. borders. The Canadian Gay Archives and the *Body Politic* sponsored international conferences of lesbian and gay historians in Toronto in 1982 and 1985, while a 1983 conference held in Amsterdam, "Among Women, Among Men," brought together Europeans and North Americans from a wide variety of disciplines.[10] Though the Toronto gatherings attracted a stronger contingent of community researchers than the university-sponsored meeting in Amsterdam, all the conferences included activists, researchers and theoreticians from many different backgrounds.

One of the knottiest contradictions in the development of the lesbian and gay history movement is the double impact of gay invisibility. Though historians have often neglected or distorted the experiences of minority groups and deprived classes, only lesbians and gay men have had their existence systematically denied and rendered invisible. The work of lesbian and gay historians makes this actively hidden past visible, and so creates enormous excitement. The simplest historical narrative about gay life is often received by lesbian and gay audiences as a profound affirmation of membership in a community with a shared past. On the other hand, lesbian and gay life is *still* invisible in many social and geographic areas. Exposure can cause individuals to lose material and social supports. Many hesitate to undertake research, or even to attend a gay event. Even those who are not gay-identified fear being "suspected" and so keep their distance from gay subjects. This dynamic greatly restricts the field for the creation and dissemination of lesbian and gay history. Thus, gay invisibility both makes historical work particularly exciting and ghettoizes it.

Because of the risks involved in being identified as lesbian or gay, gay history researchers are drawn exclusively from the ranks of those who are politically committed and willing to be "out" in public. Within these limitations, though, the recruitment of researchers is remarkably democratic. For instance, the Boston Area History Project included at its founding individuals ranging in age from the early twenties to the mid-fifties, from poor, working-class, and middle-class backgrounds, and from "old gay," contemporary gay rights and feminist movement cultures. The group included an insurance underwriter, a student, a printer, a housecleaner, a secretary, a teacher and a trained historian. As Chris Czernick explained in an article on the Boston Project in *Gay Community News*, "This exchange, or integration of skills and orientations, pushes all of us to truly listen to each other, to think more provocatively, to approach our research more creatively, and to conceptualize our history more honestly and accurately."[11]

This democratic practice has its limits, however. Though people of both genders are involved in the projects and archives, research in gay men's history remains more developed than that in lesbian history. And most projects' memberships cross but do not erase class lines. But the most stubborn barrier to a fully democratic historical practice has been the racial barrier. Most project and archive memberships are overwhelmingly white and English-speaking. Some white researchers have focused their individual projects on the history of gay people of color—Eric Garber's slide show on Harlem gay life and J. R. Roberts' bibliography of material on black lesbians, for instance.[12] Some activist groups of lesbians or gay men of color, though not history projects *per se* (such as Asian Lesbians of the East Coast and the Committee for the Visibility of the Other Black Woman), have focused attention on historical work.[13] But these efforts so far constitute a kind of ghetto-within-the-ghetto of lesbian and gay history.

The major problems built into this community-based practice of historical research are, of course, money and time. Those researchers not supported by academic jobs or student stipends find the material support for their work hard to come by. Historians such as Jonathan Katz and Judith Schwarz have had to shelve highly valued research projects in order to take draining full-time jobs, and fellow researchers and devoted audiences have deeply felt the loss.

But the democratic recruitment of researchers, in spite of its difficulties and limits, has had an enormously positive influence, not only on the nature of supporting institutions like archives and projects, but also on the very methods and sources used for research. The Lesbian Herstory Archives, for instance, is not a sterile repository of materials for use by researchers, but a kind of community center where political and social groups meet in an environment that creates a sense of a shared and meaningful past. This archive's aggressive collection of current cultural, political and personal materials also helps to generate an awareness that present accomplishments are creating a history that can shape the future.[14]

The democratic basis of research has not only helped connect historical scholarship with current concerns; it has also been indispensable in uncovering the source materials for the writing of gay and lesbian history. The problems of sources and methods for researching a group that is not just anonymous but actively hidden go far beyond those normally encountered in graduate school. Knowing where to look for sources, understanding the need for confidentiality, having some sense of the coded meanings of words and gestures, require not just training and intelligence but also diversity of experience among researchers. The Buffalo Oral History Project, for instance, found the ordinary techniques of oral history insufficient because of the interviewees' need for secrecy. Members of the project drew on experience as well as imagination in developing new techniques for generating contacts and eliciting information under these conditions. More recently, they have broadened their project's efforts to cross racial lines, drawing on the experience of project members of differing racial backgrounds.

The collective nature of much lesbian and gay historical work and the need to innovate and learn from experience have created an unusually high level of communication and cooperation among researchers. A strong informal sense of ethics about the use of colleagues' sources and the proper crediting of others' insights and information has developed. Difficulties do arise, however, as when the makers of the gay history documentary *Before Stonewall* used without proper credit unpublished material shared with them by gay historians, causing the historians to withdraw from the project.[15]

The democratic, collective nature of much lesbian and gay history has also had an impact on the form of finished work. History projects have tended to generate slide talks, lectures, radio shows, and theater presentations, rather than articles and books. These forms are both more and less accessible to popular audiences. A slide tape, for instance, may be more enjoyable, immediate and understandable than many articles, but anyone can copy an article at the public library, whereas relatively few will see any given slide tape.

The impact of community-based history on the content of finished work is less immediately clear. The quality of lesbian and gay historical work is enormously variable, and the problems of method and theory span a wide spectrum, whether the work is academic or not, and whether it is collectively or individually produced.

Much lesbian and gay history suffers from an excessive focus on "famous figures." Enormous energy is expended on the Parisian lesbian salons of the 1920s, for instance, as well as on the lives and romantic and sexual intrigues of well-known writers and artists. At its best, such work analyzes the impact of lesbian or gay identity on a small group or an individual, while making connections to the broader social meaning of that identity in a particular time and place. At its worst, a focus on the rich and famous degenerates into historical gossip about who slept with whom, and who wore what where. A concentration on the well-known is limiting, and narrows the class and racial parameters of research. Researchers continue to be drawn to the study of the well-known, however, partly because of the greater availability of sources about famous figures, and partly out of a desire to show that "we were there" among the most respected figures in Western culture.

But analytical and theoretically grounded studies coexist with these celebratory works. The class, race and gender content of research is constantly subjected to critical scrutiny. Lesbian and gay historians can expect support and encouragement from their colleagues, but they must also be prepared to be held accountable for the content of their work. At its best, such criticism is useful and enormously productive. Eric Garber's early presentations of his research, for instance, met with great enthusiasm as well as constructive criticism. Some black members of his audience pointed out that his analysis tended to focus on white gays in black Harlem rather than on Harlem's own black gay community. Garber's subsequent research benefited greatly from these early criticisms, and his emphasis shifted to reflect them. Leila Rupp's review of the work of John D'Emilio and Jonathan Katz, published in the lesbian issue of *Signs*, is another example of friendly, useful criticism—this time a lesbian's critique of the work of gay men.[16]

This critical community has also fostered work with important theoretical implications. In fact, historians have developed much of the theoretical work underlying and supporting the gay movement, in part because many gay activists had strong roots in the New Left, which emphasized a historical analysis of present political realities. Lesbian and gay historians have asked questions about the origins of gay liberation and lesbian feminism, and have come up with some surprising answers. Rather than finding a silent, oppressed, gay minority in all times and places, historians have discovered that gay identity is a recent, Western, historical construction. Jeffrey Weeks, Jonathan Katz and Lillian Faderman, for example, have traced the emergence of lesbian and gay identity in the late nineteenth century.[17] Similarly, John D'Emilio, Allan Bérubé and the Buffalo Oral History Project have described how this identity laid the basis for organized political activity in the years following World War II.[18]

The work of lesbian and gay historians has also demonstrated that human sexuality is not a natural, timeless "given," but is historically shaped and politically regulated. Their work has serious implications for the history of sexuality and the history of gender relations, the family, social movements, and cultural change and conflict. But the ghettoization of lesbian and gay history limits its impact on other fields of historical research. Few historians outside the lesbian and gay ghetto read or see lesbian and gay history. Historical research and social theory are thereby impoverished.

Enthusiastic audiences across the country have greeted this diverse work in lesbian and gay history. Slide shows in some senses "create" an audience for gay history. They are presented as social and political events, and are often attended by people otherwise unacquainted with gay history. Different portions of the audience often have different, and sometimes conflicting, expectations. Some lesbians and gay men translate their need for a sense of pride into a desire for respectability, and so expect lesbian and gay history to provide them with a "cleaned up" version of the past. The "yuppie" segments of the audience are especially embarrassed by images of gay male transvestites and street hustlers, or by images of "butch" and "femme" lesbians. This segment of the audience sometimes complains that such images are "negative" because they are not conventionally respectable. Other lesbians and gay men translate a need for pride and self-validation into the opposite expectation: they want to see the whole range of lesbian and gay life reflected in historical work, including the underground or culturally oppositional subcultures within the gay community.

This division in the audience is partly a class difference: upwardly mobile professionals project their desire for respectability onto the past, while working-class, ethnic, black, or Latino groups wish to see their own experiences reflected without apology. The division is also political. The more conservative "civil rights" wing of the gay movement emphasizes respectability, and tends to define a "positive" role model as a well-dressed, prosperous, white professional in the present as well as in the past. The more radical wing of the gay and lesbian-feminist movements, on the other hand, emphasizes inclusion, and presents political and cultural criticism of dominant class- and gender-based expectations for individual and mass behavior. Audience reception of work by lesbian and gay historians thus outlines the divisions in the lesbian and gay community at the same time that it helps to define and unify that community.

Occasionally lesbian and gay history is presented outside the arena of the "gay liberation ghetto." For example, when lesbians and gay men are fighting for a civil rights law or battling discriminatory legislation, such as the defeated Briggs initiative in California, which would have made it illegal to "advocate" homosexuality in the public schools, the cultural and intellectual resources of lesbian and gay communities are mobilized to make a public case.[19] In these circumstances the requirements of political expediency—expressed as the need for the most "positive" and publicly acceptable images of lesbians and gay men—and the need for a theoretically sophisticated, inclusive, and critical history can clash. The best history does not always seem to make the best propaganda. Nonetheless, some historians are struggling to combine complex historical analysis with pro-gay public policy efforts. John D'Emilio's affidavit, filed in the U.S. Court of Appeals in a Texas gay rights case, is one example of a successful attempt to combine these two goals.[20]

The major questions before lesbian and gay historians are these: How do we continue to grow? How do we break down the barriers that keep us under-funded and ghettoized, while maintaining our vital roots in the political communities that give us our strength? How do we continue to democratize, to more fully represent the multiple lesbian and gay communities, without fragmenting our work or sacrificing institutional cohesion? How do we learn the practice of critical historical inquiry in the context of a community under attack and in need of uplift and protection?

The answers to these questions have as much to do with the political future of the lesbian and gay movement as they do with historical practice *per se*. Right now, that future seems quite fragile. The past few years have seen increasing attacks on the basic rights of lesbians and gay men, and this repressive trend will probably continue for some years to come, eroding our gains and putting us on the defensive. At the same time, further gains continue to accrue, even in mainstream settings. The Lesbian Herstory Archives received foundation funding for a computer system; Allan

Bérubé was awarded a grant for independent historical research; the University of Chicago Press has made a continuing effort to publish gay and lesbian history. And even the ghettoized and limited accomplishments of the recent past represent a historical watershed.

The successes and limitations of the lesbian and gay history movement also have implications for community and public history efforts in general. On the positive side, lesbian and gay historians have demonstrated what can be accomplished with very slender resources when historical work is closely connected to the community being studied. They have also shown some potential for a more democratic historical practice in community settings, and have forged new ways of combining theoretically sophisticated research with a political commitment to the needs of an oppressed group. On the negative side, the experience of lesbian and gay history projects and archives shows the fragility of community-based efforts without more stable institutional supports. Many do not survive; even those that do have a limited impact on the historical consciousness of a broader public. The challenge for lesbian and gay history is essentially the same as that for community and public history more generally—how can historical work be more widely circulated, while retaining its emotional impact and political edge?

Sexual Dissent, Activism and the Academy

CHAPTER 12

Making It Perfectly Queer

LISA DUGGAN (1991)

During the past few years, the new designation "queer" has emerged from within lesbian, gay and bisexual politics and theory. "Queer Nation" and "Queer Theory," now widely familiar locations for activists and academics, are more than just new labels for old boxes. They carry with them the promise of new meanings, new ways of thinking and acting politically—a promise sometimes realized, sometimes not. In this essay I want to elucidate and advocate this new potential within politics and theory.

Because I am a Southern girl, I want to arrive at my discussion of these new meanings through a process of storytelling. From an account of concrete events—recent events that gripped and provoked me personally—I will construct a certain political history, and from that history raise certain theoretical questions. Because the position "queer" has arisen most proximately from developments in lesbian and gay politics, the trajectory I follow here reflects my own passage through those politics. Were I to follow another trajectory—through feminist or socialist politics, for example—I would arrive at a similar position, with many of the same questions and suggestions. But the stories would be different, and the "work" of those stories would be differently constructed. Here, I want to take up the position of "queer" largely in order to criticize (but not completely displace) the liberal and nationalist strategies in gay politics and to advocate the constructionist turn in lesbian and gay theories and practices.

Scene #1 New York City, March 1991;
the St. Patrick's Day Parade

The Irish Lesbian and Gay Organization (ILGO) has been denied permission to march. After much public protest of this exclusion, a deal has been struck with the march organizers. ILGO members will be permitted to march as the guests of a contingent of the Ancient Order of Hibernians, but they have had to agree not to carry any identifying banners or signs. Mayor David Dinkins, who helped to broker the deal, has decided to walk with the lesbian and gay group. On the day of the parade, this group, marked out for the curious by the presence of Dinkins, becomes the target of repeated outbursts of intense hostility on the part of spectators, parade organizers, and officials of the Catholic Church.

These events received extensive nationwide news coverage, which focused largely on the spectacle of the mayor under attack. Dinkins himself used this spectacle to frame an analogy between the treatment of the lesbian and gay marchers in the St. Patrick's Day parade and the hostile treatment of civil rights marchers in the South decades earlier. In an op-ed published in *The New York Times* several days after the parade, he extended and elaborated on this analogy:

On Saturday, despite our taking great care to see that the parade rules were observed, a fearful rage erupted—a rage of intolerance. The anger hurled at the gay and lesbian Irish Americans and me was so fierce that one man threw a filled beer can at us. Perhaps the anger from those watching the parade stemmed from a fear of a lifestyle unlike their own; perhaps it was the violent call of people frightened by a future that seems unlike the past.

It is strange that what is now my most vivid experience of mob hatred came not in the South but in New York—and was directed against me, not because I was defending the rights of African Americans but of gay and lesbian Americans.

Yet, the hostility I saw was not unfamiliar. It was the same anger that led a bus driver to tell me back in 1945, when I was en route to North Carolina in Marine uniform, that there was no place for me: "Two more white seats," he said. It was the same anger that I am sure Montgomery marchers and Birmingham demonstrators experienced when they fought for racial tolerance. It is the fury of people who want the right to deny another's identity.

We cannot flinch from our responsibility to widen the circle of tolerance. For the true evil of discrimination is not in the choice of groups to hate but in the fact that a group is chosen at all. Not only does our Bill of Rights protect us all equally, but every religious tradition I know affirms that, in the words of Dr. Martin Luther King, Jr., "Every man is somebody because he is a child of God."[1]

I quote the Dinkins op-ed extensively here even though it is in most respects formulaic and unsurprising, an invocation of the themes and images of a familiar brand of liberal politics, with its limited call for "tolerance" and an end to "discrimination." I quote it because even my most radical and cynical lesbian and gay friends found it deeply moving, because it was in one important respect quite rare. Dinkins' analogy to the civil rights movement, an analogy liberal gay organizations have outlined and pursued for decades, is still seldom heard outside lesbian and gay circles. In the hands of David Dinkins, a political figure with national visibility and a well-known record of civil rights activism, this analogy mobilizes images of noble suffering in the face of naked hatred. It invokes the culturally resonant figure of Martin Luther King, Jr. on behalf of lesbians and gay men, thereby endowing our struggle for equality with a precious and, for us, elusive political resource—moral authority.

Appeals to Liberalism

For nearly fifty years now, lesbian and gay organizations have worked to forge a politically active and effective lesbian and gay "minority" group, and to claim the liberal "rights" of privacy and formal equality on its behalf. As a rhetorical strategy, this positioning has aimed to align lesbian and gay populations with racial, ethnic, and religious minority groups and women in a quest for full economic, political and cultural participation in U.S. life. This rhetorical move, when successful, opens up avenues of political and legal recourse forged by the civil rights and feminist movements to lesbian and gay action: support for group-specific antidiscrimination statutes, participation in political coalitions to design, pass, and enforce broad civil rights provisions; application to the courts for equal protection under various constitutional provisions; organization to elect and pressure public officials; lobbying of media organizations for fair and equitable representation, and so on.

But this rhetorical overture to the logic of liberal tolerance has generally met with very limited success. The inclusion of lesbians and gay men in the pantheon of unjustly persecuted groups is everywhere unstable and contested. Political coalitions risk their legitimacy when they include lesbian and gay groups or issues. Group-specific municipal antidiscrimination ordinances are constantly subject to repeal attempts. Cultural groups from the National Endowment for the Arts to the Modern Language Association are attacked or ridiculed for the presence of lesbian and gay topics on their agendas. And the legal climate for lesbian and gay organizations has been poisoned for the rest of this century (at least) by the nasty, brutish and short 1986 decision of the U.S. Supreme Court in *Bowers vs. Hardwick* (upholding the state of Georgia's statute criminalizing consensual sodomy).

The spectacle of the suffering mayor walking with downcast gays and lesbians in the St. Patrick's Day parade brings both these failures and the important achievements of liberal gay politics into vivid relief. The hostility of the spectators, the parade organizers, and the Roman Catholic Cardinal underscored the precarious position of the ILGO and, by extension, of gay communities more generally. Inclusion could be negotiated only on humiliating terms, and even then public civility could not be enforced.

But as the subsequent press coverage and the Dinkins op-ed show, the parade was also a moment of highly visible achievement for the rhetoric of liberal gay politics. The circulation of images from the parade evoked a response supportive of Dinkins and the ILGO from nongay politicians and pundits, a response which frequently framed the issues in language that liberal gay organizations have proposed, appropriating the American Dream for the "minority" that seems to reside permanently at the bottom of the list.

At this historical moment, marked by the precarious and contested achievements illustrated by the example of the St. Patrick's Day parade, the liberal strategy has also come under increasing attack from within lesbian and gay communities. Of course, this strategy has never occupied the field of gay politics unopposed. Challenges to it have appeared from the overlapping yet distinguishable positions of militant nationalism and radical constructionism. In the 1990s, both of these positions appear to be gaining ground.

The Call to Militant Nationalism

Scene #2 New York City, Spring 1991

Posters of celebrities labeled "Absolutely Queer" appear on Manhattan walls. One, featuring an image of actress Jodie Foster, is captioned "Actress, Yalie, Dyke." These posters have not been produced by homophobic conservatives, but by gay militants engaged in the practice of "outing."

"Outing" is a political tactic inaugurated by New York City's now defunct gay weekly newspaper *Outweek* (though the term for it was coined by

Time), and associated most closely with the paper's "lifestyle" columnist, Michelangelo Signorile. As a practice, it is an extension of the early gay liberationist appeal to lesbians and gay men to "come out of the closet," reveal their hidden lives, and reject the fear and stigma attached to their identities. In "outing," this appeal is transformed from an invitation into a command. Journalists and activists expose "closeted" lesbians or gay men in public life, especially those deemed hypocritical in their approach to gay issues. Their goal is to end the secrecy and hypocrisy surrounding homosexuality, to challenge the notion that gay life is somehow shameful, and to show the world that many widely admired and respected men and women are gay.

Both "outing" and *Outweek* sprang from the efflorescence of militance surrounding the rhetoric and politics of ACT UP and its spinoff, Queer Nation. Many of these new gay militants reject the liberal value of privacy and the appeal to tolerance which dominate the agendas of more mainstream gay organizations. Instead, they emphasize publicity and self-assertion; confrontation and direct action top their list of tactical options; the rhetoric of difference replaces the more assimilationist liberal emphasis on similarity to other groups.

But the challenge that the new politics poses to the liberal strategy is not only the challenge of militance—the familiar counterposing of anger to civility, of flamboyance to respectability, often symbolized through "style"—but also the challenge of nationalism.[2]

Nationalisms have a long history in gay and lesbian politics and culture. From turn-of-the-century German homosexual emancipationist Magnus Hirschfeld to contemporary radical-feminist philosopher Mary Daly, the "nation" and its interests have been defined in varying ways. With no geographical base or kinship ties to provide boundaries, gay and lesbian nationalists have offered biological characteristics (as in the "Third Sex"), or shared experience (whether of sexual desire or gender solidarity) as common ground. Of these various nationalisms, two broadly distinguishable competing forms have appeared and reappeared since the mid-nineteenth century: (1) the ethnic model of a fixed minority of both sexes defined by biology and/or the experience of desire (most often estimated at ten percent)[3] and (2) the single-sex union of gender loyalists, the no-fixed-percentage model associated with lesbian separatism (theoretically, all women could belong to the Lesbian Nation).[4]

The ethnic model also underpins the liberal strategy, of course. The argument for "rights" is made on behalf of a relatively fixed minority constituency. It becomes the basis for a more militant nationalism when the "ethnic" group is represented as monolithic, its interests primary and utterly clear to a political vanguard. The example of "outing" serves as an illustration of this brand of gay politics. Outers generally not only believe in the existence of a gay nation, but are confident of their ability to identify its members and of their authority to do so. They have no doubts about definitions or boundaries, and do not hesitate to override the welfare and autonomy of individuals "in the national interest."[5]

Outers present their version of gay nationalism as radical but, like other nationalisms, its political implications are complex, and often actually reactionary. These new nationalists define the nation and its interests as unitary; they suppress internal difference and political conflict. Self-appointed ayatollahs explain it all.

This reactionary potential was especially apparent in the pages of *Outweek* in 1990, when Malcolm Forbes, then recently deceased, was "outed" and presented as a role model for gay youth. The same magazine had earlier reviled Tim Sweeney, a longtime gay activist and executive director of Gay Men's Health Crisis in New York City, for compromising the gay national interests by negotiating with African-American groups over the conditions for appointment of a New York City health commissioner.[6] *Outweek's* "nation," it appears, is white, values wealth and celebrity for their own sake, and pursues self-interest in the narrowest possible terms.

This particularly virulent strain of gay nationalism has been criticized with increasing vehemence by those excluded, misrepresented, or terrorized by it. C. Carr, writing in *The Village Voice* under the banner headline, "Why Outing Must Stop," called it "the most absurd excuse for political thinking I have ever encountered," and commented:

> Anyone who thinks ... that a lesbian can proclaim her sexuality in an
> industry as male-centered as Hollywood, where even straight women
> have trouble getting work ... has to be out of his fucking mind.

Voicing the sentiments of many, Carr also noted that "I'm still waiting for the news of Malcolm Forbes' homosexuality to improve my life."[7]

Carr's critique of "outing" takes up the liberal defense of "privacy"—emphasizing the continuing strategic value of a "right to privacy" for lesbians and gay men threatened with everyday persecution. But her column also echoes the criticisms of gay political discourses that women and people of color (especially, though not exclusively) have forged and developed over the past two decades.

Whose Identity?

Both the liberal assimilationist and the militant nationalist strands of gay politics posit gay identity as a unitary, unproblematic given—the political project revolves around its public articulation. But for people with multiple "marked" identities, the political project begins at the level of the very problematic construction of identities and their relation to different communities and different political projects. In Audre Lorde's much quoted words: "It was a while before we came to realize that our place was the very house of difference rather than the security of any one particular difference."[8]

Thus Carr hypothesizes that, for Jodie Foster, being a woman defines her relationship to Hollywood in a way that shifts the meaning of being "gay," and the consequences of "coming out." From this perspective, advocacy of "outing" is colonizing. Foster's situation is appropriated by a single-issue politics that cannot honor the complexity of her differences.

The charge I want to make here against both the liberal and nationalist strategies, but especially against the latter, is this: *any* gay politics based on the primacy of sexual identity defined as unitary and "essential," residing clearly, intelligibly and unalterably in the body or psyche, and fixing desire in a gendered direction, ultimately represents the view from the subject position "twentieth-century, Western, white, gay male."

Scene #3 San Francisco, February 1991; the Second Annual Lesbian and Gay Writers' Conference

> The designation of this conference as simply "lesbian and gay" is contested everywhere I look. An organized bisexual lobby is highly visible and voluble. The designation "Queer" is ubiquitous, sometimes used in the "in-your-face" manner of the many "Faggot" and "Dyke" buttons that I see, but also used to designate a more broadly inclusive "community."

Louise Sloan, reporting on this conference in the *San Francisco Bay Guardian*, wrote that it constructed a "community":

> ... of men, women, transsexuals, gay males, lesbians, bisexuals, straight men and women, African Americans, Chicanos, Asian Americans, Native Americans, people who can see and/or walk and people who cannot, welfare recipients, trust fund recipients, wage earners, Democrats, Republicans, and anarchists—to name a few.... Indeed, since difference from the "norm" is about all that many people in the "gay community" have in common with each other, these sorts of "gay and lesbian" gatherings, at their best and worst and most radical, seem to be spaces where cross-sections of the human multiverse can gather to thrash out differences and perhaps to lay the groundwork for peaceful and productive futures.... In my most naively hopeful moments, I often imagine it will be

the "queer community"—the oxymoronic community of difference—that might be able to teach the world how to get along.[9]

Sloan's description of the "oxymoronic community of difference" at the writers' conference challenges the oversimplified notion that the essentialist-versus-social-constructionist debate, now saturating the gay press, is a controversy of activist politics versus academic theory.

In its most clichéd formulations, this controversy is presented in one of two ways: valiant and dedicated activists working to get civil rights for gay and lesbian people are being undermined by a bunch of obscure, arcane, jargon-ridden academics bent on "deconstructing" the gay community before it even comes into full visibility; or theoretically informed writers at the cutting edge of the political horizon are being bashed by anti-intellectual activists who cling naively to the discursive categories of their oppressors.[10] Both these formulations fail to acknowledge the vigor and longevity of the constructionist strand in lesbian and gay politics, a strand which theorists have taken up, not produced.

From the first appearance of the homosexual/heterosexual polarity just over a hundred years ago, "essentialist" theories, both homophile and homophobic, have had to account for the observed malleability of sexual desire. Each theoretical assertion of the fixity of desire has had attached to it a residual category—a catchall explanation for those formations of pleasure that defy the proffered etiologies. In Havelock Ellis' scheme, flexible, "acquired" sexual inversion accompanied the more permanent, "congenital" type. In the lexicon of contemporary sociology, "situational" homosexuality occurs among "heterosexual" persons under special circumstances—in prisons or other single-sex institutions, for example. ("Situational" heterosexuality is seldom discussed.)[11] In each theoretical paradigm, the "essential" nature and truth of the homo/hetero dyad is shored up with a rhetoric of authenticity. The "real" is distinguished from the "copy," the "true inverts" from those merely susceptible to seduction.

Such constructionist branches on the tree of essentialism grew up on their own during the heady days of early gay liberation. Drawing on the more constructionist versions of psychoanalytic theories of sexuality, visionaries painted a utopia in which everyone was potentially polymorphously sexual with everyone else.[12] During the 1970s, lesbian-feminists outlined a somewhat more ambivalent position, with a sharper political edge. They aggressively denaturalized heterosexuality and presented it as a central apparatus in the perpetuation of patriarchy. But these same women often presented lesbianism as the naturalized alternative. When Alix Dobkin sang that "Any Woman Can Be a Lesbian," the implication was that any woman not suffering from false consciousness *would* be.[13]

The current revival of constructionist rhetoric in activist discourses is, like its constructionist predecessors, also partial and ambivalent—but in a very different sense. The new political currency of the term "bisexual," for instance, which has been added to the titles of lesbian/gay organizations from coast to coast in the United States, has had contradictory effects. Activists have used the term "bisexual" to disrupt the natural status of the dualism heterosexual/homosexual. But they have then paradoxically reinstated sexual polarity through the addition of a third naturalized term, as rigidly gendered as the original two, only doubled. The tendency of bisexual writers and organizations to appropriate wholesale the rhetoric of the lesbian and gay rights movement reinforces the latter effect.[14]

Defining a Queer Community

The notion of a "queer community" can work somewhat differently. It is often used to construct a collectivity no longer defined solely by the gender of its members' sexual partners. This new community is unified only by a shared dissent from the dominant organization of sex and gender. But not every individual or group that adopts the name "queer" means to invoke these altered boundaries. Many members of Queer Nation, a highly decentralized militant organization, use the term "queer" only as a synonym for lesbian or gay. Queer Nation, for some, is quite simply a gay nationalist organization. For others, the "queer" nation is a newly defined political entity, better able to cross boundaries and construct more fluid identities. In many other instances, various contradictory definitions coexist—in a single group, or in an individual's mind. This ambivalent mixture is illustrated in a series of interviews with Queer Nation activists published in *Out/Look*:

> **Miguel Gutierrez:** Queerness means nonassimilationist to me.
>
> **Rebecca Hensler:** A lot of what the "queer generation" is arguing for is the same stuff that was being fought for by gay liberation.
>
> **Alexander Chee:** The operant dream is of a community united in diversity, queerly ourselves.... [The facilitators] took great care to explain that everyone was welcome under the word queer.
>
> **Laura Thomas:** I don't see the queer movement as being organized to do anything beyond issues of antiassimilation and being who we want to be.
>
> **Adele Morrison:** Queer is not an "instead of," it's an "inclusive of." ... It's like the whole issue of "people of color."
>
> **Gerard Koskovich:** I think queer has been adopted here in San Francisco by people who are using their experience of marginalization to produce an aggressive critique of the prevailing social system....

I think we're seeing in its early stages a reorganization of some of those forces into a new community of people where the range of defining factors is rather fluid. People's limits have shifted significantly from the traditional urban gay community of the 1970s.[15]

Or, as former *Outweek* editor Gabriel Rotello explained to a *New York Times* reporter,

When you're trying to describe the community, and you have to list gays, lesbians, bisexuals, drag queens, transsexuals (post-op and pre-), it gets unwieldy. Queer says it all.[16]

In addition to the appearance of organizations for "bisexuals" and "queers," the boundaries of community have also been altered by a new elasticity in the meanings of "lesbian" and "gay." When Pat Califia announced that sex between lesbians and gay men is "gay sex," and *Outweek* published a cover story on "Lesbians Who Sleep With Men," the notion of a fixed sexual identity determined by a firmly gendered desire began to slip quietly away.[17]

Queer Theory on the Move

The constructionist perspective began to generate theoretical writing beginning in the 1970s. British historical sociologist Jeffrey Weeks, influenced by the earlier work of Mary McIntosh, appropriated and reworked the sociological theories known as "symbolic interactionism" or "labeling theory" to underpin his account of the emergence of a homosexual identity in Western societies during the nineteenth century. Other British writers associated with the Gay Left Collective produced work from within this same field of influence. U.S. historians Jonathan Ned Katz and John D'Emilio, influenced primarily by feminist theory and the work of Marxists such as E.P. Thompson, began to produce "social construction" theories of homosexuality by the early 1980s.[18]

This theory, though rich with implications for theoretical investigations of identity and subjectivity generally, remained severely ghettoized until relatively recently. Gay authors and gay topics, stigmatized and tabooed in the academy, have found audiences and sources of support elsewhere. But lesbian and gay history and theory have suffered from this ghettoization, as have history and theory more broadly.[19]

The figure who most clearly marks the recent movement of this theory out of the ghetto is Michel Foucault. His reputation and influence placed his investigations of the emergence of homosexual identity within a theoretical context, embedded in a body of work, that legitimated it—and ultimately served to legitimate the work of other, more stigmatized and marginalized theorists. The history of sexuality ultimately became a subject, a disciplinary location, largely as an effect of the circulation of Foucault's work through the work of (predominantly) lesbian and gay authors.[20]

Since the publication of Foucault's *History of Sexuality*, the cultural work of lesbian and gay theory has shifted. After a couple of decades of staking out a position, a territory, a locale, our theories are now preparing to travel. After defining a viewpoint, articulating a set of questions, and producing a body of knowledges, we are determined now to transport these resources across cultural boundaries. Theory is now working—finally—to get us out of the academic ghetto.

"Constructionist" theories accomplish this in a way "essentialist" theories never could. Lesbian and gay identities, theorized as fixed and borne by a minority, place certain limits on the horizon of theory as well as politics. They contain desire and naturalize gender through the operations of their very definitions. Constructionist theories, on the other hand, recognize the (constrained) mobility of desire and support a critical relation to gender. They stake out a new stance of opposition, which many theorists now call "queer." This stance is constituted through its dissent from the hegemonic, structured relations and meanings of sexuality and gender, but its actual historical forms and positions are open, constantly subject to negotiation and renegotiation.

Queer theories do their ghetto-busting work by placing the production and circulation of sexualities at the core of Western cultures, defining the emergence of the homosexual/heterosexual dyad as an issue that *no* cultural theory can afford to ignore. As Eve Sedgwick put it in the first paragraph of her book *The Epistemology of the Closet*:

> This book will argue that an understanding of virtually any aspect of modern Western culture must be, not merely incomplete, but damaged in its central substance to the degree that it does not incorporate a critical analysis of modern homo/heterosexual definition.[21]

This project works in at least two directions—taking queer questions and knowledges into the domain of mainstream theoretical paradigms, and bringing the formulations of feminist, Marxist, postmodernist and poststructuralist theories to bear on issues of queer culture and politics.

In the case of a major figure such as Foucault, the project involved the smuggling of queer questions into the very foundations of contemporary theory. Without being *completely* crude and reductive, it is possible to ask: From what subject position do prisons, mental asylums, confessionals and sexuality seem connected and central to the operations of power?

Foucault's own queerness, seldom stated but widely known, may have shaped his questions and his work in ways that endowed it with its current legitimating power.[22]

In the area of literary studies, Eve Sedgwick's work is now performing the work of legitimation and de-ghettoization. She is importing "queer readings" into the house of critical theory. She is able to accomplish this effectively in part because, as the "Judy Garland" of gay studies, she does not bear the stigma of homosexuality herself. She can be perceived (however wrongly) as in some sense "disinterested," and therefore as a more "credible" standard bearer for theoretical queerness. (This is not a criticism of Sedgwick, but of the conditions of reception for her work.)

Sedgwick's work performs its magic primarily for the benefit of gay male readers and readings, and on the texts of the traditional, white, male "canon."[23] Within the field defined by queer literary theory, lesbian visions remain profoundly ghettoized, though they are gaining ground from within feminist theory (which is itself only newly emerging from its own ghetto). Only a few literary theorists have embarked on queer readings of the texts of lesbians, especially those from less privileged class backgrounds or from communities of color.[24]

It is precisely from within feminist theory, however, that a "queer" critique of the dominant categories of sexuality and gender is emerging most imaginatively and persuasively. The work of film theorist Teresa de Lauretis, especially, has effected the de-ghettoization of a queer perspective in feminist theory. As she wrote in *Technologies of Gender* in 1987:

> The problem, which is a problem for all feminist scholars and teachers, is one we face almost daily in our work, namely, that most of the available theories of reading, writing, sexuality, ideology, or any other cultural production are built on male narratives of gender, whether oedipal or anti-oedipal, bound by the heterosexual contract; narratives which persistently tend to re-produce themselves in feminist theories. They *tend* to, and will do so unless one constantly resists, suspicious of their drift.[25]

We can surmise who is the "one" who is most likely to become and remain so relentlessly suspicious.

Following on the work of de Lauretis, feminist philosopher Judith Butler has hacked away at the heterosexual assumptions built into the foundations of theories of gender, whether feminist, nonfeminist, or antifeminist. Her *Gender Trouble: Feminism and the Subversion of Identity*, draws upon the queer practices of drag and cross-dressing (treated in the earlier work of anthropologist Esther Newton) and the queer "styles" of lesbian butch-fem to build her own conception of gender as performance, and of gender parodies as subversive bodily acts.[26]

Though neither de Lauretis nor Butler has staked out a position named specifically as "queer," the elaboration of such a locale within feminist theory could work a radical magic similar to that of the category "women of color." As many feminists have argued, the category "women of color," as proposed in such groundbreaking anthologies as *This Bridge Called My Back*, is a significant conceptual and political innovation.[27] As Donna Haraway wrote in 1985:

> This identity marks out a self-consciously constructed space that cannot affirm the capacity to act on the basis of natural identification, but only on the basis of conscious coalition, of affinity, of political kinship. Unlike the "woman" of some streams of the white women's movement in the United States, there is no naturalization of the matrix, or at least this is what [Chela] Sandoval argues is uniquely available through the power of oppositional consciousness.[28]

This description (I would argue) applies equally well to the political community and theoretical standpoint constructed by the designation "queer."

Activism Versus Academia?

The challenge for queer theory as it emerges from the academic ghetto is to engage intellectually with the political project in the best sense of "theory," while avoiding jargon and obscurantism in the worst sense of "academic." The record to date is at best uneven. On the downside, there is a tendency among some queer theorists to engage in academic debates at a high level of intellectual sophistication, while erasing the political and activist roots of their theoretical insights and concerns. Such theorists cite, modify, or dispute Foucault, Lacan, and Derrida, while feminist, lesbian, and gay innovations and political figures disappear from sight. They use formal languages to exclude all but the most specialized from the audience for theory.

On the upside, some queer theorists work in a way that disrupts the activist/theorist opposition, combining sophisticated thinking, accessible language, and an address to a broadly imagined audience. Writer/activists such as Gloria Anzaldúa, Kobena Mercer, Douglas Crimp and Gayle Rubin offer us the possibility of escape from the twin pitfalls of anti-intellectual posturing among some activists *and* the functional elitism of some would-be radical theorists.[29]

The continuing work of queer politics and theory is to open up possibilities for coalition across barriers of class, race, and gender, and to somehow satisfy the paradoxical necessity of recognizing differences, while producing (provisional) unity. Can we avoid the dead end of various nationalisms and separatisms, without producing a bankrupt universalism?

I think queer politics and theory offer us promising new directions for intervention in U.S. life—though in different ways in differing arenas. In the arena of academic cultural theory, queer theory is breaking into the mainstream, making a difference and providing (some, limited) material support in the form of careers. This is possible because queer theory shares with much academic cultural theory a critique of U.S. liberalism and a focus on the process of political marginalization. But in the arena of political activism—the kind that takes place in mass institutions from mainstream media to Congress—queer politics occupies the critical margins. This is because the language and logic of liberalism still occupy the progressive edge of the possible in mainstream U.S. politics. Lesbian and gay liberal politics offer us the best opportunities we have to make gains in courtrooms, legislatures, and TV sitcoms. Queer politics, with its critique of the categories and strategies of liberal gay politics, keeps the possibility of radical change alive at the margins. It also infuses a remarkable efflorescence of off-center cultural production—art, music, dance, theater, film and video, and more.

Jeffrey Escoffier and Allan Bérubé describe this paradoxical reality in the special *Out/Look* section on Queer Nation:

> The new generation calls itself *queer*, not *lesbian, gay, and bisexual*—awkward, narrow, and perhaps compromised words. *Queer* is meant to be confrontational—opposed to gay assimilationists and straight oppressors while inclusive of people who have been marginalized by anyone in power. Queer Nationals are undertaking an awesome task. They are trying to combine contradictory impulses: to bring together people who have been made to feel perverse, queer, odd, outcast, different, and deviant, and to affirm sameness by defining a common identity on the fringes.
>
> Queer Nationals are torn between affirming a new identity—"I am queer"—and rejecting restrictive identities—"I reject your categories," between rejecting assimilation—"I don't need your approval, just get out of my face"—and wanting to be recognized by mainstream society—"We queers are gonna get in your face."
>
> These queers are constructing a new culture by combining elements that usually don't go together. They may be the first wave of activists to embrace the retrofuture/classic contemporary styles of postmodernism. They are building their own identity from old and new elements—borrowing styles and tactics from popular culture,

communities of color, hippies, AIDS activists, the antinuclear movement, MTV, feminists, and early gay liberationists. Their new culture is slick, quick, anarchic, transgressive, ironic. They are dead serious, but they also just wanna have fun. If they manage not to blow up in contradiction or get bogged down in process, they may lead the way into new forms of activism for the 1990s.[30]

For the foreseeable future, we need both our liberal and radical fronts. But queer politics and theory, in their best guises and combinations, offer us a possible future full of provocations and possibilities.

CHAPTER 13

Scholars and Sense

LISA DUGGAN (1992)

Lesbian and gay studies—the new kid on the academic block—has a split personality, appearing by day as Queer Theory, sporting a stylish postmodern vocabulary and a huge bibliography, and by night as Queer Nation, shouting confrontational slogans and struggling (with mixed success) to create a militant, multicultural politics.

Queer Theory has crossover dreams. Academic institutions—well, English departments, to be specific—are offering jobs; publishers and journals are soliciting manuscripts. After decades of scrounging for ways to support research and writing, an unprecedented number of lesbian and gay scholars now can hope to combine visibility, intellectual recognition and material support. Within the space carved out by feminist theory, multicultural canon-busting and cultural studies, queer theory is demanding, and may find, a home.

Queer Nation, meanwhile, is mad as hell and refusing to be nice. And for good reason. National political debates resound with hateful queer-bashing, from Jesse Helms's hysteria over homoerotic art to Pat Buchanan's TV ads aimed at smearing African-American gay men. Even within the liberal wing of mainstream American political culture, the most respectable, assimilationist gay politico is treated as a rude interloper. The inclusion of lesbian and gay issues in the laundry lists of the most progressive civil rights coalitions remains everywhere contested and precarious.

Militant, multicultural, queer politics stands in angry opposition to business as usual, talking not about domestic partnership and family diversity, but about Asian fags, Chicana butches, butt-fucking, dental dams, and bashing back.

This split personality (existing not only within the field of lesbian and gay studies as a whole, but often within the same individual) expressed itself in rich profusion at the Fifth Annual Lesbian and Gay Studies Conference, held at Rutgers University last November. Postmodern theory's parodic sensibility and focus on popular culture infused panels and papers with titles like "How To Marry Marilyn Monroe" (Lisa Cohen), "Through Bette Davis Eyes: Camp Spectatorship Looks at Heterosexuality" (Hugh English), and "Madonna and the Glamour Dykes: The Politics of Lesbian Camp" (Ann Cvetkovich). Subjects of the Year: (1) The Female Phallus, or Dykes with (Strap-On) Dicks, and (2) Voguing, "Realness," or Posing for the (Moving) Pictures. Word of the Year: Phantasmatic.

Militant, multicultural politics were reflected in symposia with titles such as "Symptoms of Larger Issues: HIV/AIDS and Lesbian and Gay People of Color," "Race, Ethnicity, Sexuality," and "Activism: What Is It? Who Needs It? Who Does It?" The tone for these events was straightforward and earnest. The more playful and parodic militance associated with groups such as ACT UP was largely absent, perhaps because of the meager representation of cultural activists at the conference overall.

The range of titles was nonetheless wide, reflecting the Herculean effort of the organizers (coordinators Monica Dorenkamp and Beryle Chandler, Ed Cohen of Rutgers and Diana Fuss of Princeton, plus twenty others), who stretched the traditional boundaries of academic interest, and included more people of color on the program than the first four conferences (held at Yale for three years, then at Harvard). Organizers worked to represent participants' interests in theory and activism, cultural production as well as cultural analysis. In addition to over sixty-five panels, eight symposia and three plenaries, there were video and art exhibitions, poetry and fiction readings, comedy and performance art, the usual book exhibit and (of course) a dance.

But no amount of effort on the part of organizers could have overcome the pervasive uneasiness. Partly this was an unfortunate combination of two emotional undercurrents: the anxiety that infects all professional meetings, as participants hustle to network while worrying about their career standing, and the culture of complaint that pervades most political conferences, as multiple constituencies jostle for representation. But there was an added dimension to this uneasiness. The conference had the familiar, uncanny feel of a big, dysfunctional family holiday.

Remember those Thanksgiving dinners from hell? You were genuinely happy to be home, and couldn't wait to hear what everyone had been up to. Then, gradually, familiar feelings of dread and depression crept over you. The same old arguments with Dad, the same old put-downs from Mom, the reappearance of your childish self, feeling trapped and behaving badly. You knew you had something in common with these people, but could no longer remember what it was. The ironclad rule was always: say nothing, confront no one, preserve the fantasy of a happy family.

Such structures of hierarchy, exclusion and erasure are embedded in the field of lesbian and gay studies, as in other academic fields (perhaps less so than most), and are then denied in a rhetoric of academic freedom, openness, and inclusiveness. The stars tend to be white, and come from high-status institutions. The most highly rewarded languages are dense, steeped in technical vocabularies that require years of training to fully understand. Sophisticated theoretical discussions, rooted in and addressed to contemporary political controversies, reference Lacan, Foucault, and Bourdieu while neglecting (relatively) the contributions of the activist writers, independent scholars, and cultural producers who created the conditions for theoretical commentary. The scholar appears as authoritative (and often well-paid) voyeur, bound in hierarchial relation to her relatively impoverished subject.

Conferences could be good places to confront these structures, but they are not. Standard conference formats emphasize display of competence, not communication. It's Academic Journal Live! Or (to steal an image from Marcia Ian's paper, "The Subject of Fantasy") it's a kind of academic posturing very much like a bodybuilding competition—the goal is to appear as masterful as possible, like "a human fucking penis."

The lesbian and gay studies conferences, like other academic conferences with a political component, try to include panels addressed to activist issues, conducted in accessible language. But these really constitute a conference within the conference, as do the readings, videos, and art exhibits. People of color, activists, cultural producers, and independent scholars appear in token numbers on the numerous theory panels, but tend to be clustered on the smaller number of activist ones. The cafeteria-style smorgasbord seems to offer everything to everyone, but, by sorting similar people together onto the same panels, often segregates and separates in unacknowledged ways.

This segregation was the primary reason that the eight symposia and special group plenary put together by organizers, to address vexed issues and allow for interaction, generally failed to accomplish their ambitious goals. One particularly promising symposium, "Beyond the Gay

Community: Queer Intellectuals, Queer Publics," was a crashing disappointment. Grouped together for their "similarity" (all had one foot in the academy, one foot out—and all were white), the panelists did not disagree significantly with each other. Cindy Patton and Alisa Solomon discussed their own work. Michael Warner and Douglas Crimp praised the "diversity" of languages and audiences for gay studies. No one directly addressed the conflict-laden problem at hand: different languages and audiences bring very diverse (read: "unequal") access to resources and rewards. No one expressed, criticized or even seemed to understand the resentment that unsalaried activists sometimes feel toward academic intellectuals. The panel seemed to be promoting a queer liberal pluralism—a politics each panelist would individually reject as an uncritical fantasy.

This panel's particular mode of denial underscored a pattern of complaint and response that I heard as I walked around the conference. I kept hearing a pioneering lesbian scholar groan audibly each time Continental theorists were exclusively credited for political insights found in her own and her friends' work. A dazed gay activist friend just kept mumbling, "Where's the beef?" Those participants whose work was situated on the high end of the unspoken status hierarchy moved to resist such complaints by "deconstructing" the theory/practice, academic/activist oppositions—a welcome project, but in this case a coded way to announce that they did not feel excluded or devalued anywhere.

So how do we shed the happy family pretense, and let our split personalities meet and hash out conflicts? How can we criticize our infant field of study without engaging in mindless theory bashing and anti-intellectual posturing, or positing a moral universe in which the academy is always bad and the community (whatever that is) by definition good? How do we come to terms with the inequalities reproduced in our own practices? For instance, when we examine popular cultural forms, such as voguing, what does it mean that we speak in tongues the practitioners we write about might laugh at? Who learns or profits from our speaking? In other words, if we are transmitting cultural capital, who is (and is not) on the receiving end?

There is one possible model, available in the conference anthology *How Do I Look?: Queer Film and Video.* The conference on which this book is based brought together film- and video-makers, cultural activists, and academic critics. Papers were presented, then discussed extensively (and the often very fruitful discussions are included in the book). The collection, on the whole, represents the highest standard of politically engaged, sophisticated, queer theory. Especially notable for their self-reflexivity are Kobena Mercer's rethinking of the meanings of Robert Mapplethorpe's images of black men, "Skin Head Sex Thing: Racial Difference and the Homoerotic Imaginary," and the heated debates (about racial imagery in Sheila McLaughlin's film *She Must Be Seeing Things*, and about the felt invisibility of producers whose work is theorized in the academy) that follows Teresa de Lauretis's paper, "Film and the Visible." We get to hear theorists, activists and producers question themselves and each other, and we listen in as criticisms are voiced and directly addressed.

I have a persistent fantasy of yet another way to be critical, while avoiding blaming attacks and what Henry Louis Gates Jr. has called the "damnably virtuous solemnity" of multicultural politics. It could be a parody panel submitted to a conference in serious guise, or a whole conference at which the serious and parodic were mixed to critical effect—"Fuck Theory," pun intended. My friends and comrades have contributed ideas for such an event. Participants would be equipped with Discourse Density Meters (with Jargon Warning buzzers, set off when density of form exceeded significance of content), and their own personal card for playing Buzzword Bingo. Panels would of course address serious issues ("Pomo Postures: Are We Fucking Theory or Is Theory Fucking Us?" and, "For Colored Girls Who Have Considered Suicide at Conferences Like These") as well as simply make fun for fun ("Licking the Lack," and "Cock and Bull, or Lacan Reconsidered").

OK—it was just an idea…

CHAPTER 14

Queering the State

LISA DUGGAN (1994)

The time has come to think about queering the state.[1]

1994 is a record year for antigay initiatives in the United States. At latest count, there are between eighteen and twenty-seven ballot battles gearing up, surpassing the previous record of sixteen in 1993. This rising tide of hate is partly a backlash in the face of an increasing number of gay rights initiatives. Last year sixteen state legislatures took up measures to grant civil rights protection to gay men and lesbians or to repeal antisodomy laws (most of these proposals failed). But antigay initiatives are also part of a grander scheme to organize a right-wing voting block to take on issues such as abortion rights, school curriculums and tax policies. This fight will be a daunting challenge to the organized lesbian and gay rights movement: the combined budgets of the six largest gay organizations total only about twelve million dollars, compared to the more than 210 million dollars in the combined budgets of the six largest right-wing religious organizations.[2]

The financial clout and cultural reach of these organizations should not be underestimated. For instance, Focus on the Family, based in Colorado Springs and founded by Dr. James Dobson, formerly a member of the Meese Commission on Pornography, boasts a ninety-million-dollar annual budget and affiliated Family Councils in thirty states. It distributes the antigay video *The Gay Agenda*, publishes nine magazines, and supports sixteen hundred radio programs. The Christian Coalition of Chesapeake,

Virginia, distributed forty million voter guides in the 1992 elections in its campaign to take over state and local Republican parties. It supports the Christian Broadcasting Network, the Family Channel, and the 700 Club, which reach millions of viewers daily, as well as two newsletters, *Religious Rights Watch* and *Christian American*. The coalition's leader, Pat Robertson, situates their agenda squarely in the middle of party politics: "We want ... to see a majority of the Republican Party in the hands of profamily Christians by 1996." Finally, Citizens for Excellence in Education, an arm of the National Association of Christian Educators led by Robert Simonds and located in Costa Mesa, California, distributes the manual, "How to Elect Christians to Public Office," and claims that thirty-five hundred Christians have been elected to school boards through its efforts.

It is clear that the strategies of the religious right go well beyond the simple articulation of homophobic, racist, and antifeminist sentiments. Their targets are precise and their program well formulated, as is indicated in a statement from a fundraising letter written by Simonds: "There are 15,700 school districts in America. When we get an active Christian parent's committee in operation in all districts, we can take complete control.... This would allow us to determine all local policy: select good textbooks, good curriculum programs, superintendents, and principals."[3]

But the challenge is not only organizational and financial. The rightwing antigay zealots have mobilized new strategies and new rhetorics that challenge the customary practices, arguments and slogans of liberal gay rights organizations. Successful opposition to the onslaught on the local, state, and national levels will require more than gearing up another round of the same kind of struggle. The opposition has changed its colors, and so must we.

The crisis specifically challenges those of us who teach and write about queer issues. We have already been faced with the rhetoric of crisis in higher education, mobilized by conservatives—a rhetoric that targets teaching and scholarship in the areas of class, race, gender, and sexuality as "politically correct," and as an effort to split, fragment, and destroy the idea of a common culture transmitted through education. In right-wing attacks on the state of higher education, lesbian and gay teachers and writers are often singled out as scholars of the particularly frivolous and absurd, though we are also often represented as uniquely powerful, able to overwhelm and destroy the very conception of a common culture.

These attacks are now paralleled by similar ones launched in the arena of national politics. Lesbian and gay efforts to secure civil rights protections have quickly become central in public debates of various kinds since the election of Bill Clinton. In conservative attacks on the new administration, queers are represented as ridiculous, with trivial political concerns, but also as a frightfully controlling presence in national politics. Shrill cries of the dominance of the Gay Lobby have been mobilized with lightning speed, especially in response to the debates surrounding the military. Local and state initiatives to roll back or prevent antidiscrimination measures pick up and elaborate these themes, as they also try out new strategies and rhetorics.

Even in friendly, internal critiques of the state of progressive politics—critiques in which the problem of fragmentation is addressed—gay and lesbian politics are sometimes invoked to represent the narrowing of focus (what could be narrower?) and the neglect of the common interest. In a field of progressive alliances often pejoratively described as a conglomeration of "special interest groups," lesbian and gay organizations seem to represent the most "special" interests of all. In this way we appear, on both the right and the left, as signifiers of the "crisis" of liberal politics itself.[4]

The problem for those of us who are engaged in queer scholarship and teaching, and who have a stake in queer politics, is how to respond to these attacks at a moment in time when we have unprecedented opportunities (we are present in university curriculums and national politics as never before), yet confront perilous and paralyzing assaults. At this moment, it is imperative that we respond to these attacks in the public arena from which they are launched. We cannot defend our teaching and scholarship without engaging in public debate and addressing the nature and operations of the state upon which our jobs and futures depend. In other words, the need to turn our attention to state politics is not only theoretical (though it is also that). It is time for queer intellectuals to concentrate on the creative production of strategies at the boundary of queer and nation—strategies specifically for queering the state.[5]

In formulating the terms of address in this situation, we are also now faced with the problem of a gap between the languages of our classrooms and scholarship, and the languages of public debate on the subject of homosexuality.

To illustrate what I mean by a language gap, I will recreate a dialogue between literary critic and founding mother of queer studies, Eve Kosofsky Sedgwick, and a young fact-checker for *Rolling Stone* magazine. Stacey D'Erasmo, friend and editor at the *Voice Literary Supplement*, wrote an article on gay and lesbian studies for *Rolling Stone* in which she initially referred to Sedgwick as "straight"—a mistake she later regretted.[6] When someone's sexual identity is referred to in print, most periodicals will verify it; the article was sent to a fact-checker with no particular expertise in the subject area. The fact-checker called Sedgwick. Imagine now a split screen, with Sedgwick on one side in her office at Duke University, and on the other side, the young fact-checker, chewing gum. The dialogue—which I have recreated in the manner of a docudrama from Stacey's secondhand account—is as follows:

Fact-checker: Professor Sedgwick, the article says here that you're straight—are ya straight?
Sedgwick: Did Stacey say I'm straight? I didn't tell her that.
Fact-checker: Well, it says here you're straight. Is that true?
Sedgwick: Well, under some discursive regimes I might be considered queer.
Fact-checker: Right. So you're not straight. Then you're gay?
Sedgwick: I didn't tell Stacey I was gay.
Fact-checker: Right.... But you just said you were queer ... isn't that the same as gay?
Sedgwick: Well, as I began to explain, under some discursive regimes ...
Fact-checker: Look, Professor Sedgwick, you're married, aren't ya? So you're straight.
Sedgwick: I never told Stacey I was married ...

I tell this story not to make fun of Sedgwick, who was attempting to interrupt and resist the imperative to sexual categorization, *nor* to condescend to the fact-checker, whose frustration followed from her attempts to decipher what Sedgwick was saying, but to illustrate the difficulty of communication across the gap between the predominantly constructionist language of queer studies and the essentialist presumptions of public discourse. One might easily imagine other examples. A *Nightline* panel of queer theorists could be assembled to discuss the new military policy: Judith Butler, D. A. Miller and Leo Bersani. It is not that these figures would have nothing interesting or useful to say. They would simply have a great deal of trouble making themselves understood (as many of us in the field of queer studies would). The problems are on the levels both of cultural legibility and political palatability. Imagine Bersani: "As I argue, Ted, in my article 'Is the Rectum a Grave?' ..." The ensuing discussion of heteromasculinity's terror of penetration might put Ted in *his* grave.

Right now, several conflicting languages occupy the centers of public discourse in the U.S. In conservative politics, the language of morality and "values" predominates. This language assumes the universality and normative superiority of marital heterosexual relationships, and positions homosexuality and bisexuality as immoral and sinful threats to family values. In liberal politics, both gay and gay-supportive, the rhetoric of rights and the call for an end to discrimination against a fixed minority population of lesbians, gays and (sometimes) bisexuals hold sway. More militant gay politics stresses difference over similarity, and assertion over assimilation, but still generally posits a fixed minority political constituency, though this is changing. Queer politics is beginning to develop a strategy of public display and cultural intervention—a strategy positing a shifting, oppositional constituency. This politics is still highly contested, and only ambivalently constructionist, however.

The language of queer studies, on the other hand, is overwhelmingly constructionist. Queer studies scholars are engaged in a project of denaturalizing categories of sexual identity and mobilizing various critiques of the political practices referred to under the rubric "identity politics." Three of these critiques might be summarized as follows:

1. The homosexual/heterosexual polarity is historically recent and culturally specific. The notion that these sexual categories are fixed, mutually exclusive and mark individual bodies and personalities is a modern Western development. In other times and places, sexual acts between or among persons of the same sex have been organized and understood in dramatically different ways.

2. The production of a politics from a fixed identity position privileges those for whom that position is the primary or only marked identity. The result for lesbian and gay politics is a tendency to center prosperous white men as the representative homosexuals. (We can see this at work in the military issue. Though proportionately many more lesbians are discharged than gay men, the issue is nearly always represented as centering around men.) Every production of "identity" creates exclusions that reappear at the margins like ghosts to haunt identity-based politics. In the case of lesbian/gay politics, such exclusions have included bisexuals and transgender persons, among others.

3. Identity politics only replaces closets with ghettos. The closet as a cultural space has been defined and enforced by the existence of the ghetto. In coming out of the closet, identity politics offers us another bounded, fixed space of humiliation and another kind of social isolation. Homosexual desire is localized—projected out and isolated in the community of bodies found in the gay ghetto. In this sense, identity politics lets the larger society off the hook of anxiety about sexual difference.[7]

These critiques are now so well known and widely circulated in queer studies scholarship and classrooms that, in my own course called "Queer

Cultures" at Brown University, there are no worse epithets than to accuse someone of "essentialism," or of engaging in identity politics. This identity-bashing is presented as the progressive cutting edge of politics as well as theory—but it can also be framed in ways that are quite reactionary. It can be a way of reinventing the closet, of condescending to lesbian and gay scholars, students and activists, and of avoiding (if not outright despising) lesbian/gay/queer activism altogether—while posing as politically more progressive than thou. But the critical insights of queer theory might also be mobilized (and, I would argue, *should* be) to forge a political language that can take us beyond the limiting rhetorics of liberal gay rights and militant nationalism.

When we turn our attention to this project, we run into difficulty the moment we step outside our classrooms, books, journals and conferences. How do we represent our political concerns in public discourse? In try-ing to do this, in trying to hold the ground of the fundamental criticism of the very language of current public discourse that queer theory has enabled, in trying to translate our constructionist languages into terms that have the power to transform political practices, we are faced with sev-eral difficulties.

First, the discussion of the construction of categories of sexual identity resists translation into terms that are culturally legible and thus usable in consequential public debates. To illustrate this difficulty, let us imagine that you are asked to appear on the *Oprah Winfrey* show to talk about public school curriculums. Guest A says material on gays will influence children to think gay is okay and thus to become disgusting perverts themselves. Guest B, from Parents and Friends of Lesbians and Gays, says that this will not happen because sexual identity is fixed by the age of three, if not in utero. You are Guest C—what do you say? That "the production of queer sexualities is historically and culturally conditioned," that if gay materi-als in class are conducive to the production of queer sexualities, you are squarely in favor of their use? The difficulties here on the level of legibility and on the level of political palatability are readily apparent.

Second, the use of constructionist language to discuss homosexuality tends to leave heterosexuality in its naturalized place—it can be taken up by homophobes to feed the fantasy of a world without homosexual bodies and desires. "If history can make them, history can also *un*make them" seems to be the logic here. A decade ago, Dorothy Allison and Esther Newton suggested responding to this danger in constructionist arguments by producing buttons demanding "Deconstruct Heterosexu-ality First." Of course, we can respond as the button suggests and work to denaturalize heterosexuality (which work in queer studies is, in fact, doing), but this is unlikely to be received in current public debates without guffaws and disbelief.

The usual response to these difficulties is to resort to what is called "strategic essentialism": the use of essentialist categories and identity politics in public debates because that is all anyone can understand and we need to be effective in the political arena. I take the concerns that lead to the embrace of strategic essentialism seriously, but I think that it is ultimately an unproductive solution.[8] It allows sexual difference and queer desires to continue to be localized in homosexualized bodies. It consigns us, in the public imaginary, to the realms of the particular and the parochial, the defense team for a fixed minority, that most "special" of special interest groups—again, letting everyone else off the hook.

I would argue that we need to find a way to close the language gap in queer studies and queer politics. We need to do this especially with reference to the operations of the state. Though queer politics is presently claiming public and cultural space in imaginative new ways (kiss-ins, for example), the politics of the state are generally being left to lesbian and gay civil rights strategies. These strategies are greatly embattled at present, and there are still many gains to be made through their deployment. But they are increasingly ineffective in the face of new homophobic initiatives; they appear unable to generate new rhetorics and tactics in the face of new sorts of attacks—attacks in many ways designed specifically to disable identity-based antidiscrimination policies.[9] We cannot afford to fall back on strategic essentialism (it will not get us out of the trouble we are now in), and we cannot afford to abandon the field.

We do have some precedents. Scholars and activists working on the issues surrounding the AIDS crisis managed to transport the work of theory into the arena of politics and public policy with astonishing speed and commitment.[10] In the arts, as well, the films of Isaac Julien and the Sankofa collective and those of Marlon Riggs (*Tongues United* and *Color Adjustment*, both shown on public television) have brought into public discourse very complex ideas about the construction of racial and sexual identities and their intersections.

I have a modest proposal for attempting this translation in the context of our current political situation. We need to find ways to respond to two developing right-wing strategies: No Promo Homo and No Special Rights.

The No Promo Homo campaigns, designated as such by attorney and activist Nan D. Hunter, attempt to proscribe the public "promotion" of homosexuality, at least when state funds are involved.[11] These campaigns began appearing in 1978 with the Briggs initiative in California. The following list provides a brief history of these efforts:

- The Briggs initiative (California, 1978) would have permitted the firing of any school employee who engaged in "advocating, soliciting, imposing, encouraging, or promoting of private or public homosexual activity directed at, or likely to come to the attention of, school children and/or other employees."
- The Helms Amendment to the Labor-Health and Human Services Appropriation Act for Fiscal Year 1988 provided the caveat that "none of the funds made available under this Act to the Centers for Disease Control shall be used to provide AIDS education, information, or prevention materials and activities that promote or encourage, directly ['or indirectly' was removed], homosexual activities."
- Britain's Clause 28 of the Local Government Act of 1988 stated that local governments would not be permitted to "promote homosexuality or public material for the promotion of homosexuality" or "promote the teaching ... of the acceptability of homosexuality as a pretended family relationship." Nor could government funding go to private entities engaged in those acts.
- In 1989, in the wake of a conservative outcry over reports that the National Endowment for the Arts had supported an exhibit of Robert Mapplethorpe's photographs, the U.S. Congress enacted legislation prohibiting the NEA from funding "obscene" materials, "including but not limited to, depictions of sadomasochism, homoeroticism, the sexual exploitation of children, or individuals engaged in sex acts."
- The 1992 Oregon ballot initiative, appropriating the basic form of Clause 28, would have required that "state, regional, local governments and their properties and monies shall not be used to promote, encourage, or facilitate homosexuality." This legislation was defeated at the state level, then passed by several localities through ballot initiatives. Another effort to pass similar legislation was defeated in 1994.

Interestingly enough, No Promo Homo campaigns concede the privacy arguments advanced by lesbian/gay advocates over the past two decades. There is no attempt to police "private" behavior. Instead, there is an attempt to counter identity claims and antidiscrimination efforts based on those claims through the policing of speech, that is, "promotion" and "advocacy." These campaigns deny that lesbian/gay identities are fixed, and posit instead a contagion theory. (This may partly explain the turn to biology as a grounding for identity by some gay rights advocates and their liberal supporters, as a counter to the contagion theory at the heart of conservative strategies.) These strategies also borrow from the antiabortion movement their focus on restriction through limitation of state funding.

In addition to conceding privacy arguments, No Promo Homo campaigns also concede some right of access to "public" space, but only public space that is not supported by a state apparatus or by state revenues. This is an extremely constrained "public," in that state funds and institutions reach broadly into educational, cultural, and political life in the U.S.

The appeal in these campaigns is to some notion of a "neutral" state. The argument being made is "you can do what you want" (the concession to privacy) and "you can be who you are" (the concession to identity), but "you can't spread it around on *my* dime." This, of course, is a profoundly false neutrality. Queers are presented as those who wish illegitimately to recruit the state into "promoting" a single minority viewpoint, a parochial "special" interest.

Other campaigns that are not, strictly speaking, No Promo Homo campaigns pick up this theme as well. The Colorado ballot initiative of 1992 called for a ban on antidiscrimination legislation to protect lesbian, gay, and bisexual rights,[12] a variation on the many repeal initiatives which began with Anita Bryant's notorious Save the Children campaign in 1977. Many of the 1994 antigay initiatives are straightforward attempts to repeal existing antidiscrimination legislation; others are modeled on the more expansive Colorado effort to preempt the antidiscrimination strategy before it is mobilized. The Colorado antigay activists circulated the popular and effective slogan, "No Special Rights."

We know who really has the special rights. In fact, the state is deeply involved in regulating and "promoting" heterosexuality. It is queers who have been excluded from the benefits of state support in all kinds of areas, from tax law to education to support for cultural production, and more. As Michael Warner has argued, "The dawning realization that themes of homophobia and heterosexism may be read in almost any document of our culture means that we are only beginning to have an idea how widespread those institutions and accounts are."[13]

I therefore propose that we respond to the No Promo Homo and No Special Rights campaigns, *not* with our familiar emphases on equality (we're just like you and want the same rights) or difference (we're here, we're queer, get used to it) *only*, but with campaigns of our own: No Promo Hetero, or *Whose* Special Rights? What I am suggesting in substance is that we look beyond the language of rights claims for a fixed minority and calls for antidiscrimination (rhetorical positioning largely borrowed from the civil rights movement and feminism), and instead borrow from and transform another liberal discourse, that surrounding the effort to disestablish state religion, to separate church and state. We might become the new disestablishmentarians, the state religion we wish to disestablish being the religion of heteronormativity.[14] We might argue that public policy and public institutions may not legitimately compel, promote or prefer inter-gender relationships over intragender attachments. Without appropriat-ing too much of the liberal baggage of the discourse of religious tolerance, we might borrow from this rhetoric a strategy for reversing the terms of antigay propaganda and exposing the myriad ways that state apparatuses promote, encourage and produce "special rights" for heterosexuality.

A rhetorical move such as this has several advantages. First, it high-lights the embeddedness of heteronormativity in a wide range of state poli-cies, institutions and practices. Tracing out in a concrete way the extent of the state's involvement in promoting heterosexuality would be a useful, though enormous, project. Media materials would be effective here. For instance, under the banner of Whose Special Rights? we might use bill-boards, posters, video, film and other published material to outline the ways in which heterosexuality is endorsed through state activity (educa-tion, tax law, marriage and family life, and so on), specifying the unfair preferences that operate in each area.

Second, such a move may be articulated within the terms of a widely understood and accepted liberal discourse (the state may no more estab-lish a state sexuality than a state religion, a heterosexual presumption has no more place in public life than a presumption of Christianity). In other words, it could be framed in terms that are completely understandable within this political culture. Yet, third, its implications are much more radical and far-reaching than the rights claims we are currently forward-ing. From marriage to employment, and from health care policies to public school curricula, the aggressive deployment of this argument could trans-form the terms of public debate.

The religion analogy works better in lots of ways than analogies to liberal discourses surrounding race and gender. For instance, affirmative action strategies, which have had some limited success in relation to gender and race, would never work for us. We need strategies that do not require us to specify who is and is not a "member" of our group. If sexual desire is compared to religion, we can see it as not natural, fixed, or ahistorical, yet not trivial or shallow, as the term "lifestyle choice" implies. Religion is understood as not biological or fixed; for instance, people can and do con-vert. But it is also understood as a deep commitment. That commitment is seen as highly resistant to coerced conversion, and deserving of expression and political protection. That is why an argument for "disestablishment" might work better in many situations than calls for an end to discrimina-tion against an identifiable population.

Deconstructing heteronormativity reverses the terms of No Promo Homo and No Special Rights campaigns which try to claim that the lesbian/gay movement is seeking privilege, and which call upon the populist disdain for privilege to discredit our political efforts. Instead we point out, on *Larry King Live*, who really is trying to maintain privilege. Such a reversal has the potential to expose and disable the conservative rhetoric in ways that antidiscrimination language cannot, stripping it of its phony populist appeal.

As Dorothy Allison and Esther Newton proposed, it is a strategy that in a sense deconstructs heterosexuality first. Rather than relying on the solidification of lesbian and gay identities, it attacks the natural and preferred status of heterosexuality. No Promo Hetero and Whose Special Rights? would be, in a sense, tactical reversals (of No Promo Homo and No Special Rights), but ones that work to destabilize heteronormativity rather than to naturalize gay identities.

Moreover, this destabilization brackets debates about morality and values. As in the case of religious differences, we do not need to persuade or convert others to our view. We simply argue for "disestablishment" of state endorsement for one view over another. It brackets political differences among progressive activists (liberal assimilationists, militant nationalists, and constructionists) and debates about biology (the gay brain, the lesbian twins); we can agree on this strategic move without having to resolve our differences. And it makes a case for freedom of association (to form relationships) and freedom of speech (acknowledgment or assertion) for everyone, rather than asks for "rights" for a fixed minority. In this way, we can escape being positioned as narrow and parochial. Of course, antidiscrimination efforts work to this end as well, arguing for an end to discrimination based on anyone's sexual preference or orientation. (The success of the anti-Briggs campaign in California was partly due to such an emphasis on *everybody's* rights.) But this is becoming more difficult to do, as the No Promo Homo and No Special Rights rhetoric becomes more sophisticated at forcing gay rights activists to specify the group they represent. Turning the tables, asking right-wing activists to justify the "special rights" of heterosexuality, might help undermine this new rhetoric.

Finally, a disestablishment strategy does not require us to localize or naturalize gendered desire. But the disadvantages of such a strategy mirror the advantages. Because this case is formulated within the terms of liberalism, it may trap us in as many ways as it releases us. For instance, in some ways it seems to construct a zone of liberty in negative relation to the state (it argues about what the state can*not* do). This is not the historical moment when we want to set up a negative relation to state power, or slip into limiting forms of libertarianism. The arguments would need to be carefully framed to emphasize that state institutions must be even-handed in the arena of sexuality, not that sexuality should be removed from state action completely. Activists might also make the crucial distinction between state institutions (which must, in some sense, be neutral) and "the public" arena, where explicit advocacy is not only allowable but desirable.[15]

The radical implications of a destabilizing strategy, set in motion as they are by liberal arguments, will not be invisible to our opponents. We might very well still find ourselves beyond the pale of the *MacNeil-Lehrer Newshour* and *The New York Times*. We might expect a very strong response—perhaps the argument that the state *must* and *should* promote and prefer heterosexuality as the foundation for "the family." This response would be very difficult to reply to, given the powerful valence of "family."[16] But it would usefully put conservatives on the defensive. They would have to acknowledge and defend heterosexual privilege, rather than claim we are the ones who want unfair preferences. It would force them back into an old conservative argument, taking the *au courant* antiprivilege spin off their revamped rhetoric.

No Promo Hetero will probably not be successful in winning any kind of disestablishment of heteronormativity in the near future. Its success in the short run might be the rhetorical disabling of conservative strategies. But even in the event of this kind of success, it is not a broad solution, but only a local tactic embedded in a larger strategy of destabilizing heteronormativity. It is one among many conceivable tactics. It is not meant to replace civil rights strategies, and it would not be appropriate in all situations. There are many problems in legal and state institutions that it could not address (antiprostitution laws, for instance). We have to keep imagining new ways both to respond to attacks and to put our own vision forward.

I have one other suggestion for reconceptualizing our relation to state politics. In representing our situation in public discourse, we need a less defensive, more politically self-assertive set of linguistic and conceptual tools to talk about sexual difference. (This is the problem to which a nascent queer politics is now productively addressing itself.) We might begin to think about sexual difference, not in terms of naturalized identities, but as a form a *dissent*, understood not simply as speech, but as a constellation of nonconforming practices, expressions and beliefs.[17] Here, again, I am drawing from the arena of religion. The right to religious dissent has been understood not solely as the right to belief, but as a right to practices expressive of those beliefs. Framing our difference in this way would be useful in several contexts. First, a notion of dissent would present our difference as oppositional, bringing into the frame the illegitimacy of the social and political privilege accorded to heterosexuality. Second, this notion of dissent would join together our right to sexual conduct, both desire and expression, as well as our right to a multiplicity of possible shifting identities, and our right to state a viewpoint and promote it, to express ourselves publicly, politically, and culturally. This is useful now because of the move in both mainstream religious organizations and the military to separate "orientation" and "conduct," permitting the former (a concession to antidiscrimination arguments) but not the latter. We need to aggressively rejoin these elements, not cooperate in their separation. Some notion of "dissent" might work to that end.

Finally, the framework of "dissent" could help us think about a central paradox of sexual difference: it is both malleable—historically, culturally and in many individual lives—and yet highly resistant to coercive change. This paradox of malleability and resistance is built into the general understanding of how "dissent" works; people change their opinions and practices over time, yet will hold to them under torture. This is a paradox that neither notions of identity nor fluidity can quite capture.

Extensive transformation of these strategies will be necessary beyond the terms outlined here, if they are actually to be mobilized. If we can use the discourses of religious liberty and religious dissent at all, we must rework them into a dramatically new shape. This has been done before. The U.S. civil rights movement drew on and transformed familiar religious rhetoric, reworking it in light of new political needs and cultural practices to get it to do a kind of cultural work it was never designed to do. The question is: At this historical moment, can we transform *any* liberal rhetoric in the interests ultimately of going beyond liberal categories and solutions? Or, given the difficulty of translating our most radical insights and arguments into effective public discourse, can we afford not to try?

Whether this specific strategy will fly or not, we need to think seriously about how to formulate the insights of queer theory and transport them into public discourse. We need (I emphasize *need* here) to be both transformative *and* effective. We need not only to defend ourselves in the university, in the polity, and in the streets, but to move our political vision forward beyond the limits of lesbian and gay rights and militant nationalism. We need to do this in a way that allows us to address the general without losing sight of the particular. (We need both to specify our own situation and to reach beyond it.) We need to do this for the defense, promotion, and advocacy not only of our scholarship and teaching, but of our political, personal, and indeed our physical lives.

CHAPTER 15

The Discipline Problem

Queer Theory Meets Lesbian and Gay History

LISA DUGGAN (1994)

In 1991, I was interviewed along with three other historians of sexuality by a history department at a small, elite Northeastern college. My interview ended in disaster. Someone asked: "How could undergraduates be expected to read Foucault?" Someone else asked: "Given your, uh, interests, could we expect that you would even know who the *presidents* were?" I was sent to talk to a dean who tactfully suggested to me that my subject of research was probably really within the domain of psychology, not history. The college hired none of the historians of sexuality, canceling the search entirely for two years.[1]

In 1992, I covered the Lesbian and Gay Studies Conference at Rutgers University for *The Village Voice*.[2] I called the organizers to ask why there were so few historical or ethnographic panels. I was told that there were in fact *many* historical panels that the organizers had made special efforts to include. These were pointed out to me. Nearly all the presentations featured analyses of fictional texts, given by people employed in English departments.

I tell these two stories to make this point: lesbian and gay historians are relatively isolated from two crucial sources of support—the material and institutional support of university history departments, and the intellectual engagement and support of other scholars in the field of lesbian and gay or queer studies. And for both academic and public intellectuals, isolation leads to material as well as cultural impoverishment and decline.

Academic and intellectual isolation (though not political isolation) used to be generally shared within lesbian and gay studies. The first generation of scholars often worked outside the university, or in uneasy relationship with the few institutions supporting their scholarship.[3] During the past decade, however, a new generation of lesbian and gay scholars has been welcomed into the academy; opportunities for jobs and publication have expanded exponentially. But this welcome is both limited and far from secure. Unfortunately, history departments in particular remain largely hostile environments for new work in lesbian and gay studies. Why?

With a very few exceptions, history departments are not hiring historians of sexuality. Most of the work within history departments, particularly on lesbian and gay history in the U.S., is being done by scholars who got tenure before beginning their research in this area. And because so few have been hired, few new such historians are being trained. Again, why? I think this failure is not solely or even largely due to conservatism or stark prejudice (though I do not mean to underestimate the continuing importance of these sources of hostility). I would attribute the failure to hire and train historians of sexuality, and lesbian and gay historians specifically, to at least three other significant factors: (1) Sexuality, as a subject matter, is treated as trivial, as more about gossip than politics, more about psychology than history. The subject generates much nervous joking at faculty meetings and symposia. Even progressive and leftist historians are not exempt from treating sexuality as somehow disconnected from, and less important than, other subjects of research. (2) Lesbian and gay history, particularly, is understood as the history of a marginalized "minority" population, as the story of a small percentage of the citizenry and their doings. This history is seldom understood as linked to the study of a central historical process—the production and organization of sexualities. This is a problem that afflicts historians of race and gender as well, when their work is understood as "about" marginalized or ghettoized populations—women, African-Americans, Latinos, Asian Americans or Native Americans—rather than as concerned with the operations of social hierarchies in the broadest possible sense. (A well-known historian was quoted to me by a graduate student as saying in his U.S. history survey course: "I'm using the word 'race,' now, but it's really a code word we use for African-Americans.") (3) Historians of sexuality fit uneasily into existing job categories, and may be considered only if they have a "major" field in women's history, family history or cultural history. Search committees will often then debate whether the candidate is "really" a women's historian or a historian of sexuality, for instance. There are virtually no advertisements that even mention history of sexuality or lesbian and gay history; the most likely relevant job category for such historians is cultural history. But history of sexuality should not have to hide itself under the supposedly "broader" rubric of cultural history, any more than women's history should have to hide itself within family history.

Relations with history departments are just the first difficulty faced by the field of lesbian and gay history. In addition, as lesbian/gay studies has expanded, work has become increasingly concentrated in fields devoted to textual analysis—primarily literary and media studies based in the twentieth century. Students interested in lesbian and gay studies have turned to these growth areas, where there is acceptance and faculty support, when considering graduate studies; they are frequently warned away from history departments. Thus there has been a progressive impoverishment of the empirical, historical grounding for textual analyses of various sorts. The impressive expansion of increasingly sophisticated analyses is balanced precariously atop a stunted archive. (We get yet another article on Gertrude Stein, without any accompanying expansion of the research base for analyzing the changing discursive context for her writing at the turn of the century.[4])

The difficulty here is not merely one of imbalanced growth, however; it is also one of strained relations between what is now being called "queer theory," and lesbian and gay history. Queer theory, located within or in proximity to critical theory and cultural studies, has grown steadily in publication, sophistication and academic prestige. Queer theorists are engaged in at least three areas of critique: (1) the critique of humanist narratives which posit the progress of the self and of history, and thus tell the story of the heroic progress of gay liberationists against forces of repression, (2) the critique of empiricist methods which claim directly to represent the transparent "reality" of "experience," and claim to relate, simply and objectively, what happened, when and why, and (3) the critique of identity categories presented as stable, unitary or "authentic."

These critiques, applied to lesbian and gay history texts, might produce a fascinating discussion—but so far, they have not. Queer theorists have generally either ignored lesbian/gay history texts, or treated them with condescension. Lesbian and gay historians, in turn, have largely ignored the critical implications of queer theory for their scholarly practice.[5]

Queer theorists' condescending treatment of earlier ghettoized authors and texts has often struck me as a kind of projected shame, or perhaps a fear of the humiliation associated with the ghetto. The emphasis in much academically privileged work on the analysis of canonized literary and artistic texts or widely circulated pop culture texts implicitly aligns the critic with privilege or popularity. The relative neglect of studies of ghettoized or stigmatized populations and texts keeps the associated denigration and humiliation at a distance. When earlier, ghettoized work by lesbian and gay scholars goes unacknowledged, or is dismissed with an implied sneer, the hierarchy which has endowed the academic author with greater institutional resources and cultural privilege is reinforced. How radical! How subversive and transformative!

On the other hand, the lack of engagement by lesbian and gay historians with critical theory and cultural studies (widely shared by historians in general, especially historians of the U.S.) is proving to be a devastating mistake. Though I would not argue that it is necessary for all historians to become poststructuralists, or to write within the framework of cultural studies, I would argue that it is necessary to *engage* with cultural and critical theory across disciplinary lines in order to remain intellectually vital. And for lesbian and gay history, the need for such engagement is especially pressing—historicizing sexuality is a project that demands rigorous analysis of changing identity categories, and explication of the ideological work that such categories perform. Theoretical texts characterized by attention to the workings of systems of representation, and by close analysis of categorical imperatives and codes of language embedded in particular ideological regimes, can challenge and enrich the work of historians. Social history methods, based on empirical strategies that treat documentary sources as transparent windows onto the "real" experience of populations, hinder our ability to analyze the ideological construction of "documents," and hide the political narratives underpinning our own texts. Until lesbian and gay historians engage the critical implications of queer theory—as well as race theory, feminist theory and emerging theoretical work on nationalism and imperialism—their productions will constitute a political and intellectual backwater (a backwater within queer studies, and within intellectual life more broadly).

Let me be more concrete, and give examples of the lack of engagement I am talking about.

1

In 1990, Jeffrey Escoffier published a widely discussed article, "Inside the Ivory Closet: The Challenges Facing Lesbian and Gay Studies."[6] Jeff Escoffier, an activist and intellectual in the Bay area and now in New York City, has been an editor of *Socialist Review*, an organizer of the San Francisco Lesbian/Gay Historical Society, and a founder and editor of the now defunct national lesbian and gay quarterly *Out/Look*. He also has a

Ph.D. in sociology, and has taught and published widely in lesbian and gay studies over a period of two decades. "Inside the Ivory Closet," published in *Out/Look*, was an attempt to sketch out a generational conflict that Escoffier saw emerging in his field between Stonewall era scholars with roots in political communities (mostly historians and archivists, also some sociologists, anthropologists and journalists) and post-Stonewall academics with disciplinary concerns and university jobs (largely literary scholars and critical theorists). In this article, Escoffier carefully maps out the history and accomplishments of the first generation during the period 1969 to 1983, and includes the work of radical feminists and gay leftists, women of color and sex radicals. He argues that the major intellectual accomplishment of this diversely productive crew was the critique of essentializing, universal categories of identity, and the forging of a theory of the historical, social construction of lesbian and gay identities—identities of recent vintage which have intersected and interacted with changing identities of race, gender, class and nation. He then warns that the work of this first generation is in danger of being erased and replaced by that of the second, more privileged generation of lesbian and gay academics.

Escoffier specifically asks whether the second generation is losing touch with the political concerns of lesbian and gay communities through its deployment of an arcane and frequently obfuscating language, and its address to limited audiences who are schooled in technical vocabularies and subscribe to rarefied academic journals. He asks whether this younger generation is falling out of dialogue with broad-based publics, becoming an unrepresentative and intellectually narrow professional elite.

In asking these questions, Escoffier is expressing the anxieties and resentments of his peers—frustrated lesbian/gay historians, sociologists and anthropologists (among others) who believe that their work is being ghettoized, not just within university departments but by lesbian/gay studies scholars as well. Many of these activist-intellectuals see their pioneering work being strip-mined for research and insights, but not cited or engaged seriously by queer theorists. But in representing this frustration, Escoffier does not engage with the projects and points of view of the second generation whose work he questions. Though he offers a list of the names of scholars, including David Miller, Lee Edelman and Eve Kosofsky Sedgwick (among others), he does not map the work or lay out the accomplishments of those who have been publishing in the years since 1983, as he does for the earlier authors and publications. This is because it is the first generation on whose behalf he is writing. It is the earlier work that he wants to describe and defend, in the face of denigration or erasure.

In structuring his argument this way, Escoffier has set up an opposition between generations that overstates both the homogeneity within each group and the points of contrast between them. He neglects the possibility that many among the first generation may become narrow themselves, "out of touch" with younger activists as well as intellectuals. He omits mention of the many bridge or transition figures whose work cannot be easily slotted into his generational schema. In correctly pointing out the importance of community-based institutions for Stonewall-era scholarship (especially periodicals such as the Toronto-based newspaper, *The Body Politic*, and history projects such as the Lesbian Herstory Archives), he invents a location of imagined unity and political authenticity—"the community." And he completely omits any mention of the many theoretically informed, younger scholar-activists who exemplify precisely the sort of politically engaged work he admires in the first generation—writers such as Cindy Patton and Kobena Mercer.

Nonetheless, Escoffier's article pointed out a tension, and the existence of a hierarchy that is painfully obvious to most of those situated at its lower end. He performed the invaluable service of articulating a grievance, and offering a history and defense for a decade's worth of pioneering scholarship, much of it eked out in the margins of daily lives consumed with wage labor, and stigmatized outside of the ghettoized communities in which it was forged. Interestingly, academic scholars of Escoffier's second generation gossiped and grouched about the article, but did not respond to it seriously. Though it was being discussed nearly everywhere I went during the year it was published, those included on the post-Stonewall list ignored it in print, and occasionally shunned Escoffier in person.

Even someone as politically sensitive and personally generous as Eve Sedgwick succumbed to the mood of condescension. In a review of Cindy Patton's book, *Inventing AIDS*, for the *Lesbian and Gay Studies Newsletter* in 1991, Sedgwick responded to Escoffier's salvo. She used Patton's book as an example to correctly argue that Escoffier had completely neglected AIDS activism and scholarship, and had thus missed one of the most significant crossroads for theory and politics during the 1980s. But she then goes on to concede absolutely nothing to Escoffier's article. She recognizes no hierarchies, perceives no basis for his concerns. (It makes one wonder—are hierarchies *always* invisible to those who profit from them?) She misrepresents his arguments, quoting him out of context, and concludes her piece by calling him "anti-intellectual."[7] I wonder if this particular accusation, in an academic newsletter, would be as acceptable if Escoffier were a professor rather than a public intellectual and activist?

Sedgwick's was one of a very small number of responses to Escoffier in print. But if the article had touched such a nerve, if it was worth gossip and insult, then surely it merited acknowledgment and serious debate.[8]

2

There are very few figures who can cross over the gap between the practice of history and the arguments of critical theory, and there are few historians who can speak specifically to the ramifications for women's history of feminist theorists' work on gender. Joan Scott occupies both those roles, bringing both critical theory and the insights of feminists to an often-reluctant historical profession. The republication of her article "The Evidence of Experience" in Henry Abelove, Michele Aina Barale and David Halperin's *The Lesbian and Gay Studies Reader* is a clear indication of the importance of Scott's work for the field of lesbian and gay studies as well. This article elegantly presents the post-structuralist critique of the use of the category of "experience" by historians, and of the strategy of "giving voice to the voiceless" or "making the invisible visible."

The article begins with an extended quotation from Samuel Delany's memoir, *The Motion of Light in Water*, which describes his vision of a scene inside a gay bathhouse in 1963. Scott presents Delany's observations ("what *this* experience said was that there was a population—not of individual homosexuals ... not of hundreds, not of thousands, but rather of millions of gay men, and that history had, actively and already, created for us whole galleries of institutions, good and bad, to accommodate our sex") and interprets him to claim that,

> Knowledge is gained through vision; vision is a direct apprehension of a world of transparent objects. In this conceptualization, the visible is privileged; writing is then put at its service. Seeing is the origin of knowing. Writing is reproduction, transmission—the communication of knowledge gained through (visual, visceral) experience.[9]

She then makes an abrupt transition by arguing that, "This kind of communication has long been the mission of historians documenting the lives of those omitted or overlooked in accounts of the past." This shift from the workings of memory in memoir to the mission of history signals the logic of the rest of the article. Scott takes critical aim at the reliance of social historians on an unexamined notion of "experience," which serves as a foundational concept in their discourse.

Scott's critique, following upon her use of Delany, centers the work of historians of homosexuality as illustrative of the practices of historians of difference in general. She critiques this work in the following manner:

> Histories that document the "hidden" world of homosexuality, for example, show the impact of silence and repression on the lives of those affected by it and bring to light the history of their suppression and exploitation. But the project of making experience visible *precludes* [emphasis added] critical examination of the workings of the ideological system itself, its categories of representation (homosexual/heterosexual, man/woman, black/white as fixed immutable identities), its premises about what these categories mean and how they operate, and of its notions of subjects, origin, and cause. ... History is a chronology that makes experience visible, but in which categories appear as nonetheless ahistorical: desire, homosexuality, heterosexuality, femininity, masculinity, sex, and even sexual practices become so many fixed entities being played out over time, but not themselves historicized. Presenting the story in this way excludes, or at least understates, the historically variable interrelationship between the meanings "homosexual" and "heterosexual," the constitutive force each has for the other, and the contested and changing nature of the terrain that they simultaneously occupy.[10]

But *whom* is Scott critiquing here? Clearly, she has shifted ground away from Delany, though his memoir provides the platform she steps off from. She is evidently critiquing lesbian and gay history texts, but she does not cite or quote a single one in the text or notes to her entire article. Later in the article, she does cite feminist historians of whom she is critical (Judith Newton and Christine Stansell), and she provides an extended critique of a widely circulated article by John Toews (this article's defense of the historical concept of "experience" seems ultimately to be her central target).[11] But lesbian and gay history texts, which provide her with the initial critical focus for her arguments, appear as mute and primitive "others," spoken for but unreferenced, and profoundly misrepresented in Scott's exegesis.

For example, Scott argues that the texts she is describing present homosexual and heterosexual as "fixed immutable identities," and claims that categories appear as "ahistorical." Certainly, many lesbian/gay political texts do use these categories ahistorically; the dominant discourses of liberal lesbian and gay political action take the homosexual/heterosexual polarity as universal and axiomatic. But most lesbian and gay historians have challenged such assumptions, and have placed the historicizing and denaturalizing of categories of sexual identity at the center of their agendas. Following on the pioneering work of Jeffrey Weeks and John D'Emilio, who presented the historical emergence of the homo/hetero polarity over the last century as political, contingent and contested, Jonathan Ned Katz wrote in 1983,

> Because the homosexual/heterosexual distinction became the socially dominant usage, and is still so, it is useful to note in some detail that opposition in the process of its earliest American formulation. The homosexual/heterosexual distinction is now so deeply ingrained that it is difficult for us to think in other terms. An historical view helps us to situate the homo/hetero dualism in time, and distance ourselves from it. ...
>
> To the extent that homosexual and heterosexual represent a limiting imposition on humanity, a labeling created for the purpose, and functioning in the interest of social control, we should consider how to transcend that polarity in theory and practice. To the extent that "lesbian" and "gay" represent, simply, reverse affirmations of the old homosexuality, thereby reproducing it, we need to ask how we might transcend ... categorization. ...[12]

This kind of argument is not unique, but has appeared in lesbian and gay history texts since the late 1970s. If Scott had engaged with these texts, she would have needed to significantly alter her argument. Weeks, D'Emilio and Katz (among many others) undertake a project that Scott describes as simply impossible when she writes that "the project of making experience visible *precludes* critical examination of the workings of the ideological system itself, its categories of representation," and so on. Weeks and company set out specifically to make the historical "experience" of lesbians and gay men "visible" *at the same time* that categories of identity are presented as historical, contingent and political—as products of changing and contested systems of representation. At a minimum, including such texts would have required that Scott acknowledge and critically evaluate this project (there is much in these texts with which she might take issue, without resorting to misrepresentation), rather than dismiss it so presumptively with that little word "precludes."

Scott expends a lot of ink in "The Evidence of Experience" restating the Foucauldian critique of the repressive hypothesis, while erroneously attaching that hypothesis to lesbian and gay history texts—texts that explicitly contested the repressive hypothesis and approvingly cited Foucault themselves by the early 1980s. But she also offers an exploration of historians' use of the category of "experience" as foundational, and explores the possibilities for an antifoundationalist historical practice. These latter projects are timely, compelling and important for the future of history writing. And she supplies a model in her article for a way of returning to reconsider a text for which she had earlier provided a reductive reading. Toward the end of "The Evidence of Experience" she writes,

> The reading I offered of Delany at the beginning of this essay is an example of the kind of reading I want to avoid. I would like now to present another reading—one suggested to me by literary critic Karen Swann—as a way of indicating what might be involved in historicizing the notion of experience.[13]

The rereading Scott goes on to provide is nuanced and sensitive to the ways in which memory, history and sight are related in Delany's work. She rejects her earlier flattening of his observations into a distorted polemic. I would suggest that she return to the lesbian and gay history texts she reads with similar reductiveness, and engage in dialogue with them. Rather than an opposition, in which her own theoretical sophistication is offered as wholly superior to the mute and dominated texts she leaves uncited, she might produce instead a critical dialogue in which appreciation might play some role. As it stands, the hierarchy she produces in her article only reproduces the privilege of the elite academic voice over the writing of those who have labored with far less support, reward and recognition for their work.[14]

The lack of direct engagement that I am pointing to here is two-sided. Scott does not refer directly to the texts she implicitly critiques, and no lesbian or gay historian thus far (including myself) has responded to Scott's widely circulated article.

Lack of engagement, isolation ... for lesbian and gay history the result is a kind of homelessness. Much work goes on without consistent material or institutional support (Jonathan Ned Katz, Allan Bérubé). Other historical work takes place in English departments (Henry Abelove, Martha Vicinus) or in institutionally marginal interdisciplinary locations (especially women's studies). Major figures in the field of lesbian/gay history often teach at institutions which do not train graduate students (John D'Emilio, Henry Abelove). Venues for publication on lesbian/gay topics support a broad range of literary and media studies (from *differences* to *Discourse*, *Cultural Critique* to *Cultural Studies*), but the only journal consistently publishing lesbian/gay history is the *Journal of the History of Sexuality*. (We have yet to see what will happen with *GLQ: A Journal of Lesbian and Gay Studies*).

Clearly, this is a dismal situation. So what is to be done? I have three suggestions which track the three major complaints that I have mentioned:

- History departments should hire and train historians of sexuality. In order to accomplish this, job categories must be restructured. The current distribution of chronological, thematic and regional categories in history department divisions of labor needs fundamental rethinking to leave behind the present thoroughly colonial arrangements—in which Europe and the U.S. occupy the center and their former colonies the margins, and in which "political" history is understood narrowly but evaluated broadly, while histories of women and people of color are considered peripheral.[15] If history departments are to be forward-looking, they also should hire in areas now located oddly in English departments. For instance, why should cultural studies be consigned to English departments? Hiring in cultural studies would be one way for history departments to bring in the kind of engagement with cultural and critical theories that generate productive interdisciplinary dialogue. This would help create the kind of intellectual environment in which lesbian/gay history might thrive.
- Lesbian and gay historians must engage with queer theory, take its arguments seriously, review theoretical texts, take issue with its distortions of historical work. It is a terrible mistake to dismiss work in queer theory as jargon-ridden, elitist claptrap, as some do. Recent work on racial formations, new publications on the historical construction of nationalism, and continuing debates within feminist theory must also be engaged by lesbian and gay historians.
- Queer studies must recognize the importance of empirically grounded work in history, anthropology and social and political theory (as Michael Warner has also recently argued, in his introduction to *Fear of a Queer Planet*).[16] Scholars in this field must also acknowledge their debt to earlier, ghettoized texts. I cannot count the number of times I have read a queer studies article clearly indebted to the research and writing of Jeannette Foster, Jonathan Ned Katz or Esther Newton, that then footnotes only Continental theory, or Stuart Hall.

Like any other field, lesbian and gay historians need material support and intellectual and political exchange. For us, isolation equals cultural and professional death.

CHAPTER 16

Lawrence v. Texas as Law and Culture

NAN D. HUNTER (2005)

When the first edition of *Sex Wars* appeared in 1995, the era of *Bowers v. Hardwick*[1]—the 1986 Supreme Court decision upholding a Georgia law criminalizing homosexual sexual conduct—was already half over. In 2003, the *Hardwick* era ended when the Supreme Court emphatically reversed course in *Lawrence v. Texas*,[2] striking down a Texas sodomy law, and ruling that the state had no legitimate interest in criminalizing private, consensual sexual relations between two adults. *Lawrence* was a watershed in the history of state regulation of sexuality, albeit an overdue one, and may carry even greater import as a cultural marker than as a legal precedent.

This essay will address three questions:

- How did the *Lawrence* decision change the law?
- How is *Lawrence* likely to affect LGBT legal issues in the next generation of cases?
- How is the inter-relationship between law, political economy and culture reflected in *Lawrence*?

1. The Law of *Lawrence*

In *Bowers v. Hardwick*, the Supreme Court found that a state's interest in morality justified the criminalization of oral or anal sex (sodomy). Because what the Court treated as gay sexual conduct[3] could be made illegal, and

197

because government officials often argued that the conduct defined the class, there seemed to be few constitutional barriers to penalties that could be imposed on lesbians and gay men, including discriminatory treatment in family and employment law. *Hardwick* created a regime of categorical inequality: LGBT Americans were essentially branded as presumptive criminals and could be treated as such, regardless of whether they had ever been convicted of a crime.[4]

In 1996, the Court backed off the categorical inequality approach. Its decision in *Romer v. Evans*[5] invalidated an amendment to the Colorado state constitution that made it impossible for the state legislature or municipal councils to adopt civil rights laws protecting gay people unless the state constitution was changed—a cumbersome process. The provision singled out one group for a different political standard than any other, essentially raising the bar after gays in Colorado demonstrated that they could win legislative battles over civil rights in majoritarian votes. The uniquely high barrier to civil rights legislation left gay people susceptible to a wide range of possible negative repercussions in all the areas of life subject to antidiscrimination laws, such as employment, housing, public accommodations, and credit. The Supreme Court found that the sweep of the law made it especially likely that the motivation for it was animus toward an unpopular group. The Court reached this conclusion, however, without overturning *Hardwick*.

The reason that these two seemingly contradictory decisions could coexist was that in *Hardwick* the Court excluded gay sex from the scope of "privacy" protected under the liberty branch of the Due Process Clause of the Fourteenth Amendment,[6] while in *Romer* the Court based its ruling on equal protection law. The Texas statute that was before the Court in *Lawrence* presented both doctrinal questions: (a) whether the Court should reverse *Hardwick* and rule that criminalizing private consensual sex between men amounted to an arbitrary deprivation of liberty or privacy, and (b) whether the fact that the Texas law, by criminalizing oral and anal sex only when committed by two persons of the same sex but not when committed by a man and a woman, violated the Equal Protection Clause.

The Court chose the former route, reasoning that to focus on equal treatment would allow laws that made sodomy illegal for everyone, whether gay or straight. As a result, the *Lawrence* decision is based on meanings of liberty, not equality. The Court found that the constitutional protection for liberty includes respect for "an autonomy of self that includes … certain intimate conduct."[7]

Although the Court's analysis is about liberty, the rhetoric of the opinion is saturated with notions of equality. Within the zone of protected liberty, the Court held, are "sexual practices common to a homosexual lifestyle. The [gay] petitioners are entitled to respect for their private lives. The State cannot demean their existence or control their destiny by making their private sexual conduct a crime."[8] The Court's language explicitly invoked the principle of equality, even if not using equal protection law as such: "persons in a homosexual relationship may seek autonomy for these purposes ["intimate choices"], just as heterosexual persons do."[9] The invocation of both strains—liberty as doctrine, equality as rhetoric, like a combination of words and melody—expands traditional approaches to the idea of liberty, giving it more of a social context and a grounding in life experience. Perhaps the best summary description for *Lawrence* is that it articulates a concept of equal liberty.

Justice O'Connor chose to take only the equality route. She did not find a liberty right to engage in sexual relations. By limiting her concurrence to equal protection reasoning, O'Connor was able to avoid reversing herself: O'Connor was the only member of the six-justice majority in *Lawrence* to have also joined the majority opinion in *Hardwick*.

Justice O'Connor's concurrence is nonetheless powerful, however, because it elaborates on the equal protection analysis used in the Court's opinion in *Romer*. There, the Court found that the broad set of harms imposed by the Colorado constitutional amendment could not be justified by what the state asserted were the purposes behind it—protecting the rights of landlords and employers not to associate with gay people and conserving government funds. As a result, animus—simply the desire to harm the group—seemed the only plausible motivation. In her concurrence in *Lawrence*, O'Connor declared that there is no difference between the desire to harm a group and "moral disapproval of a group": neither is sufficient to satisfy rational basis review.[10] And she acknowledged that such situations triggered a heightened rationality test: "[w]hen a law exhibits such a desire to harm a politically unpopular group, we have applied a more searching form of rational basis review to strike down such laws under the Equal Protection Clause."[11]

From the perspective of LGBT rights advocates, the most disturbing aspect of *Lawrence* is the murky standard of review used by the Court. In constitutional cases, courts categorize challenges based on whether they require defense of a given law to meet a stringent test, such as whether it satisfies a "compelling" state interest and is "narrowly tailored" to achieve that interest, or whether the state must show only that the legislature had a "rational" basis for enacting the law. In *Lawrence*, the opinion of the Court (unlike Justice O'Connor's concurrence) does not specify which test it is using. On the one hand, the Court finds that the liberty right to private consensual sexual relations is equivalent to the right to use contraception or to obtain an abortion, both of which were found to be "fundamental" and trigger stringent standards of review. However, the Court uses language reminiscent of the rationality test: "[t]he Texas statute furthers no legitimate state interest which can justify its intrusion into the personal and private life of the individual."[12]

One result of not explicitly using a heightened standard of review is that the Court guaranteed that progress toward full equality for LGBT Americans would be slow. When heightened scrutiny is applied to a law, the law usually is declared unconstitutional, because legislative classifications are difficult to justify if the standard is that they must be precisely tailored to achieve an important goal. In essence, under the stricter standard, classifications do not receive the benefit of the doubt. Heightened scrutiny would almost certainly be fatal for classifications based on age, for example. It would be virtually impossible for a state to justify setting the eligibility age for a driver's license at 17 rather than at 16 or 18 or 19.

The Court's silence as to standard of review, in both *Romer* and *Lawrence*, signals that it was unwilling to mandate using the highest standard for sexual orientation classifications. Leaving some doubt as to how closely judges should examine the bases for laws that discriminate based on sexual orientation ensures that lower federal courts will wrestle with these issues for years. The Supreme Court seems to want to let these cases percolate, eventually producing another decision that the highest court will review.

A slow process is not unusual. Courts almost always follow, rather than lead, on issues of social change. Dramatic interventions by the Supreme Court in constitutional law tend to occur only after some other center of governmental power has taken the first step. The Court's decision in *Brown v. Board of Education* in 1954 followed President Truman's 1948 Executive Order desegregating the armed forces. *Roe v. Wade* in 1973 followed enactment by Congress of a federal law in 1964 prohibiting employment discrimination against women. In the case of sodomy law and *Lawrence*, state courts provided the tipping point. Of the twenty-five sodomy laws existing in 1986 when *Hardwick* was decided, half had disappeared, mostly by rulings of state supreme courts, by the time that the United States Supreme Court heard *Lawrence* in 2003.[13] By 2003, as many states had civil rights laws prohibiting sexual orientation discrimination as had criminal laws prohibiting sodomy.[14]

At its core, the *Lawrence* decision formalizes the acceptance of secular rationality as the appropriate conceptual paradigm for the law of sexuality, thus bringing the legal world into harmony with what has been the dominant American cultural mode for several decades. No longer is morality a sufficient basis for punishing gay sex, at least by use of criminal law. No longer is marriage the line dividing permitted from prohibited sexual conduct. Liberal law reforms modeled on a Millsian philosophy and permitting criminalization based only on harm or lack of consent, initially proposed in the 1950's, have finally been secured.[15]

2. The Next Generation of LGBT Law

As to future equality challenges, the *Lawrence* Court provided only general guidance. It was striking that there was no mention in the majority decision of the primary method by which sodomy laws have been used to silence and penalize gay people—through family and employment law. The Court noted that sodomy law *convictions* have far-reaching consequences, using those examples as illustrations of why even a misdemeanor can be significant.[16] But sodomy laws have been most frequently enforced indirectly, not directly, by the denial of custody or other parental rights to gay parents or by exclusions from certain jobs.[17] The result has been ruptured families and lost employment opportunities.

The omission of any reference to this body of case law in the majority opinion strongly suggests that all five justices who joined the opinion were not ready to rule that homosexuality is irrelevant in all those contexts. Future litigation will test whether promotion of heterosexuality is a legitimate state interest. The coming debates are likely to reveal the gap between "merely exempting [homosexual conduct] from criminal penalty" and "making it 'lawful in the full sense.'"[18]

More Liberty and More Scrutiny

The use of a rational-basis test, if that is what it was, makes the Court's conclusion in *Lawrence* even more powerful in certain respects—the interests proffered by Texas were found to be not even rational, much less compelling. A rational basis test also lowers the stakes for describing the individual's right; the Court's text makes clear that it is somehow a core right, but never crosses the line into denominating it as fundamental, with the attendant risk of providing an easier, more defined target for conservative backlash.[19] At the same time, however, a rational-basis test makes a strong decision potentially easier to distinguish in future cases—the Court can always return to an approach that gives much greater deference to state legislatures, as the typical rational-basis test does, without stepping outside the technical bounds of precedent.[20]

One important effect of the categorical inequality principle characteristic of the *Hardwick* regime was that it eliminated the need for courts to seriously question the basis for antigay laws. Treating homosexuality as properly subject to repression or *de jure* disadvantage reinforced the ideology of heterosexuality as both the natural and the normative ideal. Judicial reliance on categorical inequality precluded the contestation of that ideology. Enforcement of categorical inequality made heterosexual privilege under law virtually inevitable. The absence of serious contestation allowed the many policy choices underlying a matrix of heteronormative laws to remain disguised as mere artifacts of natural law reasoning.

Whatever standard of review it was using, the Court in *Lawrence* rejected that kind of blanket assumption. The Court's repudiation of tradition as a justification for outlawing gay sex was the rejection of a rationale that need not speak its name, since all a state needed to do under *Hardwick* was to invoke "morality." Now those who would use the state as a mechanism for privileging heterosexuality must speak, and in some detail. With the end of categorical inequality, courts will have to assess what relevance sexual orientation has in each given situation. LGBT people will win these cases more often, but the lawsuits will still need to be litigated.

Adultery law provides a useful comparison. Adultery could be considered per se immoral, as sodomy was, or it could be weighed in the context of particular facts (e.g., the impact of adulterous relationships on a given workplace). In *Marcum v. McWhorter*,[21] for example, the U.S. Court of Appeals for the Sixth Circuit debated whether firing a law enforcement officer because he engaged in an adulterous relationship could be justified because of laws prohibiting adultery, as was true for sodomy under *Hardwick,* or whether the adulterous conduct would have to be shown to produce specific harm. In that case, plaintiff's adulterous relationship was with the wife of a fellow police officer. For military personnel, the rule since 2002 has been that service members cannot be discharged for adultery without the presence of some additional factor, such as impact on the work environment.[22]

Lawrence is less important for its explicit protection of a private sphere of intimate decision-making than for its implicit unmasking of the interrelationship between sexuality and the state as a public sphere. The paradox is that the decision both granted privacy rights to intimate same-sex relations and, by creating a need for more detailed analysis by courts, simultaneously set the stage for greater judicial scrutiny of LGBT lives. For that reason, a decision thought to embody the principle of freedom from government oversight is likely to produce more, not less, intrusion by the state. In future state regulation of sexuality, discipline will replace punishment.

Protection Only for Individuals? Only for Relationships?

In the realm of cultural drama, marriage and relationship issues, for better or worse, will dominate the next generation of LGBT rights law. These are the hottest of the wedge issues, for both those most opposed to and those most committed to equality for LGBT people. Marriage also defines eligibility for a host of private and public benefits, such as forms of insurance, and operates as a linchpin for many other legal questions, such as assessing damages in a wrongful death case. None of those linkages is inevitable, of course, and most legal systems that provide stronger health and social benefits than are available in the United States do not rely on, and reinforce, marriage in that way.

For these issues, the erasure of *Hardwick* is more important than the precise content of *Lawrence*. Sodomy law operated as both a mechanism of subordination and a metaphor of heterosexual superiority. By repudiating the message of *Hardwick* that LGBT people are intrinsically second-class citizens, *Lawrence* makes it possible to imagine that they could have an equal right to access the institution of marriage. As direct or controlling precedent, however, *Lawrence* is likely to have little effect in marriage litigation.

In *Lawrence*, the Court sent multiple messages about marriage. The majority opinion notes that the sexual relationship between the two men who brought the case does not threaten to produce "abuse of an institution the law protects."[23] The Court simply holds that a gay or lesbian relationship cannot be criminalized, "*whether or not* [it is] entitled to formal recognition in the law."[24] Justice O'Connor states in her concurrence that she believes that "preserving the traditional institution of marriage" *is* a legitimate state interest and presumably would satisfy the standard that would be used to decide a gay marriage case.[25] Justice Scalia, in one of his signature blazing dissents, finds with horror that an openness to same-sex marriage crept into the logic of the majority opinions. Justice Scalia declares that nothing stands between the logic of *Lawrence* and gay marriage.[26] In particular, he finds that Justice O'Connor's "preservation" is simply a euphemism for expressing moral disapproval of homosexuality, which he reads the majority opinion as having taken out of play in constitutional analysis.[27]

The *Lawrence* Court performed the regulatory function that Gayle Rubin identified more than twenty years ago: the justices drew the line of social acceptance at a new point in the hierarchy of sexual identities, accepting the most conventional same-sex couples into the realm of "respect."[28] The problem, of course, is that those remaining in the regions of disrepute on the wrong side of the line continue to be stigmatized, perhaps even more so. Moreover, many of the most privileged persons within the community benefit from the new line.

The risk created by such partial change is not its incompleteness per se. The stages of social change are always incremental, especially in law. The risk is that the LGBT community itself will accept the new line between respect and disrepute.

Segments of the *Lawrence* opinion embody the heteronormative impulses of a court struggling to position the gay men before it as comparable to married persons. Professors Katherine Franke,[29] Teemu Ruskola,[30] and Kendall Thomas[31] argue that the Court's language seeks to subsume gay sex into the norms of domestication associated with marriage, as in the Court's statement that "[t]o say that the issue in *Bowers* was simply the right to engage in certain sexual conduct demeans the claim the individual put forward, just as it would demean a married couple were it to be said that marriage is simply about the right to have sexual intercourse."[32] The question left begging by this portion of the opinion is whether sexual acts are to be protected, and not just relationships.

The ambiguity of the Court's meaning is also reflected in its statement that "intimate conduct with another person can be but one element in a personal bond that is more enduring."[33] Some fear that this statement will be read as meaning: intimate conduct with another person can be but *one element* in a personal bond *that is more enduring.* Their concern is that long-term commitment will become a prerequisite in future cases when courts interpret the scope of liberty recognized in *Lawrence.*

However, nowhere in the record before the Court was there any indication that the parties in *Lawrence* had "an enduring personal bond." Their attorneys made no argument that they were involved in a relationship, and recent research indicates that in fact they were not.[34] There was thus no basis for the Court to condition the full protection of liberty on the existence of such a relationship. What should happen, therefore, is that the sentence will be read as meaning: intimate conduct with another person *can* be but one element in a personal bond ... *or not.* On this reading, the liberty protection attaches to the intimate conduct in a way that covers all that which *Lawrence* purports to protect: consensual, noncommercial adult sexual conduct occurring in physically sequestered locations.

Any further hierarchic ranking within that category of conduct would suggest morals-driven selection criteria. Morally neutral considerations—such as the impact of certain couples in a particular workplace—might legitimately lead to interventions such as changed job assignments. But questions of "immorality" would be irrelevant.

This debate over whether *Lawrence* protects sexual relations or just sexual relationships hints at deeply consequential strategic debates. Will advocates concerned that *Lawrence* will be "domesticated" by a limitation to respectable couples stress its application to sexual conduct outside of relationships? So far, there have been mixed results in such cases: the invalidation of fornication and discriminatory sentencing laws for youth,[35] but the refusal to strike a law barring sales of sex toys.[36] Or will the primary effort be to use *Lawrence* to stretch in the other direction, to assert coverage of more familial connections?

Some LGBT scholars argue that the risk is the opposite of what Franke, Ruskola, and Thomas fear: not that relationships will be required before the liberty right applies; but that courts will interpret *Lawrence* to cover *only* sexual acts and ignore its potential to protect family relationships.[37] On this point, too, the courts have responded unevenly: rejecting *Lawrence* as grounds to challenge a marriage law[38] or an adoption law barring gay people as adoptive parents,[39] but invoking it tangentially when protecting partner benefits for same-sex couples.[40]

The legal status of gay family bonds—whether between adults or between parent and child—has already shifted from exclusion from the protections of law to segregated systems. Legal inventions such as civil unions, domestic partnerships and second-parent adoptions provide an assortment of methods for states to recognize and regulate gay families while still barring gay couples from exercising the option to marry.[41] As states increasingly adopt systems that come closer and closer to duplicating marriage, the stranger it seems to preserve segregation qua segregation. As segregated systems fall, and same-sex couples obtain the right to choose whether to marry, the question of whether family law will protect more than marriage will become increasingly acute.

Equality, Expression, and Pluralism

The mass reception for gay equality arguments has changed from one of open hostility toward all claims made by a despised group to one of tolerance for participation in essential life activities such as work and at least some family structures. The Court's opinion in *Lawrence* established a new baseline for legal regulation: neutrality as to private consensual adult intimate relations. But the Court left unanswered countless questions of how state regulation should operate in other areas, especially those involving expression and affirmation.

At the center of most contemporary gay rights debates is the question of where the line should be drawn between neutrality/tolerance and recognition/acceptance. Perhaps the most problematic cluster of such questions involves situations where competing moral values and legal claims collide. In such cases, constitutional analysis must include weighing the First Amendment's protection for all citizens to express their points of view.

One central and persistent underlying problem in gay rights debates is the proper role of the state when adversaries invoke not just arguments over material goods, but also claims for recognition and legitimacy. In situations ranging from the broad debates over marriage to concrete instances like the Boy Scouts case, advocates on both sides argue for a right of self-expression: the right to come out as gay without sacrifice, on one side, versus the right to exclude openly gay persons as an expression of one's view that homosexuality is wrong, on the other.

Increasingly, the opponents of equality have asserted their right to ensure the continuation of important cultural spaces as exclusively heterosexual. A "no promo homo" framing implicitly concedes that "homo" is an idea which is being promoted, and ideas are entitled to First Amendment protection. But it also emphasizes the expression interests of traditional values groups and the right to promote anti-gay ideas. The result is a stalemate which permeates political discourse as well as law.

Battles between opposing cultural communities on gender and sexuality issues will only be exacerbated by increased recognition that LGBT persons are presumptively equal to those supporting anti-gay policies. Criminalization is largely off the table after *Lawrence*, but there remain countless options for using the power of the state to promote heterosexuality. Because silence = heteronormativity, many future contests will turn on who has the right to speak where and when.

3. Law, Political Economy, and Culture

To some extent, law operates in its own realm. But it is also engorged with the politics of power struggles, both struggles over state power and struggles over cultural dominance. *Lawrence* provides a window into culture as much as legal doctrine.

The Shadow on the Screen in the Mind's Eye

Probably no Supreme Court decision in history has been so linked to popular culture as *Lawrence v. Texas* has been to TV's "Will and Grace." Multiple commentators have explained the Court's equality rhetoric and its dramatic reversal of *Hardwick* by noting how culturally normal it has become to see endearing and straight-friendly depictions of (mostly) gay men and (some) lesbians in the mass media. Is that who the justices see when they envision gay people? Who is the homosexual in the collective mind's eye of the Supreme Court?

One cannot know which television programs or films any of the justices may watch, but, like other American institutions, the Court lost its "willful blindness"[42] toward gay people in the years after *Hardwick* was decided. When the life partner of a high-ranking official in the administrative section of the Court's staff died in the late 1980s, many justices expressed condolences.[43] Numerous justices are aware that one or more of their clerks have been gay men or lesbians.[44] The attorney arguing for Lawrence and Garner was himself gay. That attorney, Paul Smith, a former clerk for Justice Powell, was well known to the justices from the many cases he had argued before the Court as a member of the small number of top-flight lawyers who specialize in Supreme Court litigation.[45]

Perhaps even more than most people, the justices tend to come into contact with persons who are similar to them in social position and class. It is fair to assume that all of the justices now realize that some of the people with whom they share many characteristics are gay. That simple fact was not true in 1986.

And it is indeed quite clear that there is now a homosexual in the room as far as the Court is concerned. In both *Romer* and *Lawrence*, the Court renounced the casually contemptuous tone and language of *Bowers v. Hardwick*, in which the majority declared that any assertion of a connection between a right of privacy for gay people and a tradition of liberty to be "at best, facetious."[46] Even in cases in which the Court rules against a gay rights claim, the tone in majority opinions is now dispassionate. In *Boy Scouts of America v. Dale*, for example, Chief Justice Rehnquist writing for the Court took care to specify that the opinion was expressing no view as to whether homosexual conduct was contrary or not contrary to the terms "morally straight" and "clean" in the Scout oath, only that the organization itself had declared a position on that question.[47] This is the tone that one uses in talking about the other when the other is assumed to be present, not absent or inconsequential, and thus the well-bred speaker must be polite.

The language of *Lawrence* is by far the most positive toward LGBT persons of any majority Supreme Court opinion, for example in its insistence that gay people "are entitled to respect for their private lives."[48] "Respect" does not necessarily connote equality, and certainly does not communicate endorsement. It does, however, suggest some form of mutuality and a broadly shared ethos or community. One respects the skill or hard work of a player on an opposing team, for example; respect implicitly signals recognition that they, like me, are engaged in the same endeavor. Perhaps the homosexual in the mind's eye of the Court is a mixture of the somewhat familiar and the somewhat fuzzy. With luck, the Court will respond with a mixture of agnostic curiosity and an empirical effort at clarification.

Neoliberal Civil Rights

At a more theoretical level, *Lawrence* combines three distinct streams of political philosophy and jurisprudence: individualism, antipathy toward the state, and the ideal of equality. Correlatively, where government does not intrude or impede, liberty as the Supreme Court understands it is not threatened. Certainly nothing in this decision undermines the logic of *Harris v. McRae*[49] or *Maher v. Roe*,[50] which held that the government is not obligated to include abortion among the health care services funded by the Medicaid program, even if the right to have an abortion is protected against undue interference by the government. The Court understands the U.S. Constitution to be a charter of negative liberty rights, of protection against the government stepping into the private lives of citizens, not a source of positive liberty rights, or support for claims that government should act affirmatively to maximize social welfare.

The combination of moderate libertarianism and individualist equality reproduces norms consistent with both the American civil rights tradition and with neoliberalism. Neoliberalism is a political and cultural paradigm that stresses deregulation and greater market freedom more generally, privatization of public functions in order to achieve the assertedly greater efficiencies of private markets, and individual responsibility.[51] Unlike more traditional forms of conservative politics, however, neoliberalism is not allergic to equality.[52] As Lisa Duggan described in *Twilight of Equality*, neoliberalism and civil rights are not inconsistent, at least so long as achievement of civil rights denotes the end of prejudice and economically irrational discrimination, and not redistributive policies. A neoliberal civil rights paradigm produces a system in which liberty rights modeled on contract and property become open to all, and in which the state has become formally neutral toward the group in question. Neoliberal civil rights is negative liberty made honest.

What will come next in the broader political and legal culture is difficult to assess. The equality which is possible in a neoliberal political culture will likely provoke demands for changing norms. In the economic sphere, changing norms will not come easily. One should not expect a neoliberal model of LGBT civil rights to include mandates for employers to incur the expenses of accommodating difference (e.g., extension of insurance benefits to same-sex partners) or for government to move toward de-privatization of social costs (e.g., universal access to health care).

Culturally as well as economically, state policies operate from a baseline. The cultural baseline for the state's regulation of sexuality is a privileging of heterosexual relations, specifically within marriage, and of the social norms that have grown up around the heterosexual model. Accepting gay people into that normative universe requires both a shift in the prevailing norm so that it is stretched to include homosexuality, and a willingness by gay people to reside within the universe's new boundaries.

Moving into the mainstream inevitably produces assimilation, with both gains and losses for the newly arrived group, as well as for their long-established new neighbors. In this case, one such gain and loss is the strengthening by extension, albeit with modifications, of conventional social norms regarding sexuality. Many lesbian and gay Americans want nothing as much as they want the freedom to achieve precisely that kind of assimilation, with the attendant protections and comfort which such status carries. They are certainly correct to understand their exclusion from marriage and similar social institutions as evidence of a breathtaking assertion of superiority by those who would perpetuate the exclusion. But being allowed into the institution, and even changing it in the process, will not suffice as freedom for those who object to organizing virtually all of a society's laws regarding intimate adult relationships around marriage.

The fact that the *Lawrence* decision is consistent with the model of neoliberal civil rights does not mean, of course, that it is inherently or necessarily limited in these ways. The adjudication of *Lawrence* required no consideration of issues beyond the reach of neoliberal equality; indeed the sweep of the Court's opinion was surprising for its breadth, not its limits. It is simply important not to overstate the zone of freedom that it establishes. The decision leaves enormous flexibility as to how broadly or narrowly future courts will interpret it. Indeed, we have barely begun to create the meaning of *Lawrence*.

Conclusion

The Supreme Court's decision in *Lawrence v. Texas* turned an important corner in the history of state regulation of sexuality in the United States. In essence, the decision brought American sex law into the twentieth century, just in time for the twenty-first. Where before there had been enormous variety among state laws, there is now a key point of uniformity: private consensual sexual intimacy between adults cannot be criminalized. Future legal disputes will focus more on openness than on privacy.

Sexual Dissent in the New Millennium

CHAPTER 17

Crossing the Line

The Brandon Teena Case and the Social Psychology of Working-Class Resentment

LISA DUGGAN (2004)

As the "class war" against the working and middle class, the unemployed and underemployed, and the poor in the United States grows fiercer under "Dubya," it is encouraging when segments of the labor movement respond by expanding their agenda, and embracing diversifying constituencies and a broader range of issues. I've been especially cheered by the growing inclusion of lesbian, gay, bisexual, intersexual, transgender, and queer issues on labor's agenda. But I have also often felt frustrated at the narrow framing of those issues, hoping to see something more than antidiscrimination policies or balkanized forms of identity politics at work. Why can't issues of sexuality be more deeply connected to women's issues, race questions, and class politics? In pondering this question, I started thinking about Brandon Teena.

I was in Berlin, participating in a Green Party-sponsored conference called "Queering Democracy," when I first saw the documentary *The Brandon Teena Story* (1998). The basic outline of the events of the 1993 Nebraska rape and murder of a female-born, twenty-one-year-old legally named Teena Renae Brandon, but passing for male as Tenna Ray Brandon, Tenor Brandon, or Brandon Teena (among other aliases), was already familiar to lesbian, gay, bisexual, and transgender activists when the documentary appeared. The case became more widely known two years later with the release of the fictionalized major motion picture *Boys Don't Cry* (2000).[1] In Berlin in 1998, I was pleased to be able to view the new documentary in the company of progressive and left scholars and activists from around Europe and the United States, gathered together to discuss LGBT and queer politics. I expected a tuned-in audience, and no need to explain basic political points in this setting.

I was surprised. When the documentary, produced and directed by Susan Muska and Greta Olafsdottir, started rolling, the first scenes we saw were landscape shots, stretches of highway, and signs of the economic depression blanketing the deindustrializing U.S. Midwest. The soundtrack blared country music, and when the heads starting talking about the events leading up to the murder, the bleached blond hair, pickup trucks, and accents of working-class folks from the southern tip of Nebraska elicited sneers and laughter among the assembled conference goers. As a white southerner with family from both depressed agricultural areas and working-class enclaves in southern cities, I started to get nervous. And as the documentary continued, I never did get a chance to relax. To my eyes, the documentary itself relentlessly exoticized the "white trash" setting in which it was filmed—as if the filmmakers were metropolitan anthropologists among the "primitives." The audience response, at any rate, aligned itself seemingly seamlessly with that point of view. As the laughter and sneering continued, until the violence on screen quieted it down, I realized that this audience was comfortable projecting racism, misogyny, homophobia, and violent masculinity on to this "other" setting where it seemingly "belonged." When I returned to the United States, I discovered that urban LGBT and queer audiences, especially in New York and San Francisco, often responded similarly—with comfortable condescension and metropolitan superiority. Never mind the racism, homophobia, and violence marking the gentrifying urban settings just outside. I can only guess at the discomfort of working-class, rural midwesterners and southerners in these audiences, visitors or expatriates (like me).

But back in New York, I was also following the political rhetoric of progressive organizers who appealed to "working families" while often neglecting to address the concerns of women, youth, or LGBT and queer people who might find themselves exploited outside of families, or at risk *within* them—trapped in authoritarian, exploitative, or violent living arrangements. (And, I didn't notice that such political groups had any interest in *The Brandon Teena Story.*) I started to consider how cultural progressives focusing on feminist or queer issues have so often overlooked or misperceived the working-class or rural realities of many of their constituencies—pushing them (like me) away with class and regional prejudices. At the same time, economic populists and progressives have often ignored the plight of those without full equality or even basic safety *within* their working-class families (like the one I grew up in)—as well as outside them. Where, I wondered, was the real "progressive" impulse, and where the "conservatism" in this political landscape? And so I started thinking more about Brandon Teena. I read the 1996 true crime book about the murder by Aphrodite Jones, *All She Wanted* (1996), based on extensive interviews and police and trial transcripts, and brimming with details absent in the documentary, and ignored or fabricated in the feature film.[2]

Teena Renae Brandon, growing up in Lincoln, Nebraska during the 1970s and 1980s, wanted to be a priest, a quarterback, a race car driver, an artist, a parent. Her father died in a car crash the year she was born, when her mother was sixteen; she lived with her mother, sister, and stepfather for a while, then in a trailer with an assortment of female relatives. She went to working-class Catholic schools; she was sexually abused by a male relative. She tried to join the Army (and failed the physical exam); she worked at Bishop's Buffet (which she called the "Barffet"). She didn't want to work at girls' jobs; she wanted to avoid male sexual predators. She started calling herself Billy; she moved in with a girl named Heather who believed Billy was a boy—then the gender trouble started.

After this beginning, Billy then Tenna or Tenor or Brandon improvised. He got fake ID's with men's names, but couldn't fool employers. He undertook a long career in check forgery and credit card fraud, using the money primarily to impress girls—to give the impression that he had a good job. The girls all said he was a wonderful boyfriend, that he knew just how to treat a girl. But eventually, Billy, Tenna, Brandon, would turn to the possessive behavior plus roving eye—the customary double standard of masculine sexual privilege. That is, unless he was found out first, revealed to be female, called a lesbo or a dyke, and sent packing. In these circumstances, he would say he was a hermaphrodite, and that corrective surgery was either in progress or imminent. Teena Renae Brandon invented himself as Brandon Teena, using creative self-fashioning, lies, distortions, and theft, through a process Judith Halberstam has called "male fraud."[3]

Of course, we don't know what "really happened" or what Teena/Brandon really wanted, who she really wanted to become. We have the overlapping, conflicting, and interested stories of participants and observers of the surrounding events. Brandon's story has been claimed as the tortured coming out tale of someone "really" lesbian, or as the coming-of-age of someone "really" transgendered, female-to-male. The crisis center in Lincoln (where he sought counseling) diagnosed a "sexual identity crisis," and provided information about transsexualism. But we don't have Brandon's account, only a few notes, and the articulateness of what he did—pass as a man, and try to claim a masculine life plan—and what happened to him.

One way to grasp Teena/Brandon's life story is to think about it as a grab for masculine privilege, for the "psychological wages" or the "property" of masculinity in a complex and situated economy of gender relations. Historian David Roediger, drawing on the work of W.E.B. DuBois, has written that groups of workers accepted as white in the United States have received the psychological "wages of whiteness"—a sense of empowerment, privilege, and entitlement that partly blinds them to their own economic exploitation, and recruits them into a system of racial hierarchy in a working-class context. American Studies scholar George Lipsitz, focusing on the post-World War II period in the United States, has written of whiteness as a kind of property, through which working people have made a "possessive investment" in concrete material structures of racial inequality. Roediger and Lipsitz both examine the damage this racial reward system has wrought in the history of working-class politics—often disabling economic critique and progressive unity through racial conservatism. It is productive to think about gender hierarchy in similar terms, though the "wages" and "property" of masculinity carry different rewards than those of race, rewards that vary over time, and from one racial, class, or regional context to another.[4]

When Brandon moved to Humboldt and Falls City, Nebraska, after having been exposed and rejected by his beloved fiancée Gina Bartu in Lincoln, he found himself in smaller towns (populations 1,003 and 4,769, respectively) with few economic opportunities. As in so much of the U.S. heartland from the 1970s to the 1990s, the loss of independent family farms and good jobs had left most people dependent on low wage, no benefit, service sector work, unemployed, or on welfare. *The Brandon Teena Story* shows John Lotter, one of Brandon's killers, describing Falls City:

> There are barely any jobs, a lot of 'em are on welfare. . . . If you've got somebody who's got a job and keeps a job—especially a girl that doesn't get pregnant and end up on welfare for the rest of her life—then you're pretty damn lucky. That's Falls City for ya.

In this environment, the psychological wages and cultural property of masculinity were under pressure. Without good jobs, the capacity of men to make claims to privilege was seriously undermined. The sexual double standard—jealous possession of women by philandering men—could be aggressively enacted, but also fiercely contested in the 1990s Humboldt and Falls City households described by Aphrodite Jones. Authority within the household, control of resources, the assumption of protective superiority, all masculine privileges that might be more gently if nonetheless firmly enforced through economic advantage in more prosperous circumstances, became the center of pitched battles that found their way into divorce court, domestic violence arrests, and property disputes. Brandon stepped into the middle of this battle. In Lincoln, Humbolt, and Falls City he found some young women more than willing to accept him, to desire him, even *after* their discovery of his nonmale anatomy; he found others who rejected him with fear and disgust for his difference. He found a few gay men happy to hang out with him, until he brought violence into their world. But he found only very few rare and unusual heterosexual men who did not respond with rage once Brandon turned out to be a girl.

Why were the straight men in Brandon's world so threatened? Two of them were threatened enough to rape and kill him. Those two men, John Lotter and Marvin Thomas (Tom) Nissen, had lived hard lives, subject to deprivation, abuse, humiliation, and abandonment since birth. They had both lived in foster homes, been raised by alcoholics, experienced physical abuse, and later perpetrated it. Like Brandon, they had both attempted suicide, been diagnosed with psychiatric problems, and had difficulty keeping jobs. Tom Nissen joined a white supremacist group in prison; there were rumors that John Lotter had been repeatedly raped there. Both were heavy drinkers. They shared much of the struggle for a decent existence with the women and girls around them, but they also fought to maintain the privileges of masculinity, both in relation to women and among other men. They were possessive and controlling of their girlfriends, while they cheated on them. They evaded responsibility for the reproductive consequences of their sexual escapades; they dodged responsibility for the children they fathered. They defended their masculine pride against insult, or any inference of effeminate weakness, with verbal and physical aggression. They held men's jobs at higher wages (when they could get them), they took up space, and they inspired fear.

The prerogatives of manhood were not naturally theirs, however; they fought for them under pressure, against insults and humiliation from other men, against wayward women with minds and plans of their own. Without secure incomes or social status, their prerogatives as men were at risk. The only social capital these men had were white male bodies, so they were inclined to enforce *that* as a crucial distinction and as grounds for claiming the wages and property of white masculinity.

Brandon met John Lotter and Tom Nissen when he began dating a local girl they both had also dated—Lana Tisdale, a restless, dissatisfied girl who felt trapped, who wanted more out of life, who dreamed of travel and a singing career. When Brandon was arrested (again) for forging checks, and his nonmaleness exposed by the sheriff, every social enforcement of the gender line came into play against him. Lana's mother insulted, maligned, and ejected him from her home, the peer group he socialized with ridiculed him and the girls he had dated, and his friends John and Tom raped him on Christmas day, 1993. Then the sheriff interviewed him in an intrusive, degrading way (the documentary's audio recording of that interview is almost impossible to listen to), and refused to make timely arrests. Lotter and Nissen shot, stabbed, and killed him on New Year's Eve to prevent him from sending them to jail.

Lotter and Nissen were not typical men of their time and place. They were more damaged and more violent than most men. The working-class families of Lincoln, Humbolt, and Falls City, Nebraska, were not generally as abusive as the Lotter and Nissen families. There were, and are, many kind, generous men and nurturing families around. Lotter and Nissen were extreme examples of a nonetheless widespread form of threatened masculinity. They were lethal enforcers of the gender line that was nonetheless more or less violently policed by every social institution in town—by families, peer groups, employers, the law, the psychiatric centers, the prisons. Even the folks who most excoriated the abuse that Brandon suffered, in interviews, agreed that the gender line should hold: Girls shouldn't go around "pretending" to be boys; it's dangerous, it's wrong. Brandon suffered and died trapped in this entire matrix of regulating institutions, but he was not the only one trapped, not the only one suffering. In their own way, Lotter on death row and Nissen in prison for life following the murder were trapped and defeated by their struggles to maintain white masculine pride and privilege under stress.

In fact, Brandon was not the only one murdered. There were three murders that New Year's Eve in the Humbolt farmhouse. Lisa Lambert lived in that house with her toddler, Tanner. She worked as a nurse's aid in the nearby nursing home, and in a local bar on nights and weekends, struggling to get by as a single mother. Lisa had been Brandon's girlfriend, briefly; Brandon had wanted to adopt Tanner. But Brandon's eye wandered. He borrowed Lisa's car and drove into Falls City to go out with other girls. He lied about where he'd been. On New Year's Eve, Lisa had nonetheless offered Brandon shelter following the rape. She was shot next to him with Tanner at her side. Phillip DeVine was there as well, though his presence was minimized in the documentary (none of his family members was interviewed, though the families of the other two victims appeared) and erased in the feature film. Phillip DeVine was a black man who dated

Lana Tisdale's sister Leslie. They had met at Job Corps training in Iowa, where DeVine, president of the Business and Professional Association, was a group leader. He was visiting Leslie for the holidays, but they had had a fight. Lisa Lambert was sheltering him as well, when he was shot on New Year's Eve so that neither he nor Lisa could testify and send Lotter or Nissen to jail.

Everyone in that house who was shot on New Year's Eve had crossed a line. Brandon, the central target, was way over the gender line. Lisa Lambert and Phillip DeVine, disposable secondary targets, had also crossed lines. Lisa had been Brandon's lover, and sheltered him after his exposure as a girl. She crossed the gender line too. Phillip was a black man dating a white woman. He had crossed the racial line, and ran up against Nissen, a member of the White Americans for White Supremacy. Nearly every life in that farmhouse that day was destroyed or ruined. Brandon, Lisa Lambert, and Phillip DeVine were killed. Tom Nissen and John Lotter destroyed their own futures (they had both been suicidal for years, after all) as well as the lives of their victims. Only Tanner now has a future, but what future might that be?

Now, we can't ever know what Brandon wanted, who he might have become. But perhaps we can imagine what he needed—room to move across the gender line? Or erasure of that line's regulatory coercions? What kind of politics might speak to Brandon, or to us, with Brandon in mind? Feminist, LGBT, and queer politics surely have a lot to offer, in the form of critical exposures of the work of gender lines along with sexual policing, and visions of a world without this kind of everyday coercion and enforcing violence. But a politics that cannot grasp the constraints, coercions, pressures, and deprivations imposed through class hierarchies and economic exploitation, or that fails to imagine the realities of rural, agricultural, and other nonmetropolitan lives, cannot ultimately speak to the Brandons in our midst. Brandon needed a labor movement, a working-class politics, a critique of economic cruelties. But a progressive, class-conscious politics that cannot attend to the specific economic as well as cultural forces (and as his life shows, these cannot actually be separated) that enforce the gender line cannot speak to Brandon either. Such a politics often unintentionally reinforces the structuring cruelties in Brandon's worlds by speaking only of working families without reference to their sometimes brutal insides and outsides.

When we think about working-class conservatism, we think about Reagan Democrats. We think about the manipulative forces that recruit working people to act against their own economic self-interest, to support economic policies that ultimately exploit and impoverish them. Much writing on working-class conservatism focuses on angry white men who have been drawn into conservatism via their race and gender identifications, via their fear of racial and gender equality. Some writing focuses on the ways that "family values" and religious conviction have drawn working people into the economically conservative camp in the United States. One political response to these kinds of working-class conservatism is to ignore racial and gender inequality, not to mention sexual identity issues, and to address working families and the working class as a whole. Some populists go further to support cultural conservatism while promoting progressive economic policies, hoping to get those angry white men back on board. But this separation of the cultural and economic realms, at such a level of abstraction, obscures what this rhetorical abandonment, or recourse to cultural conservatism, means for people like Brandon, Lisa Lambert, and Phillip DeVine. It means tacit or even explicit support for their brutal exclusion from working-class families and communities. It means blindness to the incalculable price paid by many struggling to avoid such exclusions, to maintain their normative status and privileges—a price sometimes as high as that paid by John Lotter and Tom Nissen. Support for the working class as a whole must include equality and inclusion for everyone, or it leaves coercion, brutality, and suffering in the place of what might be some kind of genuine unity. The labor movement, to be an effective and engaging social movement, must be both inclusive and expansive, sometimes in ways challenging to its own constituencies. Pushing aside unpopular or stigmatized minorities leaves the vast majority of us losing the class war. Silence, about any of our lives, equals defeat ultimately for us all.

Brandon wasn't a hero; he was a young person under pressure who improvised, sometimes clumsily and insensitively, within the constraints that limited his life. We don't know what Brandon wanted, what he might have become. But perhaps we can imagine what Brandon needed—a politics that could address the interrelated workings of class, gender, race, and sexuality; a politics that could exceed nondiscrimination policies or "family values" (however progressively framed); a politics that might connect the workplace, community, and home; a politics that would link economic, social, and cultural arenas of experience, not because this has become politically correct but because such a politics is the only way to talk meaningfully about what he did, and what happened to him.

CHAPTER 18

Holy Matrimony!

LISA DUGGAN (2004)

The political storm over marriage is now intensifying as gay couples wed in San Francisco and President Bush vows to stop them with a constitutional amendment. Gay marriage threatens to wreak havoc as a "wedge issue" in the November 2004 elections, but it isn't entirely clear which party's prospects will be promoted, and which damaged, through marriage politics this year. Progressives certainly haven't figured out how best to enter the contentious and confusing public debate. Widespread anxiety over changing demographics and contested social norms is producing the background noise for a relatively volatile political calculus on all sides.

If Britney Spears's high-speed annulment and the competitive gold-digging with a sucker punch on TV's *Joe Millionaire* are any indication, concern over the state of the marital union is justified. Statistics confirm what entertainment culture spectacularizes—marriage is less stable and central to the organization of American life than ever. There are now more unmarried households than married ones, and a variety of formal and informal, permanent and transient, solemn and casual partnership and kinship arrangements have displaced any singular, static model of domestic life. Political responses to these changes have long been polarized between those who want to bring back Ozzie and Harriet and those who are fighting for the democratization of state recognition of households, along with equitable distribution of services and benefits to Americans, based on how we actually live rather than on some imagined, lost ideal. But today, in part because of the public's own ambivalence, the major political parties have been reluctant to come down firmly on either side of this divide.

What is most vexing the political parties during 2004 is same-sex marriage. The Republican electoral alliance is split on this issue. On the one hand, hard-line religious and moral conservatives have been working to rigidify the boundaries of "traditional" marriage and to shore up its privileged status. These groups are now pushing to pass a constitutional amendment defining marriage as between "a man and a woman." On the other hand, Libertarians, states' rights advocates, and social moderates prefer to retain conventional gendered marriage but support allowing some diversification of forms of partnership and household recognition at the state level. They oppose a constitutional amendment as a federal imposition on the states, or as just too mean-spirited to help Republicans during an election year. The religious and moral right appears to be winning out in the wake of the Massachusetts Supreme Judicial Court's 2003 decision that the state must extend civil marriage to same-sex couples. Bush, however grudgingly, fulfilled his promise to the Christian right when he announced on February 24, 2004 that he will support a federal marriage amendment.

With their convention in Boston, and Massachusetts Senator John Kerry the likely presidential nominee, Democrats will be fighting any "too liberal" charge associated with gay weddings by noting their opposition to same-sex marriage (the only remaining candidates who support it are Al Sharpton and Dennis Kucinich), while opposing a federal marriage amendment and emphasizing support for civil unions and domestic partnerships. Their carefully calibrated rhetoric will urge tolerance without questioning the supremacy of married, two-parent families. Indeed, the Bush Administration's recent proposal to spend $1.5 billion promoting marriage, "especially" among low-income populations, has not encountered energetic opposition from many Democrats, who have supported like-minded efforts in the past. Progressives, meanwhile, are struggling to articulate a small-d democratic politics of marriage that demands full equality for lesbians and gays without accepting the logic of the "family values" crowd.

It may be tempting to see this squabble as an example of symbolic politics, with the debate over the future of marriage potentially displacing bigger and more significant battles over war and peace, taxes and fairness, corporate greed and good government. But state regulation of households and partnerships does in fact affect the basic safety, prosperity, equality, and welfare of all Americans—it determines who will make medical decisions for us in emergencies, who may share our pensions or Social Security benefits, who may legally coparent our children, and much more. It's just hard to sort out the real issues from the smokescreens as the rhetoric heats up this election year.

Moral conservatives have so far taken the lead in the struggle to frame the meaning of the "marriage crisis." In their apocalyptic imagination, the stability of heterosexual unions and the social order they insure are threatened on all sides—by the specter of gay marriage, by women's independent choices within and outside marriage, and by government neutrality, toleration, or support of single-parent and unmarried households, especially among the poor. But wait—it gets worse. As Stanley Kurtz argued in *The Weekly Standard* (August 4/11, 2003) "Among the likeliest effects of gay marriage is to take us down a slippery slope to legalized polygamy and 'polyamory' (group marriage). Marriage will be transformed into a variety of relationship contracts, linking two, three, or more individuals (however weakly and temporarily) in every conceivable combination of male and female."

I'm not sure, given the rise of transgender activism, just how many combinations there are of male and female. But the dystopic vision is clear. Moral conservatives want to prevent courts and legislatures from opening a Pandora's box of legal options—a flexible menu of choices for forms of household and partnership recognition open to all citizens, depending on specific and varying needs. Such a menu would threaten the normative status of the nuclear family, undermining state endorsement of heterosexual privilege, the male "headed" household and "family values" moralism as social welfare policy.

The problem is not that any such flexible menu is currently available anywhere at present. What has emerged over decades of political wrangling at the municipal and state level is a hodgepodge of legal categories—civil marriage, civil union (with the same state-level benefits as civil marriage but without the portability from state to state, or federal recognition), domestic partnership (with fewer benefits than civil marriage) and reciprocal beneficiaries (which carries the fewest benefits). The categories are neither equivalent nor open to all. Civil marriage, thus far (except in Massachusetts) open only to one man and one woman who are not close blood relatives, carries the most specific benefits and mutual responsibilities (more than 1,049 automatic federal and additional state protections, benefits and responsibilities, according to the U.S. General Accounting Office). It endows couples and their children with both real and symbolic citizenship rights at the highest level. Civil union (in Vermont) or domestic partnership (in five states and over sixty municipalities) has been made available to gay and lesbian couples and sometimes to heterosexual couples who choose not to marry (or not to have to divorce) as well. Only the reciprocal beneficiaries status has been available (in different versions in Hawaii and Vermont) to close relatives, or those with no proclaimed conjugal bond. It has so far provided the most limited benefits, but it is in some senses the most radical innovation. It potentially separates state recognition of households or partnerships from the business of sexual regulation altogether.

The right wing's fear of a "slippery slope" suggests some ways that this eclectic array of statuses might move us in a progressive direction. Kurtz himself, citing Brigham Young University professor Alan Hawkins (*Weekly Standard*, August 4/11, 2003), sketches out what is to him a distasteful scenario:

> Consider the plight of an underemployed and uninsured single mother in her early 30s who sees little real prospect of marriage (to a man) in her future. Suppose she has a good friend, also female and heterosexual, who is single and childless but employed with good spousal benefits. Sooner or later, friends like this are going to start contracting same-sex marriages of convenience. The single mom will get medical and governmental benefits, will share her friend's paycheck, and will gain an additional caretaker for the kids besides. Her friend will gain companionship and a family life. The marriage would obviously be sexually open. And if lightning struck and the right man came along for one of the women, they could always divorce and marry heterosexually.
>
> In a narrow sense, the women and children in this arrangement would be better off. Yet the larger effects of such unions on the institution of marriage would be devastating. At a stroke, marriage would be severed not only from the complementarity of the sexes but also from its connection to romance and sexual exclusivity—and even from the hope of permanence.

Gee, sounds good. Then consider how such arrangements might benefit women, children, and others even more substantially. What if there were a way to separate the tax advantages of joint household recognition, or the responsibilities of joint parenting, from the next-of-kin recognition so that such rights might go to a noncoresident relative, a friend or a lover? And what if many benefits, such as health insurance, could be available to all without regard for household or partnership status? The moral conservative's nightmare vision of a flexible menu of options might become a route to progressive equality! That could happen—*if* all statuses could be opened to all without exclusions, allowing different kinds of households to fit state benefits to their changing needs; *if* no status conferred any invidious privilege or advantage over any other, or over none at all; and *if* material benefits such as health insurance were detached from partnership or household form altogether (federally guaranteed universal healthcare, for instance, would be far more democratic and egalitarian than health insurance as a partnership benefit). Meanwhile, the "sanctity" of traditional marriages could be retained and honored by religious groups and families, according to their own values and definitions.

Efforts to stop any such democratization of households have escalated steadily ever since a Hawaii state court decision conjured up visions of legitimate gay weddings in 1993. Thirty-eight states have passed legislation or constitutional amendments restricting marriage to heterosexual couples. In 1996 Bill Clinton signed the federal Defense of Marriage Act, designed to prevent any future state-level same-sex marriages from carrying the federal recognition and portability that civil marriage has so far guaranteed (though many believe DOMA is vulnerable to constitutional challenge). The proposed federal marriage amendment, with more than a hundred sponsors in the House and a handful of supporters in the Senate so far, would go much further than DOMA to write marriage restriction into the Constitution. Depending on the final wording, and the results of inevitable litigation over its interpretation, the amendment might also put a stop not solely to gay marriage but to all diversification of partnership and household recognition. In one stroke all the hard-won civil union, domestic partnership, and reciprocal beneficiary statuses could be wiped off the books, leaving civil marriage, restricted to heterosexual couples, as the sole form of recognition available at the federal, state, or municipal level (and possibly at private businesses and organizations as well) throughout the country.

Fortunately for advocates of partnership and household diversity, a marriage amendment faces a long, steep uphill battle as supporters struggle to pass it, first in Congress and then in three-fourths of the state legislatures, before it can become law. Many conservatives are clearly leery of the expensive, acrimonious battle ahead. George W. Bush withheld his own endorsement of the amendment until after his State of the Union address, in which he chose to emphasize his plan to promote conventional marriage instead.

To many, this looked like election-year strategy—an effort to pander to moral conservatives without giving them the explicit approval they craved. And surely such tactical concerns are shaping every word uttered by Bush on this issue. But it would be a mistake to attribute this Administration's interest in marriage promotion solely to such motives. There is a deeper commitment to preserving gendered marriage, on economic as well as moral grounds.

Bush's marriage-promotion initiative isn't new; it first appeared in the welfare reauthorization legislation passed by the House in 2002, which is now before the Senate and may come up for a vote as soon as this spring. Bush's $1.5 billion package, to be used to hire counselors and offer classes in marital harmony, extends the commitment contained in the 1996 welfare "reform" bill, passed under Clinton, to "end the dependence of needy parents on government benefits by promoting ... marriage." Women and children, in other words, should depend on men for basic economic support, while women care for dependents—children, elderly parents, disabled family members, etc. Under such a model, married-couple households might "relieve" the state of the expense of helping to support single-parent households, and of the cost of a wide range of social services, from childcare and disability services to home nursing. Marriage thus becomes a privatization scheme: Individual married-couple-led households give women and children access to higher men's wages, and also "privately" provide many services once offered through social welfare agencies. More specifically, the unpaid labor of married women fills the gap created by government service cuts.

Besides being sexist and outdated, this model of marriage is not exactly realistic. Relatively few men today earn a "family wage," and employed married women are not able to care fully for dependents by themselves. Marriage promotion, moreover, has not proven an effective means of alleviating poverty and reducing the need for government benefits. But even without any measurable economic impact, the effort to promote marriage among low-income populations works at the rhetorical level to shift blame for economic hardship onto the marital practices of the poor rather than on the loss of jobs, employment benefits, or government services.

Republicans and Democrats are by and large in agreement that as social programs are whittled away, gender-differentiated marriage (heterosexual, with different expectations for women and men) should take up the slack. Clinton's marriage-promoting welfare law embodied this principle, which also helps to explain the ambivalence of conservative and centrist Democrats toward genuine gender equality in marriage (illustrated in the retro discussion of the proper role of political wives in the current presidential campaign) and their opposition to gay marriage. There is an economic agenda, as well as surface moralism, attached to calls for the preservation of traditional marriage. The campaign to save gendered marriage has some rational basis, for neoliberals in both parties, as a politics of privatization.

Unwilling to support gay marriage, defend Judith Steinberg's remote relation to her husband's now-defunct presidential campaign (though Laura Bush did so), or openly attack marriage promotion as public policy, the Democrats are left with lame advocacy of second-class status for gays, mandatory secondary supportive roles for political wives, and public silence about welfare policy. No viable Democratic candidate has yet been able to shift the frame of reference to escape a weakly defensive posture on these issues. So it's left to progressives, both within the Democratic Party and outside it, to formulate a clear, positive vision of how best to address the needs of real households for state recognition and social support.

But progressives are divided, too, in their approach to marriage politics. The hateful campaign to exclude same-sex couples from full marriage rights creates tremendous pressure on gay-rights advocates and supporters to emphasize access to civil marriage as a core right of citizenship. A few marriage-equality advocates have continued to call for the multiplication of democratically accessible forms of state recognition for households and partnerships, and for the dethronement of sanctified marriage as privileged civic status, but many have couched their advocacy in language that glorifies marital bliss, sometimes echoing the "family values" rhetoric of their opponents. The "Roadmap to Equality: A Freedom to Marry Educational Guide," published by Lambda Legal Defense and Education Fund and Marriage Equality California (2002), begins with the kind of banal American Dream rhetoric that appeals to some gay people, but misdescribes, annoys, and even stigmatizes many others:

> Gay people are very much like everyone else. They grow up, fall in love, form families and have children. They mow their lawns, shop for groceries and worry about making ends meet. They want good schools for their children, and security for their families as a whole.

The guide goes on to recycle some of the more noxious views routinely spouted by conservative moralists:

> Denying marriage rights to lesbian and gay couples keeps them in a state of permanent adolescence. ... Both legally and socially, married couples are held in greater esteem than unmarried couples because of the commitment they have made in a serious, public, legally enforceable manner. For lesbian and gay couples who wish to make that very same commitment, the very same option must be available. There is no other way for gay people to be fully equal to non-gay people.

No other way? How about abolishing state endorsement of the sanctified religious wedding or ending the use of the term "marriage" altogether (as lesbian and gay progressives and queer leftists have advocated for decades)? In a bid for equality, some gay groups are producing rhetoric that insults and marginalizes unmarried people, while promoting marriage in much the same terms as the welfare reformers use to stigmatize single-parent households, divorce, and "out of wedlock" births. If pursued in this way, the drive for gay-marriage equality can undermine rather than support the broader movement for social justice and democratic diversity.

Meanwhile, critics of marriage promotion, located primarily in feminist policy and research organizations, are working to counter rosy views of the institution of marriage. The National Organization for Women's Legal Defense and Education Fund has documented the planned flow of money and services away from poor women and children and toward conservative organizations, contained in the proposed welfare reauthorization bill (see http://www.legalmomentum.org). A group of academic researchers and professors organized by Anna Marie Smith of Cornell University, Martha Albertson Fineman of Emory University, and Gwendolyn Mink of Smith College have created a Web site to circulate critiques of marriage promotion as a substitute for effective social welfare programs (http://falcon.arts. cornell.edu/ams3/npmbasis.html). As they point out, "While marriage has provided some women the cushion of emotional and economic security, it also has locked many women in unsatisfying, exploitative, abusive and even violent relationships." Their research findings and legislative analysis demonstrate that "federal and state governments are transforming the burden of caring for our needy sisters and brothers into a private obligation."

The agendas of lesbian and gay marriage-equality advocates and progressive feminist critics of marriage promotion don't necessarily or inevitably conflict, though their efforts are currently running on separate political and rhetorical tracks. Given the rising political stakes, and the narrow horizons of political possibility, it seems imperative now that progressives find ways to make room for a more integrated, broadly democratic marriage politics. To respond to widespread changes in household organization and incipient dissatisfaction with the marital status quo, progressives could begin to disentangle the religious, symbolic, kinship, and economic functions of marriage, making a case for both civil equality and the separation of church and state. They could argue that civil marriage (perhaps renamed or reconfigured), like any other household status, should be open to all who are willing to make the trek to city hall, whether or not they also choose to seek a church's blessing. Beginning with the imperfect menu of household and partnership statuses now unevenly available from state to state, it might not be such an impossibly utopian leap to suggest that we should expand and democratize what we've already got, rather than contract our options.

Such a vision, long advocated by feminist and queer progressives, may now be finding some broader support. Kay Whitlock, the national representative for LGBT issues for the American Friends Service Committee, circulated a statement to the National Religious Leadership Roundtable in 2003 that argued, "We cannot speak about equal civil marriage rights and the discrimination that currently exists without also speaking of the twin evil of coercive marriage policies promoted with federal dollars. ... For us, it is critical that the LGBT movement work for equal civil marriage rights in ways that do not further reinforce the idea that if a couple is married, they are more worthy of rights and recognition than people involved in intimate relationships who are not married." The statement continued, "We do not want to convey the message that marriage is what all queer people should aspire to. We also do not want the discussion of marriage to overwhelm and suppress discussion about a broader definition of human rights and basic benefits that ought to accompany those rights."

This seems like a good place to start. The question is, how can arguments like this be heard in the midst of the clamor against gay marriage from the Right, when Democrats are reduced to a timid whisper, and gay groups are too often sounding like the American Family Association? Might it be possible to tap into an undercurrent of dissatisfaction with the current state of the marital union—and appeal to the public's understanding of the enormous distance between rhetoric and reality on this subject? Politicians pay lip service to conservative family values, but voters do not always bolt when their actual lives fail to conform to the prescriptions—as Bill Clinton's enduring popularity despite repeated sex scandals demonstrated. Polls show widely contradictory public views on the subjects of marriage and divorce, adultery, and gay rights. Questions with only slight wording changes can yield widely differing results. Why not muster the courage to lead the public a little on this issue? Civil unions, considered beyond the pale only a few years ago, are now supported by many conservatives. The political center can and does shift—and right now, it is particularly fluid and volatile in this area.

In the current climate, progressives might profit by pointing out the multiple ways that conservative marriage politics aim to limit freedom in the most intimate aspects of our lives—through banning gay marriage as well as promoting traditional marriage. Given current demographic trends, it couldn't hurt to ask: Why do Republicans want to turn back the clock, rather than accept reality? And why can't Democrats find some way to support law and policy that advances the goals of intimate freedom and political equality, even during an election year?

CHAPTER 19

Beyond Gay Marriage

LISA DUGGAN AND RICHARD KIM (2005)

In the wake of the 2004 elections, the right moved swiftly and decisively to capitalize on its "values mandate." As many as fourteen gay marriage amendments could take effect in the next year or so. But bans on gay marriage may be only the tip of "the great iceberg," as Robert Knight of Concerned Women of America put it after the election. Parlaying anti-gay marriage campaign victories into a larger "pro-marriage" agenda, conservatives have targeted domestic partnership and reciprocal beneficiary recognition through broadly worded state ballot initiatives, launched a grassroots campaign for covenant marriages, imposed new restrictions on sex education, expanded federally funded marriage-promotion initiatives, and introduced state legislation to restrict divorce. Such initiatives appeal simultaneously to fiscal conservatives who see promoting marriage as a way to reduce state dependency, anti-gay voters who quail at the notion of same-sex unions, right-wing Christians who seek to enforce biblically determined family law, and the mass of voters anxious about the instability of marriage. Conservatives have found a way to finesse their differences through a comprehensive and reactionary program that aims to enshrine the conjugal family as the sole legally recognized household structure.

Democrats and progressives, by contrast, remain perplexed and divided, publicly bickering over the role gay marriage played in the party's defeats. Senator Dianne Feinstein chided San Francisco Mayor Gavin Newsom and the Massachusetts Supreme Court for moving "too much, too fast, too soon" on the issue and thus energizing Bush's conservative base. In rebuttal, the National Gay and Lesbian Task Force (NGLTF) pointed out that anti-gay marriage initiatives—successful in all states in which they were introduced—had negligible impact on Bush's share of the vote, particularly in swing states like Ohio, Michigan, and Oregon. Nonetheless, many gay leaders expressed deep anguish at what they felt was a surprisingly strident outpouring of homophobia at the polls and pledged to renew neglected grassroots efforts. Meanwhile, the gay movement has continued to pursue its primarily litigation-based strategy on gay marriage, winning some significant if preliminary court rulings in New York, California, Washington, and Nebraska, as well as scoring a legislative win for civil unions in Connecticut.

We believe that by engaging the marriage debate only in terms of "gay rights," both the gay movement and the Democratic Party have put themselves in a compromised and losing position. Faced with an aggressive marriage movement that has skillfully stoked and manipulated anxiety about same-sex marriage, progressive Democrats and gays must come together to reframe the issue as part of a larger campaign for household democracy and security, a campaign that responds to the diverse ways Americans actually structure their intimate lives.

The brutal central fact: ballot initiatives banning same-sex marriage passed easily in all eleven states in which they were introduced this past election, as well as in Louisiana and Missouri earlier in the year. In all, seventeen states have amended their constitutions to ban gay marriage; ten of these extend beyond marriage to eliminate other forms of partnership recognition, including civil unions and domestic partnerships. These initiatives go beyond blocking future progress for "marriage equality." Their attack on domestic partnerships and other civil contracts rolls back decades of success in winning recognition and benefits for couples of all gender combinations who could not or would not marry.

Michigan's Proposition 2 is typical of these broad state constitutional amendments. It mandates that "the union of one man and one woman in marriage shall be the only agreement recognized as a marriage or similar union for any purpose." Although Christian-right activists and Republican politicians insisted during the campaign that the Michigan amendment's vague language would only "defend marriage" and not eliminate benefits for unmarried couples, the Republican state attorney general soon announced that Prop 2 "prohibits state and local governmental entities from conferring benefits on their employees on the basis of a 'domestic partnership.'" The governor's office canceled plans to extend benefits to employees in same-sex relationships, and several public employers, from the University of Michigan to the city of Kalamazoo, will be forced, by the end of the year, to retract benefits already given to same-sex couples. Conservatives have even been pushing to have Prop 2 interpreted to bar private businesses that contract with the state from providing benefits to unmarried couples.

Although propositions like Michigan's are aimed at same-sex couples, they will impact all unmarried couples. Many of them could eliminate domestic partnership and reciprocal beneficiary statuses at state, and possibly private, institutions; revoke out-of-state and second-parent adoptions for gays and straights alike; invalidate next-of-kin arrangements, including those involving life-and-death medical decisions; and imperil joint home-ownership arrangements between unmarried people.

Is this exceedingly narrow vision of kinship and household arrangements what voters endorsed in November 2004? No, not if we take their actual living patterns as an indication of their preferences. Marriage is on the decline. Marital reproductive households are no longer in the majority, and most Americans spend half their adult lives outside marriage. The average age at which people marry has steadily risen as young people live together longer; the number of cohabiting couples rose 72 percent between 1990 and 2000. More people live alone, and many live in multigenerational, nonmarital households; 41 percent of these unmarried households include children. Increasing numbers of elderly, particularly women, live in companionate nonconjugal unions (think *Golden Girls*). Household diversity is a fact of American life rooted not just in the "cultural" revolutions of feminism and gay liberation but in long-term changes in aging, housing, childcare, and labor.

At the same time, there is increasing support for basic gay human rights. Large majorities favor employment and housing rights for gay people (89 percent in the latest 2004 Gallup poll), and a clear majority of Americans support some form of partnership recognition for same-sex couples—either marriage or civil unions (60 percent at the time of the election). In Cincinnati and Topeka, home to infamous homophobe Rev. Fred Phelps, voters defeated anti-gay ordinances, even as both Ohio and Kansas voted in favor of state-level amendments banning same-sex marriage. These victories demonstrate that decently funded and well-coordinated grassroots campaigns that reach out to other constituencies in the name of fairness and equality can secure gay rights even deep within red state territory. They also put into stark relief that gay *marriage* is the single issue trending against increasing support for gay rights. Certainly, outside the electoral arena, the entertainment industry presents lesbian and gay characters and issues as a ho-hum element of everyday life. How does this increasingly widespread acceptance of sexual diversity square with the sensational, overwhelming defeats of this election?

The answer may be that homophobia was not the sole or even central element behind voter support for the same-sex-marriage bans. The vexing, volatile issue may not have been equal rights for gay people so much as household security—the *other* security issue in this election—represented symbolically by the institution of marriage.

The net effect of the neoliberal economic policies imposed in recent decades has been to push economic and social responsibility away from employers and government and onto private households. The stress on households is intensifying, as people try to do more with less. Care for children and the elderly, for the ill and disabled, has been shifted toward unpaid women at home or to low-paid, privately employed female domestic workers. In this context, household stability becomes a life-and-death issue. On whom do we depend when we can't take care of ourselves? If Social Security shrinks or disappears and your company sheds your pension fund, what happens to you when you can no longer work? In more and more cases, the sole remaining resource is the cooperative, mutually supporting household or kinship network.

But if marriage is the symbolic and legal anchor for households and kinship networks, and marriage is increasingly unstable, how reliable will that source of support be? In the context of these questions, the big flap over marriage in the 2004 election begins to make a different kind of sense. If voters are not particularly homophobic, but they are overwhelmingly insecure, then the call to "preserve" marriage might have produced a referendum vote on the desire for household security, with the damage to gay equality caught up in its wake.

Indeed, the campaigns against same-sex marriage spewed rhetoric about the importance of "preserving" marriage, often steering away from overtly anti-gay fearmongering. For example, the Alliance for Marriage's Matt Daniels, who spearheaded the push for the Federal Marriage Amendment, has insisted that the marriage agenda is "not organized around homosexuality. Its mission is to see that more kids are raised in a home with a married mother and father." Daniels contends that "no one in the alliance believes that saving the legal status of marriage as between man and woman will alone be sufficient to stem the tide of family disintegration," but he believes that "if we lose that legal status, we lose the policy tool we need to pursue our broader agenda" (quoted in Karen S. Peterson, "Man Behind the Marriage Amendment," *USA Today*, 4/12/2004). What constitutes that "broader agenda" was made clear by another marriage movement leader, Bryce Christensen of Southern Utah University, when he said, "If those initiatives are part of a broader effort to reaffirm lifetime fidelity in marriage, they're worthwhile. If they're isolated—if we don't address cohabitation and casual divorce and deliberate childlessness—then I think they're futile and will be brushed aside" (quoted in "Gay marriage detractors urge for 'protection of marriage,'" CourtTV.com, Nov. 22, 2004).

Capitalizing on their clean sweep of November's marriage amendments, pro-marriage forces have taken Daniels and Christensen to heart. Pointing to high divorce rates in red states, social conservatives have revitalized efforts to repeal no-fault divorce and enact covenant marriage laws in Georgia, Arkansas, and other Southern states. While firmly rooted in fundamentalist Christianity, pro-marriage leaders also court more secular voters. For example, Arkansas Governor Mike Huckabee—who recently remarried his wife in a covenant marriage ceremony before a stadium packed with thousands—touts the financial gains to the state that result from pro-marriage policies. "If you start adding up the various costs—the costs of child-support enforcement, additional costs in human services, how many kids will go onto food stamps—it all adds up," he said (quoted in Rick Lyman, "Trying to Strengthen 'I do' with a more binding tie," *NY Times*, 2/15/05).

From a policy perspective, then, the anti-gay marriage initiatives are important to conservatives for a range of reasons beyond insisting upon the heterosexuality of marriage. Aiming to roll back the decades-long diversification of households, conservatives see the marriage amendments as the first step in encoding the conjugal, procreative and, for some, biblically ordained married family as the sole state-sanctioned household. Furthermore, by limiting recognition and benefits to a declining number of married families, marriage advocates are able to appeal to fiscal conservatives who might otherwise be wary of such moral legislation.

This is not to say the pro-marriage movement didn't exploit the Massachusetts Supreme Court decision and the reaction it provoked among anti-gay voters and social conservatives resentful of the so-called "liberal elite." Focusing on marriage-minded gays and lesbians and the "activist judges" who were "legislating from the bench," conservatives found an easy proxy for the decline in marriage. The "threat" of gay marriage enabled them to portray marital households as under assault (from homosexuals and judges) without addressing any of the economic factors that put marital households under stress and without directly attacking any of the related legal and social transformations (no-fault divorce, new reproductive technologies, women in the workplace) that most Americans would be reluctant to reject.

So it seems that the priority given to marriage equality by the gay movement gave the right an opening to foment a backlash that centered on gay marriage (and all that it has been made to stand for). But before gay marriage itself emerged as a viable goal, the gay movement pioneered state and local campaigns for distributing benefits through domestic partnerships and reciprocal beneficiary statuses. These statuses neither secured entitlements like Social Security nor were they portable as people switched jobs or moved, but they nonetheless marked real progress in recognizing household diversity. While some of these clauses applied to straight couples and nonconjugal households (siblings, unmarried coparents, long-term housemates, and the like), they were largely driven by the gay movement. Now, however, they are seen by many in that movement as second-class substitutes for marriage equality. What we're left with is an erratic and unevenly distributed patchwork of household statuses tied all too closely to the issue of gay marriage, with no major social movement—not labor, senior citizens, students, or gays—committed to household diversity as a primary political goal.

In order to counter conservative Republican strategy, one that promises to wreak havoc in elections to come, gay activists and progressives will have to come together to reframe the marriage debate. For gay activists, and indeed for all progressive activists, it would be far more productive to stress support for household diversity—both cultural and economic support, recognition and resources for a changing population as it actually lives—than to focus solely on gay marriage. By treating marriage as one form of household recognition among others, progressives can generate a broad vision of social justice that resonates on many fronts. If we connect this democratization of household recognition with advocacy of material support for caretaking, as well as for good jobs and adequate benefits (like universal healthcare), then what we all have in common will come into sharper relief.

Ironically, by overreaching with the state marriage amendments, the right wing may have provided the gay movement and progressives with an ideal starting point for just such a campaign. By showing the sheer number of households affected by such broad constitutional amendments, progressives can demonstrate just how narrow and extremist the pro-marriage agenda is. Defense of marriage amendments not only enshrine discrimination against gays and lesbians in state constitutions, they also severely curtail the freedom of intimate association exercised by Americans in nonmarried households—gay and straight alike. Indeed, a recent decision by a federal judge striking down Nebraska's defense of marriage amendment (the first ever at the federal level) noted that Nebraska's ban violated the rights of same-sex couples, foster parents, adopted children, and people in a host of other living arrangements. The ban "imposes significant burdens on both ... expressive and intimate associational rights" and "potentially prohibits or at least inhibits people, regardless of sexual preference, from entering into numerous relationships or living arrangements that could be interpreted as a same-sex relationship 'similar to' marriage," wrote Judge Joseph Bataillon (*Citizens for Equal Protection v. Attorney General*, Jon C. Bruning, case 4:03–cv–03155; May 12, 2005).

A campaign to expand and reform family law to account for the diversity of American households could blunt the right's moral panic about marriage and shift the entire debate in a more useful direction. Support for such a campaign might be drawn from a variety of constituencies: young adults, who are the least likely to be married as well as the least likely to have health insurance; single parents, many of whom now choose to live together in order to share housing, childcare and other costs; the elderly, who often live together after the death of a spouse or end of a marriage; caregivers, whose ability to attend to the elderly, sick, and disabled is often restricted by regulations that privilege marriage. Major corporations (almost half of which extend benefits to unmarried couples) as well as labor unions have opposed the marriage amendments on the grounds that domestic partnership agreements are necessary to provide for a diverse workforce. The nonpartisan American Law Institute has argued for blurring and eliminating distinctions between married and unmarried couples in order to simplify the laws that govern marriage, divorce, and cohabitation.

The gay movement might also do well to broaden its agenda to include Social Security preservation, reform and expansion, along with universal healthcare. According to Amber Hollibaugh, senior strategist for the NGLTF, most gay people age alone (perhaps as many as 80 percent according to her 2004 speech at NGLTF's Creating Change conference), rather than in conjugal couples. The needs of the population are better addressed through diversified forms of household recognition, guaranteed healthcare, and retirement security than through access to one-size-fits-all marriage. More broadly, progressives must lay out a vision of expanded social justice, rather than simply battle conservative initiatives that attack our limited welfare state. For instance, rather than merely criticize Republican plans to privatize Social Security, progressives might advocate reform and expansion of collective retirement provisions to include a wider range of households.

Meanwhile, a quiet social revolution is proceeding apace, as unmarried households of all ages and backgrounds work to forge collective economic and social rights. By drafting novel cohabitation contracts, pressing for state and local legislation, challenging discriminatory laws and urging employers to expand benefits, they have begun to create the kind of household recognitions that befit a genuinely pluralistic society. They have done so without an organized political infrastructure and without any major political party championing their rights. Gays and lesbians were once at the vanguard of this loosely constituted movement. It's time they rejoin it. And it's time for progressives to step forward and champion household diversity by reframing and recapturing the election's other security issue.

Appendix

The FACT Brief

NAN D. HUNTER AND SYLVIA A. LAW (1985)

The document that follows represents both a legal brief and a political statement. It was written for two purposes: to mobilize, in a highly visible way, a broad spectrum of feminist opposition to the enactment of laws expanding state suppression of sexually explicit material; and to place before the U.S. Court of Appeals for the Seventh Circuit a cogent legal argument for the constitutional invalidity of an Indianapolis municipal ordinance that would have permitted private civil suits to ban such material, purportedly to protect women.[1] Drafting this brief was one of the most demanding and exhilarating assignments that either author had undertaken.

The brief was written on behalf of the Feminist Anti-Censorship Task-force (FACT) and was cosigned by the Women's Legal Defense Fund (WLDF) and eighty individual feminists. The analysis of sexuality underlying the brief flows directly from a long tradition of nineteenth-century women's rights activists who sought sexual self-determination as an essential aspect of full liberation. From the beginning, others within the early feminist movement opposed this understanding of feminism because they viewed sexuality as a realm in which women often suffered. To protect women, they sought to restrict male sexual freedom by imposing on men the standard of sexual purity already applied to women.[2]

The modern feminist movement has continued this divergence of viewpoint. Simone de Beauvoir, for example, saw the erotic as an aspect of human liberty and insisted that sexual self-determination constitutes a fundamental part of women's liberation.[3] Since 1966, women's demands have included calls for greater sexual freedom for women and an end to double standards.[4] At the same time, the movement has fought for and won a number of reforms to curb rape and other violence directed at women.[5] A part of the feminist antiviolence movement evolved first into a campaign aimed at depictions of violence against women in a variety of media, and then into a campaign aimed at pornographic imagery, whether violent or not.[6]

Meanwhile, as feminist discourse on issues of sexuality became more elaborate, conservative forces also mobilized around issues of sexual imagery. An alliance of traditional moralists, the New Right, and some feminists promoted and defended the Indianapolis ordinance.[7] In the current political environment, the conservative voices are plainly more powerful than those of the feminists. For conservatives, the interest in suppression of pornography forms part of a larger agenda to reverse recent feminist gains through a moral crusade against abortion, lesbian and gay rights, contraceptive education and services, and women's fragile economic achievements. Conservatives and religious fundamentalists oppose pornography because it appears to depict and approve of sex outside marriage and procreation. The right seeks to use legitimate feminist concern about sexual violence and oppression to reinstate traditional sexual arrangements and the formerly inexorable link between reproduction and sexuality.

In 1985, conservative efforts to focus attention on suppression of sexual imagery culminated in the establishment of a Commission on Pornography charged to report to the Attorney General "more effective ways in which the spread of pornography could be contained."[8] Because most Americans do not share the moral view that confines sex to a solely procreative role, the commission's mission was to modernize the campaign against sexually explicit images by demonstrating that pornography causes violence. Despite the number of members chosen with a history of vehement opposition to sexually explicit material,[9] and tight control of the witness list,[10] the commission was unable to "prove" that pornography causes violence.

Social scientists, whose work the antipornography movement had previously utilized, refused in their testimony to draw the simple connections between pornography and violence that the commission sought.[11] Like FACT, these researchers urged the use of caution in the extension of artificial laboratory findings to naturalistic settings. Further, they testified that aggressive imagery and the mainstream media present more worrisome concerns than sexual imagery and X-rated channels.[12] Unable to marshal systemic evidence that pornography causes concrete injury, the commission was forced to rely upon the anecdotal testimony of carefully selected and well-prepared individual victims[13] and to invoke a vastly broadened concept of "harm."[14]

Perhaps the most significant and most telling aspect of the commission's work was its inability to agree on a definition of pornography.[15] Undaunted, the commission concluded that most commercially available pornography is "degrading" and contains "characteristics of degradation, domination, subordination, and humiliation," particularly of women.[16] An earlier draft of the commission report had even offered examples of such material.[17] For the final report, however, the commission found itself unable to agree on examples of "degradation."[18]

The Meese Commission recommended new federal and state legislation and increased prosecution to suppress sexually explicit materials to the maximum extent constitutionally possible.[19] Unfortunately, it failed to embrace the recommendation of the 1970 Commission on Obscenity and Pornography[20] to commence a serious sex education effort to empower young people to develop a healthy and balanced view of sexuality that would enable them to avoid unwanted pregnancy and sexually transmitted diseases. The Meese Commission did not recommend strengthening federal law to prohibit sexual harassment in the workplace.[21] It did not call for legislation to remove spousal immunity in sexual assault cases or for funding to improve law enforcement against domestic violence.

At the level of popular opinion, little support seems to exist for either conservative or feminist campaigns against sexual imagery. Press reaction to the Meese Commission report was uniformly negative.[22] In 1985, voters in Cambridge, Massachusetts, rejected, by a wide margin, a public referendum on an ordinance similar to the one adopted in Indianapolis.[23] A broad range of feminist organizations opposed the ordinance.[24] In 1986, citizens of Maine voted nearly three to one against adoption of an obscenity law;[25] women's organizations in Maine strongly opposed the proposal.[26]

The feminists of FACT helped to transform the contemporary dialogue about pornography. That debate no longer pits victimized women and conventional moralists against pornographers and civil libertarians. FACT affirms that sexuality is, for women, a source of pleasure and power, as well as a realm of danger and oppression. As a consequence, discussion of pornography and sexuality is more contextualized and appropriately complex. The brief that follows aspired to keep open the discussion about sexual explicitness and to assert that sexually explicit materials have both liberating and repressive qualities. The feminist analysis of these issues remains far from complete. As Carole S. Vance, one of the founders of FACT, observes, "The hallmark of sexuality is its complexity: its multiple meanings, sensations, and connections."[27]

Despite the contradictory strands in the feminist approach, the empirical and intellectual exploration of sexuality remains a central enterprise for the contemporary feminist movement.[28] Sexual ideas, images, and practices have been dominated by and oriented toward men and are often not responsive to women.[29] Many women experience sexual failure and frustration, rather than ecstasy and pleasure. Furthermore, feminism's core insight emphasizes that gender is socially defined. Social and sexual role acculturation largely determine gender differences. In Simone de Beauvoir's classic words, "One is not born, but rather becomes, a woman."[30] Social ideas and material arrangements give deep meaning to masculinity and femininity. The social significance of gender systematically favors men, through economic, political and legal structures that rest upon and reinforce gender. Sexual desire, both powerful and pliable, forms a part of that gender system. Discovering, describing and analyzing the complex interaction of gender and sexuality, of representation and reality, thus remain key projects of feminist theory and lives.

Brief Amici Curiae of Feminist Anti-Censorship Taskforce, et al., in *American Booksellers Association v. Hudnut*

Interest of Amici

Amici are feminists who sign this brief as a statement of our opposition to the Indianapolis ordinance. We believe that the ordinance reinforces rather than undercuts central sexist stereotypes in our society, and would result in state suppression of sexually explicit speech, including feminist images and literature, which does not in any way encourage violence against women. We condemn acts of violence against women; incitement to that violence; and misogyny, racism, and anti-Semitism in all media. We believe, however, that the Indianapolis ordinance will not reduce violence against women, and will censor speech and imagery that properly belong in the public realm. Some proponents of this ordinance genuinely believed that it would assist women to overcome disabling sex role stereotypes and promote greater equality for women. We who sign this brief are deeply concerned that it will have precisely the opposite effect.

The Feminist Anti-Censorship Taskforce (FACT) is a group of women, long active in the feminist movement, who organized in 1984 to oppose the enactment of Indianapolis-style antipornography laws. It is composed of community activists, writers, artists and teachers.

The Women's Legal Defense Fund, Inc. (WLDF) is a nonprofit, tax-exempt organization of over fifteen hundred members founded to further women's rights and to challenge sex-based inequities through the law, especially in the area of employment discrimination and domestic relations. WLDF volunteer and staff attorneys conduct public education about women's rights and sex discrimination; counsel thousands of individual women annually about their rights; represent victims of sex discrimination in selected precedent-setting cases; and advocate on behalf of laws guaranteeing sex-based equality before legislative and executive branch policy makers and as amicus curiae in numerous court cases.

Roberta Achtenberg is the Directing Attorney of the Lesbian Rights Project in San Francisco, and the editor of *Sexual Orientation and the Law* (Clark Boardman 1985). She was formerly Dean of New College of California School of Law.

Dennis Altman is a Policy Fellow, University of California at San Francisco, in the Institute for Health Policy Studies, and is the author of four books. He was Regents Lecturer, University of California at Santa Cruz, 1983.

Nancy K. Bereano is editor and publisher of Firebrand Books. Prior to that position, she was editor of the Feminist Series for Crossing Press.

Joan E. Biren (JEB) is a freelance photographer and the author of *Eye to Eye: Portraits of Lesbians.* She has been a feminist activist for fifteen years.

Betty Brooks, Ed.D., is the Director of the Southern California Rape Hotline Alliance Self-Defense Certification Program, a member of the American College of Sexologists, and founder of Women Against Sexual Abuse. She recently organized a FACT chapter in Los Angeles.

Rita Mae Brown is a well-known author whose works include *Rubyfruit Jungle, Southern Discomfort* and *Sudden Death.*

Arlene Carmen is Program Associate at Judson Memorial Church in New York City, where she directs a ministry to street prostitutes. She is coauthor of *Abortion Counseling and Social Change* (Judson Press 1973) and *Working Women: The Subterranean World of Street Prostitution*, scheduled to be published in August 1985.

Denise S. Carty-Bennia is a Professor of Law, Northeastern University School of Law, and an active participant in movements opposing sex and race discrimination in the United States.

Cheryl L. Clarke is a black, feminist lesbian poet, writer and member of the editorial collective of *Conditions* Magazine.

Michelle Cliff is the author of *Claiming an Identity They Taught Me to Despise* and *Abeng*. She is a member of Poets & Writers and The Authors Guild.

The Editors of Conditions Magazine—Founded in 1976, *Conditions* magazine is a feminist magazine of writing by women with an emphasis on writing by lesbians. The current editors are Dorothy Allison, Cheryl Clarke, Nancy Clarke Otter and Debby Schaubman.

Rhonda Copelon is an Associate Professor of Law, City University of New York Law School at Queens College. For the past fifteen years, she has litigated civil rights and women's rights cases as an attorney with the Center for Constitutional Rights.

Rosemary Daniell is a full-time writer. Her books include *A Sexual Tour of the Deep South* (poetry, 1975); *Fatal Flowers: On Sin, Sex, and Suicide in the Deep South* (non-fiction, 1980); and *Sleeping with Soldiers* (nonfiction, 1985).

Peggy C. Davis, Assistant Professor, New York University Law School, is a former Judge of the New York Family Court, and has worked in many efforts for racial and gender equality.

John D'Emilio, Ph.D., is an Assistant Professor of History at the University of North Carolina in Greensboro, and the author of *Sexual Politics, Sexual Communities* (University of Chicago Press 1983).

Betty Dodson is an artist, writer, publisher and teacher. She has spent eleven years organizing sexual enhancement workshops for women. Her book, *Self-Love and Orgasm*, has sold 200,000 copies.

Mary C. Dunlap is a law teacher and solo practitioner of civil law. She was cofounder and attorney-teacher at Equal Right Advocates, Inc., San Francisco, from 1973 to 1978. She is coauthor of a chapter on the First Amendment in *Sexual Orientation and the Law* (Clark Boardman 1985).

Thomas I. Emerson, Lines Professor of Law, Emeritus, Yale University School of Law, has written extensively on the First Amendment and is coauthor of "The Equal Rights Amendment: A Constitutional Basis for Equal Rights for Women," 80 *Yale Law Journal* 871 (1971).

Susan Estrich, Assistant Professor of Law, Harvard Law School, has written in the area of sex discrimination.

Mary L. Farmer is a lesbian feminist activist and bookstore owner in Washington, D.C.

Ann E. Freedman, Professor of Law, Rutgers Law School, Camden, was a cofounder of the Women's Law Project, Philadelphia. She is coauthor of "The Equal Rights Amendment: A Constitutional Basis for

Equal Rights for Women," 80 *Yale Law Journal* 871 (1971), and of *Sex Discrimination and the Law: Causes and Remedies* (1975).

Estelle B. Freedman is Associate Professor of History at Stanford University and Director of the Feminist Studies Program there. She is the author of *Their Sisters' Keepers*, a history of women's prison reform, and of articles on the history of sexuality.

Betty Friedan is the author of *The Feminine Mystique* and *The Second Stage*. She was founding president of the National Organization for Women and a founding member of the National Women's Political Caucus, and is presently cochair of the National Commission for Women's Equality of the American Jewish Congress.

Jewelle L. Gomez is a critic for *The Village Voice, Wellesley Women's Review of Books*, and *Hurricane Alice* (in Minneapolis). She is a Program Associate for the New York State Council on the Arts.

Bette Gordon is an Assistant Professor of Film at Hofstra University in New York and an independent filmmaker. Her work has been exhibited at international film festivals in Cannes, Berlin, Florence and Los Angeles, and is currently featured in New York, Paris and Sydney, Australia.

Linda Gordon is a Professor of History at the University of Wisconsin–Madison. She is the author of *Woman's Body, Woman's Right: A History of Birth Control in the US, America's Working Women*, and of numerous articles on the history of feminism and on family violence and the feminist response.

Vivian Gornick is a feminist author and journalist whose works include *Woman in Sexist Society: Essays in Feminism, In Search of Ali Mahmoud: An American Woman in Egypt*, and *Women in Science*.

Lynn A. Haanen is serving her third term on the Dane County (Wisconsin) Board of Supervisors and is a cofounder of FACT in Madison, Wisconsin, formed to raise concerns about antipornography and censorship measures.

Carolyn Heilbrun is Professor of English at Columbia University, and an author.

Donna J. Hitchens is an attorney, now in private practice in San Francisco, formerly the Directing Attorney of the Lesbian Rights Project and a staff attorney with Equal Rights Advocates.

Amber Hollibaugh was a founding member of the first Boston battered women's shelter and an organizer with Californians for Education Against the Briggs Initiative/Prop 6.

Joan W. Howarth is currently the police practices attorney for the ACLU Foundation of Southern California. In 1976, she helped to establish Women Against Violence Against Women (WAVAW) and was active in that group until 1982.

David Kairys is a writer, teacher and attorney in Philadelphia, and editor of *The Politics of Law.*

E. Ann Kaplan is an Associate Professor at Rutgers University, where she teaches literature and film. She is the author of *Women and Film: Both Sides of the Camera* (Methuen 1983) and of other books and articles dealing with women's studies.

Jonathan N. Katz is the author of *Gay American History* and the *Gay/Lesbian Almanac.*

Virginia Kerr is Assistant Professor of Law at the University of Pennsylvania Law School.

Norman Laurila co-owns and manages a gay and lesbian bookstore in New York City called "A Different Light," which also has a branch in Los Angeles.

Howard Lesnick is a Distinguished Professor of Law, City University of New York Law School at Queens College.

Long Haul Press is a lesbian-feminist press in New York.

Phyllis Lyon, Ed.D., is coauthor of *Lesbian/Woman.* She is a Human Rights Commissioner in San Francisco, and a professor at the Institute for Advanced Study in Human Sexuality.

Del Martin is the author of *Battered Wives.* She is also a member of the California Commission on Crime Control and Violence Prevention.

Judith McDaniel, Ph.D., is a poet, novelist, teacher and political activist. She is Program Director for the Albany, N.Y., Non-Violence Project.

Kate Millett is the author of *Sexual Politics, The Prostitution Papers, Flying* and *Sita.*

Joan Nestle is a writer and cofounder of the Lesbian Herstory Educational Foundation, Inc./The Lesbian Herstory Archives. For the last nineteen years she has taught writing in the SEEK Program at Queens College and at the City University of New York.

Esther Newton, Ph.D., is an Associate Professor of Anthropology and Coordinator of Women's Studies, State University of New York College at Purchase.

Lynn M. Paltrow is an attorney working at the National Abortion Rights Action League through the Georgetown University Women's Law and Public Policy Fellowship Program.

Randolph J. Peritz is a Professor of Law at Rutgers Law School, Camden.

Rosalind Petchesky is an Associate Professor of Political Theory at Ramapo College of New Jersey. She is the author of *Abortion and Wom-*

an's Choice (Northeastern University Press 1984), and has published numerous articles on women's reproductive rights and feminist theory.

Felice Picano is founder and publisher of The SeaHorse Press, and cofounder and publisher of Gay Presses of New York. He is the author of ten books, including *Eyes, The Lure* and *Slashed to Ribbons and Other Stories.*

Minnie Bruce Pratt teaches in the Women's Studies Program, University of Maryland–College Park. She is the author of two books of poetry, *The Sound of One Fork* and *We Say We Love Each Other,* and coauthor of *Yours in Struggle: Three Feminist Perspectives on Anti-Semitism and Racism.*

Jane B. Ransom has been active in reproductive rights issues as a member of the Committee for Abortion Rights and Against Sterilization Abuse, of the staff of the Center for Constitutional Rights, and of the board of the Brooklyn Teen Pregnancy Network.

Rayna Rapp, Ph.D., is an Associate Professor and Chair of the Department of anthropology Graduate Faculty at the New School for Social Research. She is editor of *Toward an Anthropology of Women* (1975), and coauthor, with Ellen Ross, of *Sex and Society: A Research Note from Cultural Anthropology and Social History* (1981).

Judith Resnick is Associate Professor of Law at the University of Southern California Law Center, and author of articles on the role of federal courts and on the problems faced by women in prison.

Adrienne Rich is widely known as a lesbian-feminist poet and writer. Her books include *Of Woman Born: Motherhood as Experience and Institution* (1974) *On Lies, Secrets and Silence* (essays, 1979) and *The Fact of a Doorframe: Poems 1950-1984.* She is an A.D. White Professor-at-Large at Cornell University (1981-1987) and has been a part-time lecturer in English at San Jose State University since 1984. Ms. Rich is a member of P.E.N. and The Authors Guild.

David A.J. Richards, Professor of Law, New York University Law School, has written prolifically on issues of morality and jurisprudence. His most recent work, *Toleration and the Constitution* (New York: Oxford University Press), is scheduled for publication in the near future.

Rand E. Rosenblatt, Professor of Law, Rutgers Law School, Camden, teaches constitutional law.

Sue Deller Ross, Clinical Professor of Law, Georgetown University Law Center, has litigated women's rights issues on the staff of the EEOC, the ACLU and the United States Justice Department. She is coauthor of *Sex Discrimination and the Law: Causes and Remedies* (1975) and *The Rights of Women* (1984).

Abby R. Rubenfeld is Managing Attorney, Lambda Legal Defense and Education Fund, Inc.

Gayle S. Rubin, Department of Anthropology at the University of Michigan, is the author of *The Traffic in Women* (1975), "Introduction," in *A Woman Appeared to Me* (1976), *The Leather Menace* (1981), and *Thinking Sex* (1984).

Vito Russo is a freelance writer and publicist. He is the author of *The Celluloid Closet: Homosexuality in the Movies* (Harper & Row 1981).

Kathy Sarris is President of Justice, Inc., the only statewide gay and lesbian civil rights organization in Indiana.

Karen Sauvigne was a cofounder of Working Women's Institute, a national research, resource, and action center that focuses on sexual harassment.

Susan Schechter is the author of *Women and Male Violence: The Visions and Struggles of the Battered Women's Movement*, and is a consultant to many organizations serving battered women.

Elizabeth Schneider, Associate Professor, Brooklyn Law School, teaches Women and the Law, and has litigated and written extensively on behalf of women's rights for over a decade.

Annamay Sheppard is a Professor of Law at Rutgers Law School, Newark.

Susan Sherman is a poet and editor of *IKON* Magazine.

Alix Kates Shulman is a Visiting Writer-in-Residence at the University of Colorado–Boulder. She is the author of three novels published by Knopf: *Memoirs of an Ex-Prom Queen* (1972), *Burning Questions* (1978) and *On the Stroll* (1981). She has also written two works on the anarchist-feminist Emma Goldman, entitled *To the Barricades* (Crowell 1971) and *Red Emma Speaks* (Schocken 1983), in addition to numerous essays and stories on feminist themes.

Barbara Smith is a black feminist activist and writer. She is cofounder of the Combahee River Collective in Boston, which does community organizing on issues such as sterilization abuse, reproductive freedom, violence against women, battering, and the murders of twelve black women in Boston from January to May, 1979. Ms. Smith is the author of *All the Women Are White, All the Blacks Are Men, But Some of Us Are Brave* and *Home Girls: A Black Feminist Anthology*.

Judith Stacey is an Associate Professor of Sociology at the University of California at Davis. She is the author of *Patriarchy and Socialist Revolution in China*, editor of *And Jill Came Tumbling After: Sexism in American Education*, and is on the editorial boards of *Feminist Studies* and *Signs*.

Catherine R. Stimpson is Professor of English and Director of the Institute for Research on Women at Rutgers University. She also edits a scholarly book series on women in culture and society for the University of Chicago Press.

Nadine Strossen, Assistant Clinical Professor, New York University Law School, has worked actively in antidiscrimination and free speech.

Amy Swerdlow, Ph.D., is Director of the Graduate Program in Women's History at Sarah Lawrence College. She is the editor and coauthor of *Households and Kin: Families in Flux* and coeditor of *Race, Class and Sex: The Dynamics of Control.*

Nadine Taub is a Professor of Law and Director of the Women's Rights Litigation Clinic at Rutgers Law School, Newark, where she teaches constitutional law, civil liberties and social welfare legislation. She has written widely in the field of women's rights on topics involving battered women, sexual harassment, and reproductive freedom.

Judith R. Walkowitz, Professor of History at Rutgers University, is the author of *Prostitution and Victorian Society: Women, Class and the State* (Cambridge University Press 1980), and a specialist on the history of commercialized sex, popular culture and themes of sexual violence. She is also the history editor of *Feminist Studies.*

Wendy Webster Williams, Professor of Law, Georgetown University Law Center, was a founding partner of Equal Rights Advocates, and has written and litigated on women's rights issues for more than a decade. She has taught sex discrimination law at several law schools, including University of California at Berkeley and Harvard.

Ellen Willis is Senior Editor of *The Village Voice* and the author of *Beginning to See the Light* (Knopf 1981).

Sarah Wunsch is a staff attorney at the Center for Constitutional Rights, where her work has included challenging laws restricting access to birth control and abortion rights, creating marital rape exemptions and restricting the expression of gay sexuality.

Diane L. Zimmerman, Professor of Law, New York University Law School, has written extensively in the areas of First Amendment rights, defamation and privacy.

Introduction

The instant case involves the constitutionality of an antipornography ordinance enacted by the City Council of Indianapolis, City-County Ordinance No. 35, 1984. The ordinance was ruled unconstitutional by the

U.S. District Court on a motion for summary judgment. *American Booksellers Ass'n v. Hudnut*, 598 F. Supp. 1316 (S.D. Ind. 1984).

Amici believe that the ordinance violates both the First Amendment guarantee of freedom of speech and the Fourteenth Amendment guarantee of equal treatment under the law. Under its trafficking provision, the ordinance would allow injunctions to issue against the distribution, sale, exhibition or production of any sexually explicit materials which fall within its definition of pornography. No showing of harm to the plaintiff (individual or class) is required as proof prior to the issuance of such an injunction. Because the trafficking provision and the definition most flagrantly violate constitutional principles, this brief concentrates its focus on those two aspects of the ordinance.

I. The Ordinance Suppresses Constitutionally Protected Speech in a Manner Particularly Detrimental to Women

Although Appellants argue that the ordinance is designed to restrict images which legitimate violence and coercion against women, the definition of pornography in the ordinance is not limited to images of violence or of coercion, or to images produced by women who were coerced. Nor is it limited to materials which advocate or depict the torture or rape of women as a form of sexual pleasure. It extends to any sexually explicit material which an agency or court finds to be "subordinating" to a claimant acting on behalf of women, and which fits within one of the descriptive categories which complete the definition of pornography.

For purposes of the trafficking cause of action, the ordinance defines pornography as the "graphic sexually explicit subordination of women, whether in pictures or in words, that also includes one or more" of the depictions described in six categories.[1] The violent and brutal images which Appellants use as illustrative examples[2] cannot obscure the fact that the ordinance authorizes suppression of material that is sexually explicit, but in no way violent. The language of the definition mixes phrases that have clear meanings and thus ascertainable applications (for instance, "cut up or mutilated") with others which are sufficiently elastic to encompass almost any sexually explicit image that someone might find offensive (for instance, "scenarios of degradation" or "abasement"). The material that could be suppressed under the latter category is virtually limitless.

While the sweep of the ordinance is breathtaking, it does not address (nor would *Amici* support) state suppression of the far more pervasive commercial images depicting women as primarily concerned with the whiteness of their wash or the softness of their toilet tissue. Commercial images, available to the most impressionable young children during prime time, depict women as people interested in inconsequential matters who are incapable of taking significant, serious roles in societal decision-making.

The constitutionality of the ordinance depends on the assumption that state agencies and courts can develop clear legal definitions of terms like "sexually explicit subordination," "sexual object," and "scenarios of degradation" and "abasement." In truth, these terms are highly contextual and of varying meanings. Worse, many of their most commonly accepted meanings would, if applied in the context of this ordinance, reinforce rather than erode archaic and untrue stereotypes about women's sexuality.

A. Historically the Law Has Incorporated a Sexual Double Standard Denying Women's Interest in Sexual Expression.

Traditionally, laws regulating sexual activity were premised upon and reinforced a gender-based double standard which assumed:

> that women are delicate, that voluntary sexual intercourse may harm them in certain circumstances and that they may be seriously injured by words as well as deeds. The statutes also suggest that, despite the generally delicate nature of most women, there exists a class of women who are not delicate or who are not worthy of protection. [By contrast, the law's treatment of male sexuality reflected] the underlying assumption that only males have aggressive sexual desires [and] hence they must be restrained.... The detail and comprehensiveness of [such] laws suggest that men are considered almost crazed by sex.
>
> K. Davidson, R. Ginsburg and H. Kay, *Sex-Based Discrimination* 892 (1st ed. 1974)

The Indianapolis ordinance is squarely within the tradition of the sexual double standard. It allows little room for women to openly express certain sexual desires, and resurrects the notion that sexually explicit materials are subordinating and degrading to women. Because the "trafficking" cause of action allows one woman to obtain a court order suppressing images which fall within the ordinance's definition of pornography, it implies that individual women are incapable of choosing for themselves what they consider to be enjoyable, sexually arousing material without being degraded or humiliated.

The legal system has used many vehicles to enforce the sexual double standard which protected "good" women from both sexual activity and explicit speech about sex. For example, the common law of libel held that "an oral imputation of unchastity to a woman is actionable without proof of damage. ... Such a rule never has been applied to a man, since the damage to his reputation is assumed not to be as great." W. Prosser, *Law of Torts*, 759-760 (1971).

The common law also reinforced the image of "good" women as asexual and vulnerable by providing the husband, but not the wife, remedies for "interference" with his right to sole possession of his wife's body and services. The early writ of "ravishment" listed the wife with the husband's chattels. To this day, the action for criminal conversation allows the husband to maintain an action for trespass, not only when his wife is raped,

> but also even though the wife had consented to it, or was herself the seducer and had invited and procured it, since it was considered that she was no more capable of giving a consent which would prejudice the husband's interests than was his horse. . . .

Id. at 874–877

While denying the possibility that "good" women could be sexual, the common law dealt harshly with the "bad" women who were. Prostitution laws often penalized only the woman, and not the man, and even facially neutral laws were and are enforced primarily against women. See, e.g., Jennings, "The Victim as Criminal: A Consideration of California's Prostitution Law," 64 *Calif. L. Rev.* 1235 (1976). Prostitution is defined as "the practice of a female offering her body to indiscriminate sexual intercourse with men," 63 Am. Jur. 2d Prostitution § 1 (1972), or submitting "to indiscriminate sexual intercourse which she invites or solicits." *Id.* A woman who has sexual relations with many men is a "common prostitute" and a criminal, while a sexually active man is considered normal.

The sexual double standard is applied with particular force to young people. Statutory rape laws often punished men for consensual intercourse with a female under a certain age. Comment, "The Constitutionality of Statutory Rape Laws," 27 *UCLA L. Rev.* 757, 762 (1980). Such laws reinforce the stereotype that in sex the man is the offender and the woman the victim, and that young men may legitimately engage in sex, at least with older people, while a young woman may not legally have sex with anyone.

The suppression of sexually explicit material most devastating to women was the restriction on dissemination of birth control information, lawful until 1972. In that year, the Supreme Court held that the constitutional right to privacy protects an unmarried person's right to access to birth control information. *Eisenstadt v. Baird*, 405 U.S. 438 (1972). To deny women access to contraception "prescribe[s] pregnancy and the birth of an unwanted child as punishment for fornication." *Id.* at 448. For most of the previous century, the federal Comstock Law, passed in 1873, had prohibited mailing, transporting or importing "obscene, lewd or lascivi-ous" items, specifically including all devices and information pertaining to "preventing contraception and producing abortion."[3] Women were jailed for distributing educational materials regarding birth control to other women because the materials were deemed sexually explicit in that they "contain[ed] pictures of certain organs of women" and because the materi-als were found to be "detrimental to public morals and welfare." *People v. Byrne*, 99 Misc. 1, 6 (N.Y. 1917).

The Mann Act was also premised on the notion that women require special protection from sexual activity. 35 Stat. 825 (1910), 18 U.S.C. §§ 2421–2422. It forbids interstate transportation of women for purposes of "prostitution, debauchery, or any other immoral purposes," and was enacted to protect women from reportedly widespread abduction by bands of "white slavers" coercing them into prostitution. As the legislative his-tory reveals, the Act reflects the assumption that women have no will of their own and must be protected against themselves. See H.R. Rep. No. 47, 61st Cong., 2d Sess. (1910), at 10–11. Like the premises underlying this ordinance, the Mann Act assumed:

> that women were naturally chaste and virtuous, and that no woman became a whore unless she had first been raped, seduced, drugged or deserted. [Its] image of the prostitute . . . was of a lonely and confused female. . . . [Its proponents] maintained that prostitutes were the passive victims of social disequilibrium and the brutality of men. . . . [Its] conception of female weakness and male domination left no room for the possibility that prostitutes might consciously choose their activities.
>
> Note, "The White Slave Traffic Act: The Historical Impact of a Criminal Law Policy on Women," 72 *Geo. L.J.* 1111 (1984)

The Mann Act initially defined a "white slave" to include "only those women or girls who are literally slaves—those women who are owned and held as property and chattels . . . those women and girls who, if given a fair chance, would, in all human probability, have been good wives and moth-ers," H.R. Rep. No. 47, 61st Cong., 2d Sess., at 9–10 (1910). Over the years, the interpretation and use of the Act changed drastically to punish volun-tary "immoral" acts even when no commercial intention or business profit was involved. See *Caminetti v. United States*, 242 U.S. 470 (1917); *Cleveland v. United States*, 329 U.S. 14 (1946).

> The term "other immoral acts" was held to apply to a variety of activities: the interstate transportation of a woman to work as a

chorus girl in a theatre where the woman was exposed to smoking, drinking, and cursing; a dentist who met his young lover in a neighboring state and shared a hotel room to discuss her pregnancy; two students at the University of Puerto Rico who had sexual intercourse on the way home from a date; and a man and woman who had lived together for four years and traveled around the country as man and wife while the man sold securities.

Note, *supra*, *72 Geo. L.J.* at 1119

Society's attempts to "protect" women's chastity through criminal and civil laws have resulted in restrictions on women's freedom to engage in sexual activity, to discuss it publicly, and to protect themselves from the risk of pregnancy. These disabling restrictions reinforced the gender roles which have oppressed women for centuries. The Indianapolis ordinance resonates with the traditional concept that sex itself degrades women, and its enforcement would reinvigorate those discriminatory moral standards which have limited women's equality in the past.

B. The Ordinance Is Unconstitutionally Vague Because Context Inescapably Determines the Effect of Sexual Texts and Images.

The ordinance authorizes court orders removing from public or private availability "graphic sexually explicit" words and images which "subordinate" women. A judge presented with a civil complaint filed pursuant to this law would be required to determine whether the material in question "subordinated" women. To equate pornography with *conduct* having the power to "subordinate" living human beings, whatever its value as a rhetorical device, requires a "certain sleight of hand" to be incorporated as a doctrine of law. *American Booksellers Ass'n v. Hudnut*, 598 F. Supp. 1316, 1330 (S.D. Ind. 1984). Words and images do influence what people think, how they feel, and what they do, both positively and negatively. Thus, pornography may have such influence. But the connection between fantasy or symbolic representation and actions in the real world is not direct or linear. Sexual imagery is not so simple to assess. In the sexual realm, perhaps more so than in any other, messages and their impact on the viewer or reader are often multiple, contradictory, layered and highly contextual.

The film *Swept Away* illustrates that serious problems of context and interpretation confound even the categories which on first reading might seem reasonably easy to apply. Made in 1975 by Italian director Lina Wertmuller, *Swept Away* tells a powerful story of dominance and submission. A rich, attractive woman and a younger, working-class man are first shown as class antagonists during a yachting trip on which the man is a deckhand and the woman a viciously rude boss, and then as sexual antagonists when they are stranded on a Mediterranean island and the man exacts his revenge. During the second part of the film, the man rapes the woman and repeatedly assaults her. She initially resists, then falls in love with him, and he with her.

Scenes in *Swept Away* clearly present the woman character as "experienc[ing] sexual pleasure" during rape. In addition, she is humiliated, graphically and sexually, and appears to grow to enjoy it. Although sexually explicit depictions are not the majority of scenes, the film as a whole has an active sexual dynamic. Given the overall and pervasive theme of sexual dominance and submission, it is improbable that the explicit scenes could be deemed "isolated." It is virtually certain that the film could be suppressed under the ordinance, since it was shown in laboratory studies cited by Appellants to measure negative impact of aggressive erotic materials.[4]

Swept Away is an example of graphic, sexually explicit images and characterizations used to treat themes of power imbalance, to push at the edges of what is thought to be acceptable or desirable, and to shock. Critical and popular opinions of the film varied, ranging from admiration to repulsion.[5] Whatever one's interpretation of the film, however, its profoundly important themes entitle it to a place in the realm of public discourse.

Context often determines meaning. Whether a specific image could be found to "subordinate" or "degrade" women may depend entirely on such factors as the purpose of the presentation; the size and nature of the audience; the surrounding messages; the expectation and attitude of the viewer; and where the presentation takes place, among others.[6] Yet the trafficking provision allows blanket suppression of images based on highly subjective criteria which masquerade as simple, delineating definitions.

C. The Ordinance Is Unconstitutionally Vague Because Its Central Terms Have No Fixed Meaning, and the Most Common Meanings of These Terms Are Sexist and Damaging to Women.

The ordinance's definition of pornography, essential to each cause of action, is fatally flawed. It relies on words often defined in ways that reinforce a constricted and constricting view of women's sexuality. Thus *Amici* fear that experimentations in feminist art which deal openly and explicitly with sexual themes will be easily targeted for suppression under this ordinance.

The central term "sexually explicit subordination" is not defined.[7] Appellants argue that "subordination" means that which "places women in positions of inferiority, loss of power, degradation and submission, among other things." Appellants' brief at 26. The core question, however, is left begging: What kinds of sexually explicit acts place a woman in an inferior status? Appellants argued in their brief to the District Court that "[t]he mere existence of pornography in society degrades and demeans all women." Defendants' memorandum at 10. To some observers, any graphic image of sexual acts is "degrading" to women and hence would subordinate them. To some, the required element of subordination or "positions of. . . . submission" might be satisfied by the image of a woman lying on her back inviting intercourse, while others might view the same image as affirming women's sexual pleasure and initiative. Some might draw the line at acts outside the bounds of marriage or with multiple partners. Others might see a simple image of the most traditional heterosexual act as subordinating in presenting the man in a physical position of superiority and the woman in a position of inferiority.

In any of these contexts, it is not clear whether the ordinance is to be interpreted with a subjective or an objective standard. If a subjective interpretation of "subordination" is contemplated, the ordinance vests in individual women a power to impose their views of politically or morally correct sexuality upon other women by calling for repression of images consistent with those views. The evaluative terms—subordination, degradation, abasement—are initially within the definitional control of the plaintiff, whose interpretation, if colorable, must be accepted by the court. An objective standard would require a court to determine whether plaintiff's reaction to the material comports with some generalized notion of which images do or do not degrade women. It would require the judiciary to impose its views of correct sexuality on a diverse community. The inevitable result would be to disapprove those images that are least conventional and privilege those that are closest to majoritarian beliefs about proper sexuality.

Whether subjective or objective, the inquiry is one that plainly and profoundly threatens First Amendment freedoms, and is totally inconsistent with feminist principles, as they are understood by *Amici*. Sexuality is particularly susceptible to extremely charged emotions, including feelings of vulnerability and power. The realm of image judgment opened by the ordinance is too contested and sensitive to be entrusted to legislative categorization and judicial enforcement.

The danger of discrimination is illustrated by the probability that some women would consider any explicit lesbian scene as subordinating, or as causing "[their] dignity [to] suffer," Appellants' brief at 36. Appellants plainly intend to include same-sex depictions, since their carefully selected trial court exhibits include such materials.[8] Lesbians and gay men[9] encounter massive discrimination based on prejudice related to their sexuality.[10] The trafficking provision of the ordinance virtually invites new manifestations of this prejudice by means of civil litigation against the erotica of sexual minorities.

The six subsections of the definition applicable to a trafficking complaint provide no clarification. The term "sexual object," for example, appears frequently in the definition. Appellants are confident that "the common man knows a sex object when he sees one." Appellants' brief at 40. Yet, although "sex object" may be a phrase which has begun to enjoy widened popular usage, its precise meaning is far from clear. Some persons maintain that any detachment of women's sexuality from procreation, marriage and family objectifies it, removing it from its "natural" web of association and context. When sex is detached from its traditional moorings, men allegedly benefit and women are the victims.[11] Feminists, on the other hand, generally use the term "sex object" to mean the absence of any indicia of personhood, a very different interpretation.

Appellants argue that the meaning of "subordination" and "degradation" can be determined in relation to "common usage and understanding." Appellants' brief at 33. But as we have seen, the common understanding of sexuality is one that incorporates a sexual double standard. Historically, virtually all sexually explicit literature and imagery has been thought to be degrading or abasing or humiliating, especially to women.

The interpretation of such morally charged terms has varied notoriously over time and place. A state supreme court thirty years ago ruled that the words "obscene, lewd, licentious, indecent, lascivious, immoral, [and] scandalous" were "neither vague nor indefinite" and had "a meaning understood by all." *State v. Becker*, 364 Mo. 1079, 1087, 272 S.E.2d 283, 288 (1954). See also *Winters v. New York*, 333 U.S. 507, 518 (1948). In *Kansas v. Great American Theatre Co.*, the court accepted as a definition for "prurient interest," an unhealthy, unwholesome, morbid, *degrading*, and shameful interest in sex," 227 Kan. 633, 633, 608 P.2d 951, 952 (1980) (emphasis added). A Florida obscenity statute which declared it to be "unlawful to publish, sell, [etc.] any obscene, lewd, lascivious, filthy, indecent, immoral, *degrading*, sadistic, masochistic or disgusting book"[12] was found to be no longer adequate after the decision in *Roth v. United States*, 354 U.S. 476 (1957), absent both a contemporary definition of those terms and a standard based on the materials' overall value and not just their explicitness.[13] After *Roth* and subsequent decisions, the statute was amended three times to incorporate these additional elements.[14] Upon amending the statute in 1961, the word "degrading" was dropped. Words like "degradation," "abasement" and "humiliation" have been used in the past synonymously with subjective, moralistic terms. There is no reason to believe that the language in this ordinance will be magically resistant to that kind of interpretation.

The First Amendment prohibits any law regulating expression which would of necessity result in such unpredictable and arbitrary interpretations. This ordinance transgresses all three of the measures of impermissible vagueness. A person of ordinary intelligence would be at a loss to predict how any of a huge range of sexually explicit materials would be interpreted by a court. *Grayned v. City of Rockford*, 408 U.S. 104, 108 (1972); *Smith v. Goguen*, 415 U.S. 566, 572–73 (1974); *Kolender v. Lawson*, 461 U.S. 352, 357 (1983). Protected expression would be chilled because the makers, distributors, and exhibitors of sexually explicit works would be induced to practice self-censorship rather than risk potentially endless lawsuits under this ordinance. *Buckley v. Valeo*, 424 U.S. 1, 41 (1976); *Smith v. Goguen*, 415 U.S. at 573. Lastly, the absence of reasonably clear guidelines for triers of fact would open the door to arbitrary and discriminatory enforcement of the ordinance. *Id.*; *Grayned v. City of Rockford*, 408 U.S. at 108; *Kolender v. Lawson*, 461 U.S. at 358; *Papachristou v. City of Jacksonville*, 405 U.S. 156, 168–169 (1972).

The ordinance requires enforcement of "common understandings" of culturally loaded terms. It perpetuates beliefs which undermine the principle that women are full, equal and active agents in every realm of life, including the sexual.

D. Sexually Explicit Speech Does Not Cause or Incite Violence in a Manner Sufficiently Direct to Justify Its Suppression under the First Amendment.

To uphold this ordinance and the potential suppression of all speech which could be found to fall within its definition of pornography, this court must invent a new exception to the First Amendment. To justify that, Appellants must show that the speech to be suppressed will lead to immediate and concrete harm. *Brandenburg v. Ohio*, 395 U.S. 444 (1969); *Collin v. Smith*, 578 F. 2d 1197 (7th Cir.), *cert. denied*, 439 U.S. 916 (1978). Only a small number of social science studies which purport to show a connection between violent pornography and negative attitudes and behavior toward women have been offered to support this position. For many reasons, their effort must fail.

Substantively, the studies relied upon do not justify the sweeping suppression authorized by the ordinance. Appellants cite the social science data in highly selective and grossly distorting ways. They fail to acknowledge that most of it is limited to studies of a narrow class of violent imagery. The ordinance, by contrast, both leaves untouched most of the images which may be said to cause negative effects, and would allow the suppression of many images which have not been shown to have any harmful effect. Appellants also fail to mention that the "debriefing" phase of the cited experiments suggests that negative changes in attitudes may be corrected through further speech. They seek to create the false impression that new social science data have completely refuted the finding in 1971 by the Presidential Commission on Obscenity and Pornography that pornography was not harmful. However, as Professor Edward Donnerstein wrote in the study placed before the District Court by Appellants as Exh. T. at 127–128,

> One should not assume . . . that all the research since the commission's time has indicated negative effects [of pornographic materials] on individuals. In fact, this is quite to the contrary. . . . [A] good amount of research strongly supports the position that exposure to certain types of erotica can reduce aggressive responses in people who are predisposed to aggression. The reader should keep in mind the fact that erotica has been shown to have many types of effects.

Lastly, whatever Appellants' claims, numerous methodological problems make these studies too unreliable as predictors of real world behavior to sustain the withdrawal of constitutional protection from what is now permitted speech.

Although the ordinance authorizes suppression of far more than simply violent images, the limited findings of a linkage between sexually explicit materials and a willingness to aggress against women under laboratory conditions have occurred only in studies of "aggressive pornography," defined as a particular scenario: "depictions in which physical force is used or threatened to coerce a woman to engage in sexual acts (e.g. rape)." Appellants' Exh. S. at 105. This limiting definition is used by both Professor Donnerstein and Professor Neil Malamuth in the recently published book, *Pornography and Sexual Aggression*. See Malamuth, "Aggression Against Women: Cultural and Individual Causes," in *Pornography and Sexual Aggression* 19, 29–30 (N. Malamuth and E. Donnerstein eds. 1984); Donnerstein, Pornography: Its Effect on Violence Against Women, in *Pornography and Sexual Aggression, supra*, at 53, 63. Where nonaggressive pornography is studied, no effect on aggression against women has been found; it is the violent, and not the sexual, content of the depiction that is said to produce the effects.[15] Further, all of the aggression studies have used visual imagery; none has studied the impact of only words. Finally, even as to violent "aggressive pornography," the results of the studies are not uniform.[16]

Violent and misogynist images are pervasive in our culture. Nothing in the research cited by Appellants proves their hypothesis that the messages are believed in a qualitatively different way when they are communicated through the medium of sexually explicit material. Both Professors Donnerstein and Malamuth have noted that regulation of imagery targeted at the sexually explicit misses the core of the problem:

> Images of violence against women are not the sole property of aggressive or violent pornography. Such images are quite pervasive in our society. *Images outside of the pornographic or X-rated market may in fact be of more concern, since they are imbued with a certain "legitimacy" surrounding them and tend to have much wider acceptance.*
>
> Sexist attitudes, callous attitudes about rape, and other misogynist values are just as likely to be reinforced by non-sexualized violent symbols as they are by violent pornography.

Donnerstein and Linz, at 35 *(emphasis added)*

> Attempts to alter the content of mass media . . . cannot be limited to pornography, since research has documented similar effects from mainstream movies. In addition, other mass media forms, such as advertisements, television soap operas, and detective magazines, to name a few, also contain undesirable images of violence against women. The most pertinent question on the issue of changing mass media content may not be where we draw the line between pornography and non-pornography but how we can best combat violence against women in its myriad forms.

Malamuth and Lindstrom, "Debate on Pornography," *Film Comment*, December 1984, at 39, 40

When "more speech" can be an effective means of countering prejudicial and discriminatory messages, the First Amendment forbids the use of censorship to suppress even the most hateful content. *Collin v. Smith*, 578 F.2d 1197 (7th Cir.), *cert denied*, 439 U.S. 916 (1978). The social science data upon which Appellants rely so heavily indicate that further speech can remove the negative effects on attitude registered after viewing certain kinds of violent pornography. Malamuth and Donnerstein both conduct "debriefing" sessions at the conclusion of their experiments. In these sessions, the purposes of the studies are explained to the subjects, and information is presented to dispel rape myths. The effectiveness of the debriefing sessions is then tested up to four months later. "The findings of these studies indicated consistently that the education interventions were successful in counteracting the effects of aggressive pornography and in reducing beliefs in rape myths." Malamuth, *supra* p. 14, at 46.

> Censorship is not the solution. Education, however, is a viable alternative. Early sex education programs which dispel myths

about sexual violence and early training in critical viewing skills could mitigate the influence of these films.

Donnerstein and Linz, "Debate on Pornography," at 35

This debriefing effect demonstrates that the changes in attitude shown from pornography are not permanent or, as Appellants contend, conditioned.

The substance of the social science data provides no support for the broad suppression of speech authorized by the ordinance. Further, even if the ordinance were narrowly limited to the "aggressive pornography" which has been studied, limits in the methodology fatally undermine Appellants' claims that even this violent material causes the sort of concrete, immediate harm that could justify creating a new exception to the First Amendment.

Behavior under laboratory conditions cannot predict behavior in life with the degree of accuracy and specificity required to justify a censorship law. The college students being studied in these laboratory tests knew that their actions would have no actual negative impact on real people. Indeed, the experimental setting may induce conduct in subjects that they would not otherwise exhibit. In the words of one theorist:

> Laboratory studies that deliberately lower restraints against aggression . . . may be seen as representing a reversal of the normal socialization process. After a subject has been angered, he is allowed (actually told) to attack his adversary. The victim emits no pain cues . . . and the subject not only feels better but learns that, in this laboratory situation, aggression is permissible and socially approved (i.e. condoned by the experimenter).

> Donnerstein, "Pornography: Its Effect on Violence Against Women," at 60

Moreover, most of the reported willingness to aggress occurs only in subjects who are previously angered as part of the experiment shortly before they are asked to administer shocks. See *generally* Donnerstein, *supra* p. 14. Some researchers believe that the anger is the primary factor producing the manifestation of aggression. See Gray, "Exposure to Pornography and Aggression Toward Women: The Case of the Angry Male," 29 *Soc. Probs.* 387 (1982).

Additionally, in most studies cited, aggressive behavior occurs only when the experimenter gives subjects disinhibitory cues indicating that such behavior is acceptable, and not when the experimenter provides an inhibitory communication.

> These data highlight the important role of situational factors in affecting aggression against women and suggest that, while cul-

tural factors such as aggressive pornography may increase some males' aggressive tendencies, the actual expression of aggressive responses may be strongly regulated by varied internal and external (i.e., situational) variables.

Malamuth, "Aggression Against Women," at 35

In life, more than in a laboratory, a multitude of interacting factors shape behavior, including early childhood experiences, family dynamics, religious training, formal education, and one's perceived relation to governmental structures and the legal system, as well as the entire range of media stimuli.[17] It is difficult even in the laboratory to identify a single "cause" for behavior.[18] Every study finding a negative effect under laboratory conditions from viewing an image cannot be grounds for rewriting the First Amendment.

Appellants and supporting *amici* also claim a causal connection between the availability of pornography and rape. Such a claim is implausible on its face. Acts of rape and coercion long preceded the mass distribution of pornography, and in many cultures pornography is unavailable, yet the incidence of rape, and of discrimination against women generally, is high.[19] The converse is also true; that is, there are places where pornography is widely available, and the incidence of rape is low compared to the United States.

Many studies have focused on Denmark to discern whether their abolition of the laws restricting pornography in the mid-1960s could be linked to any changes in behavior. Numerous conflicting arguments have been made as to the implications of the Danish experience. In 1979, the British Committee on Obscenity and Film Censorship published a report critically reviewing extensive data on the asserted linkage between pornography and sexual violence. Because it was done a decade after the American report, it includes much of the recent work published on this topic. The committee found "no support at all" for the thesis that the availability of pornography in Denmark could be linked to an increase in sexual offenses. "It is impossible to discern a significant trend in rape which could be linked in any way to the free availability of pornography since the late 1960s." *Obscenity and Film Censorship* 83 (B. Williams ed. 1979).

Appellants' argument that pornography should be precluded from First Amendment protection would require this Court to find that it causes harm in the direct, immediate way that falsely shouting fire in a crowded theater does. The social science data upon which they rely lend no support to such a claim. The findings relate to only a small portion of the material which the ordinance would suppress, results of the studies are mixed, and even the data which report laboratory findings of aggression cannot be used blithely to predict behavior in the real world.

*E. Constitutional Protection for Sexually Explicit Speech
Should Be Enhanced, Not Diminished.*

Sexually explicit speech which is judged "obscene" is not protected under the First Amendment. *Miller v. California*, 413 U.S. 15 (1973). Appellants seek to vitiate the protection currently afforded nonobscene sexual speech on the ground that any expression falling within the scope of this ordinance "is not the free exchange of ideas." Appellants' brief at 12. They ask this Court to rule that all sexually explicit speech is disfavored:

> It is essential to look at the nature of the material regulated to measure the importance of the chilling effect . . . . [T]he ordinance reaches "sexually explicit activity." . . . The Supreme Court has determined that "there is . . . a less vital interest in the uninhibited exhibition of material that is on the borderline between pornography and artistic expression than in the free dissemination of ideas of social and political significance." The message of *Young* is that it is constitutional for anyone who steps too close to the line to take the risk of crossing it when sexually explicit material is involved. The chilling effect is simply not entitled to great weight in this context.

Appellants' brief at 53 (citations omitted)

The argument that the First Amendment provides less protection for sexual images than for speech which is "political" misunderstands both the value of free expression and the political content of sexually explicit speech. Many justifications support free expression: our incapacity to determine truth without open discussion; the need for people to communicate to express self-identity and determine how to live their lives; the inability of the censor to wield power wisely.

Further, sexual speech is political. One core insight of modern feminism is that the personal is political. The question of who does the dishes and rocks the cradle affects both the nature of the home and the composition of the legislature. The dynamics of intimate relations are likewise political, both to the individuals involved and, by their multiplied effects, to the wider society.[20] To argue, as Appellants do, that sexually explicit speech is less important than other categories of discourse reinforces the conceptual structures that have identified women's concerns with relationships and intimacy as less significant and valuable precisely because those concerns are falsely regarded as having no bearing on the structure of social and political life.

Depictions of ways of living and acting that are radically different from our own can enlarge the range of human possibilities open to us, and help us grasp the potentialities of human behavior, both good and bad. Rich fantasy imagery allows us to experience in imagination ways of being that we may not wish to experience in real life. Such an enlarged vision of possible realities enhances our human potential and is highly relevant to our decision-making as citizens on a wide range of social and ethical issues.

For sexual minorities, speech describing conduct can be a means of self-affirmation in a generally hostile world. Constrictions on that speech can deny fundamental aspects of self-identity. *Cf. Gay Law Students Ass'n v. Pacific Tel. and Tel.*, 24 Cal. 3d 458, 488, 594 P.2d 592, 611, 156 Cal. Rptr. 14, 33 (1979). In *Rowland v. Mad River Local School District*, 730 F.2d 444 (6th Cir. 1984), *cert. denied*, 53 U.S.L.W. 3614 (U.S. Feb. 26, 1985), a public employee was fired from her job because she confided in coworkers that she was bisexual. Although her statement resulted in no disruption of the workplace, the Court of Appeals ruled that it was constitutionally permissible to fire her "for talking about it." *Id.* at 450. Yet, as in *Gay Law Students Association*, the speech should have been considered political:

> I think it is impossible not to note that a … public debate is currently ongoing regarding the rights of homosexuals. The fact of petitioner's bisexuality, once spoken, necessarily and ineluctably involved her in that debate. Speech that "touches upon" this explosive issue is no less deserving of constitutional attention than speech relating to more widely condemned forms of discrimination.

> *Rowland v. Mad River Local School Dist.*, 53 U.S.L.W. at 3615 (1985)
> (Brennan and Marshall, J.J., dissenting from denial of certiorari)

Sexually explicit expression, including much that is covered by the ordinance, carries many more messages than simply the misogyny described by Appellants. It may convey the message that sexuality need not be tied to reproduction, men or domesticity. It may contain themes of sex for no reason other than pleasure, sex without commitment, and sexual adventure—all of which are surely ideas. *Cf. Kingsley Corp. v. Regents*, 360 U.S. 684 (1959).

Even pornography which is problematic for women can be experienced as affirming of women's desires and of women's equality:

> Pornography can be a psychic assault, both in its content and in its public intrusions on our attention, but for women as for men it can also be a source of erotic pleasure. A woman who is raped is a victim; a woman who enjoys pornography (even if that means enjoying a rape fantasy) is in a sense a rebel, insisting on an aspect of her sexuality that has been defined as a male preserve. Insofar as pornography glorifies male supremacy and sexual alienation,

it is deeply reactionary. But in rejecting sexual repression and hypocrisy—which have inflicted even more damage on women than on men—it expresses a radical impulse.

Willis, "Feminism, Moralism and Pornography," in *Powers of Desire: The Politics of Sexuality* 460, 464 (A. Snitow, C. Stansell and S. Thompson eds. 1983). Fantasy is not the same as wish fulfillment. See N. Friday, *My Secret Garden: Women's Secret Fantasies* (1973) and *Forbidden Flowers: More Women's Sexual Fantasies* (1975). But one cannot fully discuss or analyze fantasy if the use of explicit language is precluded.

The range of feminist imagination and expression in the realm of sexuality has barely begun to find voice. Women need the freedom and the socially recognized space to appropriate for themselves the robustness of what traditionally has been male language. Laws such as the one under challenge here would constrict that freedom. See Blakely, "Is One Woman's Sexuality Another Woman's Pornography?," *Ms.* magazine, April 1985, at 37. *Amici* fear that as more women's writing and art on sexual themes[21] emerge which are unladylike, unfeminine, aggressive, power-charged, pushy, vulgar, urgent, confident, and intense, the traditional foes of women's attempts to step out of their "proper place" will find an effective tool of repression in the Indianapolis ordinance.

II. The Ordinance Unconstitutionally Discriminates on the Basis of Sex and Reinforces Sexist Stereotypes

The challenged ordinance posits a great chasm—a categorical difference— between the makeup and needs of men and of women. It goes far beyond acknowledgment of the differences in life experiences which are inevitably produced by social structures of gender inequality. The ordinance presumes women as a class (and only women) are subordinated by virtually any sexually explicit image. It presumes women as a class (and only women) are incapable of making a binding agreement to participate in the creation of sexually explicit material. And it presumes men as a class (and only men) are conditioned by sexually explicit depictions to commit acts of aggression and to believe misogynist myths.

Such assumptions reinforce and perpetuate central sexist stereotypes; they weaken, rather than enhance, women's struggles to free themselves of archaic notions of gender roles. In so doing, this ordinance itself violates the Equal Protection Clause of the Fourteenth Amendment. In treating women as a special class, it repeats the error of earlier protectionist legislation which gave women no significant benefits and denied their equality.

*A. The District Court Erred in Accepting Appellants' Assertion
That Pornography Is a Discriminatory Practice Based on Sex.*

The ordinance is predicted on a finding that:

> Pornography is a discriminatory practice based on sex which
> denies women equal opportunities in society. Pornography is
> central in creating and maintaining sex as a basis for discrimina-
> tion. . . . [It harms] women's opportunities for equality of rights
> in employment, education, access to and use of public accommo-
> dations, and acquisition of real property; promote[s] rape, bat-
> tery, child abuse, kidnapping and prostitution and inhibit[s] just
> enforcement of laws against such acts. . . .

Indianapolis, Ind., Code § 16-1(a)(2)

The District Court accepted that finding, but held that First Amendment values outweighed the asserted interest in protecting women. *American Booksellers Ass'n v. Hudnut*, 598 F. Supp. 1316, 1335–1337 (S.D. Ind.
1984). *Amici* dispute the City and County's "finding" that "pornography
is central in creating and maintaining sex as a basis for discrimination."
There was no formal, or indeed informal, legislative fact-finding process leading to this conclusion. Rather, legislators who had previously
opposed obscenity on more traditional and moralistic grounds adopted
a "model bill" incorporating this finding.[22] The model bill was in turn
based on legislative hearings, held in Minneapolis, which did not, in fairness, reflect a reasoned attempt to understand the factors "central" in
maintaining "sex as a basis for discrimination."[23] See Appellants' brief
at 15, n.6.

It is true that sex discrimination takes multiple forms, which are
reflected in the media. But the finding that "pornography is central in creating and maintaining sex as a basis for discrimination" does not represent our best understanding of the complex, deep-seated and structural
causes of gender inequality. In the past decade, many people have grappled
with the question of causation. Feminist law professors and scholars have
published and revised collections of cases and materials. K. Davidson, R.
Ginsberg and H. Kay, *supra* p. 3 (1974 and 2d ed. 1981); B. Babcock, A.
Freedman, E. Norton and S. Ross, *Sex Discrimination and the Law: Causes
and Remedies* (1974 and Supp. 1978). The factors they find most significant include: the sex-segregated wage labor market; systematic devalua-
tion of work traditionally done by women; sexist concepts of marriage and
family; inadequate income maintenance programs for women unable to
find wage work; lack of day care services and the premise that child care is

an exclusively female responsibility; barriers to reproductive freedom; and discrimination and segregation in education and athletics.[24] Numerous feminist scholars have written major works tracing the cultural, economic and psychosocial roots of women's oppression.[25]

Misogynist images, both those which are sexually explicit and the far more pervasive ones which are not, reflect and may help to reinforce the inferior social and economic status of women. But none of these studies and analyses identifies sexually explicit material as the central factor in the oppression of women. History teaches us that the answer is not so simple. Factors far more complex than pornography produced the English common-law treatment of women as chattel property and the enactment of statutes allowing a husband to rape or beat his wife with the impunity. In short, the claim that "pornography is central in creating and maintaining sex as a basis of discrimination" is flatly inconsistent with the conclusions of most who have studied the question.

Amici also dispute the "finding" that pornography, as defined by the ordinance, is "a discriminatory practice. ... which denies women equal opportunities." Images and fictional text are not the same thing as subordinating conduct. The ordinance does not target discriminatory *actions* denying access to jobs, education, public accommodations or real property. It prohibits images. Although ideas have impact, images of discrimination are not the discrimination.

Further, the ordinance is cast in a form very different from the traditional antidiscrimination principles embodied in the Constitution and federal civil rights laws. Antidiscrimination laws demand equality of treatment for men and women, blacks and whites. The ordinance, by contrast, purports to protect women. It assumes that women are subordinated by sexual images and that men act uncontrollably if exposed to them. Sexist stereotypes are thus built into its very premises, and, as we demonstrate *infra*, its effect will be to reinforce those stereotypes.

Hence, the District Court misperceived this case as one requiring the assignment of rank in a constitutional hierarchy. It is not necessary to rule that either gender equality or free speech is more important. The ordinance is fatally flawed not only because it authorizes suppression of speech protected by the First Amendment but also because it violates the constitutional guarantee of sex-based equality.

B. *The Ordinance Classifies on the Basis of Sex, and Perpetuates Sexist Stereotypes.*

The ordinance defines pornography in gender specific terms as "the graphic sexually explicit subordination of *women*" that also presents "*women*" in particular ways proscribed by the law. The District Court found:

> [t]he Ordinance seeks to protect adult women, as a group from the diminution of the legal and sociological status as women, that is from the discriminatory stigma which befalls women *as women* as a result of "pornography."

> *American Booksellers Ass'n v. Hudnut*, 598 F. Supp. at 1335 *(emphasis supplied)*

The heart of the ordinance is the suppression of sexually explicit images of women, based on a finding of "subordination," a term which is not defined. The ordinance implies that sexually explicit images of women necessarily subordinate and degrade women, and perpetuates stereotypes of women as helpless victims and people who could not seek or enjoy sex.

The ordinance also reinforces sexist stereotypes of men. It denies the possibility that graphic sexually explicit images of a man could ever subordinate or degrade him. It provides no remedy for sexually explicit images showing men as "dismembered, truncated or fragmented": nor "shown as filthy or inferior, bleeding, bruised or hurt."

The stereotype that sex degrades women, but not men, is underscored by the proviso that "the use of men, children, or transsexuals in the place of women. ... also constitutes pornography." Indianapolis, Ind., Code § 16-3(q). The proviso does not allow men to claim that they, as men, are injured by sexually explicit images of them. Rather men are degraded only when they are used "in place of women." The ordinance assumes that in sexuality, degradation is a condition that attaches to women.[26]

The ordinance authorizes any woman to file a complaint against those trafficking in pornography "as a woman acting against the subordination of women." A man, by contrast, may obtain relief only if he can "prove injury in the same way that a woman is injured." Indianapolis, Ind., Code § 16-17(a) (7) (b). Again the ordinance assumes that women as a class are subordinated and hurt by depictions of sex, and men are not.

The ordinance reinforces yet another sexist stereotype of men as aggressive beasts. Appellants assert:

> By conditioning the male orgasm to female subordination, pornography . . . makes the subordination of women pleasurable and

seemingly legitimate. Each time men are sexually aroused by pornography, they learn to connect a woman's sexual pleasure to abuse
and a woman's sexual nature to inferiority. They learn this in their
bodies, not just their minds, so that it becomes a natural physiological response. At this point pornography leaves no more room for
further debate than does shouting "kill" to an attack dog.

Appellants, brief at 21

Men are not attack dogs, but morally responsible human beings. The
ordinance reinforces a destructive sexist stereotype of men as irrespon-
sible beasts, with "natural physiological responses" which can be triggered
by sexually explicit images of women, and for which the men cannot be
held accountable. Thus, men are conditioned into violent acts or negative
beliefs by sexual images; women are not. Further, the ordinance is wholly
blind to the possibility that men could be hurt and degraded by images
presenting them as violent or sadistic.

The ordinance also reinforces sexist images of women as incapable of
consent. It creates a remedy for people "coerced" to participate in the production of pornography. Unlike existing criminal, tort and contract remedies against coercion, the ordinance provides:

> proof of the following facts or conditions shall not constitute a
> defense: that the person actually consented . . . ; or, knew that
> the purpose of the acts or events in question was to make por-
> nography; or demonstrated no resistance or appeared to cooper-
> ate actively in the photographic sessions or in the sexual events
> that produced the pornography; or . . . signed a contract, or made
> statements affirming a willingness to cooperate in the production
> of pornography.

Indianapolis, Ind., Code § 16-3.(5) (A) VIII–XI

In effect, the ordinance creates a strong presumption that women who
participate in the creation of sexually explicit materials are coerced.[27] A
woman's manifestation of consent—no matter how plain, informed, or
even self-initiated—does not constitute a defense to her subsequent claim
of coercion. Women are judged incompetent to consent to participation in
the creation of sexually explicit material, and condemned as "bad" if they
do so.

Appellants argue that this provision is justified by Supreme Court precedent allowing suppression of sexually explicit material involving children. They assert that women, like children, "are incapable of consenting
to engage in pornographic conduct, even absent a showing of physical

coercion and therefore require special protection. . . . The coercive conditions under which most pornographic models work make this part of the law one effective address to the industry." [sic.] Appellants' brief at 17.

This provision does far more than simply provide a remedy to women who are pressured into the creation of pornography which they subsequently seek to suppress. It functions to make all women incompetent to enter into legally binding contracts for the production of sexually explicit material. When women are legally disabled from making binding agreements, they are denied power to negotiate for fair treatment and decent pay. Enforcement of the ordinance would drive production of sexually explicit material even further into an underground economy, where the working conditions of women in the sex industry would worsen, not improve.

C. The Ordinance Is Unconstitutional Because It Reinforces Sexist Stereotypes and Classifies on the Basis of Sex.

In recent years, the Supreme Court has firmly and repeatedly rejected gender-based classifications, such as that embodied in the ordinance. The constitutionally protected right to sex-based equality under law demands that:

> the party seeking to uphold a statute that classifies individuals on the basis of their gender must carry the burden of showing an "exceedingly persuasive justification" for the classification. . . . The burden is met only by showing at least that the classification serves "important governmental objectives and that the discriminatory means employed" are "substantially related to the achievement of those objectives."

Mississippi Univ. for Women v. Hogan, 458 U.S. 718, 724–725 (1982)

The sex-based classifications embodied in the statute are justified on the basis of stereotypical assumptions about women's vulnerability to sexually explicit images and their production, and men's latent uncontrollability. But the Supreme Court has held that, "[This standard] must be applied free of fixed notions concerning the roles and abilities of males and females. Care must be taken in ascertaining whether the statutory objective itself reflects archaic and stereotypical notions." *Id.* Gender-based classifications cannot be upheld if they are premised on "old notions" and "archaic and overboard" generalizations "about the roles and relative abilities of men and women." *Califano v. Goldfarb*, 430 U.S. 199, 217 (1977).

The ordinance damages individuals who do not fit the stereotypes it embodies. It delegitimates and makes socially invisible women who find sexually explicit images of women "in positions of display" or "penetrated by objects" to be erotic, liberating or educational. These women are told that their perceptions are a product of "false consciousness," and that such images are so inherently degrading that they may be suppressed by the state. At the same time, it stamps the imprimatur of state approval on the belief that men are attack dogs triggered to violence by the sight of a sexually explicit image of a woman. It delegitimates and makes socially invisible those men who consider themselves gentle, respectful of women, or inhibited about expressing their sexuality.

Even worse, the stereotypes of the ordinance perpetuate traditional social views of sex-based difference. By defining sexually explicit images of woman as subordinating and degrading to them, the ordinance reinforces the stereotypical view that "good" women do not seek and enjoy sex.[28] As applied, it would deny women access to sexually explicit material at a time in our history when women have just begun to acquire the social and economic power to develop our own images of sexuality. Stereotypes of hair-trigger male susceptibility to violent imagery can be invoked as an excuse to avoid directly blaming the men who commit violent acts.

Finally, the ordinance perpetuates a stereotype of women as helpless victims, incapable of consent, and in need of protection. A core premise of contemporary sex equality doctrine is that if the objective of the law is to "'protect' members of one gender because they are presumed to suffer from an inherent handicap or to be innately inferior, the object itself is illegitimate." *Mississippi Univ. for Women v. Hogan*, 458 U.S. at 725. We have learned through hard experience that gender-based classifications protecting women from their own presumed innate vulnerability reflect "an attitude of 'romantic paternalism' which, in practical effect, puts women not on a pedestal but in a cage." *Frontiero v. Richardson*, 411 U.S. 677, 684 (1973).

The coercion provisions of the ordinance "protect" by denying women's capacity to voluntarily agree to participate in the creation of sexually explicit images. The trafficking provisions "protect" by allowing women to suppress sexually explicit speech which the ordinance presumes is damaging to them. The claim that women need protection and are incapable of voluntary action is familiar. Historically, the presumed "natural and proper timidity and delicacy" of women made them unfit "for many of the occupations of civil life," and justified denying them the power to contract. *Bradwell v. Illinois*, 83 U.S. (16 Wall.) 130, 141–142 (1872).

Until quite recently, the law commonly provided women special protections against exploitation. In 1936, the Supreme Court upheld a law establishing minimum wages for women saying; "What can be closer to the public interest than the health of women and their protection from unscrupulous and overreaching employers?" *West Coast Hotel v. Parrish*,

300 U.S. 379, 398 (1936). In 1948, the Court approved a law banning women from work as bartenders as a legitimate measure to combat the "moral and social problems" to which bartending by women might give rise. *Goesaert v. Cleary*, 335 U.S. 464, 466 (1948). The protectionist premise of these cases is now discredited, and their holdings repudiated.

Women were, and continue to be, in a position of social and economic vulnerability that inhibits their ability to negotiate fair terms and conditions of wage labor. Further, the pervasive sexism and violence of our culture make women vulnerable to exploitation, and inhibit their ability to enter into sexual or other relationships on a free and voluntary basis.

Slavery and free self-actualization are opposite poles on a continuum. Both free agency and response to external pressure are simultaneous aspects of human action. In the 1930s, employers challenged minimum wage and hour laws saying that laborers "freely consented" to work twelve hours a day, under dangerous and harmful conditions, for wages that did not provide minimal subsistence. We understand today that this concept of voluntary consent is self-serving and empty. Similarly, many women engage in sex or in the production of sexually explicit materials in response to pressures so powerful that it would be cynical to characterize their actions as simply voluntary and consensual.

Still, the laws that "protected" only women from exploitation in wage labor hurt them. B. Babcock, A. Freedman, E. Norton and S. Ross *supra* p. 25, at 48, 191–217. Many employers responded by barring women from the best-paying jobs with the greatest opportunity for advancement. Further, the protective labor laws reinforced general beliefs about women's vulnerability and incompetence. Similarly here, the protection of the ordinance reinforces the idea that women are incompetent, particularly in relation to sex.

The pervasive sexism and violence of our culture create a social climate—in the home, workplace and street—that *is* different for women than for men. But even accurate generalizations about women's need for help do not justify sex-based classifications such as those in this ordinance. It is also true that women generally are still the ones who nurture young children. Yet we understand that laws giving mothers irrebuttable "tender-years" presumption for custody, or offering child-rearing leaves only to mothers but not to fathers, ultimately hurt women and are unconstitutional.[29]

Some of the proponents of the ordinance believe that it will empower women, while others support it for more traditional, patriarchal reasons. *Supra* note 22. But many gender-based classifications are premised on a good faith intent to help or protect women. Good intent does not justify an otherwise invidious gender-based law. "Our nation has had a long and unfortunate history of sex discrimination." *Frontiero v. Richardson*, 411 U.S. at 684. The clearest lesson of that history is that sex-based classifications hurt women.

Thus, the District Court was correct to reject Appellants' claim that women are like children who need special protection from sexually explicit material. The Court found that:

> adult women as a group do not, as a matter of public policy or applicable law, stand in need of the same type of protection which has long been afforded children. . . . Adult women generally have the capacity to protect themselves from participating in and being personally victimized by pornography. . . .

> *American Booksellers Ass'n v. Hudnut*, 598 F. Supp. at 1333–1334

The gender-based classification embodied in the ordinance is unconstitutional because it assumes and perpetuates classic sexist concepts of separate gender-defined roles, which carry "the inherent risk of reinforcing the stereotypes about the 'proper place' of women and their need for special protection." *Orr v. Orr*, 440 U.S. 268, 283 (1979).

D. The Sex-Based Classification and Stereotypes Created by the Ordinance Are Not Carefully Tailored to Serve Important State Purposes.

Appellants claim that the ordinance serves the "governmental interest in promoting sex equality." Appellants' brief at 23. Certainly preventing the violent subordination of women is the sort of compelling public purpose that might justify sex-based classification. But, as is often true of classifications justified on grounds that they protect women, the benefits actually provided are minimal. The ordinance thus also fails the requirement for a "substantial relationship" between its classification and the achievement of its asserted goal. *Mississippi Univ. for Women v. Hogan*, 458 U.S. at 724.

Supporters of the ordinance describe acts of violence against women and claim that the ordinance would provide a remedy for those injuries. But the only new remedy it provides is suppression of sexually explicit materials, a wholly inadequate and misdirected response to real violence.

Amicus Marchiano, for example, has written of her marriage to a man who beat her, raped her, forced her into prostitution, and terrorized her. L. Lovelace, *Ordeal* (1980). For several years prior to the making of *Deep Throat*, she was virtually imprisoned by her husband through brute force, control of economic resources, and the fact that she believed his claim that a wife could not charge her husband with a crime. *Id.* at 82. Had this ordinance existed then, it would not have helped her. There is a compelling social need to provide more effective remedies for victims of violence and sexual coercion. But the ordinance does not protect vulnerable people against those actions already prohibited by the criminal law. Those who have worked to empower battered women and children understand that effective enforcement of existing criminal sanctions demands a multi-pronged effort. Police and prosecutors must be trained, required to take complaints seriously, and given the resources to do so. *Bruno v. McGuire*, 4 Fam. L. Rep. (BNA) 3095 (1978). Help must be available on a continuous and prompt basis. A. Boylan and N. Taub, *Adult Domestic Violence: Constitutional, Legislative and Equitable Issues* (1981). Vulnerable people must be educated and provided support by community groups and shelters. L. Bowker, *Beating Wife Beating* (1982). See generally S. Schechter, *Women and Male Violence: The Visions and Struggles of the Battered Women's Movement* (1982); Marcus, "Conjugal Violence: The Law of Force and the Force of Law," 69 *Calif. L. Rev.* 1657 (1981). The remedy this ordinance provides for violence and sexual coercion is illusory.

Individuals who commit acts of violence must be held legally and morally accountable. The law should not displace responsibility onto imagery. *Amicus* Women Against Pornography describe as victims of pornography married women coerced to perform sexual acts depicted in pornographic works, working women harassed on the job with pornographic images, and children who have pornography forced on them during acts of child abuse. Appellants' brief at 13. Each of these examples describes victims of violence and coercion, not of images. The acts are wrong, whether or not the perpetrator refers to an image. The most wholesome sex education materials, if shown to a young child as an example of what people do with those they love, could be used in a viciously harmful way. The law should punish the abuser, not the image. Title VII of the Civil Rights Act provides remedies for working women injured by sexual taunts or slurs, including sexually explicit pictures, e.g., *Barnes v. Costle*, 561 F.2d 983 (D.C. Cir. 1977), and for those injured by misogynist imagery. See e.g., *Kyriazi v. Western Elec. Co.*, 461 F. Supp. 892 (D.N.J. 1978). These legal principles apply to any images or texts which people put to discriminatory use, whether pornography or the Bible. But no law has or should assume that the same woman harassed by pornographic images in the workplace might not enjoy those very images if given the opportunity to put them to her own use.

To resist forced sex and violence, women need the material resources to enable them to reject jobs or marriages in which they are abused or assaulted, and the internal and collective strength to fight the conditions of abuse. The ordinance does nothing to enhance the concrete economic and social power of women. Further, its stereotype of women as powerless victims undermines women's ability to act affirmatively to protect themselves.

Suppression of sexually explicit material will not eliminate the pervasive sexist images of the mainstream culture or the discriminatory economic and social treatment that maintains women's second-class status. Such suppression will not empower women to enter into sexual relationships on a voluntary, consensual basis. Empowering women requires something more than suppression of texts and images. It demands "concrete material changes that enable women and men to experience sexuality less attached to and formed by gender."[30] These changes include social and economic equality; access to jobs, day care and education; more equal sharing of responsibility for children; recognition of the social and economic value of the work that women have traditionally done in the home; and access to birth control, abortion and sex education.

III. Conclusion

Sexually explicit speech is not *per se* sexist or harmful to women. Like any mode of expression, it can be used to attack women's struggle for equal rights, but it is also a category of speech from which women have been excluded. The suppression authorized by the Indianapolis ordinance of a potentially enormous range of sexual imagery and texts reinforces the notion that women are too fragile, and men too uncontrollable, absent the aid of the censor, to be trusted to reject or enjoy sexually explicit speech for themselves. By identifying "subordination of women" as the concept that distinguishes sexually explicit material which is tolerable from that to be condemned, the ordinance incorporates a vague and asymmetric standard for censorship that can as readily be used to curtail feminist speech about sexuality, or to target the speech of sexual minorities, as to halt hateful speech about women. Worse, perpetuation of the concept of gender-determined roles in regard to sexuality strengthens one of the main obstacles to achieving real change and ending sexual violence.

* * *

The F.A.C.T. brief was originally filed in the U.S. Court of Appeals for the Seventh Circuit in April, 1985. It was originally published, together with the introduction, in the *University of Michigan Journal of Law Reform* in 1988.

Notes

Notes to New Introduction of 10th Anniversary Edition

1. See "What's Queer About Queer Studies Now?," a special issue of *Social Text* edited by David Eng, Judith Halberstam and Jose Munoz (Issue #84-85, Fall/Winter 2005).

Notes to Introduction of the First Edition

1. I borrow the phrase "bridge discourse" from Wahneema Lubiano's contribution to a *Voice Literary Supplement* special section on art and theory, "Let's Get Critical: Can't Art and Theory Get Along?" No. 126 (June 1994). Lubiano refers to poststructuralist theory as a possible "bridge discourse" or *lingua franca* among writers and artists who might not have much else in common (p. 7).

2. For one of several important exceptions, see C. Carr, *On Edge: Performance at the End of the Twentieth Century* (Hanover, New Hampshire: University Press of New England for Wesleyan University Press, 1993). Carr is among a group of feminists, publishing primarily in *The Village Voice* and *Artforum*, who continually draw connections between feminist and lesbian/gay politics and arts issues.

3. See Kiss and Tell, *Her Tongue on My Theory: Images, Essays and Fantasies* (Vancouver: Press Gang Publishers, 1994), especially Persimmon Blackbridge's essay, "Against the Law: Sex Versus the Queen," pp. 75–92.

4. For an account of the WAP tour (the very same one I went on), see John D'Emilio, "Women Against Pornography: Feminist Frontier or Social Purity Crusade?" in his *Making Trouble: Essays on Gay History, Politics and the University* (New York: Routledge, 1992), pp. 202–215. For a brilliant discussion of feminism's deployment of class disgust, and the class meanings of some

pornography, see Laura Kipnis, "(Male) Desire and (Female) Disgust: Reading *Hustler*," in her *Ecstasy Unlimited: On Sex, Capital, Gender and Aesthetics* (Minneapolis: University of Minnesota Press, 1993), pp. 220–242.

5. For an important exception, see Debbie Nathan's impressive essays on the panics over Satanistic child sexual abuse in day care centers, collected in her *Women and Other Aliens: Essays from the U.S.-Mexico Border* (El Paso, Texas: Cinco Puntos Press, 1991). The relevant essays are "Sex, the Devil, and Daycare," "The Making of a Modern Witch Trial," and "The Ritual Sex Abuse Hoax."

6. Michele Landsberg, "Canada: Antipornography Breakthrough in the Law," *Ms.*, May/June, 1992, p. 14.

7. *Ibid.*

8. See Kiss and Tell, *Her Tongue on My Theory*, pp. 75–92.

9. For an indispensable analysis of this series of events, see Carole S. Vance, "Feminist Fundamentalism: Women Against Images," *Art in America*, September 1993.

10. Note Cherríe Moraga's use of the term "queer" in Moraga and Amber Hollibaugh, "What We're Rollin' Around in Bed With: Sexual Silences in Feminism," in *Powers of Desire: The Politics of Sexuality* (New York: Monthly Review Press, 1983), eds. Ann Snitow, Christine Stansell and Sharon Thompson. pp. 400, 403.

11. In *Ecstasy Unlimited*, Laura Kipnis chides Janet Wolff for writing "as if the job of the feminist theorist is to rebuke the naïveté of the nontheoretical classes" (p. 9).

Notes to Chapter 1: Contextualizing the Sexuality Debates

Revised from *Caught Looking: Feminism, Pornography and Censorship*, (NY: Caught Looking, Inc., 1986).

Sources for this chronology include:

Aegis: Magazine for Ending Violence Against Women, 1977–1982; Boston Women's Health Book Collective, file on backlash against *Our Bodies, Ourselves*; Pat Califia, "A Personal View of the History of the Lesbian S/M Community and Movement in San Francisco" in *Coming to Power*; Alice Echols, *Daring to Be Bad: Radical Feminism in America 1967–1975*; Federation of Feminist Women's Health Centers, *A New View of a Woman's Body*; Barbara Grier, interview; Judith Hole and Ellen Levine, *Rebirth of Feminism*; Shere Hite, *The Hite Report*; Anne Koedt, Ellen Levine and Anita Rapone, *Radical Feminism*; Laura Lederer, "Introduction" and "Women Have Seized the Executive Offices of Grove Press Because" in *Take Back the Night*; C. Lewis, "Television License Renewal Challenges by Women's Groups" (unpublished); Robin Morgan, *Sisterhood Is Powerful*; *off our backs*, back issues; Susan Schechter, *Women and Male Violence*; Randy Shilts, *And the Band Played On: Politics, People, and the AIDS Epidemic*; Ann Snitow, Christine

Stansell and Sharon Thompson, "Introduction" in *Powers of Desire*; and Gay Talese, *Thy Neighbor's Wife*.

Notes to Chapter 2: Censorship in the Name of Feminism

Originally published in *The Village Voice*, October 16, 1984. Reprinted with permission.

Notes to Chapter 3: False Promises

Revised and reprinted from *Women Against Censorship*, Varda Burstyn, editor. Douglas and McIntyre, Ltd. ©1985

Acknowledgments

For stimulating discussion and political comradeship, thanks to FACT (Feminist Anti-Censorship Taskforce), New York, and to members of the Scholar and the Feminist IX study group (Julie Abraham, Hannah Alderfer, Meryl Altman, Jan Boney, Frances Doughty, Kate Ellis, Faye Ginsburg, Diane Harriford, Beth Jaker, Barbara Kerr, Mary Clare Lennon, Marybeth Nelson, Ann Snitow, Paula Webster and Ellen Willis). Special thanks to Rayna Rapp and Janice Irvine for comments and criticisms, to Lawrence Krasnoff for graphics and to Ann Snitow for aid above and beyond the call of duty. We are grateful to Varda Burstyn for her helpful suggestions and patience. We remain responsible for the opinions expressed here.

1. The bracketed phrase appears in an early version of the Minneapolis ordinance but may have been removed before the bill was formally introduced in the city council. It has reappeared, however, in subsequent defenses of the ordinance by its supporters. See J. Miller, "Civil Rights, Not Censorship," *Village Voice*, Nov. 6, 1984, p. 6.

Notes to Chapter 4: Feminist Historians and Antipornography Campaigns

Adapted from a speech given at The Sex Panic: A Conference on Women, Censorship and "Pornography" on May 8, 1993, and published in *New York Law School Law Review* 38 (1993).

1. See, e.g., Catharine A. MacKinnon, "'More Than Simply a Magazine': Playboy's Money," in *Feminism Unmodified* 134, 140 (1987):

   [N]o one has yet convinced me that extending the obscenity prohibition, liberalizing its application, would do anything but further eroticize pornography. Suppressing obscenity criminally has enhanced its value, made it more attractive and more expensive and a violation to get, therefore more valuable and more sexually exciting. Censoring pornography has not yet delegitimized it; I want to delegitimize it.

2. In 1985, voters in Cambridge, Massachusetts, were presented with a ballot question which defined pornography as:

[T]he graphic sexually explicit subordination of women through pictures and/or words that also includes one or more of the following, among others: women are presented dehumanized as sexual objects, enjoying pain or humiliation or rape, tortured or maimed, penetrated by objects or animals, or in postures of sexual submission, servility or display.

On file with the *New York Law School Law Review*. The initiative, which aimed to classify certain types of pornography as sex discrimination, was defeated 13,031 to 9,419. "Anti-Pornography Law Defeated in Cambridge," *New York Times*, November 12, 1985, at A16.

3. Drafted by Catherine MacKinnon and Gloria Allred and largely modeled after the Indianapolis ordinance, see *infra* note 5, the Los Angeles ordinance was proposed in February 1985 by the County Commission for Women. See Rich Connell, "County to Explore Adoption of Tough Pornography Law," *Los Angeles Times*, February 27, 1985, § 2, at 1, 2. The proposal was considered by the local Board of Supervisors, two members of which argued for immediate approval, but was rejected when a third and deciding vote was not forthcoming. See *id*. The proposal characterized pornography as "the graphic sexually explicit subordination of women" in pictures or words that "dehumanize women, present them as sexual objects, or present them in 'postures of sexual submission, servility or display'." Cathleen Decker, "Coalition Sees Plan as Threat to Free Speech: Feminists Resist Pornography Law," *Los Angeles Times*, March 16, 1985, § 2, at 1. The proposal would have provided women who alleged they were victimized by pornography with a cause of action. *Id*. Under the proposal, actionable depictions included "graphic pictorial depictions of sexual abuse and debasement of human beings which encourage, incite or instruct in acts of sexual violence or debasement." On file with the *New York Law School Law Review*.

4. See, e.g., Appendix: Excerpts from the Minneapolis Ordinance, in this volume.

5. Indianapolis & Marion County, Ind., Code § 16–1 to –28 (1993). The City-County Council of Indianapolis and Marion County, Indiana, found an ordinance was necessary because:

[P]ornography is a discriminatory practice based on sex which denies women equal opportunities in society. Pornography is central in creating and maintaining sex as a basis for discrimination. Pornography is a systematic practice of exploitation and subordination based on sex which differentially harms women. The bigotry and contempt it promotes, with the acts of aggression it fosters, harm women's opportunities for equality of rights in employment, education, access to and use of public accommodations, and acquisition of real property; promote rape, battery, child abuse, kidnapping and prostitution and inhibit just enforcement of laws against such acts; and contribute significantly to restricting women in particular from full exercise of citizenship and participation in public life, including in neighborhoods.

> *Id.* § 16–1(a)(2).

6. See, e.g., Amicus Brief of the Feminist Anti-Censorship Taskforce, *American Booksellers Ass'n v. Hudnut*, 771 F.2d 323 (7th Cir. 1985) (No. 84–3147), reprinted in Appendix.

7. Leonore Tiefer, "Some Harms to Women from Restrictions on Sexually Related Expression," 38 *N.Y.L. Sch. L. Rev.* (1993).

8. See Judith R. Walkowitz, "Male Vice and Female Virtue: Feminism and the Politics of Prostitution in Nineteenth-Century Britain," in *Powers of Desire: The Politics of Sexuality* 419 (ed. Ann Snitow *et al.*, 1983). The author treats the history of the feminist campaigns against prostitution as a cautionary tale:

> We must struggle to live our lives freely, without humiliation and violence. But we have to be aware of the painful contradictions of our sexual strategy, not only for the sex workers who still regard commercial sex as the "best paid industry" available to them, but also for ourselves as feminists. We must take care not to play into the hands of the New Right or the Moral Majority, who are only too delighted to cast women as victims requiring male protection and control, and who desire to turn feminist protest into a politics of repression.
>
> *Id.* at 434 (citing Rosalind P. Petchesky, "Antiabortion, Antifeminism, and the Rise of the New Right," 7 *Feminist Stud.* 206 (1981)).

9. See Ellen C. DuBois and Linda Gordon, "Seeking Ecstasy on the Battlefield: Danger and Pleasure in Nineteenth-Century Feminist Sexual Thought," in *Pleasure and Danger: Exploring Female Sexuality* 31 (ed. Carole S. Vance, 1984). The authors write:

> Today, there seems to be a revival of social purity politics within feminism, and it is concern about this tendency that motivates us in recalling its history. As in the nineteenth century, there is today a feminist attack on pornography and sexual "perversion" in our time, which fails to distinguish its politics from a conservative and antifeminist version of social purity, the Moral Majority and "family protection movement."
>
> *Id.* at 43.

10. See, e.g., "Artists Confronting Lies & Underhandedness," *Artists Expose American Civil Liberties Union's Lies About Dworkin, MacKinnon, and Pornography*, (October 9, 1992) (news release, on file with the *New York Law School Law Review*) (hailing the antipornography legislation drafted by Catharine MacKinnon and Andrea Dworkin as "[c]ivil-rights legislation" designed to "extend a speech right to women, men, children, and transsexu-

als" that they did not have before: the "presently illegal" right to bring civil suits against pornographers).

11. See *id.*

12. See, e.g., Barbara L. Epstein, *The Politics of Domesticity: Women, Evangelism, and Temperance in Nineteenth-Century America* 107 (1981) (examining temperance as an important issue for women in late nineteenth-century America because "men's drinking symbolized so many of the injustices that women felt" at that time); Ruth Rosen, *The Lost Sisterhood: Prostitution in America, 1900–1918,* at xiii (1982) (explaining that women of the nineteenth century felt they must protect their purity by challenging prostitution as a source of exploitation of women).

13. See, e.g., Robert W. Gordon, "Law and Disorder," 64 *Ind. L.J.* 803, 822 (1989) (citing the purity crusades to abolish alcohol and prostitution as just one example of early twentieth-century American attempts to impose "a regime of extraordinary conformity on political culture").

14. See Epstein, *supra* note 12, at 102 (indicating that temperance supporters accused men of spending leisure time in saloons, rather than in the home, and saw alcohol as a drug that caused normally gentle men to become violent).

15. See *id.* at 103 (explaining that women in the late nineteenth century did not blame men or the structure of the family directly as causes of the vulnerability that they felt in the home as a result of excessive drinking, but rather blamed the alcohol itself because that was an easier and more socially acceptable form of attack).

16. See John Rather, "Pornography Bill Stirs Furor in Suffolk," *New York Times,* October 7, 1984, § 11 (Long Island Weekly), at 1, 21. The proposal which was ultimately enacted, Suffolk County, N.Y., Code §§ 367–1 to –5 (1993), focused on the display of obscene material, rather than on the inherent baseness of pornography itself, as had other local legislative proposals, see *supra* notes 2–5. The ordinance states:

> [T]he unobstructed display of sexual materials in the County of Suffolk which portray obscene sexual performance, deviate sexual performance or simulated sexual conduct, poses a threat to the health, safety, morals and general welfare of the people of the County of Suffolk because it can encourage and promote anti-social behavior. It is further declared that the prominent display of such obscene materials in public areas poses an intrusion upon individual privacy and constitutes a threat to impressionable young people who are indiscriminately exposed to such material.

> Suffolk County, N.Y., Code § 367-1(A).

17. See Rather, *supra* note 16, at 1, 21 (reporting that the bill was proposed by conservative Republican County Legislator Michael D'Andre of Smithtown, New York, who was quoted as saying: "Everyone hides behind the First Amendment ... but when we have a decadent society, I don't see how

we are infringing when all we want is a set of morals.... [—]a far cry from censorship.").

18. See generally DuBois and Gordon, *supra* note 9 (discussing the major concerns of the feminist movement for the past 150 years); Walkowitz, *supra* note 8 (explaining the social-purity movement in England as centered on a woman-as-victim viewpoint).

19. See Walkowitz, *supra* note 8, at 422 (noting that nineteenth-century feminists believed that many women were "forced" into prostitution because they were unable to earn adequate wages from industrial employment, and that, therefore, prostitution was seen as a "paradigm for the female condition, a symbol of women's powerlessness and sexual victimization"); DuBois and Gordon, *supra* note 9, at 33 (explaining that, in the 1860s and 1870s, feminists believed economic pressures forced women into earning their living as prostitutes).

20. See Dubois and Gordon, *supra* note 9, at 37 (describing how feminists campaigned to enforce moral standards through organizations such as the Women's Christian Temperance Union).

21. See Walkowitz, *supra* note 8, at 432–434 (concluding that by the 1880s "feminists had lost considerable authority in the public discussion over sex to a coalition of male professional experts, conservative churchmen, and social purity advocates," who changed the focus of the movement from one directed against state regulation to one that used the instruments of the state for repressive purposes, such as "crusades against prostitution, pornography, and homosexuality").

22. See generally Walkowitz, *supra* note 8 (arguing that, while feminists were able to arouse anger among women aimed at control by men, the fact that men and conservatives dominated politics prevented feminists from improving the social and economic status of women). For a more in-depth historical account of this subject, see Judith R. Walkowitz, *Prostitution and Victorian Society: Women, Class, and the State* (1980).

23. Beulah Coughenour, a conservative Republican member of the Indianapolis and Marion County City-County Council, was recruited by Mayor William Hudnut to introduce the ordinance locally. See Lisa Duggan, "Censorship in the Name of Feminism," in this volume.

24. See, e.g., Rosen, *supra* note 12, at 19–20, 25 (reporting that judges in the late nineteenth century sent female sexual offenders to reformatories or to county workhouses); Gail Pheterson, "Not Repeating History," in *A Vindication of the Rights of Whores* 3 (ed. Gail Pheterson, 1989) (discussing the repression of prostitutes on an international scale).

25. See Karen Busby, "LEAF and Pornography: Litigating on Equality and Sexual Representations" 1 n.1 (October 1, 1993) (unpublished manuscript, originally presented at the Toronto conference "Politics of Desire: Pornography, Erotica, Freedom of Expression," on file with the *New York Law School Law Review*) (stating that the Women's Legal Education and Action Fund's (LEAF) factum in *R. v. Butler*, 1 S.C.R. 452 (Can. 1992), was written in three weeks by, among others, Catharine MacKinnon). The Canadian Supreme

Court in *Butler* held that sexually explicit material that is "degrading" or "dehumanizing" is illegal in Canada because of its potential to harm women. See 1 S.C.R. at 505.

26. See "International News in Brief: Canada," *The Advocate*, June 2, 1992, at 27 (reporting that the first prosecution under Canadian obscenity law, *Glad Day Bookshop, Inc. v. Deputy of Nat'l Revenue for Customs and Excise*, 1992 Ont. C.J. LEXIS 1296 (July 14, 1992), involved a lesbian erotic magazine, *Bad Attitude*, sold at Canada's largest gay and lesbian bookstore).

27. See generally Ellen Chesler, *Woman of Valor: Margaret Sanger and the Birth Control Movement in America* (1992) (discussing the life of Margaret Sanger, who was put in jail in 1917 for distributing contraceptives to women); *Margaret Sanger, My Fight for Birth Control* (1969) (giving an autobiographical account of the author's struggle to supply women with contraceptives at the turn of the century).

28. See Carole S. Vance, "Misunderstanding Obscenity," *Art in Am.*, May 1990, at 49 (tracing the development and effect of the NEA legislation).

29. See Wendy Kaminer, "Feminists Against the First Amendment," *Atlantic*, November 1992, at 111, 114 ("The feminist case against pornography is based on the presumption that the link between pornography and sexual violence is clear, simple, and inexorable. The argument is familiar: censorship campaigns always blame unwanted speech for unwanted behavior....").

30. See, e.g., Michael S. Kimmel, "Does Pornography Cause Rape?" *Violence Update* (Sage Newsletters, Seattle, Wash.), June 1993, at 1 (noting, for example, that a study of six cities that had banned the sale of pornography showed no decrease in the incidence of rape, casting doubt on the theory that there is a correlation between rape and the sale of pornography).

31. See Kaminer, *supra* note 37, at 114 (noting that women are not necessarily safe in Saudi Arabia, although commercial pornography is illegal there).

32. S. 1226, 101st Cong., 1st Sess. (1989); S. 1521, 102d Cong., 1st Sess. (1991).

Notes to Chapter 5: Sex Panics

Originally published in *Artforum*, October, 1989. Reprinted with permission.

Notes to Chapter 6: Banned in the U.S.A.

Originally published in *The Village Voice*. Reprinted with permission.

Notes to Chapter 7: Life After Hardwick

Originally published in 27 *Harvard Civil Rights—Civil Liberties Law Review* 531 (1992).

1. 478 U.S. 186 (1986).
2. *Id.*

3. A majority of the Supreme Court in 1977 stated, "'[T]he Court has not definitively answered the difficult question whether and to what extent the Constitution prohibits state statutes regulating [private consensual sexual] behavior among adults,' n.17, *infra*, and we do not purport to answer that question now." *Carey v. Population Services*, 431 U.S. 678, 688 n.5 (1977) (citing *Id.* at 695 n.17 [referring to a statement made later in the same decision]) (brackets in the original).

4. See "*Developments in the Law—Sexual Orientation and the Law*," 102 *Harvard Law Review* 1508, 1519–21 (1989).

5. *Hardwick*, 478 U.S. at 188 n.2.

6. See, e.g., John D'Emilio and Estelle B. Freedman, *Intimate Matters: A History of Sexuality in America* (1988) [hereinafter *Intimate Matters*]; Eve Kosofsky Sedgwick, *Epistemology of the Closet* (1990); David Halperin, *One Hundred Years of Homosexuality* (1990); Martin Duberman, Martha Vicinus and George Chauncey, Jr., *Hidden from History: Reclaiming the Gay and Lesbian Past* (1990) [hereinafter *Hidden from History*]; Judith Butler, *Gender Trouble: Feminism and the Subversion of Identity* (1990); Lillian Faderman, *Odd Girls and Twilight Lovers: A History of Lesbian Life in Twentieth Century America* (1991). A lesbian, gay and bisexual studies conference has become an annual event, held to date at Yale, Harvard, Rutgers and the University of Iowa. See *Inside/Out* (ed. Diana Fuss, 1991), a collection of papers presented at the Yale conference in 1989. See also the discussion of homosexuality as biologically different from heterosexuality, *infra* note 74.

7. See, e.g., Robert Reinhold "Veto of California Job-Bias Bill Unites Gay-Rights Forces Against Governor," *New York Times*, November 12, 1991, at A16; Alessandra Stanley, "Militants Back Queer, Shoving Gay the Way of Negro," *New York Times*, April 6, 1991, at A23.

8. The phrase is Foucault's description of sodomy. Michel Foucault, *A History of Sexuality* 101 (trans. Robert Hurley, 1978).

9. *Intimate Matters, supra* note 6, at 16, 30. As one court later stated, "[A]ll unnatural acts of carnal copulation between man with man or man with woman, where a penetration is effected into any opening of the body other than those provided by nature for the reproduction of the species, are sufficiently contemplated and embraced within the term 'infamous crime against nature'...." In *Ex parte Benites*, 140 P. 436, 437 (Nev. 1914) (citing William Hawkins, *Pleas of the Crown* (1787)).

10. Prohibitions against oral sex were added later. Sodomy also sometimes referred to intercourse between a human and an animal. The fullest exposition of the history of sodomy law can be found in Anne B. Goldstein, "History, Homosexuality, and Political Values: Searching for the Hidden Determinants of *Bowers v. Hardwick*," 97 *Yale Law Journal* 1073, 1081–1087 (1988).

11. John Winthrop, *The History of New England from 1630 to 1649: Volume II* 54–55 (1853).

12. The case is described most fully in Jonathan Ned Katz, *Gay/Lesbian Almanac* 78–82 (1983).

13. See William Bradford, *Of Plymouth Plantation 1620–1647*, 318–319 (ed. Samuel Eliot Morison, 1966).

14. The colonists concluded that the men could not be punished with the death sentence for rape because there was neither a statute nor "express law in the word of God" that justified such a sentence for rape of an "unripe" girl, and because there was not sufficient proof of penetration. See Winthrop, *supra* note 11, at 56. Additionally, the colonists believed there was an issue of consent, since at least one of the girls was reported to have "grown capable of man's fellowship, and took pleasure in it." *Id.* at 55.

15. Katz, *supra*, note 12, at 79–82; Bradford, *supra* note 13, at 404–413.

16. Bradford, *supra* note 13, at 404–13. Presumably because of the disagreement over which elements were necessary to the crime, the men were eventually charged with "carnal knowledge … in a most vile & abominable manner" and with "abusing" the girls in an "unclean and wicked manner." Katz, *supra* note 12, at 78.

17. Katz *supra*, note 12, at 78. At least one commentator has read the meaning of this debate differently, as "the exception that proves the rule" that "the Puritans nearly always meant homosexuality when they used the term sodomy." Robert F. Oaks, "Things Fearful to Name": Sodomy and Buggery in Seventeenth Century New England," 12 *J. Soc. Hist.* 268, 273 (1978). However, D'Emilio and Freedman reject the Oaks interpretation of sodomy in their book, which is the leading synthesis of the historical research. *Intimate Matters, supra* note 6, at 30. If nothing else, these different readings demonstrate the enduring contestability of the term.

18. Goldstein, *supra* note 10, at 1083 n.60.

19. Katz, *supra* note 12, at 54–60; *Intimate Matters, supra* note 6, at 30–31.

20. The Georgia statute before the Supreme Court in *Hardwick* illustrates this pattern. In 1939 the state supreme court overturned the conviction of a woman charged with sodomy for oral sex with another woman on the ground that phallic penetration was a required element of the crime. *Thompson v. Aldridge*, 200 S.E.2d 799 (Ga. 1939). In *Riley v. Garret*, 133 S.E.2d 367 (Ga. 1963), the same court held that heterosexual cunnilingus also was not covered. In 1968 the legislature amended the statute to include cunnilingus. Justice Blackmun incorrectly characterized this amendment as a relatively recent decision by the legislature to include heterosexual conduct within the scope of the statue. *Bowers v. Hardwick*, 478 U.S. 186, 200 n.1 (1986) (Blackmun, J., dissenting). At the time of the amendment, heterosexual conduct was already included; it was the possibility of nonphallic conduct that constituted the modern intervention.

21. *Eisenstadt v. Baird*, 405 U.S. 438 (1972); *Griswold v. Connecticut*, 381 U.S. 479 (1965). In an earlier case in which the Court found lack of standing and thus never reached the merits, Justice Harlan in dissent noted that Connecticut asserted in defense of its ban on contraceptives that "it considers the practice of contraception immoral in itself." *Poe v. Ullman*, 367 U.S. 497, 545 (1961) (Harlan, J., dissenting).

22. 478 U.S. at 191.

23. Foucault, *supra* note 8, at 42–43 (emphasis in original).

24. Halperin, *supra* note 6, at 27.

25. In addition to the works cited in notes 6 and 12, see *Passion and Power: Sexuality in History* (Kathy Peiss and Christina Simmons eds., 1989); John D'Emilio, *Sexual Politics, Sexual Communities: The Making of a Homosexual Minority in the United States, 1940–1970* (1983); Lillian Faderman, *Surpassing the Love of Men: Romantic Friendship and Love Between Women from the Renaissance to the Present* (1981); Jonathan Ned Katz, *Gay American History: Lesbians and Gay Men in the U.S.A.* (1976). This list does not purport to be exhaustive and specifically does not include works focused solely on non-U.S. history.

26. Randolph Trumbach, "The Birth of the Queen: Sodomy and the Emergence of Gender Equality in Modern Culture, 1660–1750," in *Hidden from History, supra* note 6, at 129–140; see also David Greenberg, *The Construction of Homosexuality* 309, 333–334 (1988).

27. See, e.g., Jeffrey Weeks, *Coming Out: Homosexual Politics in Britain*, 23–32 (1977); George Chauncey, Jr., "From Sexual Inversion to Homosexuality: Medicine and the Changing Conceptualization of Female Deviance," 58–59, *Salmagundi* 114 (1982–1983).

28. Some state statutes still use phrases like "crime against nature." See, e.g., Ariz. Rev. Stat. § 13–1411 (1989); Idaho Code § 18–6605 (1989); La. Rev. Stat. Ann. 14:89 (West 1986); Mass. Gen. Laws Ann. 272:34 (West 1990); Mich. Comp. Laws Ann. § 750.158 (West 1991); N. C. Gen Stat. § 14–177 (1986); Okla. Stat. tit. 21, § 886 (1991); R.I. Gen. Laws 11–10–1 (1981); and Va. Code § 18.2–361 (1988). A Florida statute, Fla. Stat. § 800.01 (Supp. 1973), prohibiting "the abominable and detestable crime against nature" was upheld against a vagueness attack in *Wainwright v. Stone*, 414 U.S. 21 (1973) (per curiam). In a non-retroactive ruling that occurred after the conviction in *Wainwright*, the Florida Supreme Court found the same statute to be unconstitutionally vague. *Franklin v. State*, 257 So.2d 21 (Fla. 1971). The Florida court suggested that the application of the crime against nature statute to oral sex "could entrap unsuspecting citizens and subject them to 20-year sentences ... [which] would no doubt be a shocking revelation to persons who do not have an understanding of the meaning of the statute." *Id.* at 23. Decisions holding that phrases similar to "crime against nature" provide sufficient notice of which acts are penalized include *Hogan v. State*, 441 P.2d 620 (Nev. 1968) ("infamous crime against nature"); *State v. Crawford*, 478 S.W.2d 314 (Mo. 1972) ("abominable and detestable crime against nature"); *Dixon v. State*, 268 N.E.2d 84 (Ind. 1971) (same); *State v. White*, 217 A.2d 212 (Me. 1966) ("crime against nature"); and *Warner v. State*, 489 P.2d 526 (Okl. Crim. App. 1971) (same). *Cf. Balthazar v. Superior Court*, 573 F.2d 698 (1st Cir. 1978) (Massachusetts statute prohibiting "unnatural and lascivious acts" unconstitutionally vague as applied to acts of fellatio and oral-anal contact).

29. Nan D. Hunter, Sheryl L. Michaelson and Thomas B. Stoddard, *The Rights of Lesbians and Gay Men* 120 (1992).

30. Ark. Code § 5–14–122 (1987); Kan. Crim. Code Ann. § 21–3505 (Vernon 1992); Ky. Rev. Stat. Ann. § 510.100 (Michie 1990); Mo. Rev. Stat. 566.090 (1986); Mont. Code § 45–5–505 (1991); Nev. Rev. Stat. Ann. § 201.190 (Michie 1986); Tenn. Code Ann. § 39–13–510 (West 1991); and Tex. Penal Code Ann. § 21.06 (West 1989). The Kentucky statute was ruled unconstitutional on state constitutional grounds in *Commonwealth v. Wasson*, 842 S.W. 2d 487 (Ky. 1992). The amendments that constitute this specification trend were enacted in 1973 (Montana and Texas); 1974 (Kentucky); 1977 (Arkansas, Missouri and Nevada); 1983 (Kansas); and 1989 (Tennessee).

31. *Oklahoma v. Post*, 715 P.2d 1105 (Okla. Crim. App. 1986), *cert. denied*, 479 U.S. 890 (1986).

32. See e.g., *Roe v. Roe*, 324 S.E.2d 691 (Va. 1985) (finding that a gay father who had been awarded custody of his daughter by the trial court was unfit, presumably because of his sexual orientation).

33. Ronald Bayer, *Homosexuality and American Psychiatry: The Politics of Diagnosis* (1981).

34. See *Ashton v. Civiletti*, 613 F.2d 923, 927 (D.C. Cir. 1979).

35. Thomas B. Stoddard, E. Carrington Boggan, Marilyn G. Haft, Charles Lister and John P. Rupp, *The Rights of Gay People* 17 (1983). The authors also note, regretfully, that the protective ordinances adopted by Miami and St. Paul were subsequently modified or repealed.

36. *Intimate Matters, supra* note 6, 346–347. The Oklahoma statute was declared, in part, unconstitutional in *National Gay Task Force v. Board of Educ. of City of Oklahoma City*, 729 F.2d 1270 (10th Cir. 1984), *aff'd per curiam*, 470 U.S. 903 (1985).

37. *Hardwick v. Bowers*, 760 F.2d 1202, 1204–1206 (11th Cir. 1985). Standing to challenge a statute on its face, absent an actual prosecution, necessitates a showing both that the plaintiff is likely to engage in conduct that runs afoul of the statute and that the government is likely to enforce the statute. *Virginia v. American Booksellers Ass'n.*, 484 U.S. 383, 392–393 (1988). In *Hardwick*, both aspects were found to be missing for the husband-wife couple.

38. *Hardwick*, 760 F.2d at 1205.

39. *Id.*

40. *Id.* at 1206.

41. *Bowers v. Hardwick*, 478 U.S. 186, 188 n.2 (1986).

42. *Id.* at 189, 190.

43. *Id.* at 189, 190.

44. *Id.* at 190–191.

45. *Id.* at 196.

46. *Id.* at 216 (Stevens, J., dissenting).

47. *Intimate Matters, supra* note 6, at 28–30; Greenberg, *supra* note 26, at 304; Katz, *supra* note 12, at 68, 74, 76, 85, 101.

48. Judges Canby and Norris of the Ninth Circuit are on solid legal ground when they argue that *Hardwick* is not "a state license to pass 'homosexual laws'." *Watkins v. U.S. Army*, 847 F.2d 1329, 1354 (9th Cir. 1988), *vacated and aff'd on other grounds*, 875 F.2d 699 (9th Cir. 1989) (en banc), *cert. denied*, 111 S.

Ct. 384 (1990). The problem with this view is not legal but cultural—sodomy statutes are socially understood as "homosexual laws," even if in fact or in origin they are not.

49. *Bowers v. Hardwick*, 478 U.S. 186, 197 (1986) (Burger, C.J., concurring).

50. *Watkins*, 847 F.2d at 1354 (Reinhardt, J., dissenting).

51. See *High-Tech Gays v. Defense Industrial Security Clearance Office*, 895 F.2d 563 (9th Cir. 1990), *reh'g denied*, 909 F.2d 375 (9th Cir. 1990); *Ben-Shalom v. Marsh*, 881 F.2d 454 (7th Cir. 1989), *cert. denied*, 110 S. Ct. 1296 (1990); *Woodward v. United States*, 871 F.2d 1068 (Fed. Cir. 1989), *cert. denied*, 110 S. Ct. 1295 (1990); *Padula v. Webster*, 822 F.2d 97 (D.C. Cir. 1987).

52. Data indicate that 96% to 99% of gay and lesbian persons have engaged in oral sex and a smaller proportion in anal sex. Philip Blumstein and Pepper Schwartz, *American Couples* 236, 242 (1983). From 90% to 93% of heterosexual persons have engaged in oral sex and a smaller proportion in anal sex. *Id.*

53. *Watkins*, 847 F.2d at 1357 (Reinhardt, J., dissenting).

54. *Singer v. Hara*, 522 P.2d 1187, 1195 (Wash. App. 1974).

55. *Watkins*, 847 F.2d at 1340–1341. *High-Tech Gays*, 909 F.2d at 379 (dissent from rehearing en banc). *Cf. Ciechon v. City of Chicago*, 686 F.2d 511, 522–524 (7th Cir. 1982) (even under rational basis standard of review, Chicago Fire Department could not discharge only one of two paramedics who were equally involved in and equally responsible for an incident involving the death of an elderly man).

56. The government's primary argument in justification of its exclusionary policy is that other service members and the public would react negatively to the presence of openly gay men and lesbian women in the military and that barracks life would be made uncomfortable. See, e.g., *Watkins*, 847 F.2d at 1350–1352.

57. Cass Sunstein has analyzed in detail the difference in function between the Equal Protection Clause and the Due Process Clause, and argued that *Hardwick* should not be read to determine the equal protection question in cases such as *Watkins*. Cass R. Sunstein, "Sexual Orientation and the Constitution: A Note on the Relationship Between Due Process and Equal Protection," 55 *U. Chi. L. Rev.* 1161 (1988).

58. *Watkins*, 847 F.2d at 1339 n. 14.

59. *Hatheway v. Secretary of the Army*, 641 F.2d 1376 (9th Cir. 1981).

60. *Watkins v. U.S. Army*, 875 F.2d 699, 726 (9th Cir. 1989) (en banc).

61. *Jantz v. Muci*, 759 F.Supp. 1543, 1548, 1551 (D. Kan. 1991) (appeal pending).

62. *High-Tech Gays v. Defense Industrial Security Clearance Office*, 909 F.2d 375, 380 (9th Cir. 1990).

63. Carole S. Vance posed the dilemma as deconstruction versus defense in her examination of the development of a social constructionist theory of sexuality. "Social Construction Theory: Problems in the History of Sexuality," *Homosexuality, Which Homosexuality?* by Dennis Altman, Carole Vance,

Martha Vicinus and Jeffrey Weeks, International Conference on Gay and Lesbian Studies 13, 29 (1988).

64. See, e.g., Halperin, *supra* note 6, at 41–53.

65. See *Bowen v. Gilliard*, 483 U.S. 587, 602–603 (1987).

66. In *High-Tech Gays*, 895 F.2d 563, 573 (9th Cir. 1990), for example, the Ninth Circuit panel acknowledged that this requirement for heightened scrutiny had been met, but found the plaintiffs' claim deficient on other grounds.

67. For a gay historian's views of the problems posed by wishing to use historical research in the effort to secure equality, see John D'Emilio, "Making and Unmaking Minorities: The Tensions Between Gay Politics and History," 14 *N.Y.U. Rev. L. and Soc. Change 915* (1986).

68. *Jantz v. Muci*, 759 F. Supp. 1543, 1549 (D. Kan. 1991) (quoting 98 *Harv. L. Rev.* 1302 (1985)). Goldstein, *supra* note 10, succinctly summarizes the historical evidence indicating a much more nuanced history than simply "ancient prohibitions." *Id.* at 1087.

69. *United States v. Carolene Products Co.*, 304 U.S. 144, 152 n.4 (1938).

70. *High-Tech Gays*, 895 F.2d at 574; *Steffan v. Cheney*, 780 F. Supp. 1, 7–9 (D.D.C. 1991).

71. Judges Canby and Norris argue that race would never have been ruled a suspect classification under this standard. *High-Tech Gays*, 909 F.2d 378 (9th Cir. 1990) (rehearing en banc denied). That is also true with regard to women, who were granted heightened protection at a time when Congress had already enacted both the Equal Pay Act and broad antidiscrimination laws covering employment and education, numerous states had adopted equal rights amendments to their constitutions and a federal equal rights amendment was under active consideration. See *Craig v. Boren*, 429 U.S. 190 (1976); *Frontiero v. Richardson*, 411 U.S. 677 (1973) (plurality).

72. Judges Canby and Norris concluded that homosexuals in fact do constitute political pariahs. *High-Tech Gays*, 909 F.2d at 378.

73. Bruce A. Ackerman, "Beyond Carolene Products," 98 *Harvard Law Review* 713 (1985).

74. Recent support for this position can be found in two studies, one concluding that there may be a difference in brain structure based on sexual orientation and the second positing a genetic difference. Simon LeVay, "A Difference in Hypothalamic Structure Between Heterosexual and Homosexual Men," 253 *Science* 1034 (1991); J. Michael Bailey and Richard C. Pillard, "A Genetic Study of Male Sexual Orientation," 48 *Archives Gen. Psychiatry* 1089 (1991). Both have been sharply criticized on scientific grounds and sociopolitical ones. See Letters to the Editor, "The Politics of Finding Homosexuality Genetic," *New York Times*, Jan. 7, 1992, at A14 (three separate letters to the editor by Seth Manoach, John D'Emilio and Peter Kingsley responding to a December 17, 1991 op-ed piece by Michael Bailey and Richard Pillard, "Are Some People Born Gay?," *New York Times*, December 17, 1991, at A21); William Byne and Bruce Parsons, *Human Sexual Orientation: The Biological Theories Reappraised* (1991) (unpublished manuscript on file with the *Harvard Civil Rights-Civil Liberties Law Review*).

75. *Woodward v. U.S.*, 871 F.2d 1068, 1076 (Fed. Cir. 1989); *High-Tech Gays v. Defense Industrial Security Clearance Office*, 895 F2.d 563, 573–574 (9th Cir. 1990); *Steffan v. Cheney*, 780 F. Supp. 1, 8–10 (D.C. 1991).

76. *Watkins v. U.S.*, 847 F.2d 1329, 1347 (9th Cir. 1988); *High-Tech Gays v. Defense Industrial Security Clearance Office*, 909 F.2d 375, 377 (Canby, Norris, JJ., dissenting from denial of rehearing en banc).

77. Janet Halley, "The Politics of the Closet: Towards Equal Protection for Gay, Lesbian and Bisexual Identity," 36 *UCLA L. Rev.* 915 (1989).

78. The question of whether immutability is required arises in overlapping analyses under both Equal Protection Clause claims and claims under 42 U.S.C. 1985(3). In some opinions in the former line of cases, the Supreme Court has seemed to require immutability. *Lyng v. Castillo*, 477 U.S. 635, 638 (1986); *Frontiero v. Richardson*, 411 U.S. 677, 686 (1973). *Cf. Sugarman v. Dougall*, 413 U.S. 634, 657 (1973) (Rehnquist, J., dissenting). On other occasions, the Court has analyzed the criteria for heightened scrutiny without mentioning immutability. *Plyler v. Doe*, 457 U.S. 202, 216 n.14 (1982); *Graham v. Richardson*, 403 U.S. 365, 372 (1971). As to 1985(3), "[i]t is a close question" whether its protections will be extended to a group asserting a class-based animus on any ground other than race. *United Brotherhood of Carpenters and Joiners v. Scott*, 463 U.S. 825, 836 (1983).

   Some courts have rejected the search for an immutable trait, even with regard to race. "The notion of race is a taxonomic device and, as with all such constructs, it exists in the human mind, not as a division in the objective universe." *Ortiz v. Bank of America*, 547 F. Supp. 550, 565 (E.D. Cal. 1982). Professor Halley argues that the Supreme Court has recognized, at least implicitly, that race is socially constructed rather than immutable. See Halley, *supra* note 71, at 924–926, discussing *Shaare Tefila Congregation v. Cobb*, 481 U.S. 615 (1987) and *Saint Francis College v. Al-Khazraji*, 481 U.S. 604 (1987).

79. Alien status was granted heightened protection under the Equal Protection Clause in *Graham v. Richardson*, 403 U.S. 365 (1971). Religious affiliation, of course, is independently protected under the Free Exercise Clause of the First Amendment. It has also been accepted as a ground that is entitled to protection under 1985(3) despite its mutability, although "that issue is not free from doubt." *Ravenstahl v. Thomas Jefferson Hospital*, 37 Empl. Prac. Dec. (CCH) 38,330, 38,332 (E.D.Pa. 1985).

80. The animus directed toward lesbian and gay Americans as a result of their sexual orientation constitutes discrimination on the basis of gender in two respects. First, and most obviously, discrimination based on sexual orientation is a differentiation based on the gender of one's partner. In *Hardwick* the dissenting justices argued that the Court should have reached the equal protection claim that the sodomy statute was selectively enforced against persons committing homosexual acts, and decided it on gender discrimination grounds:

   I do not see why the State can defend [the statute] on the ground that individuals singled out for prosecution are of the same sex as their partners.

Thus, under the circumstances of this case, a claim under the Equal Protection Clause may well be available without having to reach the more controversial question of whether homosexuals are a suspect class.

Bowers v. Hardwick, 478 U.S. 186, 203 n.2 (1986) (Blackmun, Brennan, Marshall and Stevens, JJ., dissenting).

This theory of sex discrimination has been rejected, however, in Title VII cases. *DeSantis v. Pacific Tel. & Tel. Co.*, 608 F.2d 327 (9th Cir. 1979); *Smith v. Liberty Mutual Ins. Co.*, 569 F.2d 325 (5th Cir. 1978); *Holloway v. Arthur Andersen & Co.*, 556 F.2d 659 (9th Cir. 1977).

Second, and more fundamentally, homosexuality has long been viewed as a deviation from the proper gender norms, and thus lesbian and gay persons are often held in contempt as "queer" specifically in relation to differing codes of behavior for males and females. See *Intimate Matters, supra* note 6, at 226. Several commentators have articulated arguments that the centrality of gender norms and sex-role stereotypes to notions of homosexuality should be the basis for the invalidation of laws that differentiate on grounds of sexual orientation. Kenneth L. Karst, "The Pursuit of Manhood and the Desegregation of the Armed Forces," 38 *UCLA L. Rev.* 499 (1991); Sylvia Law, "Homosexuality and the Social Meaning of Gender," 1988 *Wis. L. Rev.* 187; I. Bennett Capers, Note, "Sex(ual Orientation) and Title VII," 91 *Colum. L. Rev.* 1158 (1991); and Andrew Koppelman, Note, "The Miscegenation Analogy: Sodomy Law as Sex Discrimination," 98 *Yale L.J.* 145 (1988).

81. I have elaborated this argument with regard to the gay marriage debate in "Marriage, Law and Gender: A Feminist Inquiry," reprinted in this volume.

82. *Gay Rights Coalition of Georgetown University Law Center v. Georgetown University*, 536 A.2d 1 (D.C. 1987); *Gay Lib. v. University of Missouri*, 558 F.2d 848 (8th Cir. 1977), *cert. denied*, 434 U.S. 1080 (1978); *Gay Alliance of Students v. Matthews*, 544 F.2d 162 (4th Cir. 1976); *Singer v. U.S. Civil Service Commission*, 530 F.2d 247 (9th Cir. 1976), *vacated*, 429 U.S. 1034 (1977); *Gay Students Organization of University of New Hampshire v. Bonner*, 509 F.2d 652 (1st Cir. 1974); *McConnell v. Anderson*, 451 F.2d 193 (8th Cir. 1971), *cert. denied*, 405 U.S. 1046 (1972); *Endsley v. Naes*, 673 F. Supp. 1032 (D. Kan. 1987).

83. *Hardwick*, 478 U.S. 186.

84. *Baker v. Wade*, 769 F.2d 289, 292 (5th Cir. 1985) (en banc), *cert. denied*, 478 U.S. 1022 (1986).

85. *Dronenburg v. Zech*, 741 F.2d 1388, 1397 (D.C. Cir. 1984), *reh'g en banc denied*, 746 F.2d 1579 (D.C. Cir. 1984).

86. The presumptively shared interest in suppressing homosexuality also underlies a New Hampshire state supreme court decision ruling that a law barring lesbians and gay men from adopting children or serving as foster parents would be constitutional. *In Re Opinion of the Justices*, 530 A.2d 21, 25 (N.H. 1987).

87. Indeed, a plurality of the Court has accepted morality as a sufficient state interest for a statute banning nude dancing, despite its admitted restrictive effects on expression. *Barnes v. Glen Theaters*, 111 S. Ct. 2456 (1991).

88. Robert Bork, Civil Rights—A Challenge, *The New Republic*, August 31, 1963, at 21.
89. 741 F.2d at 1397 n.6.

Notes to Chapter 8: Sexual Dissent and the Family

Originally published in *The Nation* magazine, The Nation Company, Inc. (October 7, 1991 issue). Reprinted with permission.

Notes to Chapter 9: Marriage, Law and Gender

Originally published in *Law and Sexuality: A Review of Lesbian and Gay Legal Issues* (Tulane University Law School) 1991. All rights reserved. Reprinted with permission.

1. Earlier versions of this paper were presented at the Law and Sexuality Symposium, "The Family in the 1990s: Strategies for Extending Lesbian and Gay Rights" at Tulane Law School on October 5, 1990, and at the Fourth Lesbian, Bisexual and Gay Studies Conference at Harvard University on October 27, 1990. I would like to thank Lisa Duggan, Ruth Colker, Susan Herman, Elizabeth Schneider, Nancy Fink and Patti Roberts for their insightful comments; Paul Finkelman for his research suggestions; and Teresa Matushaj for able assistance.
2. *Singer v. Hara*, 11 Wash. App. 247, 522 P.2d 1187 (1974); *Jones v. Hallahan*, 501 S.W.2d 588 (Ky.Ct.App. 1973); and *Baker v. Nelson*, 291 Minn. 310, 191 N.W.2d 185 (1971), *appeal dismissed* 409 U.S. 810 (1972). In two other cases, gay couples have undergone ceremonies of marriage and then sought legal recognition of the marriage to obtain collateral benefits; in each, the court found no legal marriage existed. *Adams v. Howerton*, 673 F.2d 1036 (9th Cir. 1982), *cert. denied* 458 U.S. 1111 (1982); *McConnell v. Nooner*, 547 F.2d 43 (8th Cir. 1976). In two more recent decisions, courts reached the same result. A New York appellate court denied a right of election against a will to man asserting that he was the decedent's gay spouse-equivalent. *Matter of Cooper*, 187 A.D.2d 128, 592 N.Y.S.2d 797 (1993). And a Pennsylvania trial court refused to grant a divorce to a gay male couple, after one of the men argued that they had entered into a common-law marriage, which Pennsylvania recognizes as to heterosexual couples. *DeSanto v. Barnsley*, 476 A.2d 952 (Pa. Super. Ct. 1984).
3. The primary constitutional claims, based on equal protection and privacy principles, as well as a sex discrimination challenge under a state equal rights amendment, were all pressed in the cases brought during the 1970s. Although the body of decisional law in each of these doctrinal areas has grown since then, the new case law has not lessened the difficulties of a marriage claim on behalf of lesbian or gay couples. The fundamentality of the right to marry as an aspect of personal privacy has been more fully articulated, *Zablocki v. Redhail*, 434 U.S. 374 (1978), but the same right of privacy also has been found not to encompass protection from criminal prosecution

for consensual adult homosexual conduct, *Bowers v. Hardwick*, 478 U.S. 186 (1986). Since the counsel arguing to uphold the Georgia sodomy law at issue in that case conceded during oral argument that even sexual behavior which fell within the definition of sodomy could not be subject to prosecution if it occurred between spouses, a fascinating legal anomaly would result if a state relied on *Hardwick* to prosecute a married gay or lesbian couple. Transcript of oral argument at 7–8.

4. *Baehr v. Lewin*, 852 P.2d 44 (1993).

5. *Braschi v. Stahl Associates*, 74 N.Y.2d 201, 544 N.Y.S.2d 784, 543 N.E.2d 49 (1989). The Braschi decision suggests an additional constitutional ground, not relied on in prior cases, may be available under the Constitution's protection of the freedom to form intimate associations, a branch of the liberty guarantee of the due process clauses. Exclusionary marriage laws could be stricken as violative of the principle which insulates from state infringement "family relationships ... [which] involve deep attachments and commitments to the necessarily few other individuals with whom one shares not only a special community of thoughts, experiences and beliefs, but also distinctively personal aspects of one's own life." *Roberts v. United States Jaycees*, 468 U.S. 609, 620 (1984). The Court identified the attributes of those relationships in terms strikingly similar to the language used by the *Braschi* court. *Cf. Roberts*, 468 U.S. at 620 with *Braschi*, 74 N.Y.2d at 212–213.

6. Note, "A More Perfect Union: A Legal and Social Analysis of Domestic Partnership Ordinances," 92 *Columbia Law Review* 1164 (1992).

7. Bishop, "San Francisco Grants Recognition to Couples Who Aren't Married," *New York Times*, May 31, 1989, at A-17.

8. Bishop, "Not Quite a Wedding, but Quite a Day for Couples by the Bay," *New York Times*, February 15, 1991, at A-16.

9. Act 372 of June 7, 1989.

10. Gutis, "Small Steps Toward Acceptance Renew Debate on Gay Marriage," *New York Times*, November 5, 1989 at E–24; Sullivan, "Here Comes the Groom: A (Conservative) Case for Gay Marriage," *The New Republic*, August 28, 1989, at 20; Isaacson, "Should Gays Have Marriage Rights?," *Time*, November 20, 1989, at 101 (hereafter, "Isaacson"); Lewin, "Suit Over Death Benefits Asks, What Is a Family?," *New York Times*, September 21, 1990, at 1, B7.

11. The best exposition of this debate can be found in two companion articles published under the heading "Gay Marriage: A Must or A Bust?": Ettelbrick, "Since When Was Marriage a Path to Liberation?" and Stoddard, "Why Gay People Should Seek the Right to Marry," in 2 *Out/Look* 8 (1989) (hereafter, *Out/Look*). For an account of an earlier version of the debate, see D. Teal, *The Gay Militants* 282–293 (1971) [hereafter, "Teal"].

12. Stoddard acknowledges the oppressiveness of marriage in its traditional form, but argues that legalizing gay marriage "is ... the political issue that most fully tests the dedication of people who are *not* gay to full equality for gay people, and also the issue most likely to lead ultimately to a world free

from discrimination against lesbians and gay men." *Out/Look, supra* note 11, at 12.

13. See, e.g., S. Scheingold, *The Politics of Rights* (1974).

14. See, e.g., S. Firestone, *The Dialectic of Sex* (1970); Cronan, "Marriage" in *Radical Feminism* (1973) A. Koedt, E. Levine and J. Rapone, and M. Barrett and M. McIntosh, *The Anti-Social Family* (1982). For an account of the politics of the early stage of the second wave of feminism, when criticism of marriage was at its height, see, A. Echols, *Daring to be Bad: Radical Feminism in America 1967–1975* (1989).

15. Ettelbrick counterposes "rights" with "justice," arguing that the former may lead to empty victories, and that justice requires that society validate the differentness of lesbians and gay men: "Being queer … is an identity, a culture with many variations." *Out/Look, supra* note 11, at 14. The antimarriage argument was also expressed at the time of the first round of attempts at legalizing gay marriage. Writing in 1970, Ralph Hall argued, "Homosexual marriages submitting to the guidelines of so-called conventional rites must be classed as reactionary … [I]t isn't relevant to gay liberation when we start imitating meaningless, bad habits of our oppressors … That isn't *our* liberation. That *isn't* the freedom we want." Hall, "The Church, State and Homosexuality: A Radical Analysis," *Gay Power* No. 14 (emphasis in the original), quoted in Teal, *supra* note 11, at 291.

16. See, e.g., Law, "Rethinking Sex and the Constitution," 132 *U. Pa. L. Rev.* 955 (1984) and Williams, "Equality's Riddle: Pregnancy and the Equal Treatment/Special Treatment Debate," 13 *Review of Law and Social Change* 325 (1984/1985).

17. Neither *Baker* nor *Jones* occupies more than three printed pages in the published reports. The *Jones* court found simply that "no constitutional issue is involved." 501 S.W.2d at 590. Although the court in *Singer* engaged with the issues presented, it was equally circular in its reasoning: "There is no analogous sexual classification [to the racial classification in *Loving*] involved in this case because appellants are not being denied entry into the marriage relationship because of their sex; rather, they are being denied entry … because of the recognized definition of that relationship as one which may be entered into only by … members of the opposite sex." 522 P.2d at 1192.

18. See John Boswell, *Same-Sex Unions in Pre-Modern Europe* (1994); William N. Eskridge, Jr., "A History of Same-Sex Marriage," 79 *Virginia Law Review* 1419 (1993); Amy Swerdlow, Renate Bridenthal, Joan Kelly, and Phyllis Vine, *Household and Kin: Families in Flux* (1981); Herbert G. Gutman, *The Black Family in Slavery and Freedom 1750–1925* (1976); Jane Collier, Michelle Z. Rosaldo, and Sylvia Yanagisako, "Is there A Family? New Anthropological Views," in *Rethinking the Family: Some Feminist Questions* 25 (Barrie Thorne and Marilyn Yalom eds. 1982); Mary P. Ryan, "The Explosion of Family History," 10 (No. 4) *Rev. Am. Hist.* 181, 186–87 (1982); Jessie Bernard, *The Future of Marriage* 272–280 (1973). In *Jones v. Hallahan*, plaintiffs presented evidence of cross-cultural variability through the testimony of an anthropology professor that women in other cultures, including several African tribal

communities, married each other. The trial judge retorted that he was interested only in "this culture," not the cultures of Africa. Teal, *supra* note 11, at 290.

19. Ellen Kandoian, "Cohabitation, Common Law Marriage, and the Possibility of a Shared Moral Life," 75 *Georgetown Law Journal* 1829, 1838 (1987) (footnotes omitted).

20. The Kentucky Court of Appeals went the furthest, both in invoking nature and in drawing a complete circle, when it held that:

> appellants are prevented from marrying, not by the statutes of Kentucky or the refusal of the County Court Clerk of Jefferson County to issue them a license, but rather by their own incapability of entering into a marriage as that term is defined. A license to enter into a status or a relationship [that] the parties are incapable of achieving is a nullity.
>
> *Jones*, 501 S.W.2d at 589.

The Kentucky court not only ignores the law's power to command the terms of marriage, to define and therefore to redefine it, but also completely flips the relationship, to the point of casting the law as helpless against the rule of nature. In this configuration, any marriage license that might be granted to the plaintiffs (pursuant to an amended statute, for example) would be a mere "nullity."

21. 388 U.S. 1 (1967).

22. *Baker v. Nelson*, 291 Minn. 310, 315, 191 N.W.2d 185, 187 (1971) (emphasis added).

23. *See Singer v. Hara*, 11 Wash. App. 247, 255 n.8, 522 P.2d 1187, 1192 n.8.

24. *See Singer*, 11 Wash. App. at 254, 522 P.2d at 1194.

25. See, e.g., *Malinda and Sarah v. Gardner*, 24 Ala. 719 (1854); *Frazier v. Spear*, 2 Bibb 385 (Ky. 1811); *Girod v. Lewis*, 6 Mart. 559 (La. 1819); *Johnson v. Johnson*, 45 Mo. 595 (1870); *Brewer v. Harris*, 5 Grattan 285 (Va. 1848). Despite the legal prohibition, enslaved persons formed enduring relationships that were recognized within the African-American community as marriages. See H.G. Gutman, *supra* note 18, at 270–273.

26. See *Perez v. Sharp*, 32 Cal.2d 711 (1948); *Perez v. Lippold*, 198 P.2d 17 (Cal. 1948) (same case).

27. See Isabel Drummond, *The Sex Paradox* 361–362 (1953). In addition, some states imposed heavier penalties for violation of fornication or adultery laws when partners of different races were involved. See, e.g., *McLaughlin v. Florida*, 379 U.S. 184 (1964).

28. Edward de Grazia and Roger K. Newman, *Banned Films: Movies, Censors and The First Amendment* 92 (1982).

29. See, e.g., Judith T. Younger, "Community Property, Women and the Law School Curriculum," 48 *N.Y.U. L. Rev.* 211 (1973) (describing husband's control over jointly owned property); Mary Ann Glendon, "Marriage and the State: The Withering Away of Marriage," 62 *Virginia Law Review* 663, 702–703 (1976). See generally Ann E. Freedman, Barbara Allen Babcock, Eleanor

Holmes Norton, and Susan C. Ross, "Sex Role Discrimination in the Law of the Family," in *Sex Discrimination and the Law: Causes and Remedies* 561–566 (1975) [hereinafter Freedman].

30. *The First Restatement of the Law of Contracts* (1932), § 587, for example, forbade legal enforcement of "[a] bargain between married persons or persons contemplating marriage to change the essential incidents of marriage." The courts declared void as against public policy, because they sought to alter the "essential" elements of marriage, a variety of contracts between spouses, including those to permit the wife to choose the marital domicile, *Graham v. Graham*, 33 F. Supp. 936 (E.D. Mich. 1940) and *Sacks v. Sacks*, 200 Pa. Super. 223, 225 (1938); to provide wages to the wife for care she provided to the husband, *Tellez v. Tellez*, 51 N.M. 416, 186 P.2d 390 (1947); to enforce a contract between the parties to pay the wife for work she performed as a business partner, *Standen v. Pennsylvania R.R. Co.*, 214 Pa. 189, 63 A. 467 (1906); and to end the husband's duty to support his wife, *Kershner v. Kershner*, 244 A.D. 34, 278 N.Y.S. 501 (1935), *aff'd per curiam*, 269 N.Y. 654, 200 N.E. 43 (1936). See Freedman, *supra* note 28.

Socially, the consequences of deviance have been considered cataclysmic. Role reversal between husband and wife in African-American families was so debilitating, asserted Daniel Moynihan in 1965, as to underlie what he called "the tangle of pathology" in the black community. Lee Rainwater and William L. Yangey, *The Moynihan Report and the Politics of Controversy* 30 (1967). *See* Paula Giddings, *When and Where I Enter: The Impact of Black Women on Race and Sex in America* 325–329 (1984) (analyzing the *Moynihan Report*).

31. At least in the abstract, "the test for determining the validity of a gender-based classification ... must be applied free of fixed notions concerning the roles and abilities of males and females." *Mississippi University for Women v. Hogan*, 458 U.S. 718, 724–725 (1982).

32. See *Kirchberg v. Feesntra*, 450 U.S. 455, 459–460 (1981); *Wengler v. Druggists Mutual Ins. Co.*, 446 U.S. 142, 147 (1980); *Orr v. Orr*, 440 U.S. 268, 293 (1979).

33. See *Stanton v. Stanton*, 421 U.S. 7, 14 (1975); *Reed v. Reed*, 404 U.S. 71, 74 (1971).

34. See Lenore J. Weitzman, *The Divorce Revolution: The Unexpected Social and Economic Consequences for Women and Children in America* (1985); Nan D. Hunter, "Child Support Law and Policy: The Systematic Imposition of Costs on Women," 6 *Harvard Women's Law Journal* 1 (1983).

35. See *Singer v. Hara*, 11 Wash. App. at 254, 522 P.2d at 1195 (1974).

36. Comparably powerful social inequalities of race and class, which also resonate between spouses would, of course, remain. This argument does not presume that same-sex relationships are inherently egalitarian.

37. *Singer*, 11 Wash. App. at 254, 522 P.2d at 1195.

38. See Myrna Felder, "Grounds for Divorce," in *Family Law and Practice* 4–21 (Arnold H. Rutkin, ed. 1991) (1990 revision by the Honorable John D. Mont-

gomery) (describing the grounds for divorce); Albert Momjian, "Annulment," in *Family Law and Practice* 5–6, 5–8–5–9 (ed. Arnold H. Rutkin, 1991) (describing the grounds for annulment). Most states recognize that an intent not to consummate the marriage by engaging in sexual relations does form the basis for divorce or annulment, at least if the other party was unaware of that intent. See *Rathburn v. Rathburn*, 138 Cal. App. 2d 568, 292 P.2d 274 (1956); Uniform Marriage and Divorce Act § 208(a)(2); Felder, at 4–15 and 5–8. However, neither the Uniform Act nor the treatises report infertility as a ground for annulment or divorce. Only one court has ruled otherwise, on grounds of intent rather than incapacity. See *Link v. Link*, 48 A.D.2d 902, 369 N.Y.S.2d 496 (2d Dept. 1975) (holding that secret intention not to have children is sufficient cause for annulment). There are an estimated one million married couples in the United States who have no children and who are considered infertile. William D. Mosher and William F. Pratt, "Fecundity and Infertility in the United States, 1965–88," in 192 *Advance Data From Vital and Health Statistics of the National Center for Health Statistics* 1, 5 (December 4, 1990).

39. In cases involving lesbian and gay parents, the fear that children will be exposed to the wrong "role models" is a constant refrain. In affirming a trial court's order removing custody of a daughter from her divorced mother, alleged to be lesbian, the Missouri Court of Appeals described at length:

> The evidence … of [the lover] as a powerful, a dominant personality. She had befriended [the daughter] and had won her affection and her loyalty. She had broached the idea of homosexuality to the child. Allowing that homosexuality is a permissible life style—an "alternate life style," as it is termed these days—if voluntarily chosen, yet who would place a child in a milieu where she may be inclined toward it? She may thereby be condemned, in one degree or another, to sexual disorientation. …
>
> *N.K.M. v. L.E.M.*, 606 S.W.2d 179, 186 (Mo. Ct. App. 1980).

In *Opinion of the Justices*, 525 A.2d 1095 (N.H. 1987), the New Hampshire Supreme Court (including then-state court judge David Souter) held that legislation forbidding lesbians or gay men from adopting children would be constitutional, stating that "we accept the assertion that the provision of appropriate role models is a legitimate government purpose.… [W]e believe that the legislature can rationally act on the theory that a role model can influence the child's developing sexual identity." *Id.* at 1098–1099. A similar statute exists in Florida. See Fl. Stat. Ann. § 63.042(3) (West 1985). Other custody and visitation cases in which the courts have expressed concern with the impact of lesbian or gay parents as role models include *Jacobson v. Jacobson*, 314 N.W.2d 78, 79–81 (N.D. 1981); *S. v. S.*, 608 S.W.2d 64, 66 (Ky. Ct. App. 1980), *cert. denied*, 451 U.S. 911 (1981); and *Woodruff v. Woodruff*, 44 N.C. App. 350, 260 S.E.2d 775, 776 (1979). It is notable that the Danish law permitting a form of same-sex marriage expressly forbids lesbian and gay couples from adopting children. See Danish Registered Partnership Act, *supra* note 9.

40. A Time/CNN poll found that 54% of respondents agreed that "homosexual couples should be permitted to receive medical and life insurance benefits from their partner's insurance policies," but 69% opposed the legalization of marriage for lesbian and gay couples. Isaacson, *supra* note 10, at 101.

41. "Homosexual relationships challenge dichotomous concepts of gender. These relationships challenge the notion that social traits, such as dominance and nurturance, are naturally linked to one sex or the other." Sylvia A. Law, "Homosexuality and the Social Meaning of Gender," 1988 *Wisconsin Law Review* 187, 196. Law argues that "disapprobation of homosexual behavior is a reaction to the violation of gender norms, rather than simply scorn for the violation of norms of sexual behavior." *Id.* at 187.

42. *See* Ruthann Robson and S.E. Valentine, "Lov(h)ers: Lesbians as Intimate Partners and Lesbian Legal Theory," 63 *Temple Law Review* 511, 536–537 (1990).

43. bell hooks, an African-American feminist, has written of the perspective on family life shared by many women of color:

> [M]any black women find the family the least oppressive institution. Despite sexism in the context of family, we may experience dignity, self-worth, and a humanization that is not experienced in the outside world wherein we confront all forms of oppression.... [W]e know that family ties are the only sustained support system for exploited and oppressed peoples. We wish to rid family life of the abusive dimensions created by sexist oppression without devaluing it.
>
> *bell hooks, Feminist Theory From Margin to Center* 37 (1984).

44. Indeed, tautologies in judicial reasoning may signal weakness as well as strength. Perhaps the most famous example of a court invoking "nature" to legitimize the construction of gender was the notorious dictum of Justice Bradley in *Bradwell v. Illinois.* Justice Bradley wrote:

> [T]he civil law, as well as nature herself, has always recognized a wide difference in the respective spheres and destinies of man and woman.... The natural and proper timidity and delicacy [that] belongs to the female sex evidently unfits it for many of the occupations of civil life. The constitution of the family organization, which is founded in the divine ordinance, as well as in the nature of things, indicates the domestic sphere as that which properly belongs to the domain and functions of womanhood.
>
> 83 U.S. (16 Wall.) 130, 141 (1872).

Ironically, the Illinois legislature adopted a statute that eliminated the legal principle upheld in *Bradwell* three years after the Supreme Court ruled. See Martha Minow, "'Forming Underneath Everything That Grows:' Toward a History of Family Law," 1985 *Wisconsin Law Review* 819, 849. Minow reads Justice Bradley's opinion to reflect his unease with the recognition that "[t]he law itself could change" and with "the vulnerability of his claims of natural and divine authority." *Id.* at 844–845.

Similarly, the definitional rationale that has been characterized by each court addressing a gay marriage challenge as transcendent is in fact open to change at any time by the vote of a majority of any state's legislators, as well as by judicial interpretation.

45. See Kathryn A. London, "Cohabitation, Marriage, Marital Dissolution and Remarriage: United States, 1988," in 194 *Advance Data from Vital and Health Statistics of the National Center for Health Statistics* 1, 1 (January 4, 1991).

46. London, *supra* note 45, at 2.

47. Bureau of the Census, U.S. Department of Commerce, "Marital Status and Living Arrangements: March 1989" 1, 1 (1990) (Current Population Reports, Population Characteristics Series P-20, No. 445) [hereinafter Bureau of the Census].

48. National Center for Health Statistics, "Advance Report for Final Divorce Statistics, 1987," 38 *Monthly Vital Statistics Report No. 12, Supp. 2* (1990).

49. American Psychiatric Association, *Changing Family Patterns in the United States* 5 (1986) [hereinafter *Changing Family Patterns*]; Carlee R. Scott, "As Baby Boomers Age, Fewer Couples Untie the Knot," *Wall St. J.*, November 7, 1990, at B1, col. 3.

50. *Changing Family Patterns, supra* note 49, at 9.

51. Bureau of the Census, *supra* note 47, at 2 (Table B). Interestingly, there has been little long-term change in this figure. In 1960, the comparable numbers were 6% for women and 7% for men. *Id.*

52. Bureau of the Census, *supra* note 47, at 9–10 (Table 1).

53. Criminal laws against cohabitation still exist in 13 states. Mitchell Bernard, Ellen Levine, Stefan Presser, and Marianne Stecich, *The Rights of Single People* 12 (1985). Enforcement, however, appears to be extremely selective and heavily skewed by class and race. A 1978 survey of district attorneys in one of those states—Wisconsin—found that more than 90 prosecutions for violating that state's anticohabitation law had been initiated in the preceding five years. The most common reason, accounting for a third of the prosecutions, was the desire to use the law to exert pressure on a welfare recipient—usually female—either to report income that officials suspected her of receiving from a male cohabitant, or to stop spending part of the welfare allowance to help support the man. Martha L. Fineman, "Law and Changing Patterns of Behavior: Sanctions on Non-Marital Cohabitation," 1981 *Wisconsin Law Review* 275, 287–290.

In addition, a wide range of benefits that are available to married couples are denied to unmarried couples. For a comprehensive survey, see Barbara J. Cox, "Alternative Families: Obtaining Traditional Family Benefits Through Litigation, Legislation and Collective Bargaining," 2 *Wisconsin Women's Law Journal* 1 (1986) [Hereinafter Cox].

54. See, e.g., *Hollenbough v. Carnegie Free Library*, 436 F. Supp. 1328 (W.D.Pa. 1977) (upholding firing of unmarried male and female public library

employees because of the openness of their relationship), *aff'd mem.*, 578 F.2d 1374 (3rd Cir. 1978), *cert. denied*, 439 U.S. 1052 (1978).

55. Numerous authors have described how the principles of law discussed herein have developed in response to the legal issues that arise when unmarried couples end a relationship. Of significant usefulness are Grace Ganz Blumberg, "Cohabitation Without Marriage: A Different Perspective," 28 *UCLA Law Review* 1125 (1981); Kandoian, *supra* note 19; and Glendon, *supra* note 29.

56. *Marvin v. Marvin*, 18 Cal. 3d 660, 557 P.2d 106, 134 Cal. Rptr. 815 (1976), was the case that broke this ground, and other jurisdictions have followed its lead. See *Levar v. Elkins*, 604 P.2d 602 (Alaska 1980); *Carroll v. Lee*, 148 Ariz. 10, 712 P.2d 923 (1986); *Boland v. Catalano*, 202 Conn. 333, 521 A.2d 142 (1987); *Carlson v. Olson*, 256 N.W.2d 249 (Minn. 1977); *Kinkenon v. Hue*, 207 Neb. 698, 301 N.W.2d 77 (1981); *Hay v. Hay*, 100 Nev. 196, 678 P.2d 672 (1984); *Kozlowski v. Kozlowski*, 80 N.J. 378, 403 A.2d 902 (1979); *Beal v. Beal*, 282 Or. 115, 577 P.2d 507 (1978); *Watts v. Watts*, 137 Wis. 2d 506, 405 N.W.2d 303 (1987). In at least one instance, the contract principle has been applied to a gay male couple. See *Whorton v. Dillingham*, 202 Cal. App. 3d 447, 248 Cal. Rptr. 405 (Cal. Ct. App. 1988).

57. *Contra Hewitt v. Hewitt*, 77 Ill. 2d 49, 58, 394 N.E.2d 1204, 1207–1208 (1979).

58. This phrase was first employed by the New York Court of Appeals in holding that a household consisting of two surrogate parents and seven foster children was "the functional and factual equivalent of a natural family" for purposes of the zoning law. *Group House of Port Washington, Inc. v. Bd. of Zoning and Appeals of the Town of North Hempstead*, 45 N.Y.2d 266, 272, 380 N.E.2d 207, 209, 408 N.Y.S.2d 377, 379–380 (1978).

59. Michael Grossberg, *Governing the Hearth: Law and the Family in Nineteenth-Century America* 69–78 (1985), cited in Kandoian, *supra* note 19, at 1847–1848.

60. Courts in North Carolina and Georgia utilized principles of criminal and evidentiary law applicable to spouses in cases involving *de facto* marriages between slaves. See *State v. John*, 30 N.C. (3 Ired.) 330 (1848); *William v. State*, 33 Ga. Supp. 85 (1864). See discussion in Mark Tushnet, *American Law and Slavery* 15 (1981).

61. *Moore v. City of East Cleveland*, 431 U.S. 494 (1977).

62. Blumberg points out that the state is much more likely to treat nonmarital relationships as equivalent to married couples when the result is a disqualification for governmental benefits. See Blumberg, *supra* note 55, at 1138–1139. Glendon also found much more of a blurred distinction between married and *de facto* families in the realm of public, rather than private, law. See Glendon, *supra* note 29, at 711–715.

63. 74 N.Y.2d 201, 543 N.E.2d 49, 544 N.Y.S.2d 784 (1989). The New York State Division of Housing and Community Renewal subsequently promulgated regulations that codify the *Braschi* principles in some detail, for both rent-controlled and rent-stabilized housing units.

64. *Braschi*, 74 N.Y.2d at 211, 544 N.Y.S.2d at 788–789, 543 N.E.2d at 53.

65. *Braschi*, 74 N.Y.2d at 212–213, 544 N.Y.S.2d at 790, 543 N.E.2d at 55.

66. There have been many proposals over the years for legislation reforming how the law treats unmarried couples; few have ever been enacted. See Kandoian, *supra* note 19, at 1854–1855; Fineman, *supra* note 53, at 317–320, 326.

67. All the domestic partnership laws that have been enacted to date are limited to two-individual partnerships. There is no requirement that the individuals be in a sexual relationship. San Francisco's law, for example, defines domestic partners as "two adults who have chosen to share one another's lives in an intimate and committed relationship of mutual caring, who live together, and who have agreed to be jointly responsible for basic living expenses incurred during the Domestic Partnership." San Francisco Domestic Partnership Act § 2(a) (1990).

68. Ettelbrick, for example, posits the "domestic partnership movement" as a better alternative to a campaign for lesbian and gay marriage. *Out/Look*, *supra* note 11, at 17.

69. In addition to New York and San Francisco, some version of a domestic partnership law has been adopted in Seattle, Washington; Berkeley, Santa Cruz, and West Hollywood, California; Takoma Park, Maryland; Minneapolis, Minnesota; Ithaca, New York; and Madison, Wisconsin. See District of Columbia's Commission on Domestic Partnership, Benefits for D.C. Government Employees 8–9 (1990); Wade Lambert, "Domestic Partners of Seattle Workers Get Health Benefits," *Wall St. J.*, May 7, 1990, at B4, col. 4; American Civil Liberties Union, *Introduction to Domestic Partnership* 6–7 (1990) [hereinafter ACLU]. An excellent analysis of the legal background for enactment of such laws can be found in Cox, *supra* note 53.

70. The criteria for recognition of families in the New York State housing regulations, *infra* note 73, also have been criticized for indeterminacy. See Editorial, "We Now Pronounce You a Family," *New York Times*, December 15, 1989, at A42, col. 1.

71. The San Francisco system allows persons who meet the definitional criteria for domestic partners to create a partnership either by filing a form with the county clerk or by having a declaration of domestic partnership notarized and giving a copy to a witness. San Francisco Domestic Partnership Act § 3(a) (1990). In New York, where the benefit established is bereavement leave for employees of the city, partners register by filing a form with the city's Department of Personnel. New York City, N.Y., Executive Order No. 123 § 3 (Aug. 7, 1989). New York's version also requires that the partners have lived together for one year or more on a continuous basis before registration. *Id.* § 2.

Another legal device for achieving the same end involves registration by the parties as an unincorporated association. Family diversity advocates in California have recommended the use of this provision of state law for persons living in municipalities that do not have domestic partnership ordinances. See Laurie Becklund, "The Word 'Family' Gains New Meaning," *L.A. Times*, December 13, 1990, at A3, col. 2.

72. In the San Francisco system, if a copy of the partnership declaration was kept by a witness, that person must receive a copy of the notice that the partnership has ended. Only one partner need sign the notice, but it must be sent to the other partner. San Francisco Domestic Partnership Act § 4(b) (1990).

73. Health benefits, in some cases partial coverage, are available to domestic partners under the plans in Seattle, Madison, Berkeley, Santa Cruz, and West Hollywood. Lambert, *supra* note 69; ACLU, *supra* note 69. Bereavement leave is included in the New York City, Seattle, Madison, Berkeley, Santa Cruz, and West Hollywood plans. ACLU, *supra* note 69. Housing-related benefits are covered by New York State regulations for rent-stabilized and rent-controlled apartments, 9 N.Y. St. Reg. 13 (Apr. 4, 1990), and by a city code provision in Takoma Park, Wash., Takoma Park Code, art. 8, § 6–81 (Supp. 1986). The San Francisco system establishes only a registry; it does not itself extend benefits, although it sets the stage for that possibility. San Francisco Domestic Partnership Act (1990). Registered partners can use the partnership as proof of the relationship in attempts to negotiate with private employers and businesses.

74. In Berkeley, Santa Cruz, and West Hollywood, the partners must certify that they are "responsible for [each other's] welfare." See City of Berkeley Domestic Partnership Information Sheet (January 1, 1987) and City of Berkeley Affidavit of Domestic Partnership (November 15, 1986); City of Santa Cruz Domestic Partnership Information Sheet (no date) and City of Santa Cruz Affidavit of Domestic Partnership (no date); West Hollywood, Cal., Ordinance No. 22, (February 21, 1985) (copies of materials for each city on file at the *Law and Sexuality* office). This provision was based on the 1976 San Francisco bill, the first domestic partnership proposal, which was passed by the Board of Supervisors but vetoed by then-Mayor Diane Feinstein. The primary author of that and subsequent San Francisco proposals, Matthew Coles, has stated that the mutual responsibility provisions were included as a mechanism for balancing the rights and duties aspects of the legislation. Telephone communication with Matthew Coles (January 1991).

75. The San Francisco legislation states the mutual responsibilities in its definitional section. San Francisco Domestic Partnership Act (1990) § 2 (1990). It defines the "basic living expenses" for which the partners agree to be responsible as "the cost of basic food and shelter," plus any expenses paid for in part by benefits flowing to the couple on the basis of their status as domestic partners. *Id.* § 2(c). The law provides that by signing a declaration of partnership, the two parties acknowledge "that this agreement can be enforced by anyone to whom those expenses are owed." *Id.* § 2(d). If the partnership ends, the partners incur no further obligations to each other. *Id.* § 6(b).

76. See Frances E. Olsen, "The Family and the Market: A Study of Ideology and Legal Reform," 96 *Harvard Law Review* 1497 (1983); Nadine Taub & Elizabeth M. Schneider, "Women's Subordination and the Role of Law," in *The*

Politics of Law: A Progressive Critique 151 (ed. David Kairys, 1990) [hereinafter *Politics of Law*].

77. 18 Cal. 3d 660, 557 P.2d 106, 134 Cal. Rptr. 815 (1976).

78. Blumberg argues that the majority of cohabiting heterosexual couples both believe and act as though there is no difference between marriage and cohabitation. She asserts that the failure to treat such couples according to marriage law principles systematically harms cohabiting heterosexual women who, like married women, tend to forgo income opportunities in order to perform domestic labor. She notes that in several of the reported cases, the female partner in a dissolving nonmarital union had sought marriage, but the man had refused. Blumberg proposes that heterosexual cohabitant couples who meet certain durational criteria or who have children be automatically considered as married. Those couples who mutually do intend from the outset of a relationship to avoid the state-dictated terms of matrimony could execute waivers of statutory shares and other specific instruments to achieve the same end, but the burden to act would be on those who wish to opt out of marriage. See Blumberg, *supra* note 55, at 1166–1170. Kandoian reaches essentially the same conclusion, but would use the principles of business partnerships to achieve that end. See Kandoian, *supra* note 19, at 1863–1872.

79. Neither Blumberg nor Kandoian mentions lesbian or gay relationships in her analysis. *See* Blumberg, *supra* note 55; Kandoian, *supra* note 19.

80. In fact, however, not only are the domestic partnership laws available for use by couples without regard to sexual orientation, but several cities that have adopted such plans report that the majority of the actual registrants are heterosexual couples. See Lambert, *supra* note 69 (in Seattle, almost 75% of participants are heterosexual partners); Mayor's Lesbian and Gay Task Force of Seattle, *The Impact of Domestic Partners Legislation* (1989) (no page number) (more than 80% of participants in Berkeley plan are heterosexual partners; in West Hollywood, however, about 80% are same-sex couples).

81. One positive example of changing the framework of reform to include the genuine diversity of interests involved has been suggested by Matthew Coles. In response to concerns that previous versions of domestic partnership initiatives did not address the issues of most importance to people of color, Coles has proposed a twin registry system: in addition to the one for couples, a family registry could be added to enhance the usefulness of the concept for households where the unformalized relationship was not between two adults, but existed as a form of unofficial adoption by an adult of a child who was unrelated by blood or marriage, but who was part of a larger, informal community kinship system. Telephone communication with Matthew Coles (January 1991). Advocates in Los Angeles have also sought to frame their efforts in broad "family diversity" terms, addressing issues of housing, homelessness, child care, family violence, education, disability and concerns of elders, along with those related to unmarried couples. See Los Angeles City Task Force on Family Diversity, Final Report—Strengthening Families: A Model for Community Action (1988). A similar report grew out of the San

Francisco campaign to enact a domestic partnership law. See Mayor's Task Force on Family Policy, Approaching 2000: Meeting the Challenges to San Francisco's Families (1990).

82. Frank I. Michelman, "The Supreme Court and Litigation Access Fees: The Right to Protect One's Own Rights—Part I," 1973 *Duke Law Journal* 1153, 1177.

83. The brief and partial summary presented in this article cannot, of course, do justice to the writings of CLS scholars nor to those of their critics. Two symposium editions of law reviews, from which many of the sources cited *infra* notes 84 and 85, are taken, remain excellent collections of CLS articles on the rights debate: "Critical Legal Studies Symposium," 36 *Stanford Law Review* Nos. 1 and 2 (1984), and "Symposium: A Critique of Rights," 62 *Texas Law Review* No. 8 (1984).

84. Ideas can "be taken over and falsified immediately, the same way that the appointment of Sandra Day O'Connor is an attempt to falsify the meaning of the women's movement." Peter Gabel and Duncan Kennedy, "Roll Over Beethoven," 36 *Stanford Law Review* 1, 5 (1984).

85. Allan C. Hutchinson and Patrick J. Monahan, "The "Rights" Stuff: Roberto Unger and Beyond," 62 *Texas Law Review* 1477, 1510 (1984); Staughton Lynd, "Communal Rights," 62 *Texas Law Review* 1417, 1418–1419 (1984).

86. Alan D. Freeman, "Antidiscrimination Law: The View from 1989," in *Politics of Law, supra* note 76, at 96 (recent civil rights decisions by the Supreme Court "can be best understood . . . as reaffirming the myths that normalize inequality as the outcome of impersonal, neutral forces"); Robert W. Gordon, "New Developments in Legal Theory," in *Politics of Law, supra* note 76, at 413.

87. "Law is just one among many ... systems of meaning ... [that] has the effect of making the social world as it is come to seem natural and inevitable." Gordon, *supra* note 86, at 419.

88. *See* Kimberlé Williams Crenshaw, "Race, Reform, and Retrenchment: Transformation and Legitimation in Antidiscrimination Law," 101 *Harvard Law Review* 1331, 1357 (1988) (arguing, *inter alia*, that CLS critiques have exaggerated the role of ideological constructs and underestimated the power of racial domination and coercion); Patricia J. Williams, "Alchemical Notes: Reconstructing Ideals From Deconstructed Rights," 22 *Harvard Civil Rights-Civil Liberties Law Review* 401, 424 (1987) ("This country's worst historical moments have not been attributable to rights-*assertion*, but to a failure of rights-*commitment*.") (emphasis in original); Elizabeth Schneider, "The Dialectic of Rights and Politics: Perspectives From the Women's Movement," 61 *New York University Law Review* 589 (1986).

89. Schneider argues that the assertion of rights claims "help[s] women to overcome th[e] sense of privatization and of personal blame [that] has perpetuated women's subordination." Schneider, *supra* note 88, at 626. Crenshaw points out that "[b]ecause rights that other Americans took for granted were routinely denied to Black Americans, Blacks' assertion of their rights constituted a serious ideological challenge to white supremacy. Their demand was

not just for a place in the front of a bus, but for inclusion in the American political imagination." Crenshaw, *supra* note 88, at 1365.

90. Schneider, *supra* note 88, at 648–652.
91. Crenshaw, *supra* note 88, at 1368.

Notes to Chapter 10: Identity, Speech and Equality

Originally published in 79 *Virginia Law Review* 1695 (1993). Reprinted with permission.

1. See *Gay and Lesbian Students Ass'n v. Gohn*, 850 F.2d 361 (8th Cir. 1988); *Gay Students Services v. Texas A & M Univ.*, 737 F.2d 1317 (5th Cir. 1984); *Gay Lib v. University of Mo.*, 558 F.2d 848 (8th Cir. 1977), *cert. denied*, 434 U.S. 1080 (1978); *Gay Alliance of Students v. Matthews*, 544 F.2d 162 (4th Cir. 1976); *Gay Students Org. of the Univ. of N.H. v. Bonner*, 509 F.2d 652 (1st Cir. 1974); *Student Coalition for Gay Rights v. Austin Peay State Univ.*, 477 F. Supp. 1267 (M.D. Tenn. 1979); *Wood v. Davison*, 351 F. Supp. 543 (N.D. Ga. 1972).
2. Senate Comm. on Expenditures in the Exec. Dep'ts, *Employment of Homosexuals and Other Sex Perverts in Government*, S. Doc. No. 241, 81st Cong., 2d Sess. 4 (1950) [hereinafter *Employment of Homosexuals in Government*].
3. See John D'Emilio, "The Homosexual Menace: the Politics of Sexuality in Cold War America," in *Passion and Power: Sexuality and History* 226, 226 (ed. Kathy Peiss and Christina Simmons, 1989).
4. Exec. Order No. 10,450, 18 Fed. Reg. 2489 (1953).
5. It is at best tricky and perhaps wrong to use the term "identity" in analyzing the social concepts extant during the early postwar period. Self-consciousness about a homosexual identity was then in its infancy among lesbians and gay men; although the African-American civil rights movement was starting to emerge as a political force, the idea of identity politics had yet to develop. With these reservations, I nonetheless use the idea of "identity" in describing the process by which legal arguments helped shape a new social meaning for homosexuality and "the homosexual."
6. *Employment of Homosexuals in Government*, *supra* note 2, at 9.
7. Allan Bérubé, *Coming Out Under Fire: The History of Gay Men and Women in World War Two* 13, 139–141 (1990).
8. Senate Comm. on the Judiciary, *The Immigration and Naturalization Systems of the United States*, S. Rep. No. 1515, 81st Congress, 2d Sess. 343 (1950).
9. *Id.*
10. *Id.* at 345.
11. *Id.*
12. *Id.*
13. John D'Emilio, *Sexual Politics, Sexual Communities: The Making of a Homosexual Minority in the United States 1940–1970* 31–33, 49–50, 186–188 (1983); John D'Emilio and Estelle B. Freedman, *Intimate Matters: A History of Sexuality in America* 290–294 (1988); Arthur S. Leonard, "The Gay Bar and the Right to Hang Out Together," in his *Sexuality and the Law: An Encyclopedia of Major Legal Cases* 190–196 (1993).

14. D'Emilio and Freedman, *supra* note 13, at 294. Occasionally, police attempts to record identities of gay individuals have been used tactically against the police. See, e.g., *Cyr v. Walls*, 439 F. Supp. 697, 704–05 (N.D. Tex. 1977) (allowing the individuals whose presence at various gay functions was recorded by the police to be added to the class in a civil rights action against police officers).

15. See E. Carrington Boggan, Marilyn G. Haft, Charles Lister and John P. Rupp, *The Rights of Gay People* 10–12 (1975) [hereinafter *The Rights of Gay People*]. In this edition of the ACLU's guide for laypersons, in the chapter on speech and association, there is extensive discussion of how to keep one's group membership secret, and no discussion of the law pertaining to public protest.

16. Model Penal Code § 213.2 cmt. 2 (Proposed Official Draft 1962, Revised Comments 1980).

17. *Lesbians, Gay Men and the Law* 88, 92 (ed. William B. Rubenstein, 1993).

18. See Model Penal Code § 213.2; see also H.L.A. Hart, *Law, Liberty, and Morality* 14–15 (1963) (noting how privacy concerns underlie the Model Penal Code's dropping of the prohibition against sodomy).

19. 417 F.2d 1161, 1165 (D.C.Cir. 1969) (holding that off-hours homosexual conduct could not be basis of dismissal unless it affected work performance).

20. *Ashton v. Civiletti*, 613 F.2d 923, 927 (D.C. Cir. 1979) (quoting Civil Service Bulletin, December 21, 1993).

21. 5 U.S.C. § 2302(b)(10) (1988).

22. *Roth v. United States*, 354 U.S. 476, 489 (1957), abandoned the tendency-to-corrupt-morals test, substituting a test that asked "whether to the average person, applying contemporary community standards, the dominant theme of the material taken as a whole appeals to prurient interest." The current standard, adopted in *Miller v. California*, 413 U.S. 15, 24–25 (1973), asks (1) whether the average person, applying contemporary community standards, would find that the work appeals to the prurient interest; (2) whether the work in question depicts or describes sexual conduct in a patently offensive way; and (3) whether the work as a whole lacks serious literary, artistic, political, or scientific value.

23. *People v. Friede*, 233 N.Y.S. 565, 567 (Mag. Ct. 1929).

24. *One, Inc. v. Olesen*, 241 F.2d 772, 777 (9th Cir. 1957), rev'd, 355 U.S. 371 (1958). For a description of the magazine and its role in the homophile movement, see D'Emilio, *supra* note 13, at 109–15.

25. *One, Inc.*, 241 F.2d at 777.

26. The Supreme Court's ruling consisted of one sentence reversing the lower court and a citation to *Roth v. United States*. *One, Inc.*, 355 U.S. 371, 371. The Court's opinion thus did not address the specific question of whether promotion of homosexuality, at least if eroticized, could be a component of obscenity. In *Manual Enterprises v. Day*, 370 U.S. 478 (1962), however, the Court ruled that nudity in gay-male-oriented bodybuilding magazines was no "more objectionable" than comparable female nudity "that society toler-

ates." *Id.* at 490. The *Day* decision laid the groundwork for the growth of a national gay press. See Leonard, *supra* note 13, at 209.

27. *Van Ooteghem v. Gray,* 628 F.2d 488 (5th Cir. 1980), aff'd, 654 F.2d 304 (1981) (en banc), *cert. denied,* 455 U.S. 909 (1982); *Singer v. United States Civil Serv. Comm'n,* 530 F.2d 247 (9th Cir. 1976), *vacated and remanded,* 429 U.S. 1034 (1977); *Acanfora v. Board of Educ.,* 491 F.2d 498 (4th Cir.), *cert. denied,* 419 U.S. 836 (1974); *McConnell v. Anderson,* 451 F.2d 193 (8th Cir. 1971), *cert. denied,* 405 U.S. 1046 (1972).

28. *Norton v. Macy,* 417 F.2d 1161, 1167 (D.C. Cir. 1969) (requiring a connection between employee's conduct and the efficiency of the service provided by the government agency).

29. Compare *Van Ooteghem,* 628 F.2d at 490–93 (holding that it was a violation of plaintiff's First Amendment right to free speech to fire him for addressing a public body on the civil rights of homosexuals) with *McConnell,* 451 F.2d at 196 (holding that the fact that plaintiff took activist role in implementing his unconventional ideas formed a sufficient basis for denying plaintiff employment).

30. *Brandenburg v. Ohio,* 395 U.S. 444, 447–448 (1969).

31. See *Gay Student Servs. v. Texas A&M Univ.,* 737 F.2d 1317, 1328 (5th Cir. 1984); *Gay Lib v. University of Mo.,* 558 F.2d 848, 854 (8th Cir. 1977), *cert. denied,* 434 U.S. 1080 (1978); *Gay Alliance of Students v. Matthews,* 544 F.2d 162, 166 (4th Cir. 1976); *Gay Students Org. of the Univ. of N.H. v. Bonner,* 509 F.2d 652, 662 (1st Cir. 1974).

32. One district court, however, noted that "[h]ere we are not dealing with conduct, but with the *advocacy of the acceptability* of conduct." *Student Coalition for Gay Rights v. Austin Peay State Univ.,* 477 F. Supp. 1267, 1274 (M.D. Tenn. 1979).

33. The event occurred at the Stonewall Inn in Greenwich Village, when the bar's patrons spontaneously resisted what the police no doubt considered a routine raid. The resistance was all the more dramatic because most of the patrons were drag queens in full dress, although one observer credits a lesbian among the crowd with being the first to call on her compadres to fight back. The ensuing struggle became a pitched battle between gays and police that continued for hours in the streets of the Village. For a contemporaneous discussion of Stonewall, see Lucian Truscott IV, "Gay Power Comes to Sheridan Square," *Village Voice,* July 3, 1969, at 1, 18.

34. *The Rights of Gay People, supra* note 15, at 21.

35. Randy Shilts, *The Mayor of Castro Street: The Life and Times of Harvey Milk* 221 (1982).

36. Cal. Proposition 6, § 3(b)(2), (1978).

37. Shilts, *supra* note 35, at 212–251; "Witch-hunting" *The Economist,* October 28, 1978, at 50.

38. See Shilts, *supra* note 35, at 242; David B. Goodstein, "Fighting the Briggs Brigade," *The Advocate,* June 14, 1978, at 6; "Poll Shows a Major Shift on Prop 6," *Gay Community News,* October 21, 1978, at 1.

39. See Scott Anderson, "After Victories, Leaders Ponder the Next Step," *The Advocate*, December 27, 1978, at 8–9.

40. See Shilts, *supra* note 35, at 245–249; Sasha Gregory-Lewis, "Californians Face Proposition 6" and "Will it Be Written, Mene, Mene, Tekel Upharsin?," *The Advocate*, November 15, 1978, at 7–12; "Victory in California, Seattle; Miami Defeat," *The Advocate*, December 13, 1978, at 9 [hereinafter "Victory in California"].

41. "Victory," *supra* note 40, at 9.

42. *Gay Law Students Ass'n v. Pacific Tel. and Tel. Co.*, 595 P.2d 592, 610–611 (Cal. 1979).

43. *Id.* at 611.

44. *Id.* at 610.

45. The *Pacific Telephone* case was settled with a $5 million payment to the plaintiff class and the adoption by defendant of an antidiscrimination policy. Leonard, *supra* note 13, at 417. In a later case, the California Court of Appeals ruled that the Labor Code's provisions protecting employees' fundamental rights to engage in political activity free of employer interference also applied to expressions of sexual orientation. *Soroka v. Dayton Hudson Corp.*, 1 Cal. Rptr. 2d 77, 87–88 (Cal. Ct. App. 1991) appeal docketed, No. 5024102 (Cal. 1992). In 1992, the Labor Code was amended to add an explicit protection. Cal. Lab. Code § 1102.1 (West 1993).

46. Brief for Appellees at 2–3 n. 3, *Board of Educ. of Okla. City v. National Gay Task Force*, 470 U.S. 903 (1985) (No. 83–2030).

47. *National Gay Task Force v. Board of Educ. of Okla. City*, 729 F.2d 1270, 1274 (10th Cir. 1984), *aff'd per curiam*, 470 U.S. 903 (1985). The Supreme Court ruled by an evenly divided vote; Justice Lewis Powell took no part in the case because of illness. See Leonard, *supra* note 13, at 616.

48. *National Gay Task Force*, 729 F.2d at 1277 (Barrett, J., dissenting).

49. Arthur S. Leonard, "Discrimination," in *AIDS and the Law: A Guide for the Nineties* 297 (ed. Scott Burris et al., 1993).

50. Scott Burris, "Testing, Disclosure, and the Right to Privacy," in *AIDS and the Law, supra* note 49, at 115.

51. See, e.g., *Report of the Nat'l Comm'n on Acquired Immune Deficiency Syndrome, America Living with AIDS* 19 (1991) ("Until a cure or a vaccine is found, education and prevention are the only hope for altering the course of the HIV epidemic.").

52. Dennis Altman, "Legitimation through Disaster: AIDS and the Gay Movement," in *AIDS: The Burdens of History* 305 (ed. Elizabeth Fee and Daniel M. Fox, 1988); see also *AIDS Research: Hearings on Dep'ts of Labor, Health and Human Servs., Education, and Related Agencies Appropriations for 1989*, Subcomm. of the Comm. on Appropriations, 100th Cong., 2nd Sess. 294, 299 (1988) (written testimony of Jeffrey Levi, National Gay and Lesbian Task Force) (arguing for a greater emphasis in government AIDS spending on education as compared to testing).

53. See Ronald Bayer, *Private Acts, Social Consequences: AIDS and the Politics of Public Health* 89–93 (1989); Dennis Altman, *AIDS and the New Puritanism* 74–78 (1986).

54. Almost immediately after licensure, the U.S. military began mass HIV screening of all recruits and active duty personnel. Recruits who tested positive were rejected for service and often informed of their HIV status with no counseling or information about the disease. Military use of the test was soon followed by adoption of mandatory testing programs by the Foreign Service and the Job Corps. Bayer, *supra* note 53, at 158–62; see also *American Fed'n of Gov't Employees v. Department of State*, 662 F. Supp. 50 (D.D.C. 1987) (rejecting the enjoining of the foreign service's mandatory AIDS testing).

55. Conference on the Role of AIDS Virus Antibody Testing in the Prevention and Control of AIDS, Closing Plenary Session: Reports from the Workshops, Transcript of Proceedings (February 24–25, 1987).

56. Public Health Serv. Centers for Disease Control, U.S. Dep't of Health and Human Servs., *Recommended Additional Guidelines for HIV Antibody Counseling and Testing in the Prevention of HIV Infection and AIDS*, at 9–13 (April 30, 1987).

57. See Bayer, *supra* note 53, at 164. The final recommendations were published at 36 *Morbidity and Mortality Weekly Report* 509 (August 14, 1987).

58. Marlene Cimons, "AIDS Education Grants Frozen," *L.A. Times*, December 4, 1985, at 12.

59. 51 Fed. Reg. 3431 (1986).

60. 133 Cong. Rec. 14,267 (1987). The Labor-Health and Human Services Appropriations Act for Fiscal Year 1988 provided that "none of the funds made available under this Act to the Centers for Disease Control shall be used to provide AIDS education, information, or prevention materials and activities that promote or encourage, directly, homosexual activities." Pub. L. No. 100–202, § 514(a), 101 Stat. 1329–289 (1988).

61. 133 Cong. Rec. 14,203 (1987).

62. *Id.*

63. *Id.* at 14,204.

64. *Id.* at 14,208.

65. *Id.* at 14,219.

66. The Kennedy-Cranston Amendment stated:

    Notwithstanding any other provision of this Act, AIDS education programs funded by the Centers for Disease Control and other education curricula funded under this Act dealing with sexual activity—
        (1) shall not be designed to promote or encourage, directly, intravenous drug abuse or sexual activity, homosexual or heterosexual.

67. 134 Cong. Rec. 10,025 (1988) (statement of Sen. Cranston); see also *id.* at 17,005 (statement of Sen. Kennedy) (stating that the bill was written so as to prevent funding of programs designed solely to promote or encourage sexual activity).

68. *Id.* at 10,027.

69. *Gay Men's Health Crisis v. Sullivan*, 792 F. Supp. 278, 304 (S.D.N.Y. 1992).

70. *Id.* at 302 (holding that "the grant terms are too vague to apply in a non-arbitrary manner").

71. *Id.* at 291 (finding that "in using the 'offensiveness' criteria, the CDC has contravened its statutory authority which bars funding of only obscene, not offensive material").

72. See Ariz. Rev. Stat. Ann. § 15–716(C) (1992). Specifically, the statute states: "No district shall include in its course of study instruction which:
    1. Promotes a homosexual lifestyle.
    2. Portrays homosexuality as a positive alternative lifestyle.
    3. Suggests that some methods of sex are safe methods of homosexual sex."
    Id.

73. See Ala. Code § 16–40A–2(a)(8) (1992). Alabama requires that sex education programs include "[a]n emphasis, in a factual manner and from a public health perspective, that homosexuality is not a lifestyle acceptable to the general public and that homosexual conduct is a criminal offense under the laws of the state." *Id.*

74. Simon Garfield, "The Age of Consent," *The Independent*, November 10, 1991, at 3.

75. *Id.* The basic form of Clause 28 traveled back across the Atlantic in the form of an Oregon ballot initiative, rejected by voters in November 1992, that would have required that "[s]tate, regional and local governments and their properties and monies shall not be used to promote, encourage, or facilitate homosexuality." "For the Record," *Oregonian*, October 2, 1992, at D6.

76. Rorie Sherman, "Sex Education Manual Spurs Censorship Debate," *Nat'l L.J.*, July 18, 1988, at 14; see also Clare Kittredge, "Sex-Education Dispute Settled by State, Clinic," *Boston Globe*, September 7, 1988, at 26 (discussing how a compromise was eventually reached whereby private financing was used to finance production of the manuals and a disclaimer added disavowing any government approval of its contents).

77. Rod Paul, "Sex Education Manual Prompts Moral Outrage," *N.Y. Times*, April 24, 1988, at 39.

78. 134 Cong. Rec. 10,048 (1988).

79. *Gay Rights Coalition v. Georgetown Univ.*, 536 A.2d 1, 26 (D.C. 1987).

80. District of Columbia Appropriations Act of 1989, Pub. L. No. 100–462, § 145(c)(3), 102 Stat. 2269 (1988). The attempt temporarily failed when City Council members won a ruling that the provision violated their free speech rights. *Clarke v. United States*, 886 F.2d 404 (D.C. Cir. 1989), *vacated on other grounds*, 915 F.2d 699 (D.C. Cir. 1990). Congress had the last word, however; it simply amended the D.C. human rights act directly, drawing on its residual power over local District government. See District of Columbia Appropriations Act of 1990, Pub. L. No. 101–168, § 141, 103 Stat. 1267, 1284 (1989).

81. Pub. L. No. 101–121, § 304, 103 Stat. 701, 741 (1989).

82. Carole S. Vance, "Misunderstanding Obscenity," *Art in America*, May 1990, at 49–55. As Vance notes:

> [T]he list of sexual acts simply gives examples of depictions that might fall under the legal definition of obscenity, after the three prongs of the Miller test are met. But these sexual depictions or acts are not by themselves obscene. (Or, to take another example, more easily understood because it is not about sex, consider the phrase "obscene material including but not limited to black-and-white photographs, color slides and Cibachromes.")
>
> *Id.* at 51.

83. See *Finley v. National Endowment for the Arts*, 795 F. Supp. 1457, 1461 & n.5 (C.D. Cal. 1992).
84. Memorandum from Secretary of Defense to Joint Chiefs of Staff, *Policy on Homosexual Conduct in the Armed Forces*, July 19, 1993.
85. President's Remarks Announcing the New Policy on Gays and Lesbians in the Military, 29 *Weekly Comp. Pres. Doc.* 1372 (July 26, 1993).
86. 478 U.S. 186 (1986).
87. See generally "Life After Hardwick," reprinted in this volume.
88. See *supra* note 1.
89. *Rowland v. Mad River Local Sch. Dist.*, 470 U.S. 1009, 1016 n. 11 (1985) (Brennan, J., dissenting).
90. See, e.g., *Wooley v. Maynard*, 430 U.S. 705, 717 (1977) (holding that a state statute, which forced individuals to display messages on their private property to which they were ideologically opposed, invaded their First Amendment rights).
91. Cf. *West Virginia State Bd. of Educ. v. Barnette*, 319 U.S. 624, 642 (1943) ("If there is any fixed star in our constitutional constellation, it is that no official, high or petty, can prescribe what shall be orthodox in politics, nationalism, religion, or other matters of opinion.").

Notes to Chapter 11: History's Gay Ghetto

This essay was originally published in Susan Porter Benson, Stephen Brier and Roy Rosenzweig, eds., *Presenting the Past: Essays on History and the Public* (Phila: Temple University Press, 1986).

1. Lesbian Herstory Archives, *Newsletter*, 1 (June 1975).
2. Jonathan Katz, *Gay American History* (New York, 1976). This collection of documents revealed the wealth of gay and lesbian materials in libraries and traditional archives. The footnotes and bibliographic notes were frequently as useful as the reprinted documents themselves. It was followed in 1983 by another impressive collection, Katz's *Gay/Lesbian Almanac* (New York, 1983).
3. This slide show has been updated and revised as "She Even Chewed Tobacco" by the San Francisco Lesbian and Gay History Project, from which it is now

available. An account of its contents is in Allan Bérubé, "Lesbian Masquerade," *Gay Community News*, November 17, 1979, 8–9.

4. The results have been published as Elizabeth Kennedy and Madeline Davis' *Boots of Leather Slippers of Gold* (Routledge: New York, 1993).

5. See John Boswell, *Christianity, Social Tolerance and Homosexuality: Gay People in Western Europe from the Beginning of the Christian Era to the Fourteenth Century* (Chicago, 1980); John D'Emilio, *Sexual Politics, Sexual Communities: The Making of a Homosexual Minority in the United States, 1940–1970* (Chicago, 1983); Lillian Faderman, *Surpassing the Love of Men: Romantic Friendship and Love Between Women from the Renaissance to the Present* (New York, 1981).

6. James A. Fraser and Harold A. Averill, *Organizing an Archives: The Canadian Gay Archives Experience* (Toronto, 1980).

7. All records of the New York history projects are on file at the Lesbian Herstory Archives in New York.

8. The slide show is available from the Boston Lesbian and Gay History Project. An account that includes much of the same material is Joseph Interrante, "From the Puritans to the Present: 350 Years of Lesbian and Gay History in Boston," in *Gay Jubilee: A Guidebook to Gay Boston—Its History and Resources*, ed. Richard Burns, Neuma Cradall, and Eric Rofes (Boston, 1980).

9. The *Newsletter* is available from the Committee on Lesbian and Gay History.

10. Proceedings of the Amsterdam conference were published by Gay Studies and Women's Studies of the University of Amsterdam, *Among Women, Among Men: Sociological and Historical Recognition of Homosocial Arrangements* (Amsterdam, 1983).

11. See Chris Czernick, "How the Boston History Project Began," *Gay Community News*, June 16, 1984, 14–17.

12. Eric Garber, "Tain't Nobody's Bizness." This slide show, available through the Committee on Lesbian and Gay History, is an account of gay life during the Harlem Renaissance. See also *Black Lesbians: An Annotated Bibliography*, compiled by J. R. Roberts (Tallahassee, Fla., 1981), foreword by Barbara Smith.

13. Materials collected by these groups, and reports on their activities, are on file at the Lesbian Herstory Archives.

14. For a discussion of the politics of archiving, see Joan Nestle, "Radical Archiving: A Lesbian Feminist Perspective," *Gay Insurgent*, 4–5 (Spring 1979), 10–12.

15. John D'Emilio and Allan Bérubé, among others, withdrew their cooperation from this film project when their unpublished research was used without proper permission, credit, and payment.

16. Leila Rupp, review of Katz and D'Emilio, *Signs*, 9 (1984), 712–715.

17. Katz, *Gay/Lesbian Almanac*; Faderman, *Surpassing the Love of Men*; Jeffrey Weeks, *Coming Out: Homosexual Politics in Britain from the Nineteenth Century to the Present* (London, 1977); Jeffrey Weeks, *Sex, Politics*

and Society: The Regulation of Sexuality Since 1800 (London, 1981). See also Kenneth Plummer, *The Making of the Modern Homosexual* (London, 1981).

18. D'Emilio, *Sexual Politics*; Buffalo Oral History Project file box, Lesbian Herstory Archives; Allan Bérubé, "Marching to a Different Drummer: Lesbian and Gay GIs in World War II," *Advocate*, Oct. 15, 1981, 20–24. This article gives an account of Bérubé's slide show of the same name.

19. For an account of the campaign against the Briggs initiative, see Amber Hollibaugh, "Sexuality and the State," *Socialist Review*, 9 (May–June 1979), 55–72.

20. This affidavit recounts the contributions of gay people and their special oppression in American history. D'Emilio makes a sophisticated but extremely clear historical case for an end to the legal persecution of gay people. Affidavit of John Anthony D'Emilio in the United States Court of Appeals for the Fifth Circuit (No. 82–1590).

Notes to Chapter 12: Making It Perfectly Queer

This essay was first presented at the University of Illinois at Champaign-Urbana's Unit for Criticism and Interpretive Theory Colloquium in April, 1991, then at the 5th Annual Lesbian and Gay Studies Conference at Rutgers University in November, 1991. I would like to thank Alan Hance and Lee Furey for their comments in Urbana, and Kathleen McHugh, Carole Vance, Cindy Patton, Jeff Escoffier, Jonathan Ned Katz, and especially Nan D. Hunter, for their invaluable contributions to my thinking. I would also like to thank Gayle Rubin and Larry Gross for providing me with copies of important but obscure articles from their voluminous files, and the SR Bay Area collective for their helpful editorial suggestions.

Originally published in *Socialist Review*, 92 (January-March 1992), published by Duke University Press. Reprinted with permission.

1. David N. Dinkins, "Keep Marching for Equality," the *New York Times*, March 21, 1991.

2. The ideas in this discussion of gay nationalism were generated in conversations with Jenny Terry, Jackie Urla, and Jeff Escoffier. It was Urla who first suggested to me that certain strains in gay politics could be considered nationalist discourses.

3. For a description and defense of the "ethnic model," see Steven Epstein, "Gay Politics, Ethnic Identity: The Limits of Social Constructionism," *Socialist Review*, vol. 17, no. 3/4 (May–August 1987).

4. For an account of a 1970s incarnation of this form of nationalism—based on gender rather than sexuality *per se*—see Charlotte Bunch, "Learning from Lesbian Separatism," in her *Passionate Politics: Feminist Theory in Action* (New York: St. Martin's Press, 1987).

5. See, for example, Michelangelo Signorile, "Gossip Watch," *Outweek*, April 18, 1990, pp. 55–57. For an extended discussion of these issues, see Steve Beery *et al.*, "Smashing the Closet: The Pros and Cons of Outing," *Outweek*, May 16, 1990, pp. 40–53. The many opinions expressed in this issue indicate

that not all editors of *Outweek* agreed with Signorile—though the editor-in-chief, Gabriel Rotello, was in complete agreement.

6. See Michelangelo Signorile, "The Other Side of Malcolm," *Outweek*, March 18, 1990, pp. 40–45. The Tim Sweeney controversy continued in the pages of the magazine for several months.

7. C. Carr, "Why Outing Must Stop," *The Village Voice*, March 19, 1991, p. 37. She was later joined in the letters column of the *Voice* by B. Ruby Rich, who announced the formation of DAO—Dykes Against Outing.

8. Audre Lorde, *Zami: A New Spelling of My Name* (Watertown, MA: Persephone Press, 1982), p. 226.

9. Louise Sloan, "Beyond Dialogue," *San Francisco Bay Guardian Literary Supplement*, March 1991, p. 3.

10. For an excellent account of the political ramifications of this debate, see Jeffrey Escoffier, "Inside the Ivory Closet: The Challenges Facing Lesbian and Gay Studies," *Out/Look: National Lesbian and Gay Quarterly*, no. 10 (Fall 1990), pp. 40–48. For a theoretical discussion, see Diana Fuss, "Lesbian and Gay Theory: The Question of Identity Politics" in her *Essentially Speaking: Feminism, Nature and Difference* (New York: Routledge, 1989), pp. 97–112. (Neither of these writers offers the clichéd version of the debate that I have caricatured.)

11. For discussions of the emergence of the homosexual/heterosexual dyad and its representations in various medical-scientific discourses, see Jeffrey Weeks, *Coming Out: Homosexual Politics in Britain From the Nineteenth Century to the Present* (London: Quartet Books, 1977) and his *Sex, Politics and Society: The Regulation of Sexuality Since 1800* (London: Longman, 1981). See also Jonathan Katz, "The Invention of the Homosexual, 1880–1950," in his *Gay/Lesbian Almanac* (New York: Harper & Row, 1983), pp. 137–174.

12. See Dennis Altman, *Homosexual Oppression and Liberation* (New York: Avon Books, 1971), especially Chapter 3, "Liberation: Toward the Polymorphous Whole."

13. Alix Dobkin, "Any Woman Can Be a Lesbian," from the album *Lavender Jane Loves Women*. The best known example of this move—the denaturalization of heterosexuality, and the naturalization of lesbianism—is Adrienne Rich, "Compulsory Heterosexuality and Lesbian Existence," reprinted in *Powers of Desire: The Politics of Sexuality*, ed. A. Snitow, C. Stansell and S. Thompson (New York: Monthly Review Press, 1983), pp. 177–205. It is important to note that male-dominated gay politics has seldom supported a critique of the convention of heterosexuality for most people (the 90% or so seen as "naturally" heterosexual). Lesbian-feminists *always* regarded heterosexuality as an oppressive institution, which any woman (potentially all women) might escape through lesbianism.

14. See for example the anthology edited by Loraine Hutchins and Lani Kaahumani, *Bi Any Other Name: Bisexual People Speak Out* (Boston: Alyson Publications, 1991).

15. "Birth of A Queer Nation," *Out/Look: National Lesbian and Gay Quarterly*, no. 11 (Winter 1991), pp. 14–23. The interviews and articles in this special section were collected from New York and San Francisco, though there are other groups all over the country. My account of Queer Nation is drawn from my own (limited) knowledge of the New York and Chicago groups, and from articles and interviews in the gay and lesbian press. Because Queer Nation has no central "organization," I'm not attempting to describe it exhaustively; I am pointing to several tendencies and possibilities within it.

16. 'Gay' Fades as Militants Pick 'Queer'," the *New York Times*, April 6, 1991.

17. Pat Califia, "Gay Men, Lesbians and Sex: Doing It Together," *The Advocate*, July 7, 1983, pp. 24–27; Jorjet Harper, "Lesbians Who Sleep With Men," *Outweek*, February 11, 1990, pp. 46–52.

18. These developments are summarized by Jeffrey Escoffier in "Inside the Ivory Closet." See note 9.

19. See Lisa Duggan, "History's Gay Ghetto: The Contradictions of Growth in Lesbian and Gay History," in this volume; and John D'Emilio, "Not A Simple Matter: Gay History and Gay Historians," *Journal of American History*, vol. 76, no. 2 (September 1989), pp. 435–442.

20. The most influential single text in the United States was the English translation of *The History of Sexuality: Volume 1* (New York: Pantheon, 1978). My point about the ubiquity of lesbian and gay authors in the field of "history of sexuality" can be confirmed with a glance at the list of editors for the new journal, *Journal of the History of Sexuality*. All but a few are known to be lesbian or gay.

21. Eve Kosofsky Sedgwick, *Epistemology of the Closet* (Berkeley: University of California Press, 1990), p. 1.

22. In a fascinating interview with Foucault, published in the gay periodical *The Advocate* just after his death from AIDS in 1984, he comments: "Sexuality is something that we ourselves create. . . . We have to understand that with our desires, through our desires, go new forms of relationships, new forms of love, new forms of creation." Bob Gallagher and Alexander Wilson, "Foucault and the Politics of Identity," *The Advocate*, August 7, 1984, pp. 27–30, 58.

23. See Julie Abraham's review of Sedgwick's *Epistemology of the Closet* in *The Women's Review of Books*, vol. 8, no. 7 (April 1991), pp. 17–18. Abraham concludes provocatively that "*Epistemology of the Closet* is an extraordinary book. The questions Sedgwick addresses, and those her work provokes, together create a great deal of theoretical space. But all the women are straight, all the gays are male (and all the males are, potentially, gay). The sisters are still doing it for themselves."

24. See especially Biddy Martin, "Lesbian Identity and Autobiographical Difference(s)," in *Life/lines: Theorizing Women's Autobiography*, Bella Brodzky and Celeste Schenck, eds. (Ithaca, NY: Cornell University Press, 1988), pp. 77–103. The texts of privileged lesbians such as Gertrude Stein, Radclyffe Hall and Willa Cather have received relatively more attention, of course.

25. Teresa de Lauretis, *Technologies of Gender* (Bloomington: Indiana University Press, 1987), p. 25.

26. Judith Butler, *Gender Trouble: Feminism and the Subversion of Identity* (New York: Routledge, 1990). See especially pp. 136–139.

27. Cherríe Moraga and Gloria Anzaldúa, *This Bridge Called My Back: Writings by Radical Women of Color* (Watertown, MA: Persephone Press, 1981).

28. Donna Haraway, "A Manifesto for Cyborgs: Science, Technology, and Socialist Feminism in the 1980s," *Socialist Review*, vol. 15, no. 2 (March–April, 1985), pp. 73–74. Haraway is citing Chela Sandoval, "Dis-Illusionment and the Poetry of the Future: The Making of Oppositional Consciousness," Ph.D. qualifying essay, University of California, Santa Cruz, 1984.

29. Gloria Anzaldúa, *Borderlands/La Frontera: The New Mestiza* (San Francisco: Spinsters/Aunt Lute, 1987); Kobena Mercer, "Skin Head Sex Thing: Racial Difference and the Homoerotic Imaginary," in *How Do I Look? Queer Film and Video*, ed. Bad Objects Collective (Seattle: Bay Press, 1991), pp. 169–210; Douglas Crimp with Adam Rolston, *AIDS DemoGraphics* (Seattle: Bay Press, 1990); Gayle Rubin, "Thinking Sex: Notes for a Radical Theory of the Politics of Sexuality," in *Pleasure and Danger: Explorations in Female Sexuality*, ed. Carole S. Vance (New York: Routledge, 1984), pp. 267–319.

30. Jeffrey Escoffier and Allan Bérubé, "Queer/Nation," *Out/Look: National Lesbian and Gay Quarterly*, no. 11 (Winter 1991), pp. 14–16.

Notes on Chapter 13: Scholars and Sense

Originally published in the *Voice Literary Supplement*, June 1992. Reprinted with permission.

Notes to Chapter 14: Queering the State

Originally published in *Social Text* 39 (Summer 1994). Reprinted with permission.

   I would like to thank the Humanities Research Centre at the Australian National University for a summer fellowship which supported my work on this essay. I would also like to thank Nan D. Hunter, Cindy Patton, Henry Abelove, John D'Emilio, Gayle Rubin, and Philomena Mariani for their comments and suggestions on successive drafts.

1. I borrow here from Gayle Rubin's prescient opening line to her "Thinking Sex: Notes for a Radical Theory of the Politics of Sexuality," in *Pleasure and Danger: Exploring Female Sexuality*, ed. Carole Vance (New York: Routledge, 1984). The line is: "The time has come to think about sex."

2. Lisa Keen, "Record Number of Ballot Fights Looming for Gays," *Washington Blade*, January 21, 1994; Hastings Wyman, Jr., "Strengthening Gays' Political Response in '94," *Washington Blade*, January 7, 1994; Steven Holmes, "Gay Rights Advocates Brace for Ballot Fights," *New York Times*, January 12, 1994.

3. The data on these organizations is taken from materials presented by a member of People for the American Way at a workshop on the religious right sponsored by the Texas Family Planning Association, December 1993.

4. At an April 1993 conference at the University of Illinois, radical critic Todd Gitlin attacked the emphasis on "difference" in progressive politics, and called for a return to "universalism." This kind of pointing to "fragmentation" as caused by all those "special" and parochial interests, rather than by the false "universalism" of a failing left politics, is common. See Gitlin's article in *The Crisis in Higher Education*, ed. Michael Bérubé and Cary Nelson (New York: Routledge 1995).

5. Michael Warner has called for queer intellectuals to turn their attention to theorizing the social, and for critical theorists of politics and the state to take sexuality seriously as a category of analysis. See his introduction to *Fear of a Queer Planet* (Minneapolis: University of Minnesota Press, 1993).

   The distinction I make between "lesbian and gay" and "queer" is explained in my "Making It Perfectly Queer," in this volume.

6. Stacey D'Erasmo, "The Gay Nineties: In Schools across the Country, Gay Studies Is Coming on Strong," *Rolling Stone*, October 3, 1991. The article finally referred to Sedgwick as "a bit of a puzzle—a married woman who describes herself as 'queer'" (87). I thank Stacey for allowing me to repeat this story, and I am grateful to Eve Kosofsky Sedgwick for graciously allowing me to use her name.

7. For a collection of articles in which these arguments are laid out, see Henry Abelove, Michele Aina Barale, and David Halperin, eds., *The Lesbian and Gay Studies Reader* (New York: Routledge, 1993). Their "Suggestions for Further Reading" at the end of the volume are especially helpful for a sense of the development of these arguments over time.

8. Amanda Anderson has outlined this strategy and its limits in the context of feminist politics. See "Cryptonormativism and Double Gestures: The Politics of Poststructuralism," *Cultural Critique* 21 (1992).

9. For a discussion of the ways right-wing strategies have evolved in response to progressive identity politics, see Cindy Patton, "Tremble Hetero Swine!" in *Fear of a Queer Planet*.

10. I am thinking here of the work of Douglas Crimp, Paula Treichler, and Cindy Patton, among many others.

11. Nan D. Hunter, "Identity, Speech, and Equality," in this volume.

12. The Colorado ban has been declared unconstitutional by the courts, but this decision is presently being appealed.

13. Warner, *Fear of a Queer Planet*, xiii.

14. I borrow the evocative term "heteronormativity" from Michael Warner, *ibid.*

15. For an especially helpful discussion of the importance of this distinction, see Nancy Fraser, "Rethinking the Public Sphere: A Contribution to the Critique of Actually Existing Democracy," *Social Text*, no. 25/26 (1990).

16. I am indebted to Henry Abelove, who pointed out that conservatives would no doubt respond to No Promo Hetero with a defense of "the family."

17. Gayle Rubin has used the terms "sexual dissenters," "erotic dissidents," "sexual dissidents" and "dissident sexuality" in ways similar to my use of "sexual dissent" here. See "The Leather Menace: Comments on Politics and S/M," in *Coming to Power*, ed. Samois, (Boston: Alyson Publications, 1981), and "Thinking Sex."

Notes to Chapter 15: The Discipline Problem

Originally published in *GLQ: A Journal of Lesbian and Gay Studies*, vol. 2 (1994).

An earlier version of this paper was delivered at the annual conference of the American Historical Association in San Francisco in January, 1994. I am especially grateful to Henry Abelove for his comments there and elsewhere. I would also like to thank Laura Briggs, Cindy Patton, Nan D. Hunter, John D'Emilio and Gayle Rubin for suggestions and editorial assistance. Exchanges with Judith Butler have also challenged my thinking on these issues.

1. This interview situation reflected a split within the history department. A minority of the faculty wanted to hire a historian of sexuality, and this group had managed to control the search committee for a position advertised as women's history and social/cultural history. The majority of the history department faculty were appalled when the candidates selected by the search committee turned out all to be historians of sexuality, with particular interests in aspects of lesbian and gay history.

2. See my "Scholars and Sense," in this volume, for the published account of this conference.

3. See "History's Gay Ghetto," in this volume, for an account of the early institutionalization of lesbian and gay history, largely outside the academy.

4. I do not mean to imply here that there is any such thing as "empirical grounding" or a "research base" that is free from the need for textual analysis of sources, or from the requirement to define (rather than "discover") a discursive context. I am arguing that particular, privileged texts are over-analyzed, and overbroad claims are made based on such analyses. Historians are trained to collect a large number and variety of texts before making generalizations. Reference to this larger number and variety would provide sounder grounding for the close textual readings of literary and cultural critics.

5. A notable exception can be found in the work of Henry Abelove. See his "The Queering of Lesbian/Gay History" *Radical History Review* no. 62 (Spring 1995). This article carefully and brilliantly analyzed the tensions and differences between the standard tropes and assumptions of lesbian and gay history texts, and the politics and reading strategies of his more postmodern queer students at Wesleyan University.

6. Jeffrey Escoffier, "Inside the Ivory Closet: The Challenges Facing Lesbian and Gay Studies," *Out/Look*, no. 10 (Fall 1990), pp. 40–48.

7. Eve Kosofsky Sedgwick, review of Cindy Patton's *Inventing AIDS*, *Lesbian and Gay Studies Newsletter*, July 1991, pp. 25–27. This newsletter is published by the Lesbian and Gay Caucus of the Modern Language Association.

At the beginning of the review, Sedgwick writes that Escoffier worries about "an academically more privileged generation of younger scholars whose grounding in continental critical theory makes us, he claims, 'increasingly irrelevant to the cultural and political needs of lesbians and gay men'" (p. 25). The assertion she is referring to appears on p. 48 of Escoffier's article (cited above). He writes:

> The problem is that most of the current efforts to start programs in lesbian and gay studies are primarily concerned with building up the intellectual status of the field. This step may be necessary in order to gain legitimacy for funding and support within the academic community, but it encourages lesbian and gay academics to respond more to academic and disciplinary standards than to the political and cultural concerns of the lesbian and gay communities outside the university. The intellectual work of scholars out of touch with those communities will shrink the audience and become increasingly irrelevant to the cultural and political needs of lesbians and gay men. And the intellectual style of the post-Stonewall scholars only reinforces the potential for their academic isolation.

Escoffier's argument about the impact of economic pressures and the process of professionalization is represented by Sedgwick as pure and simple theory-bashing. Sedgwick concludes her review of Patton's book by returning to Escoffier: "So long as this is what theory sounds like—so long as this is what activism sounds like—we need hardly join Jeffrey Escoffier or other anti-intellectuals in worrying that either one will become 'unrepresentative and intellectually narrow'" (p. 27). Here she is referencing Escoffier's call, at the close of his article, for serious attention to be paid to the "asymmetries" within the field of lesbian and gay studies, asymmetries including less-than-full representation of women and people of color. "Otherwise," Escoffier writes, "the field will become unrepresentative and intellectually narrow" (p. 48).

8. The only other published discussion of Escoffier's article by an academic that I have seen is by Christopher Looby, Associate Professor of English at the University of Chicago. In his "Gay Academy, Gay Communities," *Outlines* (Chicago), February 1992, pp. 34–35, Looby writes that "It is difficult to sort out the legitimate criticisms in Escoffier's manifesto from the elements of oversimplification, resentment, and invidious discrimination with which it is replete." He goes on to agree with many of Escoffier's points, however.

9. Joan W. Scott, "The Evidence of Experience," in Henry Abelove, Michele Aina Barale and David Halperin, editors, *The Lesbian and Gay Studies Reader* (New York: Routledge, 1993), p. 398.

10. Scott, "The Evidence of Experience," p. 400.

11. The article she takes aim at most extensively is John E. Toews, "Intellectual History after the Linguistic Turn: The Autonomy of Meaning and the Irreducibility of Experience," *American Historical Review* 92 (October 1987).

12. Jonathan Ned Katz, *Gay/Lesbian Almanac* (New York: Harper & Row, 1983), pp. 147, 173. See also Jeffrey Weeks, *Sex, Politics and Society: The Regulation of Sexuality Since 1800* (London: Longman, 1981), and John D'Emilio, *Sexual Politics/Sexual Communities: The Making of a Homosexual Minority in the United States, 1940–1970* (Chicago: University of Chicago Press, 1983).

13. Scott, "The Evidence of Experience," p. 401.

14. Her lack of citation withholds legitimacy and authority from already stigmatized texts. But her use of Delany and homosexuality allows her to profit from the avant-garde caché of gay sex, without being herself stigmatized by it. For an example of a respectful, productive exchange between an academic writer of theory and nonacademic texts, see Biddy Martin, "Lesbian Identity and Autobiographical Difference(s)," in Abelove, *et. al., The Lesbian and Gay Studies Reader.*

15. Ramon Gutierrez made this point in the strongest terms when he commented on an earlier version of this paper, delivered at the January 1994 conference of the American Historical Association in San Francisco. He concluded, however, that reform is impossible, and recommended flight from departments of history.

16. Michael Warner, ed. *Fear of a Queer Planet* (Minneapolis: University of Minnesota Press, 1993), pp. vii–xxxi.

Notes to Chapter 16: *Lawrence v. Texas* as Law and Culture

Portions of this chapter appeared in similar form in the *Michigan Law Review* and the *Minnesota Law Review.*

1. 478 U.S. 186 (1986).

2. 539 U.S. 558 (2003).

3. Although the statute before the Supreme Court covered oral or anal sex without regard to who the actors were, 478 U.S. at 188 n.1, the Court considered only the challenge to it brought by Michael Hardwick, a gay man. Hence, the Court limited its ruling to the constitutionality of a prohibition on same-sex sexual conduct.

4. See, e.g., *Schroeder v. Hamilton Sch. Dist.*, 282 F.3d 946, 950-51 (7th Cir. 2002) (citing Bowers for the proposition that "homosexuals do not enjoy any heightened protection under the Constitution"); *Equality Found. of Greater Cincinnati, Inc. v. City of Cincinnati*, 128 F.3d 289, 292-93 (6th Cir. 1997) ("under Bowers . . . homosexuals did not constitute either a 'suspect class' or a 'quasi-suspect class' because the conduct which defined them as homosexuals was constitutionally proscribable").

5. 517 U.S. 620 (1996).

6. The Due Process Clause states that "no State shall deprive any person of life, liberty or property without due process of law." In the birth control and abortion cases, the Court had ruled that "liberty" included the right to

make decisions regarding certain private, intimate acts; these cases formed the basis for a "right to privacy." See, *Griswold v. Connecticut*, 381 U.S. 479 (1965); *Roe v. Wade*, 410 U.S. 113 (1973).

7. 539 U.S. at 562.

8. *Id*. at 578.

9. *Id*. at 574.

10. *Id*. at 582.

11. *Id*. at 580.

12. *Id*. at 578.

13. William N. Eskridge, Jr. and Nan D. Hunter, *Sexuality, Gender and the Law*, 2nd ed. (Foundation Press, New York, 2004), 76–78.

14. *Id*. at 865.

15. In 1955, the American Law Institute circulated a draft of the Model Penal Code which decriminalized sodomy between consenting adults. Patricia A. Cain, *Rainbow Rights: The Role of Lawyers and Courts in the Lesbian and Gay Civil Rights Movements* (Boulder, Colorado: Westview Press, 2000), 136–137.

16. *Lawrence v. Texas*, 539 U.S. at 575.

17. See, e.g., *Shahar v. Bowers*, 114 F.3d 1097 (11th Cir. 1997) (employment), cert. denied 522 U.S. 1049 (1998); Ex parte J.M.F., 730 So. 2d 1190, 1196 n.5 (Ala. 1998) (custody); Ex parte D.W.W., 717 So. 2d 793, 796 (Ala. 1998) (visitation); *Weigand v. Houghton*, 730 So. 2d 581, 586–87 (Miss. 1999) (custody). See generally Diana Hassel, "The Use of Criminal Sodomy Laws in Civil Litigation," 79 *Texas Law Review*, 813 (2001) (describing how sodomy laws have been used to disadvantage homosexuals in several areas of law).

18. *Knuller, Ltd. v. Director of Public Prosecutions*, 2 All ER 898 (1972) cited in Jeffrey Weeks, *Sex, Politics and Society: The Regulation of Sexuality Since 1800*, 275 (London: Longman, 1981).

19. Indeed, almost as soon as the decision was announced, political attention switched to marriage, an issue which has hardened conservative positions.

20. The first appellate courts to interpret Lawrence used rational basis review in just this way. *Lofton v. Sec'y of Dep't of Children and Family Services*, 358 F.3d 804 (11th Cir. 2004); *State v. Limon*, 83 P.3d 229 (Kan. App. 2004); and *Standhardt v. Superior Court of Mancopa County*, 77 P.3d 451 (Ariz. App. Div. 1 2003).

21. 308 F.3d 635 (6th Cir. 2002).

22. Executive Order No. 13262, 3 C.F.R. 210 (2003).

23. *Lawrence v. Texas*, 539 U.S. at 567.

24. *Id* (emphasis added).

25. *Id*. at 585 (O'Connor, J., concurring).

26. *Id*. at 604 (Scalia, J., dissenting).

27. *Id*. at 601.

28. Gayle Rubin, "Thinking Sex: Notes for a Radical theory of the Politics of Sexuality" in *Pleasure and Danger: Exploring Female Sexuality*, ed. Carole S. Vance, (Boston: Routledge and Kegan Paul, 1984), 267, 282.

29. Katherine Franke, "The Domesticated Liberty of *Lawrence v. Texas*," 104 *Colum. L. Rev.* 1399 (2004).

30. Teemu Ruskola, "Gay Rights vs. Queer Theory: What Is Left of Sodomy After *Lawrence v. Texas*" 23 *Soc. Text* 235 (2005).

31. Kendall Thomas, *Our Brown? Reading Lawrence v. Texas* (manuscript on file with author).

32. *Lawrence v. Texas*, 539 U.S. at 567.

33. *Id.*

34. After extensive factual research into the background of the case, Dale Carpenter concluded that the two men were occasional sex partners. Dale Carpenter, "Lawrence Past", in *The Future of Gay Rights in America*, H. N. Hirsch, ed. (New York: Routledge, 2004), 107–149.

35. In re J.M., 575 S.E.2d 441 (Ga. 2003) (invalidating fornication law); *State v. Limon*, 2005 WL 2675039 (Kan. 2005) (invalidating law that imposed much harsher sentence for sex between minors if both were of the same sex than between male and female minors).

36. *Williams v. Attorney General*, 378 F.3d 1232 (11th Cir. 2004).

37. Carlos A. Ball, "The Positive in the Fundamental Right to Marry: Same-Sex Marriage in the Aftermath of *Lawrence v. Texas*," 88 *Minn. L. Rev.* 1184, 1208–1215 (2004)

38. *Standhardt v. Superior Court of Mancopa County*, 77 P.3d 451 (Ariz. App. Div. 1 2003).

39. *Lofton v. Secretary of the Dept. of Children and Social Services*, 358 F.3d 804, reh'g en banc denied 377 F.3d 1275 (11th Cir. 2004), cert. denied 125 S.Ct. 869 (2005).

40. *Citizens for Equal Protection, Inc., v. Bruning*, 368 F.Supp. 2d 980 (D.Neb. 2005) (finding unconstitutional a state constitutional amendment barring any legal recognition for same-sex partners); *Alaska Civil Liberties Union v. State*, 122 P.3d 781 (Alaska 2005) (finding that state constitution prohibits the exclusion of same-sex partners from the health benefits offered to spouses of state government employees).

41. Civil union systems now exist in some form in California, Connecticut, Hawaii, New Jersey, and Vermont. N.J. Stat. Ann. 26:8A-1, 2001 Cal. Legis. Serv. Ch. 893, 15 Vt. Stat. Ann. § 1204(a), and Haw. Rev. Stat. § 572C.

42. In his dissent in Hardwick, Justice Blackmun wrote that "[o]nly the most willful blindness could obscure the fact that sexual intimacy is 'a sensitive, key relationship of human existence.'" *Bowers v. Hardwick*, 478 U.S. at 205 (Blackmun, J., dissenting) (quotation omitted).

43. Joyce Murdoch and Deb Price, *Courting Justice: Gay Men and Lesbians v. the Supreme Court* (New York: Basic Books, 2001), 418.

44. *Id.* at 415–422.

45. Jonathan Groner, "12 Winning Arguments: D.C.–Area Lawyers Who Make Their Mark in Appellate Litigation," *Legal Times* (July 19, 2004) at 32.

46. *Bowers v. Hardwick*, 478 U.S. at 194.

47. *Boy Scouts of America v. Dale*, 530 U.S. 640, 650 (2000).

48. *Lawrence v. Texas*, 539 U.S. at 578.

49. 448 U.S. 297 (1980).
50. 432 U.S. 464 (1977).
51. See Martha T. McCluskey, "Subsidized Lives and the Ideology of Efficiency", 8 *Am. U. J. Gender Soc. Pol'y & L.* 115, 118–27 (2000) for an astute application of the political science literature on neoliberalism, most of it concerning international trade practices, to domestic political issues in the United States.
52. See Lisa Duggan, *The Twilight of Equality? Neoliberalism, Cultural Politics, and the Attack on Democracy* (Boston: Beacon Press, 2003), xviii–xix.

Notes to Chapter 17: Crossing the Line

Reprinted from *New Labor Forum*, Volume 13, No. 3, pp. 37–44, Fall 2004.

1. *The Brandon Teena Story*, produced and directed by Susan Muska and Greta Olafsdottir (Zeitgeist, 1998); *Boys Don't Cry*, produced and directed by Kimberly Peirce (Fox Searchlight, 2000).
2. Aphrodite Jones, *All She Wanted* (Pocket Books, 1996).
3. Judith Halberstam, *In a Queer Time and Pace* (New York: New York University Press, 2005). Halberstam discusses the multiple representations of the Brandon story in chapters 2 and 3.
4. David Roediger, *The Wages of Whiteness: Race and the Making of the American Working Class* (New York: Verso, 1991); George Lipsitz, *The Possessive Investment in Whiteness: How White People Profit from Identity Politics* (Philadelphia: Temple University Press, 1998).

Notes to Chapter 18: Holy Matrimony!

Reprinted from *The Nation*, March 15, 2004.

Notes to Chapter 19: Beyond Gay Marriage

Reprinted with permission from *The Nation*, July 18, 2005.

Notes to Appendix

Reprinted with permission from Nan Hunter and Sylvia Law, "Brief Amici Curiae of the Feminist Anticensorship Task Force," *Univ. of Michigan Journal of Law Reform*, Vol. 21 nos. 1 and 2 (fall 1987-winter 1988).

Introduction

1. The ordinance states:
   Pornography shall mean the sexually explicit subordination of women, graphically depicted, whether in pictures or in words, that also includes one or more of the following:

(1) Women are presented as sexual objects who enjoy pain or humiliation; or

(2) Women are presented as sexual objects who experience sexual pleasure in being raped; or

(3) Women are presented as sexual objects tied up or cut up or mutilated or bruised or physically hurt, or as dismembered or truncated or fragmented or severed into body parts; or

(4) Women are presented being penetrated by objects or animals; or

(5) Women are presented in scenarios of degradation [sic], injury, abasement, torture, shown as filthy or inferior, bleeding, bruised, or hurt in a context that makes these conditions sexual; [or]

(6) Women are presented as sexual objects for domination, conquest, violation, exploitation, possession, or use, or through postures or positions of servility or submission or display.

Indianaplis, Ind., Code § 16-3(q) (1984).

The Court of Appeals held that the Indianapolis ordinance violated the First Amendment, and the Supreme Court affirmed that ruling without issuing an opinion. American Booksellers Ass'n. v. Hudnut, 771 F.2d 323 (7th Cir. 1985), aff'd, 475 U.S. 1001 (1986). It appears that the Feminist Anti-Censorship Taskforce (FACT) analysis influenced Judge Easterbrook's approach to the constitutional issues presented. The opinion discusses concrete examples illustrating the difficulty of distinguishing images that liberate women from those that subordinate women. *Id.* at 330. It addresses the relationship between images, ideas and behavior, and the distinction between fantasy and reality, in terms that are unusually rich and thoughtful for a judicial opinion. Id. The court rightly rejects the states's claim that pornography is "low value" speech, entitled to lesser constitutional protection than "serious" talk about public issues. *Id.* at 331.

2. DuBois & Gordon, "Seeking Ecstasy on the Battlefield: Danger and Pleasure in Nineteenth-Century Feminist Sexual Thought," in *Pleasure and Danger: Exploring Female Sexuality* 31 (ed. C. Vance, 1984) [hereinafter Pleasure and Danger].

3. S. De Beauvoir, *The Second Sex* 202-203, 366-413 (trans. H. Parshley, 5th printing 1968).

4. See Hunter, "The Pornography Debate in Context: A Chronology of Sexuality, Media & Violence Issues in Feminism," reprinted in this volume; Snitow, Stansell and Thompson, Introduction, in *Powers of Desire: The Politics of Sexuality* 9 (ed. A. Snitow, C. Stansell and S. Thompson, 1983) [hereinafter Powers of Desire].

5. See S. Schechter, *Women and Male Violence: The Visions and Struggles of the Battered Women's Movement* (1982).

6. See Snitow, "Retrenchment Versus Transformation: The Politics of the Anti-pornography Movement," in *Women Against Censorship* 107 (V. Burstyn, ed. 1985).

7. See Duggan, "Censorship in the Name of Feminism," *Village Voice*, October 16, 1984, at 11, col. 1. The ordinance was introduced in the Indianapolis City

Council by a member whose career was founded on anti-ERA organizing. *Id.* at 12, col. 1. The central popular support for its passage came from fundamentalists who attended the meetings at which the Council voted on the ordinance. The Reverend Greg Dixon of the Indianapolis Baptist Temple, a former Moral Majority official, organized the fundamentalist presence. *Id.* at 16, col. 1.

8. 2 Attorney General's Comm'n on Pornography, U.S. Dep't of Just., Final Report app. A, at 1957 (1986) [hereinafter Comm'n on Pornography].

9. The commission was chaired by Henry Hudson, a prosecutor whom President Reagan praised for closing down every adult bookstore in Arlington, Va. At least six of the eleven commission members had previously taken strong public stands opposing pornography and supporting obscenity laws as a means of control. B. Lynn, *Polluting the Censorship Debate: A Summary and Critique ot the Final Report of the Attorney General's Commission on Pornography* 14–16 (1986) (ACLU Public Policy Report); Vance, "The Meese Commission on the Road," *Nation*, August 2, 1986, at 76 (also listing Commission member Frederick Schauer as having taken a public stand opposing pornography). For example, Commission member Dr. James Dobson was president of Focus on the Family, an organization that is "dedicated to the preservation of the home and the family and the traditional values growing out of the Judeo-Christian ethic." B. Lynn, *supra*, at 15. In addition, commission member Frederick Schauer had previously argued for a highly restricted application of the first amendment. *Id.* at 17; Schauer, "Speech and "Speech"—Obscenity and "Obscenity": An Exercise in the Interpretation of Constitutional Language," 67 *Georgetown Law Journal* 899, 922–923 (1979). The three people without prior established positions on pornography frequently resisted the staff's agenda. They endorsed a statement that said that while they abhorred "the exploitation of vulnerable people" in pornography, they also rejected "judgmental and condescending efforts to speak on women's behalf as though they were helpless, mindless children." 1 Comm'n on Pornography, *supra* note 8, at 194 (statement of Dr. Judith Becker, Ellen Levine, and Deanne Tilton-Durfee). Two of these three women dissented from the final report. See *id.* at 195–212 (statement of Dr. Judith Becker and Ellen Levine).

10. Over three-fourths of the witnesses urged tighter controls over sexually explicit materials. B. Lynn, *supra* note 9, at 7.

11. See generally *id.* at 57–88. Prof. Edward Donnerstein has denounced as "bizarre" the Commission's effort to use his research to buttress a claim that sexually violent material causes criminal behavior. Goleman, "Researchers Dispute Pornography Report on Its Use of Data," *New York Times*, May 17, 1986, at A1, col. 1.

12. Vance, *supra* note 9, at 79.

13. See 1 Comm'n on Pornography, *supra* note 8, at 322–349. With respect to materials regarded by the commission as nonviolent but degrading, the commission acknowledged that there was little concrete evidence "causally linking the material with sexual aggression" but nonetheless concluded that

the "absence of evidence should by no means be taken to deny the existence of the causal link." *Id.* at 332.

14. "[T]he most important harms must be seen in moral terms, and the action of moral condemnation of that which is immoral is not merely important but essential." *Id.* at 303.
15. *Id.* at 227–232.
16. See *id.* at 331.
17. B. Lynn *supra* note 9, at 71–72. These examples included:

> [D]epictions of a woman lying on the ground while two standing men ejaculate on her; two women engaged in sexual activity with each other while a man looks on and masturbates; a woman nonphysically coerced into engaging in sexual activity with a male authority figure, such as a boss, teacher, or priest, and then begs for more; ... a woman with legs spread wide open holding her labia open with her fingers; a man shaving the hair from the pubic area of a woman; a woman dressed in a dog costume being penetrated from the rear by a man. ...
> *Id.* at 71–72.

18. *Id.* at 72.
19. Two commission members, both women, filed a sharp and cogent dissent. 1 Comm'n on Pornography, supra note 8, at 195–212 (statement of Dr. Judith Becker and Ellen Levine).
20. Commission on Obscenity and Pornography, *The Report of The Commission on Obscenity and Pornography* (1970).
21. For a case illustrating an inadequacy of the present antidiscrimination law, see *Rabidue v. Osceola Refining Co.*, 805 F.2d 611, 622 (1986) (holding that posters of nude women on workplace walls and supervisors' obscene comments do not constitute actionable sexual harassment).
22. P. Nobile and E. Nadler, *United States of America vs. Sex: How The Meese Commission Lied About Pornography* 224–225 (1986). The *New York Times* opined, "[T]he report, widely circulated without formal publication, must be faulted for relying on questionable evidence and recklessly encouraging censorship." "Defeated by Pornography," *New York Times*, June 21, 1986, at A16, col. 1.
23. "Anti-Pornography Law Defeated in Cambridge," *New York Times*, Nov. 12, 1985, at A16, col. 6.
24. FACT, Boston Chapter; The Boston Women's Health Book Collective; Boston NOW; Women Against Violence Against Women, Boston Chapter; Cambridge Commission on the Status of Women; No Bad Women, Just Bad Laws (statements on file with the U. Mich. J.L. Ref.).
25. Wald, "Voters in Maine Defeat Anti-Obscenity Plan," *New York Times*, June 11, 1986, at A32, col. 4. For ballot purposes, the four-and-a-half-page statute was reduced to the proposition, "Do you want to make it a crime to make, sell, give for value or otherwise promote obscene material in Maine?" *Id.*

26. Wald, "Obscenity Debate Focuses Attention on Maine, Where Voters Weigh Issue," *New York Times*, June 10, 1986, at A18, col. 1.
27. Vance, "Pleasure and Danger: Toward a Politics of Sexuality," in *Pleasure and Danger, supra* note 2, at 5.
28. See *Powers of Desire, supra* note 4; *Pleasure and Danger, supra* note 2; *Women Against* Censorship, *supra* note 6.
29. See Keodt, "The Myth of the Vaginal Orgasm," in *Notes From the Second Year: Women's Liberation* 37 (S. Firestone ed. 1970), and in *Voices From Women's Liberation* 158 (L. Tanner ed. 1971); M. Sherfrey, *The Nature and Evolution of Female Sexuality* (1972); L. Barbach, *For Yourself: The Fulfillment of Female Sexuality* (1971).
30. S. De Beavoir, *supra* note 3, at 273.

Brief Amici Curiae

1. (1) Women are presented as sexual objects who enjoy pain or humiliation; or
   (2) Women are presented as sexual objects who experience sexual pleasure in being raped; or
   (3) Women are presented as sexual objects tied up or cut up or mutilated or bruised or physically hurt, or dismembered or truncated or fragmented or severed into body parts; or
   (4) Women are presented being penetrated by objects or animals; or
   (5) Women are presented in scenarios of degradation, injury, abasement, torture, shown as filthy or inferior, bleeding, bruised or hurt in a context that makes these conditions sexual; or
   (6) Women are presented as sexual objects for domination, conquest, violation, exploitation, possession, or use, or through postures or positions of servility or submission or display.
      Indianapolis, Ind., Code § 16-3(q) (1984)
2. By the use of highly selected examples, Appellants and supporting *amici* convey the impression that the great majority of materials considered pornographic are brutal. Although most commercial pornography, like much of all media, is sexist, most is not violent. A study of pictorials and cartoons in *Playboy* and *Penthouse* between 1973 and 1977 found that, by 1977, about 5% of the pictorials were rated as sexually violent. "No significant changes in the percentage of sexually violent cartoons were found over the years." Malamuth and Spinner, "*A Longitudinal Content Analysis of Sexual Violence in the Best-Selling Erotic Magazines*," 16 J. Sex. Research 226, 237 (1980). The Women Against Pornography (W.A.P.) *amicus* brief, in particular, totally mischaracterizes content analyses of pornography. It asserts, at p. 8 n. 14, that one study found the depictions of rape in "adults only" paperbacks has doubled from 1968 to 1974, a statement which is simply false. The study found that the amount of explicit sexual content had doubled, but also "that the plots, themes, and stories have remained much the same in these books throughout the years measured in this study." Smith, "The Social Content of Pornography," 26 J. Comm. 16, 23 (1976). The brief then cites a study find-

ing that depictions of bondage and domination in Times Square pornography stores "had increased dramatically in frequency in 1982," but neglects to mention that the increase was to 17.2%. The same study also concluded that "many bondage and domination magazines do not depict suffering or bodily injury." Dietz and Evans, "Pornographic Imagery and Prevalence of Paraphilia," 139 *Am. J. Psychiatry* 1493, 1495 (1982). That some pornography would be found by *amici* on both sides to be offensive to women does support this legislative approach to curtailing that pornography, which is overbroad and dependent on suppression of speech.

3. 18 U.S.C.A. §§ 1461–1462 (West 1984); 19 U.S.C.A. § 1305 (West 1980 & Supp. 1984); see *United States v. One Obscene Book Entitled "Married Love,"* 48 F.2d 821 (S.D.N.Y. 1931); *United States v. One Book Entitled "Contraceptions,"* 51 F.2d 525 (S.D.N.Y. 1931) (prosecution for distribution of books by Marie Stopes on contraception); *United States v. Dennett*, 39 F.2d 564 (2d Cir. 1930) (prosecution of Mary Ware Dennett for publication of pamphlet explaining sexual physiology and functions to children); and *Bours v. United States*, 229 F. 960 (7th Cir. 1915) (prosecution of physician for mailing a letter indicating that he might perform a therapeutic abortion). It was not until 1971 that an amendment was passed deleting the prohibition as to contraception, Pub. L. No. 91–662, 84 Stat. 1973 (1971); and the ban as to abortion remains in the current codification of the law.

4. See Appellants' Exh. S. at 114–115.

5. The reviewer for *Ms.* magazine wrote:

> At several points I was very offended by the idea of love won by brute force. . . . I'd like to explain this away by stressing that this is an allegory of class war, not sex war. But that is not true. For the brilliance of *Swept Away* is that it is everything at once. As a description of what capitalism does to us it is sophisticated and deep. At the same time, it comes to grips with the "war" between the sexes better than anything I've seen or read. . . . It has shocking scenes linking sex and violence and yet it is about tenderness. . . . [It] is a funny, beautiful, emotional movie about a somber, ugly, intellectual subject.

Garson, "A Reviewer Under the Influence," *Ms.*, December 1975, at 37, 38.

Other reviewers strongly disagreed:

> I really don't know what is more distasteful about this film—its slavish adherence to the barroom credo that all women really want is to be beaten, to be shown who's boss, or the readiness with which it has been accepted by the critics. Yes, it is effective enough in parts, but strictly on the level of slick pornography.

Turan, "Not Swept Away," *The Progressive*, May 1976, at 39, 40.

6. The same theme may be perceived very differently in different contexts. In her novel, *A Sea Change*, feminist author Lois Gould repeatedly invokes fantasies and images of rape and submission in order to make more dramatic

her story of women transforming their sexual lives. One striking passage narrates the main female character being stroked and then entered by the gun held by a fantasy male character, B.G. L. Gould, *A Sea Change* 95 (1977). At the end of the novel, the woman character becomes B.G. This graphic depiction of penetration by an object, undoubtedly suppressible under the ordinance, especially since there are several scenes in the book which could meet the definition of pornography, is one of the fantasies Gould explores and uses in her treatment of the theme of sexual power.

7. To define "pornography" as that which subordinates women, and then prohibit as pornographic that which subordinates, makes the claim that pornography subordinates either circular or logically trivial.

8. See, e.g., Appellants' Exhs. N., M., and W. These exhibits, like most commercial pornography which depicts sex between women, were not produced by or primarily for lesbians. Yet part of the shock value of such images in contemporary society may be attributable to their depiction of sexual explicitness between women. When the door is opened to suppress "scenarios of degradation," for example, there is no guarantee that this shock value of any graphic depiction of homosexual acts will not spill over to images and texts which authentically express lesbian sexuality.

9. The provision that "the use of men . . . in the place of women . . . shall also constitute pornography" makes clear that same–sex male images and texts could fall within the scope of the ordinance, especially so, one supposes, if one male partner is depicted as effeminate.

10. See, e.g., *Baker v. Wade*, 553 F. Supp. 1121 (N. D. Tex 1982), on appeal; *People v. Onofre*, 51 N.Y.2d 476 (1980), *cert. denied*, 451 U.S. 987 (1980); *National Gay Task Force v. Board of Educ.*, 729 F.2d 1270 (10th Cir. 1984), *aff'd per curiam*, 53 U.S.L.W. 4408 (U.S. March 26, 1985).

11. See, e.g., G. Gilder, *Sexual Suicide* (1973).

12. Act of June 20, 1957 ch. 57–779, § 1, 1957 Fla. Laws vol. 1, pt. 1, 1102, 1103–1104 (amending Fla. Stat. § 847.01) (amended 1959, repealed 1961) (emphasis added).

13. See *State v. Cohen*, 125 So. 2d 560 (Fla. 1960); *State v. Reese*, 222 So. 2d 732 (Fla. 1969); and *Rhodes v. State*, 283 So. 2d 351 (Fla. 1973).

14. See Act of May 5, 1961, ch. 61–67, 1961 Fla. Laws vol. 1, pt. 1, 13; Act of June 3, 1969, ch. 69–41, 1969 Fla. Laws vol. 1, pt. 1, 164; Act of June 7, 1973, ch. 73–120, 1973 Fla. Laws 185.

15. Studies have indicated that if you take out the explicit sexual content from aggressive pornographic films, leaving just the violence (which could be shown on any network television show), you find desensitization to violent acts in some subjects. However, if you take out the aggressive component and leave just the sexual, you do not seem to observe negative effects of desensitization to violence against women. Thus, violence is at issue here. That is why restrictions or censorship solutions are problematical.

Donnerstein and Linz, "Debate on Pornography," *Film Comment*, December 1984, at 34, 35.

16. Malamuth describes a study he did in which *no* evidence was found of changes in perceptions or attitudes following exposure to this type of pornography:

> One group of male and female subjects looked at issues of *Penthouse* and *Playboy* magazines that showed incidents of sadomasochism and rape. A second group examined issues of these magazines that contained only non-aggressive pornography and a third group was given only neutral materials. Shortly afterward, subjects watched an actual videotaped interview with a rape victim and responded to a questionnaire assessing their perceptions of a rape victim and her experience. Weeks later . . . subjects indicated their views on rape in response to a newspaper article. Exposure to the aggressive pornography did not affect perceptions of rape either in response to the videotaped interview with a rape victim or to the newspaper article.
> Appellants' Exh. S. at 113.

17. See also Abramson and Hayashi, "Pornography in Japan: Cross–Cultural and Theoretical Considerations," in *Pornography and Sexual Aggression* 173, N. Malamuth and E. Donnerstein, eds. (1984). Japanese pornography contains more depictions of rape and bondage than does American pornography and is also more readily available in popular magazines and on television. Yet Japan has a substantially lower incidence of rape than any Western country, and a lower incidence of violent crime generally. The authors attribute the lower crime rate to cultural factors unrelated to pornography.

18. A good example of the limitations of laboratory studies is provided by the study described in Appellants' Exh. R. Male subjects viewed violent "slasher" movies, one a day for five consecutive days, and answered questions each day about the extent to which the film was degrading to women. The subjects clearly knew that attitudes related to sexual violence against women were being measured. On the last day of the experiment, subjects were informed that the sixth and final film had not arrived. They were told since their original film did not arrive they would watch a law school documentary about a rape trial. After viewing the rape documentary, subjects completed questionnaires. The authors concluded that "exposed subjects later judged the victim of a violent assault and rape to be significantly less injured and generally more worthless than a control group of subjects who saw no films." Appellants' Exh. R., abstract.

   Appellants cite this study in support of their claim that "pornography" makes men "less able to perceive that an account of rape is an account of rape." Appellants' brief at 20. The study is of limited value. First, the images used in the slasher films are not within the ordinance's definition of pornography. Second, there is a high probability that "demand characteristics"— where subjects understand the purpose of a study and give the experimenter what he or she is thought to be looking for—skewed the responses. Third, the term "worthless" did not occur spontaneously to the subjects, but was suggested by a question asking, "I felt [the victim] was: valuable 1 2 3 4 5 6

7 8 9 worthless." Thus, when the authors state that subjects who viewed the films found the victim "more worthless," they mean that the subjects circled the number 6, say, instead of the number 4. The question regarding the perception of the victim's injury was presented in a similar manner. What is being measured in studies of this type are not complex sets of attitudes, such as all of us have in real life, but gross responses on a questionnaire. Fourth, although the author found "significant differences" between subjects who had viewed the films and those who had not on the "injury" and "worthlessness" measures, they did *not* find significant differences on other measures, including defendant intention, victim resistance, victim responsibility, victim sympathy and victim unattractiveness. Finally, an hypothesized correlation between perception of violence and perception of degradation proved to be nonsignificant, as did the expected correlation between perception of degradation and enjoyment of the film. The point is not that this is poor social science research, but that this kind of research does not produce evidence sufficiently strong to justify censorship.

19. Even the Baron and Strauss chapter, *Sexual Stratification, Pornography, and Rape in the United States*, in *Pornography and Sexual Aggression*, cited by the W.A.P. amicus brief at 16, which found, in a state-by-state analysis, a positive correlation between circulation rates for mainstream pornographic magazines (e.g., *Playboy*) and incidents of rape, could not explain some strikingly anomalous results, such as, for example, Utah, which ranked 51st (last) in per capita readership of sex magazines, but 25th in per capita rate of rape.

20. Even clearly misogynist pornography is political speech. Indeed, antipornography activists have often argued that pornography is political propaganda for male dominance. One lawyer then associated with Women Against Pornography pointed out that the political message of pornography hostile to women results in its entitlement to heightened, not lesser, First Amendment protection as a form of advocacy, albeit of noxious ideas. Kaminer, "Pornography and the First Amendment: Prior Restraints and Private Action," in *Take Back the Night: Women and Pornography* 239–246 (1980).

21. The following are among the works which could fall within the scope of the ordinance's definition and thus be suppressed pursuant to the trafficking cause of action: K. Acker, *Blood and Guts in High School* (1984); *Bad Attitude* (Quarterly, Boston); L. Barbach, *Pleasures: Women Write Erotica* (1984); *A Woman's Touch* (Cedar and Nelly eds. 1979); J. Chicago, *The Dinner Party* (1979); T. Corinne & J. Lapidus, *Yantras of Women Love* (1982); N. Friday, *My Secret Garden: Women's Sexual Fantasies* (1973) and *Forbidden Flowers: More Women's Sexual Fantasies* (1975); L. Gould, *A Sea Change* (1977); E. Jong, *Fear of Flying* (1973) and *How to Save Your Own Life* (1976); Kensington Ladies Erotica Society, *Ladies Home Erotica* (1984); S. Kitzinger, *Women's Experience of Sex* (1983); R. Mapplethorpe, *Lady Lisa Lyon* (1983); K. Millett, *Sita* (1976); A. Nin, *Delta of Venus* (1977); Olds, "Bestiary" in *Powers of Desire: The Politics of Sexuality supra* p. 22, at 409; A. Oakgrove, *The Raging Peace* (1984); J. Rechy, *City of Night* (1963); *Coming to Power* (Samois ed.

1982); Shulman, "A Story of a Girl and Her Dog," in *Powers of Desire: The Politics of Sexuality, supra*, p. 22 at 410.

22. Duggan, "Censorship in the Name of Feminism," *Village Voice*, October 16, 1984, at 15, col. 1.

23. Courts may not defer to legislative determination of fact when the supposed "facts" are marshaled to suppress free speech or to justify sex discrimination. "Deference to a legislative finding cannot limit judicial inquiry when First Amendment rights are at stake," *Landmark Communications, Inc. v. Virginia*, 435 U.S. 829, 843 (1978). See also, *Craig v. Boren*, 429 U.S. 190 (1976).

24. See also U.S. Commission on Civil Rights, *Women and Poverty* (1974); *Women Still in Poverty* (1979); and *Child Care and Equal Opportunity for Women* (1981) and National Advisory Council on Economic Opportunity, *Final Report: The American Promise: Equal Justice and Economic Opportunity* (1981).

25. See, e.g., *Toward an Anthropology of Women* (R. Reiter ed. 1975); M. Rosaldo and L. Lamphere, *Women, Culture and Society* (1974); M. Ryan, *Womanhood in America: From Colonial Times to the Present* (1979); N. Chodorow, *The Reproduction of Mothering: Psychoanalysis and the Sociology of Gender* (1978); D. Dinnerstein, *The Mermaid and the Minotaur: Sexual Arrangements and Human Malaise* (1976); J. Mitchell, *Women's Estate* (1972).

26. Appellants explain that the proviso is needed because "without it, pornographers could circumvent the ordinance by producing the exact same material using models other than adult biological females, i.e., men, children, and transsexuals, to portray women." Appellants' brief at 45.

27. The provisions negating common law defenses to coercion are cast in facially neutral terms. But since "pornography" is defined in gender-specific terms, the provisions abrogating defenses to coercion also apply to women or to others used "in the place of women."

28. Perpetuating the stereotype that "good girls" do not enjoy sex, and suppressing images of women's sexuality, is particularly tragic for teenagers. A recent study by the prestigious Alan Guttmacher Institute identifies factors explaining why teenagers in the United States experience unwanted pregnancy at rates significantly higher than those in any other developed nation. This extensive study found that the single most important factor associated with low rates of unwanted pregnancy is "openness about sex (defined on the basis of four items; media presentations of female nudity, the extent of nudity on public beaches, sales of sexually explicit literature and media advertising of condoms)." Jones, Forrest, Goldman, Heusbaw, Livecloer, Rosoff, Westoff, and Wolf, "Teenage Pregnancy in Developed Countries: Determinants and Policy Implications," 17 *Family Plan. Persp.*, March–April 1985, at 53, 61.

29. On the dangers and unconstitutionality of a blanket "tender years" presumption, see *Devine v. Devine*, 398 So. 2d 686 (Ala. 1981); "Developments in the Law: The Constitution and the Family," 93 *Harv. L. Rev.* 1156, 1334–1338 (1980); S. Ross and A. Barcher, *The Rights of Women*, 229–230 (1983). On the danger and illegality of a mother-only child-rearing leave, see

Danielson v. Board of Higher Educ., 358 F. Supp.22 (S.D.N.Y. 1972). *See also Phillips v. Martin Marietta Corp.*, 400 U.S. 542 (1971) (company policy prohibiting the hiring of mothers, but not fathers, of preschool–aged children violates section 703(n) of Title VII of the Civil Rights Act of 1964). Williams, "Reflections on Culture, Courts and Feminism," 7 *Women's Rts. L. Rep.* 175, 198 (1982).

30. Vance and Snitow, "Toward a Conversation About Sex in Feminism: A Modest Proposal," 10 *Signs: J. of Women in Culture and Soc.* 126, 131 (1984).

Index

A

Abelove, Henry, 191
Abortion clinics, 18
Abortion rights, 3, 19, 103, 171
Ackerman, Bruce, 96
ACLU, 30
Activism, 3, 51, 147, 161
Adult businesses, 29
The Advocate, 22
Affirmative action, 38, 79
Against Our Will, 20
AIDS, 125, 129
Aiken, Susan, 10
Albertson, Martha, 228
Alito, Samuel, 28
Allen, Paula, 10
Allison, Dorothy, 176, 181
All She Wanted, 215
American Communist Party, 77
American Dream, 152
American Family Association, 74
American Historical Association, 140
American Newspaper Guild, 18
Anal sex, 93
Ancient Order of Hibernians, 150
Angelina Foxy, 10
Annenberg, Walter, 74
Antiabuse laws, 34

Antidiscrimination ordinances, 4
Antigay personnel policy, 98
Antigay referenda, 3
Antiporn politics, 22, 65–70
Antipornography campaigns, 65–70
Antipornography legislation, 2, 29, 65–70
Antirape organizations, 18
Antisodomy laws, 4
Anzaldua, Gloria, 22
Aparicio, Carlos, 10

B

Bad Attitude, 9, 23, 25
Barale, Michele Aina, 191
Barker, Sarah Evans, 30
Before Stonewall, 142
Bersani, Leo, 174
Berubes, Allan, 137
The Bitch Goddesses, 51
"A Black Feminist Statement," 20
Body Politic, 138, 190
Boston Area History Project, 141
Boswell, John, 139
Bowers vs. Hardwick, 10, 24, 28, 77–82, 133
Boy Scouts of America v. Dale, 207
Boys Don't Cry, 214

Bradenburg test, 123, 126
Brandon Teena Case, 213–220
The Brandon Teena Story, 213
Braschi v. Stahl Associates, 113
Brennan, William, 134
Bridal fair exposition, 17
Brides, 19
Briggs Initiative, 124, 128, 178
Brownmiller, Susan, 20
Brown v. Board of Education, 78, 200
Bryant, Anita, 126, 179
Buffalo Oral History Project, 138, 142
The Burning Bed, 61
Burstyn, Varda, 6
Bush, George W., 27, 30
Butler, Judith, 160, 174

C

Califia, Pat, 22
Campbell, Robert, 101
Canadian Gay Archives, 139
Capital punishment, 87
Carr, C., 154
Caught Looking: Feminism, Pornography, and Censorship, 2
Censorship, 7, 29–40
Center for Disease Control, 127, 128
Chandler, Beryle, 166
Chee, Alexander, 157
Child pornography, 74
Christian American, 172
Citizens for Decency, 45
Citizens for Excellence in Education, 172
Civil liberties, 3, 86
Civil rights, 151
Civil Rights Act of 1964, 59
Civil Service directive, 122
Class, 3
Clean Community day, 31
Clinton, Bill, 26
Coalition for a Clean Community, 45
Cohen, Ed, 166
Colonialism, 3
Color Adjustment, 177
The Color Purple, 22
Coming to Power, 22, 23, 49

Committee on Lesbian and Gay History, 140
Concerned Women of America, 231
Conduct, 86
Conservatism, 30
Constructionism, 152, 159
Cosmopolitan, 17
Coughenour, Beulah, 32, 45
Court of Appeals, 90
Crenshaw, Kimberle Williams, 117
Crimp, Douglas, 168
Critical Legal Studies (CLS), 116
Cultural theory, 2
Czernick, Chris, 141

D

Daly, Mary, 153
D'Andre, Michael, 39
Deep Throat, 50, 58
Defense of Marriage Act (DoMA), 26, 225
Delany, Samuel, 191
D'Emilio, John, 139
Department of Health and Human Sources, 129
D'Erasmo, Stacey, 173
DeVine, Phillip, 219
The Dialectic of Sex, 17
Diary of a Conference, 22
Dinkins, David, 150
Discipline problem, 185–196
Dissent, 182
Dixon, Greg, 30–31, 33, 36, 67
Dobkin Alix, 156
Dodson, Betty, 19
Domestic partnership laws, 115
Domestic partners ordinance, 106
Domestic Policy Council, 128
Donald, Wildmon, 24
Donald Butler vs. Her Majesty the Queen, 9
Donnerstein, Edward, 34
Dorenkamp, Monica, 166
DuBois, Ellen, 66
Due process clause, 198
Dworkin, Andrea, 6, 16, 23, 28, 43

E

Eagle Forum, 20
Economic class, 115
Edelman, Lee, 189
Eight Amendment, 78
Elitists, 35
Ellis, Havelock, 156
The Epistemology of the Closet, 159
Equal Opportunity Board, 34, 46
Equal Protection clause, 94, 198
Equal rights admendment, 19, 110
Escoffier, Jeffrey, 162, 189
Essentialist theory, 156
Executive Order 10,450, 121
Explicit, sexually, 53

F

Factionalism, 79
Faderman, Lillian, 139
Fait accompli, 35
Falwell, Jerry, 22
Family Circle, 17
Family law theorists, 111, 205
Family Protection Act, 39
Family values, 100
Fear of a Queer Planet, 195
Federal Marriage Admendment, 28, 234
Fellatio, 51
Feminism, 11, 29–40, 66
Feminist Anti-Censorship Taskforce
    (FACT), 1
Feminist antipornography legislation,
    43–64
Feminist Historians and
    antipornography campaigns,
    65–70
Feminist Women's Health Center, 19
Finley, Karen, 3, 16, 24
Fire, 26
Firestone, Shulamith, 17
First Admendment, 30, 57, 75, 119
Fleck, John, 24
Food and Drug Administration, 127
Forbes, Malcolm, 154
Forced sterilization, 18
Forcing provision, 59

*For Colored Girls Who Have Considered
    Suicide When the Rainbow is
    Enuf,* 20
Foster, Jodie, 155
Foucault, Michel, 89
Franke, Katherine, 204
Fraser, Donald, 23
Free choice, 59
Free market economy, 26
Free speech, 30, 57, 120, 134
Frohnmayer, John, 132
Functionalists, 113
Fundamentalists, 33, 44, 90
The Furies, 18
Fuss, Diana, 166

G

Gag rule, 24, 27
Garber, Eric, 141
Garcia, Inez, 20
Gates, Henry Louis Jr., 169
The Gay Agenda, 171
Gay American History, 137
Gay Community News, 138, 141
Gay Left Collective, 158
"Gay liberation ghetto," 145
Gay Men's Health Crisis, 1, 128, 154
Gay-related immune deficiency (GRID),
    22
Gay rights, 3, 106, 171
Gender dissent, 118
*Gender Trouble: Feminism and the
    Subversion of Identity,* 160
Globalism, 35
Gonzalez, Alberto, 28
Gordon, Linda, 66
Griswold-Eisenstadt principle, 93
Grove Press, 18
Gutierrez, Miguel, 157

H

Habitual criminal, 77
Hackler, Ron, 31, 36
Halberstam, Judith, 215
Hall, Radclyffes, 122
Halley, Janet, 96

Halperin, David, 191
Haraway, Donna, 161
Hardwick, Michael, 91
Hardwick ruling, effects of, 77–82
Harris v. McRae, 208
Hart-Delvin debate, 120
Harvey Milk Archives, 139
Hay, Harry, 28
Helms, Jesse, 24, 30, 129
Helms Amendment, 178
Hensler, Rebecca, 157
Heresies 12: The Sex Issues, 22
Hill, Anita, 25
History of Sexuality, 159
Hite, Shere, 19
HIV testing debate, 126
Hodgson v. Minnesota, 103
Hollibaugh, Amber, 237
Homoeroticism, 132
Homosexuality, 24, 72, 86
How Do I Look?: Queer Film and Video,
    168
Hudnut, William III, 31, 34
Hudson, Rock, 24
Hughes, Holly, 3, 16, 24
Human Sexual Response, 16
Humphrey, Gordon, 132
Hunter, Nan, 10, 15

I

Identity, speech, and equality, 119–136
    Briggs initiative, 124
    evolution of, 133
    HIV testing and, 126
    right to privacy, 120
Identity politics, 175
Inventing AIDS, 190
Irish Lesbian and Gay Organization
    (ILGO), 150

J

Jackson, Janet, 28
Jackson State college, 18
Jacobsen, Carol, 10
Jantz v. Muci, 95
John, Elton, 28

Jones, Aphrodite, 215
Jones, Paula, 26
Journalism, 2
Journal of the History of Sexuality, 194
The Joy of Sex, 49
Julien, Isaac, 177
Justice, Inc., 34
Justice Department Task Force of
    Obscenity, 28

K

Katz, Jonathan Ned, 87, 137
Kennedy, Robert, 17
Kennedy, Sheila Suess, 33
Kennedy-Cranston Amendment, 130
Kent State University, 18
Kerry, John, 222
King, Martin Luther, 17, 151
Kitchen Table Press, 22
Knight, Robert, 231
Koedt, Anne, 17
Koop, C. Everett, 128
Koskovich, Gerard, 157
Kowalski, Sharon, 11, 99

L

Labeling theory, 158
Labor movement, 220
Ladies Home Journal, 17
Lambert, Lisa, 219
Larry King Live, 181
Lauretis, Teresa de, 160
Law, Bernard Cardinal, 28
Lawrence v. Texas, 28, 197–209
    law and, 197
    marriage and, 204
    morality and, 202
    politics and culture, 206
Lee, Rex, 79
Legislation, 43
    antipornography, 65–70
    civil, 43, 46
    trafficking, 55
Leigh, Carol, 10
Lesbian and Gay Historical Society, 139

Lesbian and Gay history, growth of, 137–147
Lesbian and Gay Researchers Network, 140
The Lesbian and Gay Studies Reader, 191
Lesbian/gay politics, 3, 96, 119, 124
Lesbian Herstory Archives, 137, 142
Lesbian History Project, 140
"Lesbian Masquerade," 137
Lesbian Sex Mafia, 22
"Lesbians Who Sleep With Men," 158
Lewinsky, Monica, 27
Libel, 56
Liberal groups, 2, 79, 114, 151
Liberating Masturbation, 19
Libertarian, 114
Liberty of privacy, 198
Lifestyle choices, 180
Lipsitz, George, 216
Little, Joanne, 20
Lorde, Audre, 155
Los Angeles Times, 101
Lotter, John, 216
Lowell, Amy, 140

Media, 2
Meese commission, 2, 28, 74
Mehta, Deepa, 26
Mental illness, 121
Mercer, Kobena, 168, 190
Michael H. v. Gerald D., 103
Military service, 97
Miller, D.A., 174, 189
Miller, Tim, 24
Miller v. California, 19
Millet, Kate, 6, 17
Mink, Gwendolyn, 228
Misogyny, 69
Miss american pageant, 17
Model Penal Code, 89, 122
Modern Language Association, 152
Moraga, Cherrie, 22
Moral Majority, 30, 36, 44, 67
Moral regulation, 26
Morgan, Robing, 18
Morrison, Adele, 157
Mother Jones, 21
The Motion of Light in Water, 191
"The Myth of the Vaginal Orgasm," 17

M

MacKinnon, Catharine, 6, 9, 16, 43
Mademoiselle, 19
Maher v. Roe, 208
Mahoney, Kathleen, 9
Mainardi, Pat, 18
Male fraud, 215
Mapplethorpe, Robert, 8, 24
Marchiano, Linda, 50, 58
Marcum v. McWhorter, 202
Marriage law, 11, 105, 118
    current debate of, 221–230
    function and contract of, 111
    nature of, 107
    rights under, 116
Marvin v. Marvin, 112
Marxists, 158
Masturbation, 22
Mattachine Society, 28
McCarthysim, 77
McIntosh, Mary, 158
McLaughlin, Sheila, 169

N

National Abortion Conference, 18
National Association of Christian Educators, 172
National Black Feminists Organization, 19
National Coalition Against Censorship, 8
National Coalition Against Sexual Assault, 21
National Conference for New Politics, 16
National Endowment for the Arts (NEA), 1, 24, 71, 132
Nationalism, 152, 153
Nationalists politics, 4
National Organization of Women (NOW), 16, 65
National security, 121
Neoliberalism, 208
New Left press, 16, 144
New Right, 30
Newsday, 19

Newsweek, 19
Newton, Esther, 160, 176, 181
New York Times, 19, 74, 101, 150
Nissen, Tom, 217
Norton v. Macy, 122
Notes from the Second Year, 17
Nunn, Sam, 133

O

Obscenity law, 25, 51, 57, 68
O'Connor, Sandra Day, 28, 199
One Institute Library, 139
On Our Backs, 23
Oprah Winfrey, 176
Oral sex, 91
Organizing an Archives: The Canadian Gay Archives Experience, 139
Our Bodies, Ourselves, 19
"Our Boston Heritage," 140
Outlaw Poverty, Not Prostitutes, 10
Outweek, 152

P

Parental relationship, 103
Paris is Burning, 25
Patton, Cindy, 168, 190
Penetration, 88
Playboy philosophy, 17
Pleasure and Danger, 23
Policy Institute, 26
Political activism, 35
Political/sexual expression, 12
"The Politics of Housework," 18
Pornography: Men Possessing Women, 21
Pornography, regulation of, 1
Pornography Victims' Compensation Act, 69
Post modern politics, 4
Powers of Desire: The Politics of Sexuality, 23
President's Commission on Obscenity and Pornography, 18
Privacy right, sexual, 78, 94, 151
Progressive groups, 2
Progressive politics, 173

"Prostitution: From Academia to Activism," 10
"Psychology Constructs the Female," 18
Psychopathic personality, 121

Q

Queer, 12
"Queer community," 157
"Queer nation," 149, 153
Queer theory, 12
"Queer theory," 149, 165, 187

R

Race, 3, 30
Radical groups, 2, 30
Ramsey, Jon-Benet, 26
Rape, study of, 20
Reader's Digest, 19
Reagan, Ronald, 21, 125
Registered partnerships, 106
Rehnquist, William, 28, 80
Reinhardt, Stephen, 92
Religious Rights Watch, 172
Rent control law, 106, 113
Resiman, Judith, 74
Rich, Adrienne, 6
Riggs, Marlon, 25, 177
"Right to know" campaigns, 127
Rivera, Sylvia, 28
Roberts, J. R., 141
Roberts, John, 28
Robertson, Pat, 172
Roediger, David, 216
Roe v. Wade, 19, 25, 78, 200
Rolling Stone magazine, 173
Romer v. Evans, 198
Rotello, Gabriel, 158
Rubin, Gayle, 6
Rubyfruit Jungle, 19
Rupp, Leila, 143
Ruskola, Teemu, 204

S

Safe-sex education, 1, 16, 127
The Salt Mines, 10

Same-sex conduct, 88
San Francisco Bay Guardian, 155
Sanger, Margaret, 68
*Sapphistry: The Book of Lesbian
    Sexuality,* 22
Sarris, Kathy, 34
Schlafly, Phyllis, 20, 32
Scholar and studies, 165–170
Schwarz, Judith, 142
Schwarzenegger, Arnold, 28
Scott, Joan, 191
Sedgwick, Eve, 160
Segregation, 30
Self-defense, 11, 20
Self-examination, 19
Self-representation, 12
Sex, 3
Sex descrimination, 29, 110
Sexism, 48, 61
Sex objects, 52
Sex panics, 1, 71–76
Sexual acts, 54
Sexual dissent, 5, 41, 83, 99–104
Sexual expression, freedom of, 18
Sexual freedom, 21
Sexual identity, 96, 120
Sexual identity crisis, 216
Sexuality, 2, 22
    expression, 43
    issues of, 95
    self discovery, 22
    social regulation of, 89
    subordination, 50
    women and, 19
Sexuality debates, contextualizing of,
    15–28
Sexual pervasion, 121
Sexual politics, 17
Sexual representation, 41
"Sex Wars," 65
Shange, Ntozake, 20
She Must Be Seeing Things, 169
Shepard, Mathew, 27
Show Me, 74
Signorile, Michelangelo, 153
Simonds, Robert, 172
Sims, Alice, 74
Singer v. Hara, 93

Sisterhood is Powerful, 17
Sloan, Louise, 155
Smith, Anna Marie, 228
Smith, Barbara, 6
Snuff, 20
Social analysis, 2
Social anxiety, 90
Social construction, 158
Social control, 193
Social groups, 117
Social legislation, 38
Social-purity campaign, 67
Social regulation, 89
Social security, 234
Social value, 19
Sodomy, 11, 34, 73, 78, 85
Solomon, Alisa, 168
Special interests groups, 173
Special protection, 59
Special rights, 180
Specter, Arlen, 39
Speech, sexual, 55
Stonewall rebellion, 124, 131
Stonewall riots, 17
Street Sex, 10
Students for Democratic Society (SDS),
    16
Subordination, 52, 58
Supreme court, 9, 77, 103
Swank, Hilary, 27
Sweeney, Tim, 154
Symbolic interactionism, 158
Symbols, 17

T

Take Back The Night, 21
"Take Back the Night" march, 20
Technologies of Gender, 160
Teena, Brandon, 25
Temperance campaign, 67
Testing campaigns, 127
*This Bridge Called My Back: Writings
        By Radical Women of Color,*
    22, 161
Thomas, Clarence, 25
Thomas, Kendall, 204
Thomas, Laura, 157

Thompson, E. P., 158
Thompson, Karen, 100
Thompson, Sharon, 11
Title VII, 59
Toews, John, 192
Tolerance, 151
Tomberlin, Karen, 101
Tongues United, 25, 177
Twilight of Equalitiy, 208

U

Unions, 111
University of Michigan, 10
Unnatural acts, 34
Urban League, 34

V

Vance, Carole S., 6, 132
The Village Voice, 6, 19, 21, 154
Violence, sexual, 47, 69, 126
Voice Literary Supplement, 173

W

Walker, Alice, 22

Walkowitz, Judith, 66
Warner, Michael, 168, 179
Warren Court, 79
Washington Court of Appeals, 93
Washington Post, 19
Washington Times, 74
Water Babies, 74
Weeks, Jeffrey, 144, 158
Weisstein, Naomi, 18
The Well of Loneliness, 122
What Color Is Your Hankerchief, 21
Willis, Ellen, 21
Winthrop, John, 87
Women Against Censorship, 6
Women Against Pornography (WAP), 30
Women Against Violence Against
    Women, 16, 20
Women's Legal Defense Fund, 6
Women's Legal Education and Action
    Fund (LEAF), 9
Women's liberation, 16
Women's Liberation Front, 18